murach's
HTML,
XHTML,
and CSS

Anne Boehm

MIKE MURACH & ASSOCIATES, INC.

1-800-221-5528 • (559) 440-9071 • Fax: (559) 440-0963
murachbooks@murach.com • www.murach.com

Authors:	Anne Boehm
Editor:	Mike Murach
	Ben Murach
Cover Design:	Zylka Design
Production:	Tom Murach
	Cynthia Vasquez

Books for web developers

Murach's JavaScript and DOM Scripting
Murach's ASP.NET 3.5 Web Programming with VB 2008
Murach's ASP.NET 3.5 Web Programming with C# 2008
Murach's Java Servlets and JSP (Second Edition)

Books for database programmers

Murach's ADO.NET 3.5, LINQ, and the Entity Framework with VB 2008
Murach's ADO.NET 3.5, LINQ, and the Entity Framework with C# 2008
Murach's SQL Server 2008 for Developers
Murach's Oracle SQL and PL/SQL

Books on Visual Basic, C#, C++, and Java

Murach's Visual Basic 2008
Murach's C# 2008
Murach's C++ 2008
Murach's Java SE 6

Books for IBM mainframe programmers

Murach's OS/390 and z/OS JCL
Murach's Mainframe COBOL
Murach's CICS for the COBOL Programmer
DB2 for the COBOL Programmer, Part 1

For more on Murach books, please visit us at www.murach.com

10 9 8 7 6 5 4 3 2 1
ISBN-13: 978-1-890774-57-8

Contents

Introduction

Expanded contents

Chapter 4   How to use CSS to format the elements of a web page

Chapter 5   How to use the CSS box model for spacing, borders, and backgrounds

Chapter 6 How to use CSS for page layout

Section 2 Other HTML and CSS skills as you need them

Chapter 7 How to work with links and lists

Introduction

If you have anything to do with web development, you should know how to use HTML, XHTML, and CSS the modern, professional way. That's true if you want to become a web designer. That's true for web designers who still use tables for page layout when they should be using CSS. That's true for JavaScript programmers. And that's true for server-side programmers who use PHP, ASP.NET, Java servlets and JSPs, or other server-side languages.

Our crash course in HTML, XHTML, and CSS

To get you started right, section 1 in this book shows you use to HTML, XHTML, and CSS to develop web pages at a professional level. As we see it, anyone who has anything to do with web development should read the six chapters in this section. These chapters are designed to teach you what you need to know faster and better than ever, and they work like this:

- For those readers who are completely new to web development, chapter 1 shows how static and dynamic web pages work, and it gives a first view of how HTML and CSS are intended to work together in a modern web site.

- Chapter 2 presents the basic syntax for HTML, XHTML, and CSS, and also shows how to test, debug, and validate these files. This chapter also shows the differences between HTML and XHTML, which are minimal. At this point, you're ready to learn the coding details.

- Chapter 3 presents a professional subset of HTML/XHTML that will run on both Internet Explorer and standard browsers like Firefox. Here, you'll learn that HTML and XHTML should present only the content and structure for a web page, because CSS should be used for the formatting and page layout.

- Chapters 4 and 5 present a professional subset of CSS for formatting your HTML/XHTML elements. In chapter 4, you'll learn the basics of CSS. And in chapter 5, you'll learn how to use the CSS box model so you can set the margins, spacing, borders, and backgrounds for a web page just the way you want them.

- Chapter 6 completes the professional subset by showing how to use CSS for page layout. Here, you'll learn how to develop two- and three-column pages that have headers and footers. To develop pages like that, you'll learn how to float elements on a page. But you'll also learn how to use absolute and relative positioning for those occasional layout problems that require them.

When you finish these chapters, you'll have the perspective and skills you need for developing professional web pages whether you're a web designer, client-side programmer, or server-side programmer. Then, you can add to those skills by reading any of the chapters in the next two sections.

Just-in-time training and on-the-job reference

After you finish the crash course in section 1, you have the background you need for reading any of the other chapters in this book. In other words, you don't have to read them in sequence. If, for example, you want to learn how to use forms after you complete section 1, you can skip to chapter 10. If you want to know how to develop style sheets for printing or how to develop pages for mobile devices, you can skip to chapter 12. And if you want to know how to design or deploy a web site, you can skip to chapter 14 or chapter 15.

In other words, the chapters in sections 2 and 3 provide the training you need when you need it…or, as trainers call it, "just-in-time" training. These chapters present all of the HTML/XHTML/CSS skills that you're going to find yourself wishing you had as you develop web pages. And because of our unique "paired pages" format, all of the chapters in this book are ideal for on-the-job reference after you've used them for training.

Why you'll learn faster and better with this book

Like all our books, this one has features that you won't find in competing books. That's why we believe you'll learn faster and better with our book than with any other. Here are a few of those features.

- From the first page to the last, this book shows you how to use HTML, XHTML, and CSS the modern, professional way, with HTML for the content of each page and CSS for the formatting and page layout. That way, your web pages and your web sites will be easier to create and maintain.

- Because section 1 presents a complete subset of HTML, XHTML, and CSS in just 6 chapters and 216 pages, you are ready for productive work much faster than you are when you use competing books. In most competing books, for example, you won't learn how to use CSS for page layout until late in the book, even though that's a critical part of web page development.

- Unlike other books, sections 2 and 3 present all of the other HTML, XHMTL, and CSS skills that you need most for designing, developing, and deploying a web site: everything from using an image editor for sizing your images to using tested JavaScript code for image rollovers and swaps. To confirm that, just look at the table of contents and the expanded table of contents for this book.

- If you page through this book, you'll see that all of the information is presented in "paired pages," with the essential syntax, guidelines, and examples on the right page and the perspective and extra explanation on the left page. This helps you learn faster by reading less...and this is the ideal reference format when you need to refresh your memory about how to do something.

- To show you how the HTML and CSS work together, this book presents all the code for complete web pages that range from the simple to the complex. To see what I'm talking about, take a quick look at the four sets of web pages and code that start in figures 4-14, 5-6, 5-11, and 6-4. As we see it, studying complete examples is the best way to master HTML, XHTML, and CSS because they show the relationships between the segments of code. And yet, most competing books limit themselves to snippets of code that don't show these relationships.

- Of course, this book also presents dozens of short examples. So it's easy to find an example that shows you how to do whatever you need to do as you develop your web pages. And our "paired pages" presentation method makes it much easier to find the example that you're looking for than it is with traditional presentations in which the code is embedded in the text.

What software you need

To develop web pages with HTML, XHTML, and CSS, you can use any text editor that you like. However, a text editor that includes syntax coloring and auto-completion will help you develop applications more quickly and with fewer errors. That's why we recommend Notepad++ for Windows users and TextWrangler for Mac OS users. Both are available for free, and both can be used for entering HTML, XHTML, and CSS.

Then, to test a web page, you need one or more web browsers. Because Internet Explorer is the most widely-used browser and the one that deviates the most from the standards, you should always test your pages in it. But we also recommend that you test your pages in a standard browser like Mozilla Firefox. Here again, both browsers are free.

To help you install these products, Appendix A provides the web site addresses and procedures that you'll need. In addition, chapter 2 provides a quick guide to using Notepad++.

How our downloadable files can help you learn

If you go to our web site at www.murach.com, you can download all the files that you need for getting the most from this book. These files include:

- the HTML/XHTML and CSS files for all of the examples in this book

- the HTML/XHTML and CSS files that you will use as the starting points for the exercises

These files let you test, review, and experiment with the code. They also let you copy and paste any of the source code into your own files. Here again, appendix A shows you how to download and install these files.

Support materials for trainers and instructors

If you're a corporate trainer or a college instructor who would like to use this book for a course, we offer an Instructor's CD that includes: (1) a complete set of PowerPoint slides that you can use to review and reinforce the content of the book; (2) instructional objectives that describe the skills a student should have upon completion of each chapter; (3) test banks that measure mastery of those skills; and (4) solutions to the exercises in this book.

To learn more about this Instructor's CD and to find out how to get it, please go to our web site at www.murach.com and click on the Trainers link or the Instructors link. Or, if you prefer, you can call Kelly at 1-800-221-5528 or send an email to kelly@murach.com.

Related books

If you want to learn client-side or server-side web programming when you finish this book, we offer several books that will help you. Our JavaScript and DOM Scripting book will help you get the most from JavaScript. Our ASP.NET books will show you how to develop web applications with C# or Visual Basic. Our servlets and JSP book will show you how to develop web applications with Java. And in the Fall of 2010, we'll be publishing a book that shows you how to use PHP and MySQL for server-side programming.

To find out more about our new books and latest editions, please go to our web site at www.murach.com. There, you'll find the details for all of our books, including complete tables of contents.

Please let us know how this book works for you

From the start of this project, I had two goals for this book. First, I wanted to make it easier than ever for you to learn how to use HTML, XHTML, and CSS the right way…that is, by using HTML or XHTML to define the structure and content of a web page and by using CSS to provide the formatting and layout. Second, I wanted to build on that foundation to raise your skills to a professional level.

Now, I thank you for buying this book. I wish you all the best with your web development. And if you have any comments about this book, I would appreciate hearing from you.

Anne Boehm

Anne Boehm, Author
anne@murach.com

Section 1

A crash course in HTML and CSS

The six chapters in this section are designed to get you off to a fast start. First, chapter 1 presents the concepts and terms that you need for using HTML and CSS. Then, chapter 2 shows you how to enter, edit, test, and validate the HTML and CSS for the web pages of a web site. These chapters provide all of the background that you need for learning the coding details of HTML and CSS.

Then, chapter 3 shows you how to code the HTML that defines the content and structure for a web page. Chapter 4 shows you how to code the CSS that does basic formatting to the HTML content. Chapter 5 shows you how to use the CSS box model for spacing, borders, and backgrounds. And chapter 6 shows you how to use CSS for page layout.

When you complete these chapters, you'll be able to develop web pages at a professional level. Then, you can expand your skills by reading the other chapters in this book.

Please note, however, that you don't have to read the chapters in the other sections in sequence. Instead, you can skip to the chapter that presents the skills that you want to learn next. In other words, the six chapters in this section present the prerequisites for all of the other chapters, and all of the other chapters are written as independent learning modules. As a result, you can read any of these chapters whenever you need its skills.

1

Introduction to web development

This chapter introduces you to the concepts and terms that you need to work with HTML and CSS. First, you'll learn how web browsers and web servers interact to display web pages. Next, you'll learn how HTML and CSS work together to create formatted web pages. Then, you'll be introduced to the tools that you use for developing web sites. When you're finished with this chapter, you'll have the background you need for building web sites.

How web applications work

The *World Wide Web*, or web, consists of many components that work together to bring a web page to your desktop over the *Internet*. Before you start web pages of your own, you should have a basic understanding of how these components work together.

The components of a web application

The first diagram in figure 1-1 shows that web applications consist of *clients* and *web servers*. The clients are the computers that use the web applications. They access the web pages through programs known as *web browsers*. The web servers hold the files that make up each web application.

A *network* is a system that allows clients and servers to communicate. The Internet in turn is a large network that consists of many smaller networks. In a diagram like this, the "cloud" represents the network or Internet that connects the clients and servers.

In general, you don't need to know how the cloud works. But you should have a general idea of what's going on. That's why the second diagram in this figure gives you a conceptual view of the architecture of the Internet.

To start, networks can be categorized by size. A *local area network* (*LAN*) is a small network of computers that are near each other and can communicate with each other over short distances. Computers on a LAN are typically in the same building or in adjacent buildings. This type of network is often called an *intranet*, and it can be used to run web applications for use by employees only.

In contrast, a *wide area network* (*WAN*) consists of multiple LANs that have been connected together over long distances using *routers*. To pass information from one client to another, a router determines which network is closest to the destination and sends the information over that network. A WAN can be owned privately by one company or it can be shared by multiple companies.

An *Internet service provider* (*ISP*) is a company that owns a WAN that is connected to the Internet. An ISP leases access to its network to other companies that need to be connected to the Internet.

The Internet is a global network consisting of multiple WANs that have been connected together. ISPs connect their WANs together at large routers called *Internet exchange points* (*IXP*). This allows anyone connected to the Internet to exchange information with anyone else.

This diagram shows an example of data crossing the Internet. Here, data is being sent from the client in the top left to the server in the bottom right. First, the data leaves the client's LAN and enters the WAN owned by the client's ISP. Next, the data is routed through an IXP to the WAN owned by the server's ISP. Then, it enters the server's LAN and finally reaches the server. All of this can happen in less than $1/10^{th}$ of a second.

The components of a web application

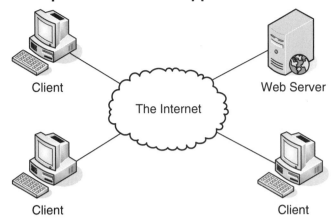

The architecture of the Internet

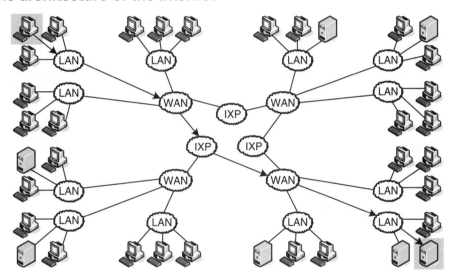

Description

- A web application consists of clients, a web server, and a network. The *clients* use programs known as *web browsers* to request web pages from the web server. The *web server* returns the pages that are requested to the browser.

- A *local area network* (LAN) directly connects computers that are near each other. This kind of network is often called an *intranet*.

- A *wide area network* (WAN) consists of two or more LANs that are connected by *routers*. The routers route information from one network to another.

- The *Internet* consists of many WANs that have been connected together at *Internet exchange points* (IXP). There are several dozen IXPs located throughout the world.

- An *Internet service provider* (ISP) owns a WAN and leases access to its network. It connects its WAN to the rest of the Intenet at one or more IXPs.

Figure 1-1   The components of a web application

How static web pages are processed

A *static web page* like the one at the top of figure 1-2 is a web page that only changes when the web developer changes it. This web page is sent directly from the web server to the web browser when the browser requests it.

The diagram in this figure shows how a web server processes a request for a static web page. This process begins when a user requests a web page in a web browser. To that, the user can either type in the address of the page into the browser's address bar or click a link in the current page that specifies the next page to load.

In either case, the web browser builds a request for the web page and sends it to the web server. This request, known as an *HTTP request*, is formatted using the *hypertext transport protocol* (HTTP), which lets the web server know which file is being requested.

When the web server receives the HTTP request, it retrieves the requested web page from the hard drive and sends it back to the browser as an *HTTP response*. This response includes the HTML for displaying the requested page.

When the browser receives the HTTP response, it *renders* (translates) the HTML into a web page that is displayed in the browser. Then, the user can view the content. If the user requests another page, either by clicking a link or typing another web address in the browser's address bar, the process begins again.

In this book, you'll learn how to use HTML and CSS to create static web pages. You can spot these pages in a web browser by looking at the extension in the address bar. If the extension is .htm or .html, the page is a static web page.

A static web page at http://www.techno-solis.com/whytechno.html

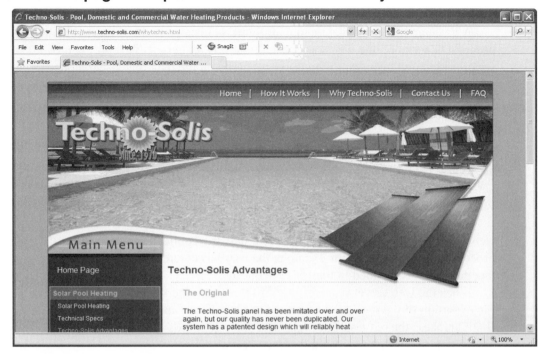

How a web server processes a static web page

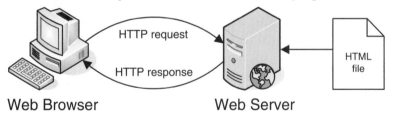

Web Browser   Web Server

Description

- *Hypertext Markup Language* (*HTML*) is the language used to design the web pages of an application.
- A *static web page* is an HTML document that's stored on the web server and doesn't change. The file names for static web pages have .htm or .html extensions.
- When the user requests a static web page, the browser sends an *HTTP request* to the web server that includes the name of the file that's being requested.
- When the web server receives the request, it retrieves the web page and sends it back to the browser in an *HTTP response*. This response includes the HTML for the page.
- When the browser receives the HTTP response, it *renders* the HTML into a web page that is displayed in the browser.

Figure 1-2   How static web pages are processed

How dynamic web pages are processed

A *dynamic web page* like the one in figure 1-3 is a page that's created by a program or script on the web server each time it is requested. This program or script is executed by an *application server* based on the data that's sent along with the HTTP request. In this example, the HTTP request identified the book that's shown. Then, the program or script retrieved the image and data for that book from a *database server*.

The diagram in this figure shows how a web server processes a dynamic web page. The process begins when the user requests a page in a web browser. To do that, the user can either type the URL of the page in the browser's address bar, click a link that specifies the dynamic page to load, or click a button that submits a form that contains the data that the dynamic page should process.

In each case, the web browser builds an HTTP request and sends it to the web server. This request includes whatever data the application needs for processing the request. If, for example, the user has entered data into a form, that data will be included in the HTTP request.

When the web server receives the HTTP request, the server examines the file extension of the requested web page to identify the application server that should process the request. The web server then forwards the request to the application server that processes that type of web page.

Next, the application server retrieves the appropriate program or script from the hard drive. It also loads any form data that the user submitted. Then, it executes the script. As the script executes, it generates the HTML for the web page. If necessary, the script will request data from a database server and use that data as part of the web page it is generating.

When the script is finished, the application server sends the dynamically generated HTML back to the web server. Then, the web server sends the page back to the browser in an HTTP response that includes the HTML for the page.

When the web browser receives the HTTP response, it renders the web page. Note, however, that the web browser has no way to tell whether the HTML in the HTTP response was for a static page or a dynamic page. It just renders the HTML.

When the page is displayed, the user can view the content. Then, when the user requests another page, the process begins again. The process that begins with the user requesting a web page and ends with the server sending a response back to the client is called a *round trip*.

Dynamic web pages let you create interactive *web applications* that do all of the types of processing that you find on the Internet including eCommerce applications. Although you won't learn how to develop dynamic web pages in this book, you will learn how to create the HTML forms that send user data to the web server. Once you master HTML, you can learn how to use server-side languages like JSP, ASP, or PHP to create the dynamic pages that a web site needs.

A dynamic web page at amazon.com

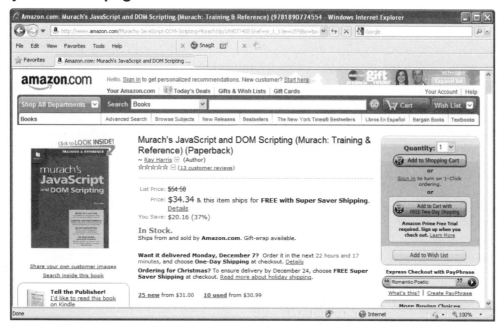

How a web server processes a dynamic web page

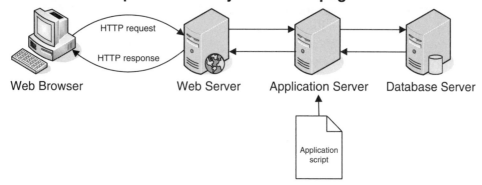

Description

- A *dynamic web page* is a web page that's generated by a server-side program or script.

- When a web server receives a request for a dynamic web page, it looks up the extension of the requested file to find out which *application server* should process the request.

- When the application server receives a request, it runs the specified script. Often, this script uses the data that it gets from the web browser to get the appropriate data from a *database server*. This script can also store the data that it receives in the database.

- When the application server finishes processing the data, it generates a web page and returns it to the web server. Then, the web server returns the web page to the web browser.

Figure 1-3   How dynamic web pages are processed

How JavaScript fits into web development

In contrast to the *server-side processing* that's done for dynamic web pages, JavaScript provides for *client-side processing*. In the web site in figure 1-4, for example, JavaScript is used to change the images that are shown without using server-side processing.

To make this work, all of the required images are loaded into the browser when the page is requested. Then, if the user clicks on one of the color swatches below a shirt, the shirt image is changed to the one with the right color. This is called an *image swap*. Similarly, if the user moves the mouse over a shirt, the image is replaced by a closeup image of the shirt. This is called an *image rollover*.

The diagram in this figure shows how JavaScript processing works. In contrast to server-side processing, JavaScript code is executed in the web browser by the browser's *JavaScript engine*. This takes some of the processing burden off the server and makes the application run faster. As this diagram shows, JavaScript can be used in conjunction with dynamic web pages, but it can also be used with static web pages.

Besides image swaps and rollovers, there are many other uses for JavaScript. For instance, another common use is to validate the data that the user enters into an HTML form before it is sent to the server for processing. This saves unnecessary trips to the server. Other common uses of JavaScript are to run slide shows, rotate headlines or products in one area of a web page, and provide animation. In fact, whenever you see a portion of a web page cycle through a series of text blocks or images, that's probably being done by JavaScript.

In this book, you won't learn how to code JavaScript. However, chapter 13 presents an introduction to JavaScript that shows how you can use JavaScript that someone else has written to do tasks like printing a page, swapping an image, and validating a page. Then, when you finish this book, we recommend that you read *Murach's JavaScript and DOM Scripting* by Ray Harris. It will show you how to write your own JavaScript code for the tasks you want to do.

A web page with image swaps and rollovers

Image swap

Image rollover

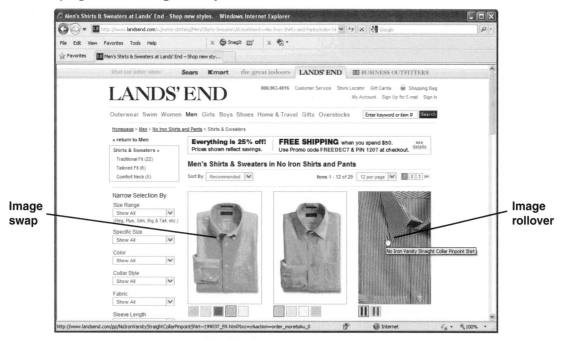

How JavaScript fits into this architecture

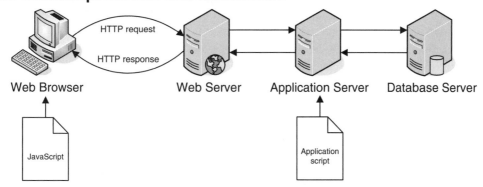

Three of the common uses of JavaScript

- Data validation
- Image swaps and rollovers
- Slide shows

Description

- *JavaScript* is a *client-side scripting language* that is run by the *JavaScript engine* of a web browser and controls the operation of the browser. As a result, the work is done on the client, not the server.

Figure 1-4   How JavaScript fits into web development

A survey of browsers, servers, and scripting languages

Figure 1-5 summarizes the five web browsers that are used the most today. When you develop Internet web sites for a general audience, you usually need to test the pages on all five of these browsers including all versions that are still in common use. On the other hand, if you're developing a web site for a company's internal use that runs on an intranet, you can sometimes specify the browser and version that has to be used.

Microsoft's Internet Explorer (IE) is the most widely used browser. It is currently available only for Windows, but an earlier version for Mac OS was available until January 2006. Although IE 8 was released in September 2008, IE 7 and even 6 are still in widespread use.

Firefox is the second most popular web browser. It is available for Windows, Mac OS, Linux, and other operating systems. Firefox was built using source code from the original Netscape Navigator web browser, and many web developers use it as their primary browser because they like its many features including its debugging features.

Safari and Opera are used by a small percentage of users. Safari is the default web browser on Mac OS, but it is also available for Windows. Opera is available for Windows, Mac OS, Linux, and other operating systems.

Google's Chrome is a recent addition to the most popular web browsers, and its popularity is growing fast. Chrome is based on the WebKit rendering engine, which is the same one that Safari uses.

Next, this figure summarizes the two web servers that are used the most. The *Apache* web server, which was developed by the Apache Software Foundation, is the most widely used. It is an open-source software project that's available for free. Although there are Apache versions for most operating systems, it is typically used on a Linux server.

The other widely used web server is Microsoft's *Internet Information Services (IIS)*. It is included as part of the Windows Server operating system, and it supports the ASP.NET scripting language. This web server isn't open source, and new features other than scripting languages must be released by Microsoft.

Last, this figure summarizes the most common *scripting languages* for web servers. These are the languages that let you develop dynamic web pages. For instance, ASP.NET is a Microsoft product that is designed for the IIS web server. JSP is a free, open-source language that is commonly used with Java servlets and runs on an Apache server. And PHP is another free, open-source language that typically runs on an Apache server.

To develop dynamic web pages, you need to choose one of these languages. To learn how to use ASP.NET, JSP, or PHP, please check our web site for our latest books on these subjects.

Web browsers

Browser	Description
Internet Explorer	Published by Microsoft, the latest version is IE 8 released in September 2008. It is only available on the Windows platform.
Firefox	Published by the Mozilla Corporation, the latest version is 3.5 released in June 2009. It is available for all major operating systems.
Safari	Published by Apple, the latest version is 4.0.4 released in November 2009. It is available for OS X and Windows.
Opera	Published by Opera Software, the latest version is 10 released in September 2009. It is available for all major operating systems.
Chrome	Published by Google, the latest version is 3.0 released in September 2009. It will eventually be available for all major operating systems.

Web servers

Server	Description
Apache	An open-source web server that can run on any major operating system. It supports many server-side languages and can interact with many database servers.
IIS	This is the Microsoft web server. It primarily supports the ASP.NET scripting language and Microsoft's SQL Server database, but it can be used with other server-side scripting languages and databases.

Server-side scripting languages

Language	Description
ASP.NET	Included with the Microsoft IIS web server, its pages have the .aspx extension.
JSP	A free, open-source language that is commonly used with Java servlets. It runs on an Apache web server, and its pages have the .jsp extension.
PHP	A free, open-source language that is typically used with an Apache web server, but is also available for IIS. Its pages have the .php extension.
ColdFusion	A commercial scripting language from Adobe that integrates well with Adobe Flash and Flex. It is available for both IIS and Apache, and its pages have the .cfml file extension.
Ruby	A free, open-source language that is typically used with Apache and combined with the Rails framework to simplify development. Its pages have the .rb extension.
Perl	A free, open-source language that was originally designed for use at the UNIX command line to manipulate text. Its pages have the .pl extension.
Python	A free, open-source language that can be used to develop many types of applications besides web applications. Typically used with an Apache server, its pages have the .py extension.

Description

- When you develop a web site for general use, you need to test it on all five of the web browsers listed above including all versions that are still in common use.
- To develop dynamic web pages, you use a language like ASP.NET, JSP, or PHP.

Figure 1-5   A survey of browsers, servers, and server-side scripting languages

An introduction to HTML, XHTML, and CSS

To develop a web page, you use HTML or XHTML to define the content and structure of the page. Then, you use CSS to format that content. The topics that follow introduce you to HTML, XHTML, and CSS.

The HTML for a web page

HyperText Markup Language (*HTML*) is used to define the content and structure of a web page. *Extensible HTML (XHTML)* is a modified version of HTML that supports the same features as HTML but uses a syntax that is somewhat stricter. From a practical point of view, you choose which of the two markup languages you're going to use when you start a web site and stick with it. More about that in a moment.

In figure 1-6, you can see the HTML for a web page followed by a browser that shows how that page is displayed in Internet Explorer. Although you're going to learn how to code every aspect of an HTML page in this book, here's a brief introduction to what's going on.

The code for the entire page is called an *HTML document*. This document starts with a *DOCTYPE declaration* that indicates whether the document is coded with HTML or XHTML. In this example, this declaration says that the document is using XHTML 1.0.

The DOCTYPE declaration is followed by *tags* that identify the *HTML elements* within the document. The *opening tag* for each element consists of the element name surrounded by angle brackets, as in <html>. And the *closing tag* consists of a left angle bracket, a forward slash, the element name, and the right angle bracket, as in </html>.

The basic structure of an HTML document consists of head and body elements that are coded within the html element. The head section contains elements that provide information about the document. The body section contains the elements that will be displayed in the web browser. For instance, the title element in the head section provides the title that's shown in the title bar of the web browser, while the h1 element in the body section provides the heading that's displayed in the browser window.

Many elements can be coded with *attributes* that identify the element and define the way the content in the element is displayed. These attributes are coded within the opening tag, and each attribute consists of an attribute name, an equals sign, and the attribute value. For instance, the opening <div> tag in this example has an attribute called id with *page* as its value, and the <img> tag has two attributes named src and alt. In this case, the src attribute provides the name of the image file that should be displayed and the alt attribute provides the text that should be displayed if the image can't be found.

The code for an HTML file named book.html

```
<!DOCTYPE html PUBLIC "-//W3C//DTD XHTML 1.0 Transitional//EN"
    "http://www.w3.org/TR/xhtml1/DTD/xhtml1-transitional.dtd">
<html xmlns="http://www.w3.org/1999/xhtml">
    <head>
        <title>JavaScript book</title>
    </head>
    <body>
        <div id="page">
            <h1>JavaScript and DOM Scripting</h1>
            <img src="javascriptbook.jpg" alt="JavaScript Book" />

            <p>Today, web users expect web sites to provide advanced
            features, dynamic user interfaces, and fast response times.
            To deliver that, web developers need to know the JavaScript
            language. Beyond that, though, they need to know how to use
            JavaScript to script the Document Object Model (or DOM).</p>
            <p>Now, at last, your trainees can learn both JavaScript and
            DOM scripting in this one great book. To find out how this
            book does it, <a href="">read more...</a></p><br /><br />
        </div>
    </body>
</html>
```

The HTML displayed in a web browser

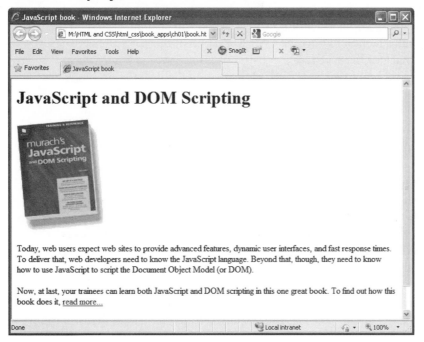

Description

- *HTML (HyperText Markup Language)* or *XHTML (eXtensible HyperText Markup Language)* is used to define the content and structure of a web page.

Figure 1-6   The HTML for a web page

The CSS for a web page

Until recently, most HTML documents were coded so the HTML not only defined the content and structure of the web page but also the formatting of that content. However, this mix of structural and formatting elements made it hard to edit, maintain, and reformat the web pages.

Today, however, *Cascading Style Sheets* (*CSS*) let you separate the formatting from the content and structure of a web page. As a result, most of the formatting that was once done in the HTML should now be done in the CSS.

The best way to apply a *style sheet* to an HTML document is to code the styles in a separate file called an *external style sheet*. Then, to apply the style sheet, you code a link element in the head section of the HTML document as shown at the top of figure 1-7. Here, the href attribute of the tag says that the style sheet in the file named book.css should be applied to the HTML document.

After this link element, you can see the CSS that's in the book.css file. This is followed by a browser that shows how the web page is displayed after the style sheet has been applied to it. If you compare this to the screen shot in the last figure, you can see that the page is now centered with a border around it, the heading is larger, the font for the text has been changed, there's less spacing between paragraphs, and the text is displayed to the right of the book image. This gives you a quick idea of how much you can do with CSS.

Although you're going to learn how to code CSS in chapters 4, 5, and 6, here's a brief introduction to how the CSS works. First, this CSS file consists of five *rule sets*. Each of these rule sets consists of a *selector* and a *declaration block*. The selector identifies an HTML element, and the declaration block specifies the formatting for the element. Within the declaration block are one or more *declarations* (or *rules*) that specify the formatting for the element.

For instance, the first rule set applies to the body element. It says that the body should have no margins and that the font family for the content should be Arial, Helvetica, or the default sans-serif type, in that order of preference. This changes the font for the elements that are coded within the body.

In contrast, the second rule set applies to the div element with "page" as its id. If you look back to the HTML, you can see that this element encloses all of the other elements. Then, this rule set sets the top and bottom margins to zero and the left and right margins to auto, which centers the page in the browser window. It also adds a solid border with navy as its color.

Then, the third rule set formats all of the h1 elements in the HTML with a larger font size and the navy color. The fourth rule set formats the image by floating it to the left so the <p> tags are displayed to its right. And the fifth rule set changes the spacing between <p> tags.

You will of course learn all of the details for coding rule sets in this book, but this should give you an idea of what's going on. In short, the HTML defines the content and structure of the document, and the CSS defines the formatting of the content. This separates the content from the formatting, which makes it easier to create and maintain web pages.

The element in the head section of the HTML file that links it to a CSS file

```
<link rel="stylesheet" type="text/css" href="book.css" />
```

The code for the CSS file named book.css

```css
body {
    margin: 0 0;
    font-family: Arial, Helvetica, sans-serif;
    font-size: 82.5%;
}
#page {
    width: 500px;
    margin: 0 auto;
    padding: 1em;
    border: 1px solid navy;
}
h1 {
    margin: 0;
    padding: .25em;
    font-size: 250%;
    color: navy;
}
img  {
    float: left;
    margin: 0 1em;
}
p {
    margin: 0;
    padding-bottom: .5em;
}
```

The web page displayed in a web browser

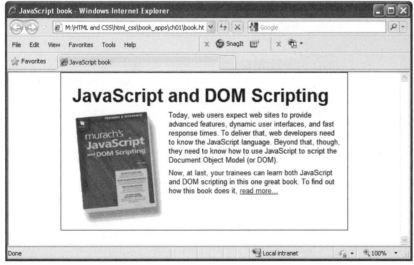

Description

- *Cascading Style Sheets* (*CSS*) are used to control how web pages are displayed by specifying the fonts, colors, borders, spacing, and layout of the pages.

Figure 1-7   The CSS for a web page

The HTML, XHTML, and CSS standards

As figure 1-8 shows, the standards for HTML, XHTML, and CSS continue to change. As a web developer, you need to keep track of these changes for two reasons. First, you want to make sure that your current web pages will continue to work with new browsers. Second, you want take advantage of new features as they become widely available.

As this figure shows, HTML has been around since the early 1990's. The last version of HTML was HTML 4.01, which was released in December 1999. Then, XHTML 1.0 was introduced in January 2000.

XHTML is a modified version of HTML that supports the same elements as HTML 4.01, but uses the syntax of XML. This is a stricter syntax that allows XHTML to be read and manipulated by automated tools. This also allows XHTML editors to identify errors in the document structure more easily.

Work is currently underway to develop HTML 5. This standard includes a new version of XHTML known as XHTML 5. Some browsers already support parts of the HTML 5 specification, but you should avoid using these features in production web sites until the specification is supported by most browsers.

As this figure shows, CSS 2.1 is the most stable version of CSS. It was released as a candidate standard in February 2004, but it was returned to a working draft for further modification. In July 2007, it was released again as a candidate standard.

Because of the revisions to the standards, CSS has been inconsistently supported. However, the major web browsers support most of CSS 2.1. As a result, this is the version of CSS that you will learn in this book.

What version of HTML we use in this book

At present, web developers debate whether you should use HTML 4.01 or XHTML 1.0 as you develop your web sites. Since Internet Explorer still doesn't support XHTML, you would think you would have to use HTML 4.01. However, as you will see in the next chapter, the differences between HTML 4.01 and XHTML 1.0 are minimal. As a result, you can easily code a version of XHTML 1.0 that is compatible with Internet Explorer.

So what we recommend in this book is that you use XHTML 1.0, but code it in a way that is compatible with Internet Explorer. That way, you will get the benefits of using the stricter syntax of XHTML, but your code will be compatible with HTML 4.01 so it will run on all modern browsers including Internet Explorer. This will also prepare you for HTML 5, which will probably end the debate about whether you should use HTML or XHTML by bringing them closer together.

With that as background, we're going to use the term *HTML* to refer to either HTML or XHTML in the rest of this book. We will only use the term *XHTML* to identify some aspect of coding that applies just to XHTML.

Highlights in the history of the HTML and XHTML standards

Version	Description
HTML 1.0	A draft specification released in January 1993 that was never adopted as a standard.
HTML 2.0	Adopted in November 1995.
HTML 3.2	Adopted in January 1997. It formalized new features that were used by web browsers.
HTML 4.0	Adopted in December 1997. It formalized new features that were used by web browsers and deprecated older features. It had three versions: Strict, Transitional, and Frameset.
HTML 4.01	Adopted in December 1999 and updated through May 2001. It maintained the Strict, Transitional, and Frameset versions.
XHTML 1.0	Adopted in January 2000 and revised in August 2002. It reformulates HTML 4 using the syntax of XML, which makes it easier to parse the web page. This allows automated tools to find errors in a web page. It maintained the Strict, Transitional, and Frameset versions.
XHTML 1.1	Adopted in May 2001. The control of the presentation of content is now done through CSS.
XHTML 2	Released as a working draft in July 2006. It is intended to be a new version of XHTML, but it may be replaced by XHTML 5 before becoming a standard.
HTML 5	Released as a working draft in January 2008. It is a new version of HTML 4 and XHTML 1 that defines an HTML version called HTML 5 and an XHTML version called XHTML 5.

The CSS standards

Version	Description
1.0	Adopted in December 1996.
2.0	Adopted in May 1998.
2.1	First released as a candidate standard in February 2004, it was returned to working draft status in June 2005. It became a candidate standard again in July 2007.
3.0	A modularized version of CSS with the earliest drafts in June 1999. Only a few modules have been released as candidate standards; some reverted to working drafts.

HTML vs. XHTML

- By default, all pages are sent to the browser, or served, as HTML. In fact, Internet Explorer won't display pages that are served as XHTML.
- Because the syntax of XHTML is stricter than the syntax of HTML, XHTML encourages good coding practices.

What version of HTML we use in this book

- In this book, we use a form of XHTML 1.0 that is compatible with HTML 4.01.
- This works for all browsers including Internet Explorer because XHTML 1.0 is backward-compatible with HTML 4.01.

Figure 1-8   The HTML, XHTML, and CSS standards

Tools for web development

To create and edit the HTML and CSS files for a web site, you need either a text editor or an IDE for web development. To deploy a web site on the Internet, you also need an FTP program to upload the files from your computer or network server to the web server. You'll learn about these tools next.

Text editors for HTML and CSS

Although you can use any text editor to enter and edit HTML and CSS files, a better editor can speed development time and reduce coding errors. For that reason, we recommend that Windows users start with Notepad++. It is a free editor that uses color to show the syntax in HTML and CSS code. It also provides auto-completion lists that let you select an item after you enter the first characters.

The auto-completion feature is illustrated by the Notepad++ window in figure 1-9. Here, the developer has entered the first two letters of an <img> tag, and the auto-completion list shows the words that start with those letters. Then, the developer can move the cursor to the right word in the list and press the Tab key to enter that word into the code. In the next chapter, you'll learn how to use Notepad++.

If you're a Mac OS user, we recommend that you start with TextWrangler as your editor. This is a free editor that provides syntax highlighting, but doesn't provide auto-completion. If you want auto-completion, we recommend the commercial version of TextWrangler, which is called BBEdit.

Another alternative for both Windows and Mac users is Komodo Edit. This is a free editor that provides color coding, tag completion, code snippets, and more.

Notepad++ with open HTML and CSS files

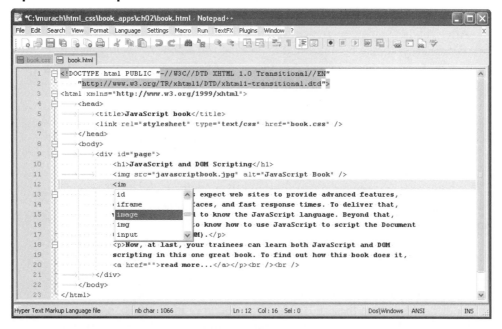

Popular text editors that are free

Editor	Runs on
Notepad++	Windows
TextWrangler	Macintosh
Komodo Edit	Windows, Macintosh, and Linux/UNIX

Description

- A text editor lets you enter and edit the HTML and CSS files for a web application.
- Some common features of a text editor for HTML and CSS are syntax highlighting and auto-completion.

Figure 1-9   Text editors for HTML and CSS

IDEs for web development

After you get some experience with a text editor like Notepad++ or TextWrangler, you may be interested in an *Integrated Development Environment* (*IDE*) for web development. For instance, Adobe DreamWeaver has long been the most popular commercial IDE for web development.

As you can see in figure 1-10, DreamWeaver lets you edit HTML or CSS code in one panel of its window while it shows you how the web page will look in another panel. DreamWeaver also lets you generate code instead of entering it by dragging the symbols for common elements onto the HTML document. It provides the starting code for an HTML document whenever you start a new file. It helps you manage the directories and files for the web site. It provides an FTP program that uploads the pages from your development server to your Internet server. And it has many other features.

In general, an IDE like DreamWeaver can help you make dramatic improvements in your productivity. That's why professional web developers often use IDEs for web development. Two other popular IDEs that you might want to consider are Komodo IDE and Microsoft Expression Web.

Note, however, that these IDEs vary considerably in features and price. For instance, Komodo IDE offers features that let you integrate your HTML and CSS development with JavaScript and server-side scripting languages like PHP, Perl, and Python. So before you buy an IDE, you need to find the IDE that best suits your requirements and budget.

At the highest level, an IDE for web development can include all of the programs that are required for developing a web site. IDEs like this are often referred to as *suites*. For example, the Design Premium edition of the Adobe Creative Suite includes Photoshop for editing photos and images, Illustrator for creating and editing illustrations, Flash for adding animation and interactivity to web pages, and several other programs that are related to web development. Similarly, Microsoft Expression Studio provides a variety of related products for developing web pages.

Here again, suites vary considerably in price and features. So you need to find the one that best suits your requirements and budget.

Adobe DreamWeaver

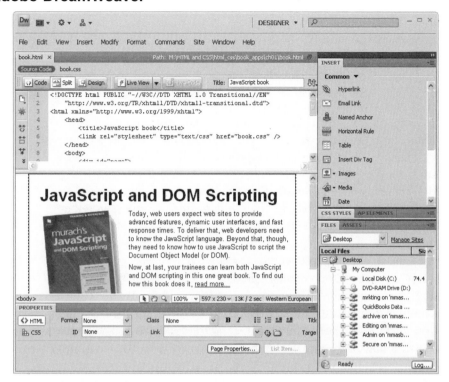

Popular IDEs for web development

IDE	Runs on
Adobe DreamWeaver	Windows and Macintosh
Komodo IDE	Windows, Macintosh, and Linux/UNIX
Microsoft Expression Web	Windows

Popular suites for web development

IDE	Runs on
Adobe Creative Suite	Windows and Macintosh
Microsoft Expression Studio	Windows

Description

- An *Integrated Development Environment* (*IDE*) goes beyond text editing to provide other features for the development of web sites.

- *Suites* are IDEs that provide all of the software components that you need for the development of a web site.

Figure 1-10   IDEs for web development

FTP programs

If you want to *deploy* (or *publish*) your web site on the Internet, you need to transfer the directories and files for your web site from your computer or network to a web server with Internet access. To do that, you use an *FTP program* like one of those listed in figure 1-11. This type of program uses *File Transfer Protocol* to transfer files to or from the web server.

If you're using an IDE like DreamWeaver for web development, it will probably include an FTP program. And if you're using a text editor, you may be able to find a *plug-in* or *add-in* for an FTP program. Then, you can access the FTP program from your text editor.

If you don't already have an Internet web server, one option is to find an *Internet Service Provider* (*ISP*) that provides *web hosting*. If you search the web, you'll be able to find many ISPs that provide web hosting, often for a small monthly fee.

If you're going to use dynamic web pages on your web site, you need to find an ISP that supports the server-side language and the database that you're going to use. If, for example, you're going to use PHP with a MySQL database, which is a common combination, you need to find an ISP that supports that.

When you select a web host, you get an *IP address* like 64.71.179.86 that uniquely identifies your web site (IP stands for Internet Protocol). Then, you can get a *domain name* like www.murach.com. To do that, you can use any number of companies that you can find on the Internet, and sometimes you can get the domain name from your ISP. Until you get your domain name, you can use the IP address to access your site.

After you get a web host, you use your FTP program to upload the files for your web site to the web server of the web host. Then, you can test your web site on the Internet. When you're through testing, you can announce your web site to the world and let it go live.

An FTP program that uploads files to the web server

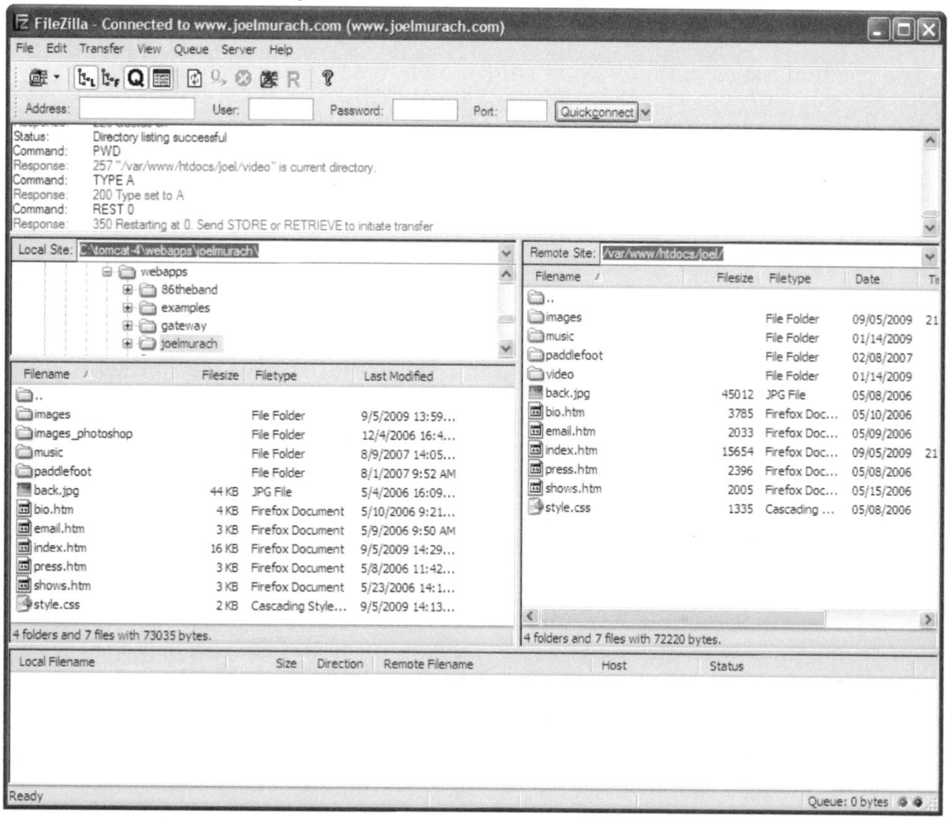

Popular FTP programs

Program	Description
FileZilla	A free program available for Windows, Macintosh, and Linux.
FTP Voyager	An inexpensive program for Windows.
CuteFTP	An inexpensive program for Windows and Macintosh.
Fetch	An inexpensive program for Macintosh.

Description

- To *deploy* (or *publish*) a web site on the Internet, you need to transfer the directories and files for the web site from your computer or network to a web server on the Internet. To do that, you use an *FTP program* that uses *File Transfer Protocol*.

- An FTP program not only lets you transfer files from a client to a web server but also from a web server to a client. Most IDEs have a built-in FTP program.

- If you're using a text editor, you may have to use a separate FTP program or add a plug-in FTP program to your editor. For example, there's a plug-in program for Notepad++.

- For more information on deploying an application to a web server, please see chapter 15.

Figure 1-11   FTP programs for uploading files to the web server

How to view deployed web pages

The last two topics in this chapter show you how to view a web page in a web browser and how to view the source code for a web page that's displayed in the browser. These are valuable skills as you test your own web pages or study the pages on other sites.

How to view a web page

Figure 1-12 shows you how to view a web page on the Internet. One way is to enter a *uniform resource locator* (*URL*) into the address bar of your browser. The other is to click on a link on a web page that requests another page.

As the diagram in this figure shows, the URL for an Internet page consists of four components. In most cases, the *protocol* is HTTP. If you omit the protocol, the browser uses HTTP as the default.

The second component is the *domain name* that identifies the web server that the HTTP request will be sent to. The web browser uses this name to look up the address of the web server for the domain. Although you can't omit the domain name, most web sites let you omit "www." from the domain name.

The third component is the *path* where the file resides on the server. This path lists the directories that contain the file. Forward slashes are used to separate the names in the path and to represent the server's top-level directory at the start of the path. In this example, the path is "/books/". If you omit the path, you must also omit the file name. Then, the web server will return the web site's home page.

The last component is the name of the file. In this example, the file is named index.htm. If you omit the file name, the web server will search for a default document in the path. Depending on the web server, this file will be named index.html, default.htm, or some variation of the two.

In general, directory and file names should only contain lowercase letters, numbers, the period, and the underscore character. Lowercase letters are recommended because on some web servers, the names in the path may be case sensitive. Then, if a URL specifies a directory named "Images", but the directory on the server is actually named "images", the web server will report that it cannot find the file.

Now that you know the components of a URL, you can see that the domain name for the page in the browser in this figure is www.riverparkway.org and its file name is default.asp. Here, the file extension indicates that this is a dynamic web page created by the ASP scripting language, which is the predecessor to ASP.NET. In contrast, ASP.NET files have aspx as the extension.

If you want to view an HTML page that's on your own computer or an intranet, you can use the Open command (IE) or Open File command (Firefox) in the File menu of the browser. You'll learn more about this in the next chapter.

The components of an HTTP URL

http://www.murach.com/books/index.htm

  protocol   domain name   path   filename

The web page at http://www.riverparkway.org/default.asp

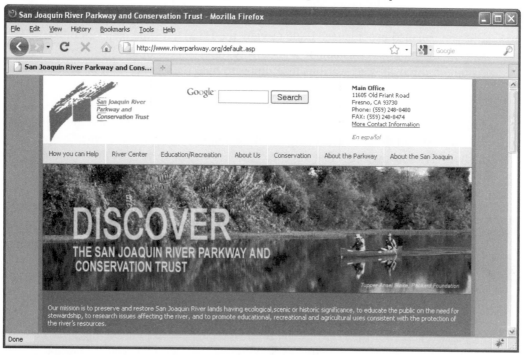

What happens if you omit parts of a URL

- If you omit the protocol, the default of http:// will be used.
- If you omit the filename, the default document name for the web server will be used. This is typically index.html, default.htm, or some variation.
- If you omit the path, you must also omit the filename. Then, the home page for the site will be requested.

Two ways to access a web page on the Internet

- Enter the URL of a web page into the browser's address bar.
- Click on a link in the current web page to load the next web page.

How to access a web page on your own server or computer

- Use the File→Open command with Internet Explorer or the File→File Open command with Firefox.

Figure 1-12   How to view a web page

How to view the source code for a web page

When a web page is displayed by a browser, you can use the techniques in figure 1-13 to view the HTML code for the page in a separate window. If, for example, you're using the Firefox browser, you can use the View→Page Source command to see the HTML code. In this example, the HTML code for the page in the previous figure is shown.

Viewing the source code can be useful when you're testing an application. But you can also use this technique to view the HTML for the pages of other sites on the Internet. This can be a good way to learn how other sites work. Although some sites use various techniques to hide their code, a lot of the code for Internet sites is available.

If the CSS for an HTML page is stored in an external file, you can sometimes use the Firefox browser to open that file by clicking on the path in the HTML code. In the code in this figure, for example, you can click on include/style.css to access that css file. This lets you analyze how the CSS code works.

If you're using Internet Explorer, you can view the CSS code in an external file by entering the URL for the CSS file in the browser's address bar. For instance, for the CSS file that's identified by the link element in the HTML code in this figure, you can enter this address into the browser:

`http://www.riverparkway.org/include/style.css`

Then, when you press the Enter key, the file is opened in another browser window. In chapter 3, you'll learn more about the relative addresses that are used in HTML code so you'll be able to determine what their URLs are.

When you view the HTML code for a web page, keep in mind that it may include embedded CSS code or JavaScript code. Beyond that, you'll find that all but the simplest sites are quite complicated. Once you finish this book, though, you should be able to figure out how the HTML and CSS for most sites work. And you'll learn a lot by studying how the best sites are coded.

The HTML source code for the page in figure 1-12

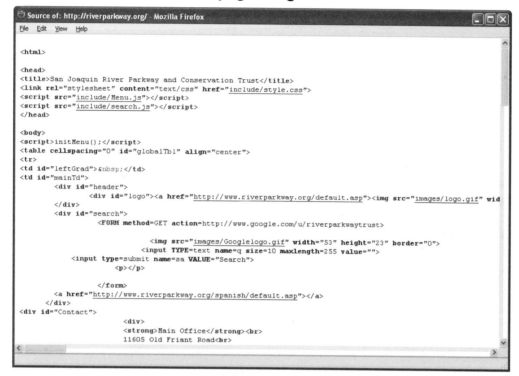

How to view the HTML source code for a web page

- In Firefox, use the View→Page Source command.
- In Internet Explorer, use the View→Source command.

How to view the CSS code in an external CSS file

- In Firefox, click on the link in the link element that refers to it.
- In Internet Explorer, enter the URL for the CSS file in your web browser.

Description

- When you view the source code for a web page in a web browser, the HTML code is opened in a separate window.
- If the CSS for the page is stored in an external file, you can often view that file by using the techniques above.
- Often, CSS is stored in the HTML file instead of an external file. That makes it easier to see how the HTML and CSS work together, but that isn't the best way to use CSS.

Figure 1-13   How to view the source code for a web page

Perspective

Now that you know the concepts and terms that you need for developing web sites with HTML and CSS, you're ready to learn how to develop a web page. So in the next chapter, you'll learn how to enter, edit, test, and validate a web page. After that, you'll be ready to learn all the details of HTML and CSS that you need for developing the pages of a web site.

Terms

World Wide Web	server-side scripting language
Internet	HTML (HyperText Markup Language)
client	XHTML (eXtensible HTML)
web browser	HTML document
web server	DOCTYPE declaration
network	HTML element
local area network (LAN)	tag
intranet	opening tag
wide area network (WAN)	closing tag
router	attribute
Internet service provider (ISP)	CSS (Cascading Style Sheets)
Internet exchange point (IXP)	style sheet
static web page	external style sheet
HTTP request	rule set
HTTP (HyperText Transport Protocol)	selector
HTTP response	declarative block
render a web page	declaration
dynamic web page	rule
application server	IDE (Integrated Development Environment)
database server	suite
round trip	deploy
web application	publish
server-side processing	File Transfer Protocol (FTP)
JavaScript	FTP program
client-side processing	web host
client-side scripting language	IP address
image swap	domain name
image rollover	URL (Uniform Resource Locator)
JavaScript engine	

Summary

- A web application consists of clients, a web server, and a network. *Clients* use *web browsers* to request web pages from the web server. The *web server* returns the requested pages.

- A *local area network* (*LAN*) connects computers that are near to each other. This is often called an *intranet*. In contrast, a *wide area network* (*WAN*) uses *routers* to connect two or more LANs. The *Internet* consists of many WANs that are connected at *Internet exchange points*.

- To request a web page, the web browser sends an *HTTP request* to the web server that includes the name of the requested file. Then, the web server retrieves the HTML for the requested web page and sends it back to the browser in an *HTTP response*. Last, the browser *renders* the HTML into a web page.

- A *static web page* is a page that is the same each time it's retrieved. The file for this type of page has html or htm as its extension, and its HTML doesn't change.

- The HTML for a *dynamic web page* is generated by a server-side program or script, so its HTML can change from one request to another. When a web server receives a request for a dynamic web page, it uses the extension of the requested file to find out which *application server* should process the request.

- *JavaScript* is a *scripting language* that is run by the *JavaScript engine* of a web browser. It provides for client-side processing, and it is commonly used in modern web applications.

- *HTML* (*HyperText Markup Language*) is the language that defines the structure and contents of a web page. *CSS* (*Cascading Style Sheets*) are used to control how the web pages are formatted.

- *HTML* has been around since the early 1990's. *XHTML* is a modified version of HTML that uses a stricter syntax than HTML. In this book, we use a form of XHTML 1.0 that is compatible with HTML 4.01 so it runs on Internet Explorer as well as all modern browsers.

- To develop web pages, you can use a text editor like Notepad++, TextWrangler, or Komodo Edit. You can also use an *Integrated Development Environment* (*IDE*) like Adobe DreamWeaver or Komodo IDE that combines text editing with other development functions.

- To *deploy* (or *publish*) a web site on the Internet, you need to transfer the directories and files for your site from your computer or server to a web server with Internet access. To do that, you use an *FTP program* that uses *File Transfer Protocol* to transfer the files.

- To view a web page, you can enter the *URL* (*Uniform Resource Locator*) into a browser's address bar. A URL consists of the *protocol*, *domain name*, *path*, and *filename*.

- To view a web page that's on your own computer or server, you can use the browser's File→Open or File→File Open command.

- To view the HTML for a web page, you can use your browser's View→Page Source or View→Source command. Then, to view the CSS for a page, you can either click on the link for it in the source code (Firefox) or enter the URL for the CSS file in the address bar (Internet Explorer).

Before you do the exercises for this book...

Before you do the exercises for this book, you should download and install the Firefox browser. You should also download and install the applications for this book. The procedures for installing the software and applications for this book are described in appendix A.

Exercise 1-1   Visit some Internet web sites

In this exercise, you'll visit some Internet web sites and view the source code for those sites.

Visit the River Parkway web site with Firefox

1.   Start Firefox.

2.   Enter *www.riverparkway.org* into the address bar and press the Enter key or click on the arrow at the right side of the address bar. That should display the home page for this web site.

3.   Enter just *riverparkway* into the address bar and press the Enter key. Note how Firefox adds www. and .com. But you want org, not com. So click the Back button to return to the site in step 2.

4.   Use the View→Page Source command to view the HTML file for the home page. In the fourth line, you can see a link element that identifies the CSS file that does the formatting. This is followed by two script elements that identify JavaScript files.

5.   If you scroll through this code, it probably looks overwhelming, even though this site is relatively simple. By the time you complete this book, though, you should understand this code.

6.   Click on the underlined value of the href attribute in the link element. That should open the CSS file for this page. This shows how easy it is to access the HTML and CSS code for many (but not all) sites.

Visit the River Parkway web site with Internet Explorer

7.   Start Internet Explorer. Then, repeat steps 2 through 4, but use the View→Source command to view the source code. In the source code, note that the links aren't underlined as they are in Firefox so you can't click on one to view the related code or file.

8.   Enter this URL into the browser's address bar and press the Enter key:

     `http://www.riverparkway.org/include/style.css`

     This should display the CSS code in a new window. Note, however, that if you have DreamWeaver installed on your system, this may open the CSS file in DreamWeaver. Either way, though, you can review the CSS code.

Visit other web sites

9. Use either Firefox or Internet Explorer to visit other web sites and view the source code of those sites. When you're through experimenting, go on to the next exercise.

Exercise 1-2   View the example in this chapter

In this exercise, you'll visit the book page that was used as an example in figures 1-6 and 1-7.

Open the book page in Firefox

1. Start Firefox if it isn't already open.

2. Use the File→Open File command to open this HTML file:

   ```
   c:\html_css\ch01\book.html
   ```

3. Use the View→Page Source command to display the HTML file for this page. Note that the DOCTYPE declaration specifies XHTML 1.0 Transitional.

4. Click on *book.css* in the link element in the HTML code to display the CSS file for this page.

Open the book page in Internet Explorer

5. Start Internet Explorer if it isn't already open.

6. Use the File→Open command to open the same HTML file as in step 2. Note that this page is displayed the same way even though the DOCTYPE declaration specifies XHTML 1.0, which isn't supported by IE. That's because the HTML file uses a version of XHTML 1.0 that's compatible with HTML 4.01.

7. Use the View→Source command to open the HTML file for this page. Then, click on *book.css* in the link element in the HTML code to try to display the CSS file for this page. Here again, this doesn't work with IE.

2

How to code, test, and validate a web page

In this chapter, you'll learn how to create and edit HTML and CSS files. Then, you'll learn how to test those files to make sure they work correctly. Last, you'll learn how to validate the code in HTML and CSS files to make sure that it doesn't have any errors. When you're through with this chapter, you'll be ready to learn all the details of HTML and CSS coding.

The HTML syntax

When you code an HTML document, you need to adhere to the rules for creating the HTML elements. These rules are referred to as the *syntax* of the language.

In the four topics that follow, you'll learn the HTML syntax as well as the variations between HTML 4.01 and XHTML 1.0. As you read these topics, remember that we recommend that you use a version of XHTML 1.0 that is compatible with HTML 4.01.

The basic structure of an HTML document

Figure 2-1 presents the basic structure of an *HTML document*. This structure starts with the DOCTYPE declaration that specifies the HTML or XHTML standard that you're going to use. This declaration is followed by *HTML elements* that define the content and structure of the web page.

When you use XHTML, the DOCTYPE declaration must be followed by an html element that includes the xmlns (XML name space) attribute. Then, within the opening and closing tags for that element, there must be a head element and a body element.

In chapter 3, you'll learn more about coding the DOCTYPE declaration. But usually, you'll use the declaration and HTML elements that are shown in this figure in every document that you create. As a result, you can start every document from a template that contains this code or you can copy this code into any new HTML file that you create.

This figure also summarizes the differences between the structure of an HTML document and the structure of an XHTML document. In short, the html, head, and body elements aren't required in HTML, and the xmlns attribute isn't allowed if you do code an html element. This illustrates that XHTML has a stricter syntax than HTML.

You may remember from chapter 1 that all of the examples in this book use XHTML code that's written in a way that will run on Internet Explorer, even though IE doesn't support XHTML. We think this will prepare you for the next releases of the HTML and XHTML standards. This will also make it easier for you to validate your files as shown at the end of this chapter. On the other hand, if you're working on a project that uses some version of HTML instead of XHTML, it's easy to make the required adjustments.

The basic structure of an XHTML document

```
<!DOCTYPE html PUBLIC "-//W3C//DTD XHTML 1.0 Transitional//EN"
    "http://www.w3.org/TR/xhtml1/DTD/xhtml1-transitional.dtd">

<html xmlns="http://www.w3.org/1999/xhtml">
    <head>
        .
        .                ── head element
    </head>
                                                    ── html (root) element
    <body>
        .
        .                ── body element
    </body>
</html>
```

A simple XHTML document

```
<!DOCTYPE html PUBLIC "-//W3C//DTD XHTML 1.0 Transitional//EN"
    "http://www.w3.org/TR/xhtml1/DTD/xhtml1-transitional.dtd">
<html xmlns="http://www.w3.org/1999/xhtml">
    <head>
        <title>San Joaquin Valley Town Hall</title>
    </head>
    <body>
        <h1>San Joaquin Valley Town Hall</h1>
        <p>Welcome to San Joaquin Valley Town Hall.</p>
        <p>We have some amazing speakers in store for you this
        season!</p>
        <p><a href="speakers.html">Speaker information</a></p>
    </body>
</html>
```

Differences between the structure of an XHTML and an HTML document

- In XHTML, the <!DOCTYPE> declaration and the html, head, and body elements are required. In HTML, these elements can be omitted, although that will make validation (see figure 2-13) more difficult.

- In XHTML, the html element requires an xmlns attribute that's coded exactly as shown above. In HTML, this attribute isn't allowed.

Description

- An *HTML document* contains *HTML elements* that define the content and structure of a web page.

- Each HTML document should start with a <!DOCTYPE> declaration that specifies the HTML or XHTML standard that's used by the document.

- In an XHTML document, the first element must be the html element, which is called the *root element*. This element marks the beginning and end of the HTML code.

- Within the html element of an XHTML document, you must code a head element that marks the beginning and end of the document heading, followed by a body element that marks the beginning and end of the document body.

Figure 2-1   The basic structure of an HTML document

How to code elements and tags

Figure 2-2 shows you how to code elements and tags. As you have already seen, most HTML elements start with an *opening tag* and end with a *closing tag* that is like the opening tag but has a slash within it. Thus, <h1> is the opening tag for a level-1 heading, and </h1> is the closing tag. Between those tags, you code the *content* of the element, which is usually displayed when the page is rendered.

Some elements, however, have no content or closing tag. These tags are referred to as *self-closing tags*. For instance, the <br /> tag is a self-closing tag that starts a new a line when the document is displayed, and the img tag is a self-closing tag that identifies an image that should be displayed.

In this book, we refer to elements by the code used in the opening tag. For instance, we refer to head elements, h1 elements, a elements, p elements, img elements, and so on. We do that without any special typography to mark the type of element. Although this may cause you to misread a few times in the early going, especially the one-letter element names, you will soon get used to it.

The third set of examples in this figure shows the right way and the wrong way to code tags when one element is *nested* within another. In short, the tags for one element shouldn't overlap with the tags for another element. That is, you can't close the outer element before you close the inner element.

After the examples, you can see the differences between the XHTML and HTML requirements for tags. Here again, the XHTML requirements are stricter, and they lead to better code and fewer errors. Please note, however, that it's easy to code HTML in a way that is consistent with XHTML because the differences are minimal. All you have to do is adhere to the requirements of XHTML.

Two elements with opening and closing tags

```
<h1>San Joaquin Valley Town Hall</h1>
<p>Here is a list of links:</p>
```

Two self-closing tags

```
<br />
<img src="logo.gif" alt="Murach Logo" />
```

Correct and incorrect nesting of tags

Correct nesting

```
<p>Order your copy <i>today!</i></p>
```

Incorrect nesting

```
<p>Order your copy <i>today!</p></i>
```

Differences between XHTML tags and HTML tags

- In HTML, tag names can be coded in lowercase, uppercase, or mixed case. In XHTML, tag names must be coded in lowercase.

- In HTML, the closing tags for some elements can be omitted. For example, a <p> tag doesn't require a closing </p> tag. In XHTML, a closing tag is always required.

- In HTML, a self-closing tag can be coded without the slash (i.e.
 instead of <br />). In XHTML, the slash is required. In addition, a space is typically coded before the slash.

- In HTML, you can nest tags incorrectly. In XHTML, you can't.

Description

- Most HTML elements have three parts: an opening tag, content, and a closing tag. Each tag is coded within a set of brackets (<>).

- An element's *opening tag* includes the tag name, which must be lowercase. The *closing tag* includes the tag name preceded by a slash. And the *content* includes everything that appears between the opening and closing tags.

- Some XHTML elements have no content or closing tag. For example, the <br /> element, which forces a line break, consists of just one tag. This type of tag is called a *self-closing tag*.

- HTML elements can be *nested* within each other. To nest elements correctly, make sure to close the inner set of tags before closing the outer set of tags.

Figure 2-2   How to code elements and tags

How to code attributes

Figure 2-3 shows how to code the *attributes* for an HTML element. These attributes are coded within the opening tag of an element or within a self-closing tag. For each attribute, you code the attribute name, an equals sign, and the attribute value in quotation marks. Although you can use either double or single quotes for the value, you should be consistent.

In the first set of examples, you can see how one or more attributes can be coded. For instance, the third example is an img element that contains a src attribute that gives the name of the image file that should be displayed plus an alt attribute that gives the text that should be displayed if the image file can't be found.

The next example illustrates the use of a *Boolean attribute*. That is an attribute that can have just two values, which represent either on or off. In this case, the checked attribute applies to a check box, which can either be checked or unchecked. To check the box, you code the name of the attribute as the value for the attribute, as in checked="checked".

The next set of examples illustrates the use of two attributes that are commonly used to identify HTML elements. The id attribute is used to uniquely identify just one element, so each id attribute must have a unique value. In contrast, the class attribute can be used to mark one or more elements, so the same value can used for more than one class attribute. You'll see these attributes in a complete example in figure 2-6.

Once again, the differences between HTML and XHTML are trivial. Although the XHTML is stricter, it's easy to write HTML code that adheres to the stricter syntax.

How to code attributes

An opening tag with one attribute

```
<a href="contact.html">
```

An opening tag with three attributes

```
<a href="contact.html" title="Click to Contact Us" class="nav_link">
```

A self-closing tag with two attributes

```
<img src="logo.gif" alt="Murach Logo" />
```

A self-closing tag with a Boolean attribute named checked

```
<input type="checkbox" name="mailList" checked="checked" />
```

Two common attributes for identifying HTML elements

An opening tag with an id attribute

```
<div id="page">
```

An opening tag with a class attribute

```
<a href="contact.html" title="Click to Contact Us" class="nav_link">
```

Differences between XHTML attributes and HTML attributes

- In HTML, attribute names can be coded in lowercase, uppercase, or mixed case. In XHTML, attribute names must be coded in lowercase.

- In XHTML, attribute values must be enclosed in single or double quotes. In HTML, they don't have to be.

- In HTML, the name of a Boolean attribute and the equals sign can be omitted when you want to represent an on value. In XHTML, you must code both a name and a value.

Description

- *Attributes* can appear within an opening or self-closing tag to supply optional values.

- To code an attribute, code the name of the attribute, an equals sign (=), and the value for the attribute enclosed in quotes.

- To code multiple attributes, separate each attribute with a space.

- A *Boolean attribute* represents either an on or off value. To code the on value, you use the name of the attribute as the value for the attribute.

- The id attribute is used to identify a single HTML element so its value can only be applied to one HTML element.

- A class attribute with the same name can be applied to more than one HTML element.

Figure 2-3   How to code attributes

How to code comments and whitespace

Figure 2-4 shows you how to code *comments*. Here, the starting and ending characters for the two comments are highlighted. Then, everything within those characters is ignored when the page is rendered.

One common use of comments is to describe or explain portions of code. That is illustrated by the first comment.

Another common use of comments is to *comment out* a portion of the code. This is illustrated by the second comment. This is useful when you're testing and debugging a web page and you want to temporarily disable a portion of code that you're having trouble with. Then, after you test the rest of the code, you can remove the comments and test that portion of the code.

This figure also illustrates the use of *whitespace*, which consists of characters like tab characters, return characters, and extra spaces. For instance, the return character after the <body> tag and all of the spaces between that tag and the next tag are whitespace.

Since whitespace is ignored when an HTML document is rendered, you can use the whitespace characters to format your HTML so it is easier to read. In this figure, for example, you can see how whitespace has been used to indent and align the HTML elements.

That of course is a good coding practice, and you'll see that in all of the examples in this book. Note, however, that the code will work the same if all of the whitespace is removed. In fact, you could code all of the HTML for a document in a single line.

An XHTML document with comments and whitespace

```
<!DOCTYPE html PUBLIC "-//W3C//DTD XHTML 1.0 Transitional//EN"
    "http://www.w3.org/TR/xhtml1/DTD/xhtml1-transitional.dtd">

<!--
    This document displays the home page
    for the web site
-->

<html xmlns="http://www.w3.org/1999/xhtml">
    <head>
        <title>San Joaquin Valley Town Hall</title>
    </head>

    <body>
        <h1>San Joaquin Valley Town Hall</h1>
        <h3>Bringing cutting-edge speakers to the valley</h3>
        <h2>2009-2010 guest speakers</h2>
<!-- This comments out all of the HTML code in the unordered list
        <ul>
            <li>October 14, 2009: Dr. Alan J. Russell</li>
            <li>November 18, 2009: Dr. Edward Diener</li>
            <li>January 20, 2010: David Brancaccio</li>
            <li>February 17, 2010: Robert Fitzpatrick</li>
            <li>March 17, 2010: Juan Williams</li>
            <li>April 21, 2010: Steve Coll</li>
        </ul>
    The code after the end of this comment is active -->
        <p>Contact us by phone at (559) 444-2180 for ticket
        information.</p>
    </body>
</html>
```

Description

- An HTML *comment* is text that appears between the <!-- and --> characters. Since web browsers ignore comments, you can use them to describe or explain portions of your HTML code that might otherwise be confusing.

- You can also use comments to *comment out* elements that you don't want the browser to display. This can be useful when you're testing and debugging a web page.

- An HTML comment can be coded on a single line or it can span two or more lines.

- *Whitespace* consists of characters like tab characters, line return characters, and extra spaces.

- Since whitespace is ignored by browsers, you can use it to indent lines of code and separate elements from one another by putting them on separate lines. This is a good coding practice because it makes your code easier to read.

Figure 2-4   How to code comments and whitespace

The CSS syntax

Like HTML, CSS also has a syntax that must be adhered to when you create a CSS file. This syntax is presented next.

How to code CSS rule sets and comments

A CSS file consists of *rule sets*. As the diagram in figure 2-5 shows, a rule set consists of a *selector* followed by a set of braces. Within the braces are one or more *declarations*, and each declaration consists of a *property* and a *value*. Note that the property is followed by a colon and the value is followed by a semicolon.

In this diagram, the selector is h1 so it applies to all h1 elements. Then, the rule set consists of a single property named color that is set to the color navy. The result is that the content of all h1 elements will be displayed in navy blue.

In the CSS code that follows, you can see four other rule sets. Three of these contain only one declaration (or *rule*), but the third example is a rule set that consists of two rules: one for the font-style property, and one for the border-bottom property.

Within a CSS file, you can also code comments that describe or explain what the CSS code is doing. For each comment, you start with /* and end with */, and anything between those characters is ignored. In the example in this figure, you can see how CSS comments can be coded on separate lines or after the lines that make up a rule set.

You can also use comments to comment out portions of code that you want disabled. This can be useful when you're testing and debugging your CSS code just as it is when you're testing and debugging your HTML code.

The parts of a CSS rule set

selector

```
h1 {
    color: navy;  ◄── declaration
}
    ▲        ▲
```

property value

A simple CSS document with comments

```css
/**********************************************************
 * Description: Primary style sheet for valleytownhall.com
 * Author:      Anne Boehm
 **********************************************************/
/* Adjust the styles for the body */
body {
    background-color: #FACD8A;          /* This is a shade of orange. */
}
/* Adjust the styles for the headings */
h1 {
    color: #363636;
}
h3 {
    font-style: italic;
    border-bottom: 3px solid #EF9C00;  /* Adds a line below h3 headings */
}

/* Adjust the styles for the unordered list */
ul {
    list-style-type: square;           /* Changes the bullets to squares */
}
```

Description

- A CSS *rule set* consists of a selector and a declaration block.
- A CSS *selector* consists of the identifiers that are coded at the beginning of the rule set.
- A CSS *declaration block* consists of an opening brace, zero or more declarations, and a closing brace.
- A CSS *declaration* consists of a *property*, a colon, a *value*, and a semicolon. Although the semicolon for the last declaration in a block is optional, it's a best practice to code it.
- To make your code easier to read, you can use spaces, indentation, and blank lines within a rule set.
- CSS *comments* begin with the characters /* and end with the characters */. A CSS comment can be coded on a single line, or it can span multiple lines.

Figure 2-5   How to code CSS rule sets and comments

How to code basic selectors

The selector of a rule set identifies the HTML element or elements that the rules should be applied to. To give you a better idea of how this works, figure 2-6 shows how to use the three basic selectors for CSS rule sets. Then, in chapter 4, you'll learn how to code all types of selectors.

The first type of selector identifies HTML elements like body, h1, or p elements. For instance, the selector in the first example applies to the body element. But if h1 were coded instead of body, the rule set would apply to all h1 elements.

The second type of selector starts with the pound sign (#) and applies to a single HTML element that's identified by an id attribute. For instance, #main applies to the HTML element that has an id attribute with a value of main. As you can see, that's the div element in the HTML code. Similarly, #footer applies to the last p element in the HTML code.

The third type of selector starts with a period (.) and applies to all of the HTML elements that are identified by the class attribute with the named value. For instance, .base_color applies to all elements with class attributes that have a value of base_color. In the HTML code, this includes the h1 element and the last p element.

Starting with chapter 4, you'll learn all the details of coding the rules for a rule set. But to give you an idea of what's going on in this example, here's a quick review of the code.

In the rule set for the body element, the font-family is set either to Arial (if the browser has access to that font) or the sans-serif type that is the default for the browser. This font is then used for all text that's displayed within the body element, unless it's overridden later on by some other rule set. So in this example, all of the text will be Arial or sans-serif, and you can see that font-family in the browser display.

In the rule set for the div element (#main), the width of the division is set to 300 pixels, a solid black border that's two pixels wide is placed around the contents of the division, and the padding between the contents and the border is set to 1 em, which is the height of the default font . Then, in the rule set for the second p element (#footer), the font size is set to 75% of the default font size, and the text is right-aligned. In this figure, you can see how both of these rule sets are applied in the browser display, and you'll learn more about specifying measurements in chapter 4.

Last, in the rule set for the class named base_color, the color is set to blue. This means that both of the HTML elements that have that class name (the h1 element and the second p element) are displayed in blue.

This example shows how easy it is to identify the elements that you want to apply CSS formatting to. This also shows how the use of CSS separates the formatting from the content and structure that is defined by the HTML.

HTML elements that can be selected by element, id, or class

```
<body>
    <div id="main">
        <h1 class="base_color">Student materials</h1>
        <p>Here are the links for the downloads:</p>
        <ul>
            <li><a href="exercises.html">Exercises</a></li>
            <li><a href="solutions.html">Solutions</a></li>
        </ul>
        <p id="footer" class="base_color">Copyright 2009</p>
    </div>
</body>
```

CSS rule sets that select by HTML element, id, and class

HTML element

```
body {
    font-family: Arial, sans-serif;
}
```

ID

```
#main {
    width: 300px;
    border: 2px solid black;
    padding: 1em;
}
#footer {
    font-size: 75%;
    text-align: right;
}
```

Class

```
.base_color {
    color: blue;
}
```

The elements in a browser

Description

- To code a selector for an HTML element, you simply name the element.
- If an element is coded with an id attribute, you can code a selector for that id by coding a pound sign (#) followed by the id value, as in #main.
- If an element is coded with a class attribute, you can code a selector for that class by coding a period followed by the class name, as in .base_color.

Figure 2-6   How to code basic selectors

How to use Notepad++ with HTML and CSS files

In chapter 1, you were introduced to text editors like Notepad++. Now, you'll learn how to use Notepad++ as you create and edit HTML and CSS files. If you're using some other text editor for HTML and CSS, you should still browse these topics so you can see the tasks that you should be able to do with your editor.

How to open an HTML file

Figure 2-7 shows two ways to open an HTML file with Notepad++. First, you can use the File→Open command, which is just like the Open command for any other Windows program. Second, you can find the file in Windows Explorer, right-click on it, and select the Edit with Notepad++ command. An HTML file will of course have either htm or html as its extension.

When you open an HTML file, it is opened into a new tab within Notepad++. This means that you can have several files open at the same time and move from one to another by clicking on a tab. This makes it easy to switch back and forth between the HTML and CSS files for a web page. This also makes it easy to copy code from one file to another.

Notepad++ as it's about to open an existing HTML file

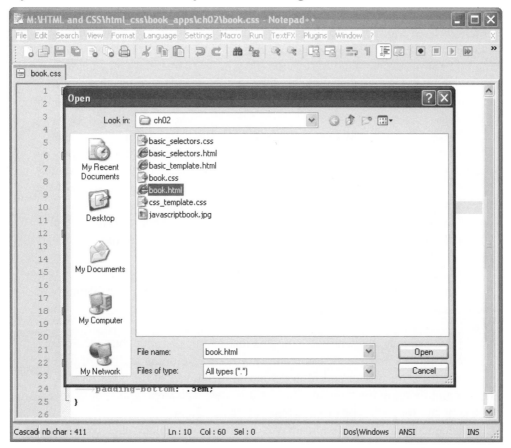

The directory that contains the files for this chapter

```
C:\murach\html_css\book_apps\ch02
```

Two ways to open an HTML file

- Start Notepad++, select the File→Open command, and use the Open dialog box to open the HTML file.
- Start Windows Explorer, navigate to the HTML file, right-click on the file, and select the Edit with Notepad++ command.

Description

- When you open an HTML file, the file is opened in a new tab.

Figure 2-7   How to open an HTML file

How to start a new HTML file

Figure 2-8 shows how to start a new HTML file. To do that, you can use the File→New command, which starts an empty file in a new tab. Then, you can use the File→Save As command to save the file with the name that you want to use and the html extension. Once you've done that, Notepad++ knows that you're creating an html file so it will properly highlight the code that you enter into the file.

However, a better way to start a new HTML file is by opening a *template* file that contains the starting code for the new file. This is illustrated by the code in the Notepad++ window at the top of this figure. Here, the code includes the DOCTYPE declaration; the html, head, and body elements; and some of the lines within those elements that you code every time. This saves you the time that it would take to enter those lines of code or to copy them in from another file. It also helps you avoid coding errors because those lines are the same every time.

As soon as you open the template, you should use the File→Save As command to save the file with a new name. That way, you won't accidentally modify the code in the template. Then, you can modify and add to the starting code.

In this example, the template contains just 13 lines of code, but a template can be far more extensive. If, for example, you're developing a series of pages that have the same header and footer, you can include all of the code for the header and footer in the template. In fact, for most web sites, you should have one template for each type of page that you're developing.

Incidentally, an IDE like DreamWeaver provides templates that you can use for a wide variety of page layouts. For instance, there's a template for a page that has a header, a footer, and a two-column body as well as a template for a page that has a header, a footer, and a three-column body. Templates like those give you both the HTML and CSS files that you need, which not only increases your productivity but helps you learn the right way to code those layouts.

As you become more familiar with HTML, you'll start to create your own templates. If, for example, you're going to develop several pages that have the same general content, you can create an HTML template for those pages. That will make it easier for you to develop those pages.

Notepad++ after a new HTML file has been started from a template

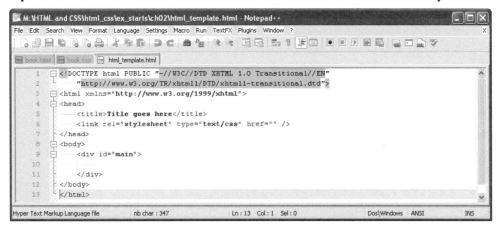

The Save As dialog box

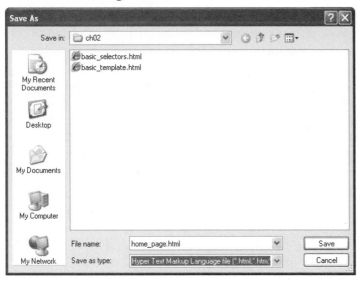

How to start a new file from scratch

- Select the File→New command. This starts an empty file in a new tab.
- Use the File→Save As command to display the Save As dialog box. Then, select the directory for the file, enter a file name, select the file type (html is the default), and click the Save button.

How to start a new file from a template

- Open the file that contains the *template* that you want to use. Then, before you change anything, use the File→Save As command to save the file with a new name.

Figure 2-8   How to start a new HTML file

How to edit an HTML file

Figure 2-9 shows how to edit an HTML file. After you save a new file with the html or htm extension, Notepad++ knows what type of file you're working with so it can use color to highlight the syntax components. That makes it easier to spot errors in your code.

As you enter a new line of code, the auto-completion feature presents lists of words that start with the letters that you've entered. This type of list is illustrated by this figure. Here, the list shows the choices after the letters *hr* have been entered. Then, you can select a word and press the Tab key to insert it into your code.

If necessary, you can also press Ctrl+Space at any time to display an auto-completion list. To enable auto-completion, though, you may have to use the Settings→Preferences command as described in this figure.

This figure also lists some common coding errors. Often, the color coding will help you spot the first four types of errors. If, for example, you misspell an attribute name or if you forget to code a closing quotation mark, the color coding will indicate that the code isn't correct. And if you click on an opening tag, both the opening and closing tag will be highlighted so you can be sure that they're matched correctly.

On the other hand, Notepad++ has no way of knowing what the correct code should be for file references in link, img, or a elements. As a result, you must discover those errors when you test the web page. If the file reference for a style sheet in a link element is incorrect, the CSS won't be applied. If the file reference in an image element is incorrect, the image won't be displayed and the alt text will be displayed. And if the file reference for an a element is incorrect, the browser won't access the correct page.

Notepad++ with an auto-completion list

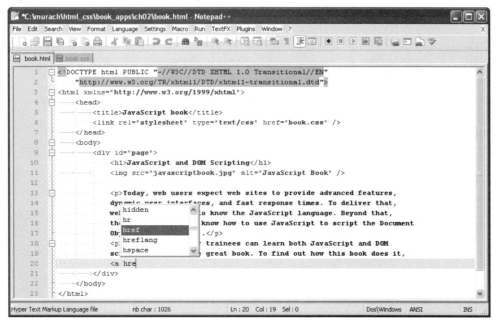

Common coding errors

- An opening tag with no closing tag.
- Attribute values that aren't enclosed in quotation marks.
- Quotation marks that aren't paired.
- Misspelled tag or attribute names.
- Incorrect file references in link, img, or a elements.

How to enable auto-completion

- Use the Settings→Preferences command, click the Backup/Auto-completion tab, and check the "Enable Auto-completion on each input" box.

Description

- Notepad++ displays the different parts of a file in different colors so they're easy to recognize. This helps you spot some of the common errors. For this to work, the file must have a supported extension.

- The auto-completion feature displays a list of terms that start with what you've typed. To insert one of those terms, double-click on it or use the arrow keys to highlight it and press the Tab key.

- You can display an auto-completion list at any time by pressing Ctrl+Space.

Figure 2-9   How to edit an HTML file

How to open or start a CSS file

As figure 2-10 shows, you use the same methods for opening and starting CSS files that you use for opening and starting HTML files. But here again, it's best to start a new CSS file from a template that contains the code that you're likely to use for the page you're developing. When you're creating a web site, for example, you will often use the same rule sets for many of the pages. Those are likely to include rule sets for the body element, for the div element that contains all of the code for a page, and for common elements like the h1, h2, p, and a elements.

Notepad++ after a new CSS file has been started from a template

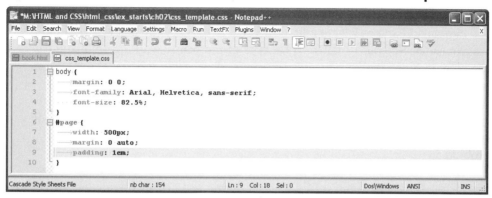

The Save As dialog box

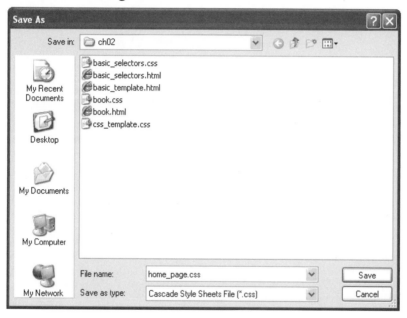

How to open CSS files or start new CSS files from scratch

- Use the same methods that you use for HTML files, but use css extensions.

How to start a new CSS file from a template

- Open the file that contains the *template* that you want to use. Then, before you change anything, use the File→Save As command to save the file with a new name and the css extension.

Figure 2-10   How to open or start a CSS file

How to edit a CSS file

Figure 2-11 shows how to edit a CSS file. After you save a new file with the css extension, Notepad++ knows what type of file you're working with so it can use color to highlight the syntax components. That makes it easier to spot errors in your code.

Because CSS code is simpler than HTML code, the color coding makes it easy to spot the common errors in CSS code. If, for example, you forget to code a brace or a semicolon, the color coding will clearly indicate that there's a problem.

On the other hand, Notepad++ has no way of knowing if you code an id or class name incorrectly. You'll find that out during testing by noticing that the rule sets that you've specified for some of the elements haven't been applied.

Notepad++ with an open CSS file

```
M:\HTML and CSS\html_css\ex_starts\ch02\book.css - Notepad++

File  Edit  Search  View  Format  Language  Settings  Macro  Run  TextFX  Plugins  Window  ?                    X

 book.html    book.css

  1    body {
  2        margin: 0 0;
  3        font-family: Arial, Helvetica, sans-serif;
  4        font-size: 82.5%;
  5    }
  6    #page {
  7        width: 500px;
  8        margin: 0 auto;
  9        padding: 1em;
 10        border: 1px solid navy;
 11    }
 12    h1 {
 13        margin: 0;
 14        padding: .25em;
 15        color: navy;
 16        font-size: 250%;
 17    }
 18    img {
 19        float: left;
 20        margin: 0 1em;
 21    }
 22    p {
 23        margin: 0;
 24        padding-bottom: .5em;
 25    }
 26

Cascade Style Sheet: nb char : 344           Ln : 1   Col : 1   Sel : 0        Dos\Windows   ANSI        INS
```

Common coding errors

- Braces that aren't paired correctly.
- Missing semicolons.
- Equal signs instead of colons.
- Id or class names that don't match the names used in the HTML.

Description

- To edit a CSS file, you can use the same techniques you use to edit an HTML file. Here again, the color coding will help you spot syntax errors.

Figure 2-11   How to edit a CSS file

How to test, debug, and validate HTML and CSS files

Now that you know how to create and edit HTML and CSS files, you're ready to learn how to test and validate those files.

How to test and debug a web page

When you finish editing your HTML and CSS files, you need to save them. To do that with Notepad++, you can click on the Save All button in the toolbar. Then, to test the web page, you open the page in your web browser. To do that you can use one of the techniques listed in figure 2-12. If you're using Windows or a text editor with launch commands, the last two techniques are usually the quickest.

Once the page is displayed in the browser, you study it to make sure that it looks the way you want it to. If it doesn't, you need to change the HTML, the CSS, or both, and test the page again. When you test a page for the second time, though, you don't need to open it again. Instead, you can click on the Reload or Refresh button in the browser's toolbar.

Often, the changes you make as you test a web page are just minor adjustments or improvements. Sometimes, though, you need to debug your code because it isn't working the way you want it to. That means you have to find the coding errors. Usually, these errors are caused by trivial coding problems like missing tags, quotation marks, and braces, but finding these problems can be hard to do when your files consist of dozens of lines of code.

If you're developing web pages for a general audience over the Internet, you need to test your pages on all of the browsers that your audience is likely to use. At the least, this means you should test your web pages with Internet Explorer and with Firefox.

When you do this testing, you will often find that a web page will work on one browser, only to find that it doesn't work on another. That's usually because one of the browsers makes some assumptions that the other browser doesn't. If, for example, you have a slight coding error in an HTML file, one browser might make an assumption that fixes the problem, while the other doesn't.

To fix this type of problem, look for an error in the code. If you can't find any, you may want to validate the file as shown in the next figure.

The HTML file displayed in the Firefox browser

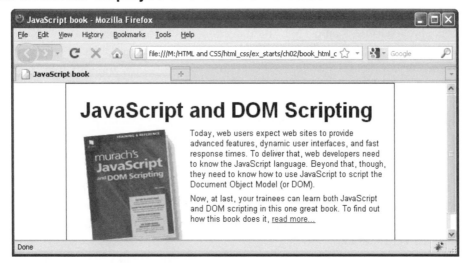

The Open File dialog box for Firefox

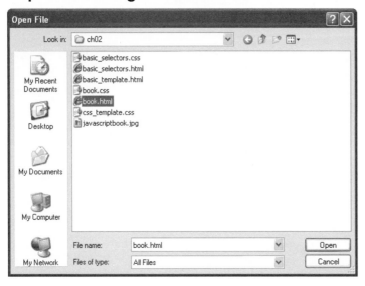

Four ways to test a web page that's on an intranet or your own computer

- Start your browser, and use the File→Open or Open File command to open the file.
- Start your browser and type the complete path and filename into the address bar.
- If you're using Windows, use Windows Explorer to find the file, and double-click on it.
- If you're using Notepad++, use the Run→Launch commands to open the file in Firefox or Internet Explorer. If you're using another text editor, look for similar commands.

How to retest a web page after you change the source code

- Click the Reload or Refresh button.

Figure 2-12   How to test the HTML and CSS for a web page

How to validate an HTML file

When a browser opens an HTML file that contains errors, it ignores the errors and does its best to render the page. Often, the errors are obvious so you can find and correct them. Other times, the errors aren't obvious, and they may cause problems with some browsers.

One solution to this problem is to use a validating program to *validate* your HTML documents. Some web development IDEs provide validation programs, and some web sites provide them. One of the most popular web sites for validating HTML is the one for the W3C Markup Validation Service that's shown at the top of figure 2-13.

When you use this web site, you can provide the HTML document that you want to validate in three ways. You can provide the URL for the page. You can upload the document. And you can copy and paste the document into their Validate by Direct Input tab.

In this figure, the Validate by File Upload tab is shown. Then, you click on the Browse button to find the file that you want to validate. Once that's done, you click on the Check button to validate the document.

The web address of the W3C Markup Validation Service

`http://validator.w3.org/`

The home page for the W3C validator

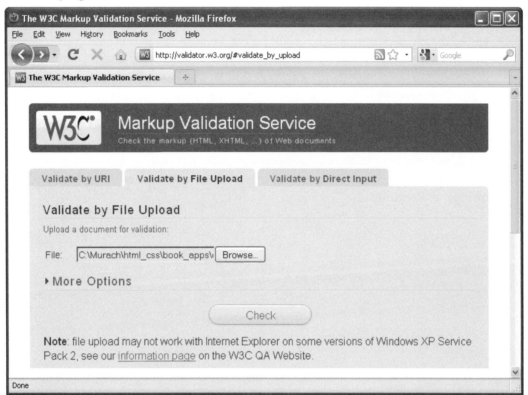

Description

- When an HTML file is opened in a browser, the browser ignores any errors and renders the web page as well as it can.

- To *validate* the HTML for a page, you can use a program or web site for that purpose. One of the most popular is the web site for the W3C Markup Validation Service.

- If the page you want to validate has already been uploaded to a web server, you can validate it by entering its URL on the Validate by URI tab.

- If the page you want to validate hasn't been uploaded to a web server, you can validate it by entering its address on the Validate by File Upload tab.

- You can also validate the HTML for a page by copying and pasting it into the Validate by Direct Input tab.

Figure 2-13   How to validate an HTML file (part 1 of 2)

If the HTML code is valid when a document is validated, the MarkUp Validation Service displays a message that indicates that. But if the code contains errors, the message will indicate the number of errors that were detected. Then, you can scroll down to a list of the errors like the one in the second part of this figure.

In this example, all of the error messages were caused by a missing /> at the end of the img element, which is right before a p element. In this case, you would catch that error when you test the web page because the image wouldn't be displayed. But sometimes, a web page will be displayed okay even though it contains an error or two.

Incidentally, a web page may display correctly in all of the browsers that you test it on and still not pass a validation test. In fact, some XHTML coding requirements are more for validation than for browser rendering. For instance, the alt attribute for the img element is required for XHTML validation, but all of the current browsers will render the img element correctly, even if it doesn't include an alt attribute.

The error listing for an HTML file with a missing tag ending

Description

- If the HTML document is valid, the Markup Validation Service will indicate that the document passed the validation. In that case, warnings may still be displayed.

- If the HTML document isn't valid, the Markup Validation Service will indicate the number of errors that were detected. Then, you can scroll down to a description of the errors.

- The Markup Validation Service may also display warnings that indicate areas where you can improve your HTML.

Figure 2-13   How to validate an HTML file (part 2 of 2)

How to validate a CSS file

You can validate a CSS file the same way you validate an HTML file, either with a validation program that may be part of an IDE for web development or with a web site service like the W3C CSS Validation Service. If you use the W3C Validation Service, the opening page looks like the one for markup validation. Then, you can use any one of the three tabs to validate a CSS file.

If the file contains errors, the validation service will display a screen like the one in figure 2-14. Here, both errors were caused by a missing closing brace. If you're using a text editor like Notepad++, though, the color coding makes it easy to identify and avoid errors like that.

The web address of the W3C CSS Validation Service

`http://jigsaw.w3.org/css-validator/`

The CSS Validation Service with errors displayed

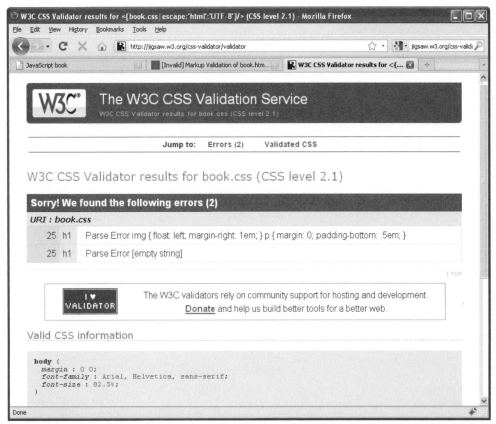

Description

- To validate the CSS for a page, you can use a program or web site for that purpose. One of the most popular is the web site for the W3C CSS Validation Service. This web site works the same as the W3C Markup Validation Service.

- If the CSS for a page is valid, the CSS Validation Service displays a message that indicates that no errors were found.

- If the CSS for a page isn't valid, the CSS Validation Service displays a message that indicates that errors were found. In addition, it displays information about the errors to help you fix them.

- The CSS Validation Service may also display warnings that indicate areas where you can improve your CSS.

Figure 2-14   How to validate a CSS file

Perspective

Now that you've completed this chapter, you should be able to create and edit HTML and CSS files using Notepad++ or some other text editor. Then, you should be able to test those files by displaying their web pages in your web browser and in any other web browsers that your users might use. In some cases, you may also want to validate the HTML and CSS files for a web page.

At this point, you should also be able to create the HTML and CSS files for simple web pages of your own just by following the examples that you've seen so far. Then, in chapter 3, you'll learn the details for coding the HTML elements that define and structure the content for a web page. And in chapters 4, 5, and 6, you'll learn the details for coding the CSS rule sets that format the HTML content.

Terms

HTML document	comment out
HTML element	whitespace
root element	rule set
opening tag	selector
closing tag	declaration block
content of an element	property
self-closing tag	value
nested elements	template
attribute	HTML validation
Boolean attribute	CSS validation
comment	

Summary

- An *HTML document* contains *HTML elements* that define the content and structure of a web page. The basic structural elements in an XHTML file are the html element (or *root element*), the head element, and the body element.

- Most HTML elements consist of an *opening tag* and a *closing tag* with *content* between these tags. These tags are enclosed by brackets as in the <h1> opening tag and the </h1> closing tag. When you *nest* elements with XHTML, the inner set of tags must be closed before the outer set.

- *Attributes* can be coded in an opening tag to supply optional values. An attribute consists of the name of the attribute, an equal sign, and the attribute value. In XHTML, the attribute value must be enclosed in single or double quotation marks. To code multiple attributes, you separate them with spaces.

- An *HTML comment* can be used to describe or explain a portion of code. Because comments are ignored, you can also use comments to *comment out* a portion of HTML code so it isn't rendered by the browser. This can be helpful when you're testing your HTML code.

- *Whitespace* consists of characters like tab characters, line return characters, and extra spaces that are ignored by browsers. As a result, you can use whitespace to indent and align your code.

- A *CSS rule set* consists of a selector and a declaration block. The *selector* identifies the html elements that are going to be formatted. Three of the common CSS selectors select by HTML element, ID, and class.

- The *declaration block* contains one or more *declarations* that do the formatting. Each declaration (or *rule*) consists of a *property*, a colon, a *value*, and a semicolon.

- *CSS comments* work like HTML comments. However, CSS comments start with /* and end with */, and HTML comments start with <!-- and end with -->.

- Notepad++ is a text editor that can be used to edit HTML or CSS code. To help you read the code, Notepad++ displays different parts of the code in different colors. It also provides auto-completion lists to make it easier to enter code.

- When you start a new HTML or CSS file, it's usually best to start it from a *template* that provides the starting code for the file.

- To test an HTML file, you display it in a browser. Then, if the display isn't the way you want it, you need to correct the HTML or CSS code and test the file again. You also need to test each file on all of the types of browsers that your clients will use.

- To *validate* an HTML or CSS file, you can use a program or web site for that purpose. Often, a validation program will detect errors in a file, even though the web page displays the way you want it to on all browsers.

Before you do the exercises for this book...

If you haven't already done it, you should download and install the Firefox browser. You should also download and install the applications for this book. The procedures for doing both are in appendix A.

Exercise 2-1   Edit and test the book page

In this exercise, you'll edit and test the book page that is shown in figure 2-12.

Open the HTML and CSS files for the book page

1. Start Notepad++ or your text editor.

2. Use one of the methods in figure 2-7 to open this HTML file:

   `c:\html_css\ch02\book.html`

3. Use the same method to open the CSS file named book.css that's in the same directory. This should open in a new tab.

Test the book page in Internet Explorer and Firefox

4. Start Internet Explorer. Then, use the File→Open command to open the same HTML file as in step 2.

5. Start Firefox. Then, use the File→Open File command to open the same HTML file. Notice that the page looks the same in both browsers.

Modify the HTML and CSS code and test again

6. Go to the book.html file in your text editor, and delete the two <br /> tags at the end of the division. Then, save the file.

7. Refresh the web page in the IE browser by clicking on the Refresh button in the toolbar. Then, refresh the page in the Firefox browser by clicking on the Reload button. Is there a difference in the displays? If so, this illustrates why you need to test a web page in more than one browser.

8. Go back to your text editor, and undo the changes that you made in step 6. Then, save the file and test the page in the Firefox browser to make sure that the page has been corrected.

9. Go back to your text editor and click on the tab for the book.css file. Then, change the float property for the img element from left to right, and save the file. Now, test this change in one or both browsers.

10. Go back to the book.css file, and change the color for the h1 element to "red" and change the font-size to 200%. Then, test that change in one or both browsers.

11. Go back to the book.html file, and add a p element at the bottom of the page that has this content:

    `For customer service, call us at 1-555-555-5555.`

    Then, save the file and test this change.

12. Go to the book.html file and add an id attribute with the value "service" to the p element that you just entered. Then, go to the book.css file and enter a rule set for the p element with that id. This rule set should use the color property to change the text to red. If you need help doing this, refer back to figure 2-6. Now, save both the html and css files, and test these changes.

Experiment on your own and close the files

13. By now, you should have the general idea of how HTML and CSS work together. But you may want to continue experimenting on your own.

14. When you're through experimenting, close both of the files in your text editor.

Exercise 2-2   Start a new web page

In this exercise, you'll start HTML and CSS files from templates that are stored in this directory:

`c:\html_css\ch02\`

Start your files from templates

1. Start your text editor, and open the template named html_template.html. Then, save the file in the same directory with the name testpage.html.

2. Use your text editor to open the template named css_template.css. Then, save the file in the same directory with the name testpage.css.

Add some content to the HTML file and test it

3. In the title element, change the content to "Test page".

4. In the link element, change the value of the href attribute to "testpage.css".

5. Add an h1 element to the HTML file that says: "This is a test page." Then, save the file, and test the page by opening it in Firefox or IE.

6. This illustrates how fast you can get started with a new web page when you start the html and css files from templates. Now, if you want to add more elements to the HTML or more rules or rule sets to the CSS, give it a try.

7. When you're through experimenting, close the files in your editor.

Exercise 2-3   Validate an HTML and a CSS file

In this exercise, you'll use the validation web sites in figures 2-13 and 2-14 to validate an HTML and a CSS file. These files are named book_error.html and book_error.css, and they're stored in this directory:

```
c:\html_css\ch02\
```

1. Go to the site specified in figure 2-13, and use the Validate by File Upload tab to validate the book_error.html file. If you scroll down the page after the validation is finished, you'll see 11 error messages, even though the file contains just two errors.

2. Open the file in your text editor, and note that the errors aren't that easy to find. Then, use the validation messages to find and fix the errors. When you think you've got them fixed, validate the file again by first clicking on the browser's Back button and then on the web site's Check button.

3. Go to the site specified in figure 2-14, and use the Validate by File Upload tab to validate the book_error.css file. This time, you'll see just 2 error messages.

4. Open the file in your text editor, and note that these errors are relatively easy to find due to the color coding. Then, fix the errors, and validate the file again.

5. To make sure you've got everything right, test the html file in your browser. It should look like the book page that you opened in step 4 of exercise 2-1.

3

How to use HTML to structure a web page

In chapter 2, you saw the basic structure of an HTML document, you learned the basic techniques for coding the elements that make up a document, and you learned that these elements specify the structure and content of a page when it's displayed in a browser. Now, in this chapter, you'll learn how to code the HTML elements that you'll use in most of the documents you create. Then, in the next chapter, you'll learn how to use CSS to format those HTML elements.

How to start an HTML document

Every HTML document should start with a DOCTYPE declaration. In the topics that follow, you'll learn how to code this declaration.

How to code the DOCTYPE declaration

The main function of the *DOCTYPE declaration* is to indicate which version of HTML or XHTML a document uses. To do that, it uses a *Document Type Definition, or DTD*. In most cases, you'll use HTML 4.01 or XHTML 1.0 as indicated by the DTDs in the first four examples in figure 3-1.

If you use HTML 4.01 or XHTML 1.0, the DTD must also indicate which *flavor* of HTML or XHTML the document uses. If you want to be able to use *deprecated* elements and attributes, which may be dropped in future versions, you should use the Transitional flavor. If you don't want to use them, you can use the Strict flavor.

The third flavor is the Frameset flavor, but this flavor is rarely needed or used in modern web sites. As a result, it isn't presented in this book.

Notice that the last DOCTYPE declaration in this figure is for XHTML 1.1. Because this version of XHTML doesn't have different flavors, the DOCTYPE declaration doesn't include a flavor.

How quirks mode works

If you code a proper DOCTYPE declaration, the browser assumes that the document follows the standards specified by the DTD. In that case, the document is displayed in *standards mode*. In contrast, if no DTD is specified in the DOCTYPE declaration or if this declaration is omitted, the document is displayed in *quirks mode*.

This mode is designed for code that was written for older browsers that interpreted HTML and CSS code in "quirky" ways. To get around these quirks, web developers coded special "workarounds" that got the results that they wanted. As the browsers improved, though, these workarounds were no longer needed. Unfortunately, that meant that pages that still used the workarounds didn't always display properly in newer browsers.

Today, when quirks mode is used, the browser assumes that the document includes workarounds that were designed for older browsers. If, for example, a page that uses quirks mode is displayed in Internet Explorer 6 or later, it will appear as if it's being displayed in Internet Explorer 5.5. A better approach, however, is to update all of the pages in a web site so they follow the current standards and don't have to use quirks mode.

The three flavors of HTML 4.01 and XHTML 1.0

Flavor	Description
Strict	Disallows the use of deprecated elements and attributes.
Transitional	Allows the use of deprecated elements and attributes.
Frameset	Similar to Transitional, but provides for the use of frames, which are rendered in separate browser windows. In general, frames aren't used in modern web sites, so they aren't presented in this book.

Some common DOCTYPE declarations

HTML 4.01 Strict

```
<!DOCTYPE html PUBLIC "-//W3C//DTD HTML 4.01//EN"
    "http://www.w3.org/TR/html4/strict.dtd">
```

HTML 4.01 Transitional

```
<!DOCTYPE html PUBLIC "-//W3C//DTD HTML 4.01 Transitional//EN"
    "http://www.w3.org/TR/html4/loose.dtd">
```

XHTML 1.0 Strict

```
<!DOCTYPE html PUBLIC "-//W3C//DTD XHTML 1.0 Strict//EN"
    "http://www.w3.org/TR/xhtml1/DTD/xhtml1-strict.dtd">
```

XHTML 1.0 Transitional

```
<!DOCTYPE html PUBLIC "-//W3C//DTD XHTML 1.0 Transitional//EN"
    "http://www.w3.org/TR/xhtml1/DTD/xhtml1-transitional.dtd">
```

XHTML 1.1

```
<!DOCTYPE html PUBLIC "-//W3C//DTD XHTML 1.1//EN"
    "http://www.w3.org/TR/xhtml11/DTD/xhtml11.dtd">
```

Description

- The *DOCTYPE declaration* indicates which version of HTML or XHTML the document uses. To do that, it refers to a *Document Type Definition*, or DTD, that defines the rules that must be followed.

- Some of the elements and attributes for HTML 4.01 and XHTML 1.0 have been *deprecated*, which means that they will be removed from future releases. If you want to use these deprecated elements and attributes, you'll need to use the Transitional flavor.

- If you don't include a DTD in your DOCTTYPE declaration, a modern browser will display the page in *quirks mode*. In this mode, the browser assumes that the document includes workarounds. For a modern web site, though, you should upgrade old pages so quirks mode isn't needed.

What HTML version we use in this book

- In this book, we use XHTML 1.0 because we think the stricter syntax helps you write better code. We use the Transitional flavor because it allows some coding flexibility.

- If you use HTML 4.01, we recommend you follow the syntax for XHTML 1.0. The only difference is that you must omit the slash for a self-closing tag, as in <br>.

Figure 3-1   How to code the DOCTYPE declaration

How to code the head section

The head section of an HTML document contains elements that provide information about the web page rather than the content of the page itself. In chapter 1, for example, you learned that the title element sets the text that's displayed in the browser's title bar. Now, you'll learn more about this element as well as some other elements you can code in the head section.

How to specify the title for a page

At a minimum, the head element must contain a title element. The content of this element is displayed in the browser's title bar. You can see how this works in figure 3-2. Note here that the title is also displayed in the tab for the page. It may also be used for the other purposes described in this figure. However, this element can't contain any other elements, even simple formatting elements.

How to identify a linked file

The link element is an optional element that you can use to specify a file that should be linked to the web page. For example, you can use this element to identify a style sheet for the page. You'll learn how to do that in the next chapter.

In figure 3-2, the link element is used to link a custom icon, called a *favicon*, to the web page. This causes the icon to be displayed at the left side of the URL in the browser's address bar and to the left of the title in the tab for the page. Note that you typically name this icon favicon.ico as shown in this figure.

When you code the link element, you typically include three attributes. The rel attribute indicates the relationship of the linked resource to the document. For a favicon, you use the value "shortcut icon".

The href attribute provides the URL of the resource. In this example, the favicon is in the same directory as the HTML file, so the URL is just the file name. If the file is in a different location, though, you can use an absolute or relative URL to identify that location. You'll learn how to code absolute and relative URLs later in this chapter.

The type attribute is optional, but it's typically used to indicate the media type of the resource. If you're linking a favicon, for example, you typically code this attribute with the value "favicon/ico".

If you're using Internet Explorer, you should realize that it won't display a favicon if the page is displayed from your local file system. To test a favicon in this browser, then, you need to upload the page to a server and display it from that server. You'll learn how to do that in chapter 15.

A head section with a title and a linked icon file

```
<head>
    <title>San Joaquin Valley Town Hall</title>
    <link rel="shortcut icon" href="favicon.ico" type="favicon/ico" />
</head>
```

A browser that shows the title and icon

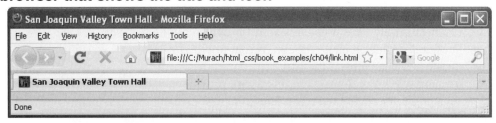

How to use the title element

- The title element specifies the text that's displayed in the browser's title bar and is a required element. This element can't contain any other elements.

- The title may also be displayed in the tab for the web page and in the Windows taskbar. It may be used as the name of a favorite or bookmark for the page. And it may be used as the name for the page in search engine results.

The attributes of the link element

Attribute	Description
`rel`	Specifies the relationship of the resource being linked to the document. Typical values are "stylesheet" for a CSS and "shortcut icon" for a favicon.
`href`	Specifies the URL of the resource being linked to the web page.
`type`	Specifies the media type of the resource being linked. When the rel attribute is "stylesheet", the type should be "text/css". When the rel attribute is "shortcut icon", the type should be "favicon/ico".

How to use the link element

- The link element identifies a file that's linked to the web page, like a CSS file or a custom icon file. See chapter 4 for more information on linking to a CSS file.

- A custom icon, called a *favicon*, is typically named favicon and must have the extension .ico to work correctly with Internet Explorer. A favicon typically appears to the left of the URL in the browser's address bar. It may also appear to the left of the title in a tab, and it may be used for a favorite or bookmark.

- You can create an ico file by using an icon editor, a program that converts an image to an ico file, or a web-based converter. You may also be able to find an icon on the Internet by searching for "web icons".

Internet Explorer note

- To display a favicon in Internet Explorer, the page must be displayed from the web server, not from your local file system.

Figure 3-2   How to specify a title and identify a linked file

How to include metadata

The meta element is another optional element that you can code within the head element. You use it to specify *metadata*, which provides information about the content of the document.

The head element in figure 3-3 includes three meta elements. The first one provides values for the HTTP headers in an HTTP response. Note, however, that this metadata is only used if headers aren't provided by the web server. One benefit of coding this element, though, is that it will eliminate two warning messages when you validate the file.

The next two meta elements in this figure provide metadata that can be used by search engines to index the page. Here, the first element uses the name attribute with the value "description" to indicate that the content attribute contains a brief description of the web page. The second element uses the name attribute with the value "keywords" to indicate that the content attribute contains a list of keywords related to the page.

At present, there is some debate about how search engines use this metadata. In fact, the algorithms that search engines use are frequently changed, so it's hard to know what the best use of metadata is. There is also the danger that you might change the content of a page and forget to change the metadata. In that case, a search engine might index the page incorrectly. Nevertheless, it's a good practice to provide the "description" and "keywords" metadata for at least the important pages of a web site.

A head section that includes metadata

```
<head>
    <title>San Joaquin Valley Town Hall</title>
    <meta http-equiv="content-type" content="text/html; charset=utf-8" />
    <meta name="description"
          content="San Joaquin Valley Town Hall speakers for 2009-2010" />
    <meta name="keywords" content="san joaquin, town hall, speaker" />
</head>
```

How to use NotePad++ to specify the character encoding

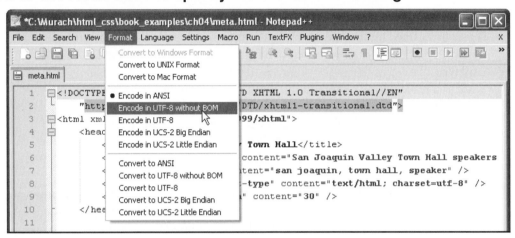

Three attributes of the <meta> tag

Attribute	Description
name	Specifies the type of metadata being added to the document. The values "description" and "keywords" can be used to specify content for some search engines.
http-equiv	Specifies the name of the metadata in an HTTP header. The value "content-type" is the most common and is used to indicate the content type of the document.
content	Specifies the value to be used for the item specified by the name or http-equiv attribute.

Description

- The meta element provides information about the HTML document that's called *metadata*.

- The "content-type" metadata is used in HTTP response headers, but only if the web server doesn't provide its own headers. Here, the content is usually coded as text/html so the page is served as HTML, and UTF-8 is typically used for documents in English speaking countries. If you include a statement like this, two warning messages are eliminated when the file is validated.

- The "description" and "keywords" metadata is used by some search engines to determine how the page is indexed. Although the search algorithms for using this data are changed frequently, it's a good practice to include this data for at least the important pages of your site.

Figure 3-3   How to include metadata

How to code text elements

Within the body of a document, you can code two types of elements: block elements and inline elements. In the topics that follow, you'll learn how to code a variety of block and inline elements that define the text for a document.

How to code headings and paragraphs

Headings and paragraphs are the most common content of a web page. These are defined by the HTML elements shown in figure 3-4. These elements are called *block elements*, and each one begins on a new line when it is displayed.

If you review the example in this figure, you shouldn't have any trouble understanding how these elements work. Here, the HTML uses the h1, h2, and p elements to generate the text that's shown. When these elements are displayed by a browser, each element has a default font and size that's determined by the base font of the browser. This base font is typically Times New Roman in 16 pixels.

When you use the h1 through h6 elements, you should use them to provide a logical structure for your document, not to format the text. For example, the h1 element in this figure is used to mark the most important heading on the page, and the h2 element is used to mark the second most important heading. This helps search engines index your site properly, and it makes your pages more accessible to devices like screen readers. Then, you can use CSS to size and format the text in these elements, as shown in the next chapter.

Common block elements for headings and paragraphs

Element	Description
h1	Creates a level-1 heading with content in bold at 200% of the base font size.
h2	Creates a level-2 heading with content in bold at 150% of the base font size.
h3	Creates a level-3 heading with content in bold at 117% of the base font size.
h4	Creates a level-4 heading with content in bold at 100% of the base font size.
h5	Creates a level-5 heading with content in bold at 83% of the base font size.
h6	Creates a level-6 heading with content in bold at 67% of the base font size.
p	Creates a paragraph of text at 100% of the base font size.

HTML that uses the block elements

```
<h1>San Joaquin Valley Town Hall Programs</h1>
<h2>Pre-lecture coffee at the Saroyan</h2>
<p>Join us for a complimentary coffee hour, 9:15 to 10:15 a.m.
on the day of each lecture. The speakers usually attend this very
special event.</p>
<h2>Post-lecture luncheon at the Saroyan</h2>
<p>Extend the excitement of Town Hall by purchasing tickets to the
luncheons. This unique opportunity allows you to ask more questions
of the speakers--plus spend extra time meeting new Town Hall
friends.</p>
<p>A limited number of tickets are available. Call
(559) 555-1212 for reservations by the Friday preceding the event.</p>
```

The block elements in a web browser

San Joaquin Valley Town Hall Programs

Pre-lecture coffee at the Saroyan

Join us for a complimentary coffee hour, 9:15 to 10:15 a.m. on the day of each lecture. The speakers usually attend this very special event.

Post-lecture luncheon at the Saroyan

Extend the excitement of Town Hall by purchasing tickets to the luncheons. This unique opportunity allows you to ask more questions of the speakers--plus spend extra time meeting new Town Hall friends.

A limited number of tickets are available. Call (559) 555-1212 for reservations by the Friday preceding the event.

Description

- *Block elements* are the main building blocks of a web site and can contain other elements. Each block element begins on a new line.
- The base font size and the spacing above and below headings and paragraphs are determined by the browser. You can change these values using CSS.

Figure 3-4   How to code headings and paragraphs

How to code special blocks of text

In addition to the elements for headings and paragraphs, HTML provides some elements that you can use to code special blocks of text. The three most common elements are described in figure 3-5.

You typically use the pre element to display preformatted blocks of code. When you use this element, any whitespace or line breaks that appear in the content is maintained. In addition, the content is displayed in a monospaced font. In this figure, the pre element is used to display two lines of JavaScript code.

You typically use the blockquote element to display an actual quote like the one shown in this figure. Depending on the browser, this element may cause the content to be indented from the left side of the block element that contains it or from both the left and right sides. Which brings up another point: the blockquote element must always be coded within another block element.

You can use the address element to display contact information for the developer or owner of a web site. In this figure, the address element is used to display a phone number and web address. As you can see, this information is displayed in italics.

Although these elements provide some default HTML formatting, you shouldn't think of these elements that way. Instead, you should use these elements to identify elements that need a specific type of formatting. Then, you can use CSS to format these elements so they look the way you want them to.

Block elements for special types of text

Element	Description
pre	Creates a block of preformatted text that preserves whitespace and is displayed in a monospaced font. Typically used for sections of code that are already formatted with line breaks and spaces.
blockquote	Creates a block of text that's indented. Typically used for actual quotes. The blockquote element must be enclosed in another block element such as the p element.
address	Creates a block of text that's displayed in italics. Typically used to provide contact information for the developer or owner of a web site.

HTML that uses the block elements

```
<p>How to use JavaScript to display the year:</p>
<pre>
        var today = new Date();
        document.writeln( today.getFullYear() );
</pre>

<p>Ernest Hemingway wrote:
    <blockquote>"Cowardice, as distinguished from panic, is almost
    always simply a lack of ability to suspend the functioning of the
    imagination."</blockquote>
</p><br />

<p>How to contact Mike Murach &amp; Associates:</p>
<address>1-800-221-5528<br />
    <a href="murachbooks@murach.com">murachbooks@murach.com</a>
</address>
```

The block elements in a web browser

```
How to use JavaScript to display the year:

        var today = new Date();
        document.writeln( today.getFullYear() );

Ernest Hemingway wrote:

    "Cowardice, as distinguished from panic, is almost always simply a lack of ability to suspend the
    functioning of the imagination."


How to contact Mike Murach & Associates:

1-800-221-5528
murachbooks@murach.com
```

Description

- For most web pages, you won't need to use these elements. If you do need them, you can use the examples above to get started. Then, if you need more information about these elements, you can search the Internet.

Figure 3-5   How to code special blocks of text

How to code inline elements for formatting and emphasizing text

In contrast to a block element, an *inline element* doesn't start on a new line. Instead, an inline element appears within a block element. In this topic, you'll learn how to code some of the most common inline elements for emphasizing text.

Figure 3-6 presents these elements and shows how to use them. As you can see in the examples, each inline element must be coded within a block element. In addition, except for the br element, each element must have both an opening and a closing tag. Then, the appropriate formatting is applied to the content between these tags.

As you review these elements, you'll notice that both the i and em elements cause the content to be displayed in italics. Similarly, both the b and strong elements cause the content to be displayed in bold. The difference is that the i and b elements don't assign any meaning to the content; they simply apply formatting. In contrast, the em element indicates that the content should be emphasized, and the strong element indicates that the content should be strongly emphasized.

Because of that, you should only use i and b when you don't need to associate any meaning with the content. In this figure, for example, you can see that the i element is used to italicize the term "Hypertext Markup Language", but the em element is used to emphasize the words "you won't pass the class". The examples for the b and strong elements are similar.

Please note that the way the i and b elements are used have changed since CSS has become available. Previously, these elements were commonly used to apply formatting. Now, it's more common to use em and strong and to use CSS to apply the appropriate formatting.

The next element, code, displays text in a monospaced font. Unlike the pre element that you use to display a block of code, you typically use the code element to display short pieces of code within other text on a web page. In this figure, for example, the code element is used to display the names of the strong and em elements in a monospaced font.

If you ever need to display subscripted or superscripted text, you can use the sub and sup elements. The examples in this figure show how this works. Although these elements don't provide meaning, it's still common to use them.

The last element shown here, br, forces a new line of text. Note, however, that you shouldn't use this element to provide space between block elements; your CSS should do that. Instead, you should use it only to force a new line within a block element. In the last paragraph in this figure, for example, the br element is used to force a new line between two lines of poetry.

Common inline elements for formatting and emphasizing text

Element	Description
i	Displays the content in italics.
em	Indicates that the content should be emphasized by being displayed in italics.
b	Displays the content in bold.
strong	Indicates that the content should be strongly emphasized by being displayed in bold.
code	Displays the content in a monospaced font.
sub	Displays the content as a subscript.
sup	Displays the content as a superscript.
br	Starts a new line of text.

HTML that uses the inline elements

```
<p>If you don't get 78% on your final, <em>you won't pass the class.</em>
</p>
<p>Save a bundle at our <strong>big yearend sale</strong>.</p>
<p>HTML stands for <i>Hypertext Markup Language</i>.</p>
<p>Please be sure to boldface <b>Murach</b> in the company logo.</p>
<p>You can use <code>strong</code> or <code>em</code> to emphasize text.
</p>
<p>The chemical symbol for water is H<sub>2</sub>O.</p>
<p>Your payment is due on the 4<sup>th</sup> of each month.</p>
<p>"To sleep, perchance to dream-<br />ay, there's the rub."</p>
```

The inline elements in a web browser

If you don't get at least 78% on your final, *you won't pass the class.*

Save a bundle at our **big yearend sale**.

HTML stands for *Hypertext Markup Language*.

Please be sure to boldface **Murach** in the company logo.

You can use strong or em to emphasize text.

The chemical symbol for water is H_2O.

Your payment is due on the 4th of each month.

"To sleep, perchance to dream-
ay, there's the rub."

Description

- An *inline element* is coded within a block element and doesn't begin on a new line. Many of the inline elements, such as the ones shown above, are used to format or emphasize text.
- HTML provides inline elements for formatting text in addition to the ones shown above. However, you'll rarely, if ever, need to use these elements.

Figure 3-6   How to code inline elements for formatting and emphasizing text

How to code character entities

Many of the web pages you develop will require special characters such as a copyright symbol and opening and closing "curly" quotes. To display these special characters, you use *character entities*. Figure 3-7 presents the most common of these entities.

As you can see, all character entities start with an ampersand (&) and end with a semicolon (;). Then, the rest of the entity identifies the character it represents. To insert the copyright symbol (©), for example, you use the © character entity.

Because the & character marks the start of each character entity, you shouldn't use this character within an HTML document to represent an ampersand. Instead, you should use the & entity. Similarly, because the left bracket (<) and right bracket (>) are used to identify HTML tags, you shouldn't use those characters within an HTML document to represent less-than and greater-than signs. Instead, you should use the < and > entities.

Besides the entities for characters, you may sometimes need to insert a non-breaking space to force a browser to display a space. To do that, you use the   character entity. In the third paragraph in this figure, for example, this character entity is used to indent the first line of the paragraph four spaces. Note that because you can accomplish the same thing using CSS, you probably won't use the   character entity this way. Later in this chapter, though, you'll see how to use this entity to provide space between an inline element and the content of the block element that contains it.

Common HTML character entities

Entity	Character
`&amp;`	&
`&lt;`	<
`&gt;`	>
`&copy;`	©
`&reg;`	®
`&trade;`	™
`&cent;`	¢
`&deg;`	°
`&plusmn;`	±
`&lsquo;`	' (opening single quote).
`&rsquo;`	' (closing single quote or apostrophe).
`&ldquo;`	" (opening double quote).
`&rdquo;`	" (closing double quote).
` `	A non-breaking space. It will always be displayed.

Examples of character entities

```
<p>It&rsquo;s time to start your Christmas shopping!</p>

<p>President John F. Kennedy said, &ldquo;And so, my fellow Americans,
ask not what your country can do for you; ask what you can do for
your country.&rdquo;</p>

<p>    Turning fear into hope, medical futurist
Dr. Alan J. Russell will discuss the science of regenerating damaged
or diseased human body parts, while offering real hope for the future
of human health.</p>

<p>&copy; 2009 Mike Murach &amp; Associates, Inc.</p>
```

The character entities in a web browser

It's time to start your Christmas shopping!

President John F. Kennedy said, "And so, my fellow Americans, ask not what your country can do for you; ask what you can do for your country."

    Turning fear into hope, medical futurist Dr. Alan J. Russell will discuss the science of regenerating damaged or diseased human body parts, while offering real hope for the future of human health.

© 2009 Mike Murach & Associates, Inc.

Description

- *Character entities* can be used to display special characters in an HTML document.
- HTML provides a variety of character entities in addition to the ones shown above. These are the ones you'll use most often, though.

Figure 3-7   How to code character entities

How to code div and span elements

The div element is a block element that you use to divide an HTML document into logical divisions. The span element is an inline element that you can use to apply formatting within a block element. Figure 3-8 shows how these elements are used.

In the example in this figure, you can see that the content of the document is structured into three divisions. The first division contains the entire web page, and it is divided into two other divisions: one for the main portion of the web page, and one for the footer.

If you look at this web page as it's displayed in the browser, you can see that the div elements don't affect the appearance of the page. But as you'll see in the next chapter, you can use CSS to format these divisions by referring to their id attributes.

In the p element in the main division, you can see an inline span element. Like the div element, the span element doesn't affect the appearance of the page. But as you'll see in the next chapter, you can use CSS to format span elements.

A block element for structuring a web page

Element	Description
div	Lets you structure a page into logical divisions that can be formatted and positioned with CSS. This element can contain text, inline elements, and other block elements.

An inline element for structuring text

Element	Description
span	Lets you identify text that can be formatted with CSS.

A page that's structured with div and span elements

```
<body>
    <div id="page">
        <div id="main">
            <h1>San Joaquin Valley Town Hall</h1>
            <p><span id="welcome">Welcome to San Joaquin Valley Town
                Hall.</span>
            We have some amazing speakers in store for you this season!</p>
        </div>
        <div id="footer">
            <p>&copy; Copyright 2009 San Joaquin Valley Town Hall.</p>
        </div>
    </div>
</body>
```

The page displayed in a web browser

San Joaquin Valley Town Hall

Welcome to San Joaquin Valley Town Hall. We have some amazing speakers in store for you
this season!

© Copyright 2009 San Joaquin Valley Town Hall.

Description

- You can use div elements to define divisions within the body of a document. This can help indicate the structure of the page.

- You can use span elements to identify sections of text within a block that you want to apply special formatting to.

- You can use CSS to apply formatting to div and span elements as described in chapter 4.

Figure 3-8   How to code div and span elements

How to code the core attributes

Besides the attributes you've learned about so far, HTML provides some core attributes that you can use with most elements. In figure 3-9, you can see the five core attributes that you're most likely to use.

You use the id attribute to uniquely identify an HTML element. Then, you can use CSS to work with the element.

The class attribute is similar, except it doesn't have to be unique. That lets you assign more than one element to the same class. Then, you can use CSS to apply the same formatting to all the elements in the class. Note that when you use the class attribute, you can assign an element to more than one class.

In the example in this figure, you can see that the div element includes an id attribute with the value "main". Also, the input element has an id attribute with the value "email". As you'll see in the next chapter, CSS can be used to apply unique formatting to elements with id attributes.

A class attribute is used in this example to assign a class named "first" to the first p element. Then, another class attribute is used to assign two classes to the second p element. These classes are "first" and "field". Later, you can use CSS to apply the formatting to the elements in these classes.

You can use the title attribute to provide additional information for an element. In the example in this figure, this attribute is used to provide a tooltip for an input field that lets the user enter an email address (you'll learn more about input fields in chapter 10). Then, when the cursor is moved over this field in the browser, the tooltip is displayed. For some elements, though, a tooltip isn't displayed so the title attribute has no purpose.

The lang and xml:lang attributes let you override the default language used by a document. The difference between the two is that you can code the xml:lang attribute only within an XHTML document, but you can code the lang attribute in either an HTML or an XHTML document.

In most cases, you'll code this attribute on the html element to specify the language for the entire document, but you can also code it for individual elements. For English-speaking countries, for example, you typically code the lang attribute like this:

```
lang="en"
```

and the xml:lang attribute like this:

```
xml:lang="en"
```

This can help a screen reader pronounce words correctly. If a sentence on a web page is written in French, for example, you can code this attribute for the element that contains the sentence.

Core HTML attributes

Attribute	Description
id	Specifies a unique identifier for an element that can be referred to by CSS. This identifier can also be used in an a element to jump to that element (see chapter 7).
class	Specifies one or more classes for an element that can be referred to by CSS, and more than one element can belong to the same class. To code more than one class for an element, separate the class names with spaces.
title	Specifies additional information about an element. For some elements, the title appears in a tooltip when the user hovers the mouse over the element.
lang	Identifies the language that the content of the element is written in.
xml:lang	Same as the lang attribute, but can only be used within an XHTML document.

HTML that uses these attributes

```
<div id="main">
    <h1>San Joaquin Valley Town Hall</h1>
    <p class="first">Welcome to San Joaquin Valley Town Hall.</p>
    <form action="subscribe.php" method="post">
        <p>Please enter your e-mail address to subscribe to our
        newsletter.</p>
        <p class="first field">E-Mail:
            <input type="text" name="email" id="email"
            title="Enter e-mail here." /></p>
        <p><input type="submit" value="Subscribe"/></p>
    </form>
</div>
```

The HTML in a web browser with a tooltip displayed

Description

- The core attributes can be coded for most HTML elements.
- ID and class names are case sensitive, should start with a letter, and can include letters, numbers, underscores, hyphens, colons, and periods.
- The lang and xml:lang attributes are typically used to assist screen readers to read content correctly and to provide for searches that are restricted by language.

Figure 3-9   How to code the core attributes

How to code links, lists, and images

Because you'll use links, lists, and images in most of the web pages that you develop, the topics that follow introduce you to their elements. But first, you need to know how to code absolute and relative URLs so you can use them with your links and images.

How to code absolute and relative URLs

Figure 3-10 presents some examples of absolute and relative URLs. To help you understand how these examples work, the diagram at the top of this figure shows the directory structure for the web site used in the examples. As you can see, the directories for this web site are organized into three levels. The root directory for the site contains five subdirectories, including the directories that contain the images and styles for the site. Then, two of the other subdirectories contain subdirectories of their own.

In chapter 1, you learned about the basic components of a URL. The URL you saw in that chapter was an *absolute URL*, which includes the domain name of the web site. For example, the first two URLs in this figure refer to a page at the web site with the domain name www.murach.com. The first URL points to the index.html file in the root directory of this web site, and the second URL points to the toc.html file in the root\books\javascript directory.

When used within the code for the web pages of a site, an absolute URL is typically used to refer to a file in another web site. In contrast, a *relative URL* can only be used to refer to a file within the same web site. This type of URL specifies the location of the file relative to the directory that contains the current page.

This is illustrated by the third and fourth examples. Here, the third URL refers to a file in the same directory as the current page. The fourth URL refers to a file in the javascript subdirectory of the directory that contains the current page.

The next two examples show how you can use a relative URL to navigate up the directory structure from the current directory, which is root\books\javascript. To navigate up one directory, you code two periods followed by a slash as in the fifth example. This URL refers to the index.html file in the root\books directory. To navigate up two directories, you code two periods and a slash followed by two more periods and a slash as in the sixth example. This URL refers to the index.html file in the root directory. To navigate up additional directories, you code two periods and a slash for each directory level.

Another way to navigate to the root directory for a web site is to code a slash as in the seventh example. This URL refers to the login.html file in the root directory. You can also navigate to a directory within the root directory by coding the path for that directory after the slash as in the eighth example. This URL refers to the murachlogo.gif file in the images subdirectory of the root directory.

A simple web site directory structure

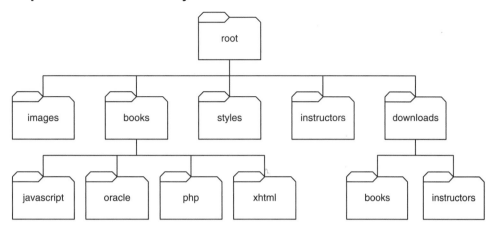

Examples of absolute and relative URLs

Absolute URLs

```
http://www.murach.com/index.html
http://www.murach.com/books/javascript/toc.html
```

Relative URLs that are based on the root\books directory

```
index.html                 (refers to root\books\index.html)
javascript/overview.html   (refers to root\books\javascript\overview.html)
```

Relative URLs that navigate up from the root\books\javascript directory

```
../index.html             (refers to root\books\index.html)
../../index.html          (refers to root\index.html)
/login.html               (refers to root\login.html)
/images/murachlogo.gif    (refers to root\images\murachlogo.gif)
```

Description

- When you code an *absolute URL*, you code the complete URL including the domain name for the site. Absolute URLs let you display pages at other web sites.

- When you code a *relative URL*, you base it on the current directory, which is the directory that contains the current page.

- To go up one level from the current directory, you code two periods and a slash. To go up two levels, you code two periods and a slash followed by two more periods and a slash. And so on.

- To go to the root directory for the web site, you code a slash. Then, you can code one or more directories after the slash.

Figure 3-10   How to code absolute and relative URLs

How to code links

Most web pages contain *links* that go to other web pages or web resources. To code a link, you use the a element as shown in figure 3-11. Because this element is an inline element, you usually code it within a block element like a p element.

In most cases, you'll code only the href attribute for the a element. This attribute specifies the URL for the resource you want to link to. The examples in this figure illustrate how this works. The first three examples use relative URLs to link to a page in the same directory as the current page, to link to a page in a subdirectory of the parent directory, and to link to a page based on the root directory. In contrast, the last example uses an absolute URL to link to a page at another web site.

By default, links are underlined when they're displayed in a browser to indicate that they're clickable. As a result, most web users have been conditioned to associate underlined text with links. Because of that, you should avoid underlining any other text.

When a link is displayed, it has a default color depending on its state. For instance, a link that hasn't been visited is displayed in blue. A link that has been visited is displayed in purple. And an active link, one that the user has clicked down on but hasn't released, is displayed in red. In addition, if a link contains an image, most browsers display it with a border around it. Note, however, that you can use CSS as described in the next chapter to change these settings.

When you create a link that contains text, it's a good practice to use text that indicates the function of the link. For example, you shouldn't use text like "click here" because it doesn't indicate what the link does. Instead, you should use text like that shown in this figure. In short, if you can't tell what a link does by reading its text, you should rewrite the text. This improves the accessibility of your site, and it helps search engines index your site.

Basic attribute of the \<a> tag

Attribute	Description
href	Specifies a relative or absolute URL for a link.

A link to a web page in the same directory

```
<p>Go view our <a href="products.html">product list</a>.</p>
```

A link to a web page in a subdirectory of the parent directory

```
<p>Read about the <a href="../company/services.html">services we
provide</a>.</p>
```

A link to a web page based on the root directory

```
<p>View your <a href="/orders/cart.html">shopping cart</a>.</p>
```

A link to a web page at another web site

```
<p>To learn more about JavaScript, visit the
<a href="http://www.javascript.com/">official JavaScript web site</a>.</p>
```

The links in a web browser

Description

- The a element is an inline element that creates a *link* that loads another web page. The href attribute of this element identifies the page to be loaded.

- The content of an a element can be text as shown above, an image, or text and an image. See figure 3-13 for an introduction to images.

- The text content of a link is underlined by default to indicate that it's clickable. If a link hasn't been visited, it's displayed in blue. If it has been visited, it's displayed in purple. If it's active, it's displayed in red. You can change these values using CSS.

- If a link contains an image, most browsers display the image with a border. However, you can remove the border by using CSS.

- See chapters 4 and 7 for more information on coding and formatting the a element.

Figure 3-11   How to code links

How to code lists

Figure 3-12 shows how to code the two basic types of lists: ordered lists and unordered lists. To create an *unordered list*, you use the ul element. Then, within this element, you code one li element for each item in the list. The content of each li element is the text that's displayed in the list. By default, when a list is displayed in a browser, each item in an unordered list is preceded by a bullet. However, you can change that bullet with CSS.

To create an *ordered list*, you use the ol element, along with one li element for each item in the list. This works like the ul element, except that the items are preceded by numbers rather than bullets when they're displayed in a browser. In this case, you can change the type of numbers that are used with CSS.

The two lists shown in this figure illustrate how this works. Here, the first list simply displays the names of several programming languages, so these items don't need to reflect any order. In contrast, the second list identifies three steps for completing an order. Because these steps must be completed in a prescribed sequence, they're displayed in an ordered list.

When you work with the li element, you should be aware that it can contain text, inline elements, or block elements. For example, an li element can contain an a element that defines a link. You'll see an example of that later in this chapter.

Elements that create ordered and unordered lists

Element	Description
`<ul>`	Creates an unordered list.
`<ol>`	Creates an ordered list.
`<li>`	Creates a list item for an unordered or ordered list.

HTML that creates two lists

```html
<p>We have books on a variety of languages, including</p>
<ul>
    <li>Java</li>
    <li>JavaScript</li>
    <li>Visual Basic</li>
    <li>C#</li>
    <li>C++</li>
</ul>

<p>You will need to complete the following steps:</p>
<ol>
    <li>Enter your billing information.</li>
    <li>Enter your shipping information.</li>
    <li>Confirm your order.</li>
</ol>
```

The lists in a web browser

We have books on a variety of languages, including

- Java
- JavaScript
- Visual Basic
- C#
- C++

You will need to complete the following steps:

1. Enter your billing information.
2. Enter your shipping information.
3. Confirm your order.

Description

- The two basic types of lists are *ordered lists* and *unordered lists*. By default, an unordered list is displayed as a bulleted list and an ordered list is displayed as a numbered list.
- See chapters 4 and 7 for more information on coding and formatting lists.

Figure 3-12   How to code lists

How to include images

Images are an important part of most web pages. To display an image, you use the img element shown in figure 3-13. This is an inline element that's coded as a self-closing tag. In the example in this figure, this tag is coded within an h2 element. Also notice that to add space between the image and the text for the heading, I used two   character entities. In chapter 5, though, you'll see a better way to do this by using CSS.

The most important attribute for an img element is the src attribute. This attribute specifies the URL of the image you want to display, and it is required. For instance, the src attribute for the image in the example indicates that the image named murachlogo.gif can be found in the images subdirectory of the current directory.

The alt attribute is also a required attribute in XHTML. You typically use this attribute to provide information about the image in case it can't be displayed or the page is being accessed using a screen reader. For instance, because the image in this figure is our company's logo, the value of the alt attribute is set to "Murach Logo". If an image doesn't provide any meaning, however, you can code the value of the alt attribute as an empty string (""). You might want to do that, for example, when an image is only used for decoration.

The images that you include in a web page need to be in one of the formats that modern web browsers support. Currently, most web browsers support the JPEG, GIF, and PNG formats. Typically, a web designer uses imaging software such as Adobe Photoshop to create and maintain these files for a web site. In particular, you use imaging software to create images that are the right size for your web pages.

Then, you can use the height and width attributes of an img element to tell the browser what the size of an image is. That can help the browser lay out the page as the image is being loaded. Although you can also use the height and width attributes to render an image larger or smaller than the original image, it's better to use your image editor to make the image the right size. You'll learn more about working with images in chapter 8.

As a good practice, you should only use the img element to link to images on the current web site. However, it's possible to link to an image that's stored on another web site by coding an absolute URL for the value of the alt attribute. This is known as *hot linking*, and it's highly discouraged.

Attributes of the <img> tag

Attribute	Description
src	Specifies the relative or absolute URL of the image to display. It is a required attribute.
alt	Specifies alternate text to display in place of the image. This text is also read aloud by screen readers for users with disabilities. It is required.
longdesc	Specifies a long description of the image.
height	Specifies the height of the image in pixels.
width	Specifies the width of the image in pixels.

An img element

```
<h2><img src="images/murachlogo.gif" alt="Murach Logo" height="75px" />
  Mike Murach &amp; Associates, Inc.</h2>
```

The image in a web browser

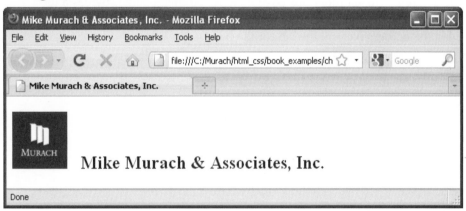

The image formats that are supported by most browsers

- JPEG (Joint Photographic Experts Group)
- GIF (Graphic Interchange Format)
- PNG (Portable Network Graphics)

Description

- The img element is an inline element that is used to display an image that's identified by the src attribute.
- The height and width attributes can be used to indicate the size of a image so the browser can allocate the correct amount of space on the page. These attributes can also be used to size an image, but it's usually better to use an image editor to do that.
- JPEG files commonly use the JPG extension and are typically used for photographs and scans. GIF files are typically used for small illustrations and logos. And PNG files combine aspects of JPEG and GIF files.
- See chapters 4 and 8 for more information on coding, formatting, and using img tags.

Figure 3-13   How to include images

A structured web page

Now that you've seen the HTML elements for structuring a web page, you're ready to see a simple web page that uses these elements.

The page layout

The web page shown in figure 3-14 uses many of the HTML elements you learned about in this chapter. The main purpose of this page is to display information about a series of lectures being presented by a non-profit organization.

To start, this page uses three different levels of headings, a list, and two paragraphs. The first paragraph uses an inline element to apply italics to a portion of the text, and the second paragraph uses a character entity to include a copyright symbol. In addition, this page includes an image that provides a logo for the site, and each item in the list includes a link. Finally, a favicon is displayed in the address bar and the tab for the page.

A web page that uses some of the HTML presented in this chapter

Description

- This web page provides information for a non-profit organization that arranges lectures by renowned speakers. The speakers are presented in an unordered list, and additional information about each speaker can be displayed by clicking on the link for that speaker.

- This web page contains block elements that define the headings and paragraphs and divide the page into sections. It also contains an inline element that applies italics to part of the text in the next to last paragraph.

- This page uses a character entity to include the copyright symbol in the last paragraph. It also uses a character entity to provide space between the image at the top of the page and the text to its right.

- This page includes a favicon that's displayed to the left of the URL in the address bar and to the left of the page title in the tab.

Figure 3-14   The page layout for a structured web page

The HTML file

Figure 3-15 presents the HTML file for the web page. The first thing you should notice is that this document uses XHTML 1.0 Transitional. Because of that, the html element includes an xmlns attribute. This attribute is always coded the same way when XHTML is used, but it isn't allowed when HTML is used.

The head section includes the required title element, followed by a link element that links to the favicon for the page. In addition, the head section includes a meta element for the content-type HTTP header. This header indicates that the document should be served as HTML and that the character set used by the document is UTF-8.

The body section starts with a div element that contains all of the contents of the web page. In chapter 5, you'll see how this lets you use CSS to apply formatting to the entire web page. That's why starting the body element with a div element for the entire page is a common practice.

Within the div element for the entire page are three other div elements that divide the page into three components. The first div element defines the header for the page. It consists of an h1 element that contains the logo image as well as text. Notice that the image and text are separated by two   character entities. Also notice that the height of the image is set so the image will be the correct size. The h1 element is followed by an h3 element.

The next div element defines the main content of the page. This content begins with an h2 element, followed by an unordered list of the speakers who will be giving lectures. Notice that each li element includes an a element that defines a link to a page that provides more information about the speaker. This list is followed by a paragraph that includes contact information. An em element is used within this paragraph to emphasize some of the text.

The last div element defines the copyright at the bottom of the page. This division consists of a single paragraph that contains the copyright information. The character entity that's used at the start of this paragraph is for the copyright symbol.

Each division in this document is uniquely identified by an id attribute. That way, different formatting can be applied to each division. You'll learn how to use CSS to apply formatting in the next chapter.

The HTML file for the web page

```
<!DOCTYPE html PUBLIC "-//W3C//DTD XHTML 1.0 Transitional//EN"
    "http://www.w3.org/TR/xhtml1/DTD/xhtml1-transitional.dtd">
<html xmlns="http://www.w3.org/1999/xhtml">

    <head>
        <title>San Joaquin Valley Town Hall</title>
        <link rel="shortcut icon" href="images/favicon.ico"
            type="favicon/ico" />
        <meta http-equiv="content-type" content="text/html; charset=utf-8" />
    </head>

    <body>
        <div id="page">
            <div id="header">
                <h1><img src="images/logo.jpg" alt="Town Hall Logo"
                    width="50px" />  San Joaquin Valley Town Hall</h1>
                <h3>Bringing cutting-edge speakers to the valley</h3>
            </div>

            <div id="main">
                <h2>2009-2010 guest speakers</h2>
                <ul>
                    <li>October 14, 2009: <a href="speakers/russell.html">
                        Dr. Alan J. Russell</a></li>
                    <li>November 18, 2009: <a href="speakers/diener.html">
                        Dr. Edward Diener</a></li>
                    <li>January 20, 2010: <a href="speakers/brancaccio.html">
                        David Brancaccio</a></li>
                    <li>February 17, 2010:
                        <a href="speakers/fitzpatrick.html">
                        Robert Fitzpatrick</a></li>
                    <li>March 17, 2010: <a href="speakers/williams.html">
                        Juan Williams</a></li>
                    <li>April 21, 2010: <a href="speakers/coll.html">
                        Steve Coll</a></li>
                </ul>
                <p><em>Contact us by phone</em> at (559) 555-1212 for ticket
                information.</p>
            </div>

            <div id="footer">
                <p>&copy; Copyright 2009 San Joaquin Valley Town Hall.</p>
            </div>
        </div>
    </body>
</html>
```

Figure 3-15   The HTML file for a structured web page

Perspective

This chapter has presented many of the HTML elements that you need for developing web pages. In particular, it has presented the main block elements that you use to structure a document, as well as the inline elements that you use to format and emphasize text.

With these skills, you can create web pages with the default formatting of the browser. As I've mentioned throughout this chapter, though, the right way to format and lay out your web pages is to use CSS. That's why the next three chapters show you how to do that.

Terms

DOCTYPE declaration	character entity
Document Type Definition (DTD)	absolute URL
deprecated	relative URL
standards mode	link
quirks mode	ordered list
favicon	unordered list
metadata	hot linking
Internet media type	JPEG (Joint Photographic Experts Group)
block element	GIF (Graphic Interchange Format)
inline element	PNG (Portable Network Graphics)

Summary

- The *DOCTYPE declaration* for an HTML document should include a *Document Type Definition* that indicates which version of HTML or XHTML the document is using along with the *flavor* of that version. In this book, the examples use XHTML 1.0 in the Transitional flavor. That flavor allows the use of the *deprecated* elements that will be removed from future releases.

- If a document doesn't include a DTD, the browsers assume that the document should be rendered in *quirks mode*. This means that the HTML includes workarounds that were designed for older browsers. Today, however, you should avoid using quirks mode.

- In the head section of an HTML document, the title element provides the text that's displayed in the browser's title bar, and the link element identifies a file that's linked to the web page.

- One common use of the link element in the head section is to identify a custom icon called a *favicon* that appears in the browser's address bar. This icon may also appear in the browser tab for the document or as part of a bookmark.

- *Block elements* are the primary content elements of a web site, and each block element starts on a new line when it is rendered by a browser. Headings and paragraphs are common block elements.

- *Inline elements* are coded within block elements, and they don't start on new lines when they are rendered. Some common inline elements are i (for italics), b (for bold), and em (for emphasize), which are used for formatting text. Another is the br element, which starts the text that follows on a new line.

- *Character entities* are used to display special characters like the ampersand and copyright symbols in an HTML document. In code, character entities start with an ampersand and end with a semicolon as in   (a non-breaking space).

- The div element is used to divide the code for an HTML document into divisions. The span element is used to identify a portion of text within a block element so special formatting can be applied to it.

- The core attributes that are commonly used for most HTML elements are the id, class, and title attributes. The id attribute uniquely identifies one element. The class attribute can be used to identify one or more elements. And the title attribute can provide other information about an element like the text that should be displayed in a tooltip.

- When you code an *absolute URL*, you code the complete URL including the domain name. When you code a *relative URL*, you base it on the current directory, which is the directory that contains the current page.

- The a element is an inline element that creates a link that loads another page. By default, the text of an a element is underlined. Also, an unvisited link is displayed in blue, a visited link in purple, and an active link in red. If a link contains an image, most browsers display the image with a border.

- Lists are block elements that can be used to display both *unordered lists* and *ordered lists*. By default, these lists are indented with bullets before the items in an unordered list and numbers before the items in an ordered list.

- The img element is used to display an image file. The three common formats for images are JPEG (for photographs and scans), GIF (for small illustrations and logos), and PNG, which combines aspects of JPEG and GIF.

Exercise 3-1   Create a simple web page

In this exercise, you'll develop the web page shown below. To make that easier, you'll start from a template.

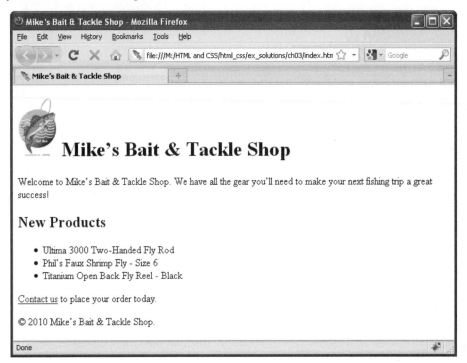

Complete the head section

1. Use your text editor to open this template:

    `c:\html_css\ch03\template.html`

    Then, save this file in the same directory as index.html.

2. Notice that the DOCTYPE declaration indicates that the document is written in XHTML 1.0 Transitional. Note also that this file contains a meta element for "content-type" metadata that serves the page as HTML with UTF-8 (English) coding. However, this file doesn't provide for other types of metadata.

3. Enter a title for the page as shown above. Be sure to use character entities for the apostrophe and ampersand in the title and throughout the document.

4. Add a link element to the head section to link the favicon that's in the images subdirectory of the ch03 directory to the document. To do that, you can use this relative address:

    `images/favicon.ico`

    This points to this directory:

    `c:\html_css\ch03\images\favicon.ico`

Enter the body section

5. Define the body section with four div elements. The first element is already there because it came from the template. It will contain everything in the body section, and its id is "page". Within this div element, code three more div elements with the ids "header", "main", and "footer".

6. Add an h1 element to the header division. Within this element, include the image and the text that will be displayed at the top of the page. You'll find the image in the images subdirectory of the ch03 directory. To start, don't include a height or width attribute for the img element.

7. Test your page in the Firefox browser to see how it looks so far, and fix any problems that you discover. Note that the image has a specific size of its own.

8. Set the height for the img element to 90 pixels, and test the page again.

9. Add the first p element to the main division with the text shown above, and test again.

10. Add an h2 element with "New Products" as its content, followed by the unordered list. Then, test again.

11. Add the second paragraph, which should include a link that displays a page named contact.html, and test again.

12. Add a paragraph to the footer division that includes the copyright symbol and information shown above. Then, test again.

13. While you're testing, click on the contact link and see that your browser isn't able to display the page because you haven't created it yet. Then, click on the Back button to return to the index page.

Create the contact.html page

14. Open the template.html file that you used in step 1. Then, save it as contact.html in the same directory.

15. Add a title element in the head section that displays "Contact us." Then, code an h1 element that says "This page under construction." Last, add a link that says "Return to index page."

16. Test this page by clicking on the link in the index page. Then, click on the "Return to index page" link to make sure that it takes you back to the index page. If necessary, fix any errors in the index or contact page.

Test in IE and validate the document

17. Test the index and contact pages in the Internet Explorer browser. If necessary, fix any problems and test again in both the Firefox and IE browsers.

18. Validate the HTML for the index page as shown in figure 2-13 of chapter 2 just to make sure no errors are present. If any are detected, fix them and validate the HTML again.

4

How to use CSS to format the elements of a web page

After you code the HTML that defines the structure of a web page, you're ready to code the CSS rule sets that determine how the page is formatted. To do that, you need to learn how to code selectors, and you need to learn how to code the properties and values for rule sets.

In this chapter, you'll learn how to code all types of selectors, and you'll learn how to apply the CSS properties for formatting text and links. Then, in the next chapter, you'll learn how to use the CSS box model for doing other types of formatting.

Basic skills for using CSS

Before you code the CSS for a web page, you need to know how to include CSS in a web page. You also need to know how to code the measurements and colors that you can use as values for some properties.

Three ways to include CSS in a web page

Figure 4-1 starts by showing two ways to include the CSS that's stored in an *external style sheet* in a web page. The first way is to use the link element. This is currently considered a best practice because it's more efficient when you load more than one external style sheet for a page.

The second way is to use the style element with the @import rule. This was considered a best practice until recently, so it's still widely used.

As you learned in chapter 3, when you code a relative URL in a link or style element, the URL is relative to the current file. For instance, the two dots and slash (../) in the URL in the first example in this figure navigate up one directory from the current file. Then, this URL navigates down to the styles directory and selects a file named main.css.

Although it isn't recommended, you can also use *embedded style sheets* and *inline styles* within an HTML document as shown by the second set of examples in this figure. When you embed a style sheet, the CSS rule sets are coded in a style element. For instance, the embedded style sheet in the first example in this group contains a rule set for the h1 element.

When you use an inline style, you code a style attribute for the HTML element with a value that contains all the CSS declarations that apply to the element. For instance, the inline style in the second example in this group applies two CSS declarations to the span element.

If you do use embedded style sheets or inline styles, the styles in the embedded style sheets override the styles in the external style sheets, and the inline styles override the styles in the embedded style sheet. If, for example, you code the embedded style sheet in this figure, the declarations for the h1 element will override those in the external style sheet.

Remember, though, that using external style sheets is a best practice. When you use them, the CSS declarations are in a separate CSS file, which separates the formatting for a web page from its content. This also makes it possible for more than one web page to share the same CSS file, which has several benefits. First, the HTML files are smaller. Second, you can provide consistent formatting for all the pages that use the same style sheet. Third, you can modify the formatting for all those pages by modifying a single style sheet.

The last example shows that you can include more than one style sheet in a single document. You might do that to include more styles for a page. You might also do that to include style sheets for different types of media. For instance, the first two style sheets in this example will be used if the page is displayed on a computer screen, and the last style sheet will be used if the page is printed.

Two ways to include an external style sheet

With the link element (currently considered the best practice)

```
<link rel="stylesheet" type="text/css" href="../styles/main.css" />
```

With the style element and the @import directive

```
<style type="text/css">
    @import "../styles/main.css";
</style>
```

How to embed styles in an HTML document (not recommended)

By embedding a style sheet in a style element in the head section

```
<style type="text/css">
    h1 {
        color: blue;
        font-size: 14pt;
    }
</style>
```

By using the style attribute of an inline element

```
<span style="color: red; font-size: 14pt;">Warning!</span>
```

Part of an HTML document that uses three style sheets

```
<head>
    <title>San Joaquin Valley Town Hall</title>
    <link rel="stylesheet" type="text/css" href="../styles/main.css"
        media="screen" />
    <link rel="stylesheet" type="text/css" href="../styles/speaker.css"
        media="screen" />
    <link rel="stylesheet" type="text/css" href="../styles/print.css"
        media="print" />
</head>
```

Description

- It's a best practice to use *external style sheets* whenever possible. To do that, you can use either the link element or the style element with the @import rule.

- Currently, the best practice for including external style sheets is to use the link element because it's more efficient when you use more then one style sheet for a web page. This is a recent change, though, so style elements are still commonly used.

- When you specify a relative URL for an external CSS file, the URL is relative to the current file.

- You can include two or more external style sheets in a single document. Then, if the styles are for the same medium, the styles in the first style sheet are applied first, followed by the styles in the second style sheet, and so on.

- You can use the media attribute of the link or style element to specify the type of medium that a style sheet will be used for. Common media types are screen (the default), print, handheld (for devices like smart phones), speech (the content is read by a screen reader), Braille (the content is displayed on a tactile device), and embossed (the content is printed in Braille).

Figure 4-1   How to include CSS in a web page

How to specify measurements

Figure 4-2 shows the four units of measure that are commonly used with CSS: pixels, points, ems, and percent. Here, the first two are *absolute units of measure*, and the second two are *relative units of measure*. Other absolute units are inches and picas, but they aren't used as often.

When you use relative units of measure like ems or a percent, the measurement will change if the user changes the browser's font size. If, for example, you set the size of a font to 80 percent of the browser's default font size, that element will change if the user changes the font size in the browser. Because this lets the users adjust the font sizes to their own preferences, we recommend that you use relative measurements for font sizes.

In contrast, when you use an absolute unit of measure like pixels or points, the measurement won't change even if the user changes the font size in the browser. If, for example, you set the width of an element in pixels and the font size in points, the width and font size won't change.

When you use pixels, though, the size will change if the screen resolution changes. That's because the screen resolution determines the number of pixels that are displayed on the monitor. For instance, the pixels on a monitor with a screen resolution of 1280 x 1024 are closer together than the pixels on the same monitor with a screen resolution of 1152 x 864. That means that a measurement of 10 pixels will be smaller on the screen with the higher resolution. In contrast, a point is 1/72nd of an inch no matter what the screen resolution is.

The examples in this figure show how you can use pixels and relative measurements in your CSS. Here, the bottom border for the header is set to 3 pixels. In contrast, the font sizes are set as percentages, and the margins and padding are set as ems. This is a typical way to use these measurements.

To start, a font size of 87.5% is applied to the body element. This means that the font will be set to 87.5% of the default font size for the browser, which is usually 16 pixels. In that case, the font size for the body element will be 14 pixels.

A left margin of 2 ems is also applied to the body element. Because an em is equal to the current font size, that means that the body of the document is indented 28 pixels (2 times 14 pixels).

Next, the padding below the div element with an id of "header" is set to .75 em, or 10.5 pixels (14 times .75). Then, a solid black border that's 3 pixels wide is added below the padding. Finally, a margin of 1.5 ems, or 21 pixels (14 times 1.5), is added below the border. You'll learn more about padding, borders, and margins in the next chapter.

The last rule set indicates that the h1 element should be 200% of the base font, which was set in the rule set for the body element. In addition, no margin should be added below the h1 element. Notice here that no unit of measure is specified for the margin-bottom property. That's because when the value is zero, it doesn't matter what the unit of measure is.

Common units of measure

Symbol	Name	Type	Description
px	pixels	absolute	A pixel represents a single dot on a monitor. The number of dots per inch depends on the resolution of the monitor.
pt	points	absolute	A point is 1/72 of an inch.
em	ems	relative	One em is equal to the font size for the current font.
%	percent	relative	A percent specifies a value relative to the current value.

The HTML for a web page

```
<body>
    <div id="page">
        <div id="header">
            <h1>San Joaquin Valley Town Hall</h1>
        </div>
        <div id="main">
            <p>Welcome to San Joaquin Valley Town Hall. We have some
            amazing speakers in store for you this season!</p>
        </div>
    </div>
</body>
```

CSS that uses relative units of measure with a fixed border

```
body {
    font-size: 87.5%;
    margin-left: 2em; }
#header {
    padding-bottom: .75em;
    border-bottom: 3px solid black;
    margin-bottom: 0; }
h1 {
    font-size: 200%;
    margin-bottom: 0; }
```

The web page in a web browser

San Joaquin Valley Town Hall

Welcome to San Joaquin Valley Town Hall. We have some amazing speakers in store for you this season!

Description

- You can use the units of measure to specify a variety of CSS properties, including font-size, line-height, width, height, margin, and padding.
- To specify an *absolute measurement*, you can use pixels or points.
- To specify a *relative measurement*, you can use ems or percents. This type of measurement is relative to the size of another element.

Figure 4-2   How to specify measurements

How to specify colors

Figure 4-3 shows three ways to specify colors. The easiest way is to specify a color name, and this figure lists the names for 16 colors that are supported by all browsers. In addition to these names, though, most browsers support the color names in the draft CSS 3 Color specification. To find a complete list of these color names, you can go to the web site listed in this figure.

Note that when you use color names that contain "gray", most web browsers allow you to spell the name using either "gray" or "grey". Internet Explorer, however, requires that you spell most names with "gray" only. The exception is that you must use "lightgrey" instead of "lightgray".

Another way to specify a color is to use an *RGB* (red, green, blue) *value*. One way to do that is to specify the percent of red, green, and blue that make up the color. For instance, the example in this figure specifies 50% red, 25% green, and 25% blue. When you use this method, you can also use values from 0 through 255 instead of percents. Then, 0 is equivalent to 0% and 255 is equivalent to 100%. This gives you more precision over the resulting colors.

The third way to specify a color is to use *hexadecimal*, or *hex*, *values* for the red, green, and blue values, and this is the method that's preferred by most web designers. Then, each two-digit hex value is equivalent to a decimal value from 0 through 255. When you use this technique, the entire value must be preceded by the pound sign (#).

When you use hex values for colors, you usually get the hex value that you want from a chart or palette that shows all of the colors along with their hex values. For instance, you can get a complete list of the hex values for colors by going to the web site listed in this figure. Or, if you're using an IDE like DreamWeaver, you may also be able to choose a color from a palette and then have the IDE insert the hex value for that color into your code. A third alternative is to get the right hex values from printed color charts, which are commonly found in graphics design books.

Before I go on, you should realize that the color property shown here determines the foreground color, which is the color of the text. In the CSS in this figure, for example, the color of the header is set to blue (#00008b), and the background color of the body is set to a light orange (#facd8a). You'll learn more about setting background colors in the next chapter.

You should also realize that the color property for an element is *inherited* by any child elements. If, for example, you set the color property of the body element to navy, that color will be inherited by all of the elements in the body of the document. However, you can override an inherited property by coding a rule set with a different value for that property. Throughout this chapter and book, I'll point out the properties that are inherited as well as those that aren't.

16 descriptive color names

black	silver	white	aqua
red	lime	green	maroon
yellow	olive	purple	teal
gray	blue	fuchsia	navy

Three ways to specify colors

With a color name

```
color: silver;
```

With an RGB (red-green-blue) value

```
color: rgb(50%, 25%, 25%);
color: rgb(128, 64, 64);   /* Using three integers from 0 to 255 */
```

With an RGB value that uses hexadecimal numbers

```
color: #cd5c5c;
color: #a6f;                /* Expands to #aa66ff */
```

CSS that uses hexadecimal values to specify colors

```
body {
    font-size: 87.5%;
    margin-left: 2em;
    background-color: #facd8a; }
#header {
    color: #00008b; }
h1 {
    font-size: 200%; }
```

The HTML in a web browser

San Joaquin Valley Town Hall

Welcome to San Joaquin Valley Town Hall. We have some amazing speakers in store for you this season!

Description

- All browsers support the 16 color names shown above, and most browsers support many more. These are okay for getting started with the use of colors.

- Most graphic designers use *hexadecimal*, or *hex*, values to specify an *RGB value* because that lets them specify the exact colors that they want.

- You can find a list of color names and their corresponding hex values at http://www.w3.org/TR/css3-color.

- Some IDEs like DreamWeaver let you select a color from a palette of colors and then insert the right hex value into your code.

Figure 4-3   How to specify colors

How to code selectors

Now, you're ready to learn how to code selectors. Once you understand that, you will be able to apply CSS formatting to any part of a web page.

How to code selectors for elements, ids, and classes

In chapter 2, you were introduced to the basic selectors shown in figure 4-4. These are the selectors that you'll use the most.

To start, this figure shows the body of an HTML document that contains two div elements. The first div element is assigned an id of "main". Within this division is an h4 element followed by an unordered list. The unordered list contains two list items, each containing a link to another page.

The second div element is assigned an id of "footer". This division contains a single paragraph with copyright information, and the paragraph includes a class attribute with the value "copyright inactive". This means that this paragraph belongs to two classes named copyright and inactive.

Next, this figure shows the CSS rule sets that are used to format the HTML. The first rule set selects HTML elements by type. To do that, the selector is simply the name of the element. As a result, this rule set selects h4 elements. Within this rule set, the first rule sets the font-family property to Arial or a generic sans-serif font if Arial isn't available. Then, the second rule sets the margin above any h4 elements to .5 em, and the third rule sets the margin below any h4 elements to zero.

The second CSS rule set selects an HTML element by its id. To do that, the selector is a pound sign (#) followed by an id value that uniquely identifies the element. As a result, this rule set selects the div element that has an id of "main". Then, the first rule adds a border around the division; the second rule puts a 1 em margin outside of the border; and the third rule puts 1 em of padding between the border and the content of the division.

The last two rule sets select HTML elements by their class. To do that, the selector is a period (.) followed by a class name. As a result, the first rule set selects any elements that have been assigned to the copyright class. Here, the only element assigned to this class is the paragraph in the footer division. Then, the rule in this rule set right-aligns the text in the paragraph.

Similarly, the last rule set selects any elements that have been assigned to the inactive class. This, too, applies to the paragraph in the footer division. In this case, the text for this paragraph is set to gray.

You may remember from the last chapter that you can code a class attribute with the same value for more than one element on a page. That means that if you code a selector for that class, it will be used to format all the elements with that class. In contrast, the value of an id attribute on a page must be unique. That means that an id selector can only be used to format a single element.

HTML that can be selected by element, id, or class

```
<body>
    <div id="main">
        <h4>For more information:</h4>
        <ul>
            <li> View our <a href="products.html"> product list</a>.
            </li>
            <li>Read about the <a href="services.html">
            services we provide</a>.</li>
        </ul>
    </div>
    <div id="footer">
        <p class="copyright inactive">Copyright 2010</p>
    </div>
</body>
```

CSS rule sets that select by element, id, and class

Element

```
h4 { font-family: Arial, sans-serif;
    margin-top: .5em;
    margin-bottom: 0; }
```

ID

```
#main {
    border: 2px solid black;
    margin: 1em;
    padding: 1em; }
```

Class

```
.copyright { text-align: right; }
.inactive { color: gray; }
```

The elements displayed in a browser

For more information:

- View our product list.
- Read about the services we provide.

Copyright 2010

Description

- You code a selector for an element simply by naming the element.

- You code a selector for an element with an id attribute by coding a pound sign (#) followed by the id value.

- You code a selector for an element with a class attribute by coding a period followed by the class name. Then, the rule set applies to all elements with that class name.

Figure 4-4   How to code selectors for elements, ids, and classes

How to code selectors for descendants, combinations, and siblings

Figure 4-5 shows how to code selectors for descendants, combinations, and siblings. These are other types of selectors that you are likely to use.

As you read about these selectors and the ones in the next figure, keep in mind that terms like *parent*, *child*, *sibling*, and *descendent* are used in the same way that they are in a family tree. Child elements are at the first level below a parent element. Sibling elements are at the same level. And descendent elements can be one or more levels below a parent element.

That means a *descendant selector* selects the elements that are contained within another element. For instance, all of elements in the HTML in this figure are descendents of the div element, the li elements are also descendents of the ul element, and the a elements are descendents of the li, ul, and div element.

To code a descendant selector, you code a selector for the parent element, followed by a space and a selector for the descendent element. This is illustrated by the first group of examples. Here, the first selector selects all li elements in the division with the id "main". Then, the second descendant selector selects all the a elements that are descendants of the ul element.

The second group of examples in this figure shows how to select elements by element and class. To do that, you code the element name, followed by a period and the class name. Here, the selector selects ul elements that have a class of "speakers".

The third group of examples shows how to code multiple selectors for the same rule set. To do that, you separate the selectors with commas. Here, the first rule set uses multiple selectors to apply its rules to all h1, h2, and h3 elements. Then, the second rule set uses multiple selectors to apply its rules to all p elements and to li elements that are descendents of the ul elements that are assigned to the speakers class.

The last group of examples shows how to use an *adjacent sibling selector* to select an element that's coded at the same level as another element and is also coded right next to it. For instance, the h3, ul, and p elements in the HTML are all siblings, and the first h3 element and the ul element are adjacent siblings. In contrast, the first h3 element and the p elements aren't adjacent siblings.

To code an *adjacent sibling selector*, you code a selector for the first element, followed by a plus sign and a selector for the sibling element. In the example in this group, the selector will select any p elements that are adjacent to h3 elements. In this case, that means it will select the first p element that follows the second h3 element.

HTML that can be selected by descendants, combinations, and siblings

```
<div id="main">
    <h3>Winter 2010 Town Hall speakers</h3>
    <ul class="speakers">
        <li>January 20, 2010: <a href="speakers/brancaccio.html">
        David Brancaccio</a></li>
        <li>February 17, 2010: <a href="speakers/fitzpatrick.html">
        Robert Fitzpatrick</a></li>
        <li>March 17, 2010: <a href="speakers/williams.html">
        Juan Williams</a></li>
    </ul>
    <h3>Post-lecture luncheons</h3>
    <p>Extend the excitement of Town Hall by purchasing tickets to
    the luncheons. This unique opportunity allows you to ask more
    questions of the speakers.</p>
    <p>A limited number of tickets are available. Call now for
    reservations.</p>
    <p><em>Contact us by phone</em> at (559) 555-1212.</p>
</div>
```

CSS rule sets for descendants, combinations, and siblings

Descendant
```
#main li { font-size: 14pt; }
ul a { color: green; }
```

Element and class
```
ul.speakers { list-style-type: square; }
```

Multiple selectors
```
h1, h2, h3 { color: blue; }
p, ul.speakers li { font-family: "Times New Roman", serif; }
```

Adjacent sibling
```
h3+p { margin-top: .5em; }
```

Description

- To select elements only when they are descendants of a higher-level element, use a *descendant selector* that consists of the higher element, a space, and the descendent element.

- To code a selector for an element and class, code the element name, a period, and the class name.

- To code multiple selectors for the same rule set, use commas to separate the selectors.

- To select a sibling element that's adjacent to another element, use an *adjacent sibling selector* that consists of the first element, a plus sign (+), and the sibling element.

Figure 4-5   How to code selectors for descendants, combinations, and siblings

How to code other types of selectors

Figure 4-6 shows how to code other types of selectors. Note, however, that some of these selectors won't work in older browsers like IE6 and some won't work in new browsers that don't support the CSS 3.0 standards. As a result, you probably shouldn't use any of these selectors until the older browsers are phased out and the new browsers support CSS 3.0. With that in mind, you may want to skip this topic. But if you're curious, read on.

To start, you can select all HTML elements by using the *universal selector*. To do that, you code an asterisk (*). In the example in this figure, the universal selector changes the foreground color of all elements on the web page to green. Although this selector works on all browsers, you probably won't need to use it.

If you want to select elements only when they're direct child elements of a parent element, you can code a *child selector*. To do that, you separate the parent and child selectors with a greater than (>) sign. In this figure, for example, the first child selector selects the p elements that are children of the main division, and the second selector selects the a elements that are children of the li elements.

Unlike the adjacent sibling selector, a *general sibling selector* selects any sibling element whether or not the elements are adjacent. To code this type of selector, you separate the selector for the first element and the selector for the sibling element by a tilde (~). In this figure, the general sibling selector selects all the p elements that follow any h3 element.

An *attribute selector* selects elements based on an attribute or attribute value. The three examples in this figure illustrate how this selector works. To code an attribute selector that selects elements that have an attribute, you code an element selector followed by the name of the attribute in brackets [ ]. For instance, the first attribute selector selects all of the a elements that have an href attribute. Then, the second selector uses the universal selector to select all elements that have an href attribute. Note, however, that you can also omit the universal selector and code just the attribute in brackets to select all elements with that attribute.

To code an attribute selector that selects elements with the specified attribute value, you follow the attribute name with an equals sign and the value enclosed in quotation marks. This is illustrated in the third example. This selector will select all input elements with a type attribute whose value is set to "submit".

Other ways to code selectors

The universal selector

```
* { color: green; }
```

Child (not supported by some older browsers like IE 6)

```
#main>p { font-size: 11pt; }
li>a { color: green; }
```

General sibling (a new feature of CSS 3.0)

```
h3~p { margin-left: 2em; }
```

Attribute (not supported by some older browsers like IE 6)

```
a[href] { font-family: Arial, sans-serif; }
*[href] { font-size: 95%; }
input[type="submit"] {
    border: 1px solid black;
    color: #ef9c00;
    background-color: #facd8a;
}
```

Description

- Note that child, general sibling, and attribute selectors won't work in all browsers. As a result, you shouldn't use these selectors until the old browsers are no longer used and all current browsers support CSS 3.0.

- To select all elements, you can use the *universal selector* (*). This works with all browsers, but you may never need to use it.

- To select elements only when they are direct child elements of the parent element, you can use a *child selector* that consists of the parent element, the greater than sign (>), and the child element, but this isn't supported by some of the older browsers.

- To select any elements that are siblings to another element, you can use a *general sibling selector* that consists of the first element, a tilde (~), and the sibling element, but this can only be used by browsers that support CSS 3.0.

- To select an element with a specific attribute, you can use an *attribute selector* that consists of the element followed by the attribute name within brackets, but this isn't supported by some of the older browsers.

- To select all elements with a specific attribute, you can use an attribute selector that consists of the universal selector followed by the attribute name in brackets. If you do use this type of selector, you can omit the universal selector and code just the attribute name in brackets.

- To select an element with a specific attribute value, you can use an attribute selector that consists of the element followed by the attribute name, an equals sign, and a value within quotation marks.

Figure 4-6   How to code other types of selectors

How to code pseudo-class selectors

Figure 4-7 shows how to code *pseudo-class selectors*. To do that, you use one of the *pseudo-classes* listed at the top of this figure. These classes represent various conditions that apply to the elements on a page. For example, you can use the :link pseudo-class to refer to a link that hasn't been visited, and you can use the :visited pseudo-class to refer to a link that has been visited. Although you can use these two pseudo-classes only with links, you can use the other pseudo-classes with most HTML elements. For example, you can use the :hover pseudo-class with a or p elements.

To code a pseudo-class selector, you code the selector for an element followed by the pseudo-class. For instance, the first pseudo-class selector in this figure causes all unvisited links to be displayed in blue. Then, the second selector causes all visited links to be displayed in navy, the third selector causes a link to be displayed in bold when you point to it with the mouse, and the fourth selector causes a link to be displayed in purple when it's active, which means that you've pressed the mouse button down on it but haven't released it.

The fifth pseudo-class selector causes the text in the first p element in the main division to be indented 2 ems. Note here that the second p element in the main division isn't indented because it isn't the first child element of the division. Also note that the id isn't required in this selector since the HTML consists of a single division. In most cases, though, you'll want to identify the division so the rule set applies only to that division.

After the CSS examples, you can see how the formatting looks in a web browser. Here, the first line of the first paragraph is indented, but not the first line of the second paragraph. Also, the mouse is hovering over the second link so it's displayed in bold.

When working with pseudo-class selectors, you may find that different browsers support them differently or not at all. That's the case with the :first-child selector. However, the :visited and :hover selectors have been commonly used with links since the early days of the web. As a result, most browsers support these selectors when they're used with links.

Although we won't present them here, you should know that CSS also provides *pseudo-elements* that you can use in selectors. Pseudo-elements are similar to pseudo-classes in that they're predefined. However, you use pseudo-elements to format part of an element. For example, you can use the :first-letter pseudo-element to format the first character of an element, and you can use the :first-line pseudo-element to format the first line of text for an element. For more information on how to use pseudo-elements, see the W3C documentation at www.w3.org/TR/CSS2.

CSS pseudo-classes

Name	Description
`:link`	A link that hasn't been visited.
`:visited`	A link that has been visited.
`:hover`	An element when the mouse is hovering over it.
`:active`	An element that's currently active. For example, a link is active after the user presses the mouse button but before the user releases the mouse button.
`:first-child`	An element that's the first child element of its parent element.

HTML that can be used by pseudo-class selectors

```
<div id="main">
    <p>Welcome to San Joaquin Valley Town Hall. We have some amazing
    speakers in store for you this season!</p>
    <ul class="speakers">
        <li>January 20, 2010: <a href="brancaccio.html">
        David Brancaccio</a></li>
        <li>February 17, 2010: <a href="fitzpatrick.html">
        Robert Fitzpatrick</a></li>
        <li>March 17, 2010: <a href="williams.html">Juan Williams</a></li>
    </ul>
    <p><a href="contact.html">Contact us</a> to purchase your tickets
    today!</p>
</div>
```

The CSS for pseudo-class selectors

```
a:link { color: blue; }
a:visited { color: navy; }
a:hover { font-weight: bold; }
a:active { color: purple; }
#main p:first-child { text-indent: 2em; }
```

The pseudo-class selectors in a web browser

Welcome to San Joaquin Valley Town Hall. We have some amazing speakers in store for you this season!

- January 20, 2010: David Brancaccio
- February 17, 2010: **Robert Fitzpatrick**
- March 17, 2010: Juan Williams

Contact us to purchase your tickets today!

Description

- A *pseudo-class* is a predefined class that's applied when a certain condition occurs. A pseudo-class starts with a colon and is immediately followed by the class name.

Figure 4-7   How to code pseudo-class selectors

How the cascade rules work

The term *Cascading Style Sheets* refers to the fact that more than one style sheet can be applied to a single web page. Then, if two or more rule sets are applied to the same element, the cascade order and rules determine which rule set takes precedence.

Before you can understand the cascade rules, though, you need to know that a user can create a *user style sheet* that provides default rule sets for web pages. Because most users don't create user style sheets, this usually isn't an issue. But some users do. For instance, users with poor vision often create user style sheets that provide for large font sizes. In that case, you need to consider how the user style sheets could affect your web pages.

You should also know how to identify one of your rules as important so it has precedence over other rules. To do that, you code "!important" as part of the rule. This is shown by the example in figure 4-8.

With that as background, this figure lists the five levels of the cascade order from highest to lowest. As you can see, the important rules in a user style sheet override the important rules in a web page, but the normal rules in a web page override the normal rules in a user style sheet. Below these rules are the default rules in the web browser.

But what happens if an element has more than one rule applied to it at the same level? To start, the rule with the highest specificity takes precedence, and this figure shows you which parts of a selector are more specific. For instance, the #main selector is more specific than the .speakers selector because an id is more specific than a class.

If a selector contains multiple parts, the additional parts add to that selector's specificity. This means that a selector with a class and an element is more specific than a selector with just a class. For instance, the p.highlight selector is more specific than the .highlight selector. As a result, p.highlight takes precedence.

If that doesn't settle the conflict, the rule that's specified last is applied. Earlier in this chapter, for example, you learned that if you include two or more style sheets to a document, the rule sets in each style sheet will override the rule sets in the preceding style sheets. This notion also applies if you accidentally code two rule sets for the same element in a single style sheet. Then, the one that is last takes precedence. In addition, because inline styles are specified after an external style sheet or an embedded style sheet, inline styles take precedence.

If this sounds complicated, it usually isn't a problem if you do a good job of organizing your style sheets. You'll see one way to do that in the application that's presented at the end of this chapter. Then, if a conflict does occur, you can usually resolve it by identifying one of the rules as important.

How to identify a rule as important

```
.highlight {
    font-weight: bold !important;
}
```

The cascade order for applying CSS rule sets

Search for the rule sets that apply to an element in the sequence that follows and apply the rule set from the first group in which it's found:

- !important rules in a user style sheet
- !important rules in a web page
- Normal rules in a web page
- Normal rules in a user style sheet
- Default rules in the web browser

If more than one rule set in a group is applied to an element...

- Use the rule set with the highest specificity. For example, the p.highlight selector is more specific than the .highlight selector.
- If the specificity is the same for two or more rule sets in a group, use the rule set that's specified last.

How to determine the specificity of a selector

- An id is the most specific.
- A class, attribute selector, or pseudo-class selector is less specific.
- An element or pseudo-element selector is least specific.

Description

- When two or more rule sets are applied to an HTML element, CSS uses the cascade order and rules shown above to determine which rule set to apply.
- A user can create a *user style sheet* that provides a default set of rules for web pages. Users with poor vision often do this so the type for a page is displayed in a large font.
- Since most users don't create user style sheets, you usually can control the way the rules are applied for your web applications. But you should keep in mind how your web pages could be affected by user style sheets.
- If you want to create or remove a user style sheet, you can search the Internet for the procedures that your browser requires.

Figure 4-8   How the cascade rules work

How to work with text and links

Now that you know how to select the elements that you want to format, you're ready to learn how to use CSS to apply that formatting. To start, you'll learn how to style fonts and format text.

How to set the font family and font size

Figure 4-9 shows how to set the *font family* and font size for text elements. The table at the top of this figure lists the five generic font families, and the examples below that table show what typical fonts in these families look like.

When you develop a web site, your primary font family should be a sans-serif font family. That's because sans-serif fonts are easier to read in a browser than the other types of fonts, including serif fonts, even though serif fonts have long been considered the best for printed text. You can also use serif and monospace fonts for special purposes, but you should avoid the use of cursive and fantasy fonts.

When you code the values for the font-family property, you code a list of the fonts that you want to use. For instance, the first example in this figure lists Arial, Helvetica, and sans-serif as the fonts, and sans-serif is a generic font name. Then, the browser will use the first font in the list that is available to it. But if none of the fonts are available, the browser will substitute its default font for the generic font that's coded last in the list.

If the name of a font family contains spaces, like "Times New Roman", you need to enclose the name in quotation marks when you code the list. This is illustrated by the second and third examples in the first group.

To set the font size for a font, you use the font-size property as illustrated by the second group of examples. For this property, we recommend that you use relative measurements so the users will be able to change the font sizes in their browsers.

When you use a relative measurement, it's relative to the parent element. For example, the second rule in the second set of examples will cause the font to be 150% larger than its parent element. So if the parent element is 12 points, this element will be 18 points. Similarly, the third rule specifies 1.5 ems so it will also be 150% of the parent font.

The next example shows how the font family and font size can be set in the body element. Here, the default font family for the browser is changed to a sans-serif font, and the default font size is changed to 87.5 percent of the browser's default size. Remember that most browsers use Times New Roman and 16 pixels as the defaults, and these defaults are typically changed.

Like colors, the font properties that you set in an element are inherited by all of its descendents. Note, however, that it's not the relative value that's inherited when you use a relative measurement for the font size. Instead, it's the actual size that's calculated for the font. If, for example, the default font size is 16 pixels and you set the font-size property to 125%, the size of the element and any descendents will be 20 pixels.

The five generic font families

Name	Description
serif	Fonts with tapered, flared, or slab stroke ends.
sans-serif	Fonts with plain stroke ends.
monospace	Fonts that use the same width for each character.
cursive	Fonts with connected, flowing letters that look like handwriting.
fantasy	Fonts with decorative styling.

Examples of the five generic font families

Times New Roman is a serif font. It is the default for most web browsers.

Arial is a sans-serif font that is widely used, and sans-serif fonts are best for web pages.

Courier New is a monospace font that is used for code examples.

Lucida Handwriting is a cursive font that is not frequently used.

Impact is a fantasy font that is rarely used.

How to specify a font family

```
font-family: Arial, Helvetica, sans-serif;
font-family: "Times New Roman", Times, serif;
font-family: "Courier New", Courier, monospace;
```

How to specify the font size

```
font-size: 12pt;          /* in points */
font-size: 150%;          /* as a percent of the parent element */
font-size: 1.5em;         /* same as 150% */
```

A font-family rule in the body element that is inherited by all descendents

```
body {
    font-family: Arial, Helvetica, sans-serif;
    font-size: 87.5%; }
```

A font-family rule in a descendent that overrides the inherited font-family

```
p { font-family: "Times New Roman", Times, serif; }
```

Description

- The fonts specified for the font-family property are searched in the order listed. If you include a font name that contains spaces, the name must be enclosed in quotes.
- If you specify a generic font last and the web browser can't find any of the other fonts in the list, it will use its default font for the generic font that you specified.
- The font properties that you set for an element are inherited by all of its descendents.
- If you use relative font sizes, the users will be able to vary the sizes by using their browsers. If you use pixels, the font size will vary based on the screen resolution.

Figure 4-9   How to set the font family and font size

How to set the other properties for styling fonts

The table in figure 4-10 summarizes the other properties that you can use for styling a font. Like the font-family and font-size properties, these properties are also inherited by their descendants.

In this figure, the first group of examples shows how italics and small caps can be applied to a font by using the font-style and font-variant properties. Then, the second group of examples shows how font weights can be applied to a font. In most cases, you'll use the bold keyword to boldface a font. But if you want to use varying degrees of boldness, you can use multiples of 100. You can also specify the boldness of a font relative to the boldness of the parent font by using the lighter or bolder keyword as shown in the last example.

The third group of examples shows how to set the line height for a font. This property lets you increase or decrease the amount of vertical space that's used for a font. If, for example, you set the line height to 14 points for a font that is set to 12 points, there will be two extra points of space for the font. This space will be divided equally above and below the font. This provides extra spacing for block elements that are displayed on more than one line.

Like the font-size property, it's usually better to set the line-height property with a relative measurement like a percent or ems. That way, all modern browsers will be able to adjust the line height relative to the font size. The first three examples illustrate that. The fourth example is similar, but it specifies a number that is used to calculate the line height.

Note that when you use a percent or ems as in the second and third examples, the actual line height will be inherited by descendent elements. When you use a number, however, the number itself will be inherited. If a descendent element has a smaller font size, then, the line height will also be smaller, which is usually what you want.

Often, you code each of the font properties that you've just learned about in a separate rule. However, you can also use the *shorthand property* for fonts that's shown in figure 4-10. If you look at the syntax for this property, you can see that it provides for all six font properties. In this syntax summary, the properties in brackets [ ] are optional, which means that only the font-size and font-family are required.

When you use this property, you code the font properties separated by spaces without coding the property names. You combine the font-size and line-height properties separated by a slash. And you separate the list of fonts for the font-family property with commas. This is illustrated by the three examples after the syntax summary.

Here, the first rule includes all the font properties except for font-variant. The second rule includes the font-variant, font-size, and font-family properties. And the third rule includes the font-size, line-height, and font-family properties.

Other properties for styling fonts

Property	Description
font-style	A keyword that determines how the font is slanted: normal, italic, and oblique.
font-weight	A keyword or number that determines the boldness of the font: normal, bold, bolder, lighter, or multiples of 100 from 100 through 900. Bolder and lighter are relative to the parent element.
font-variant	A keyword that specifies whether small caps will be used: normal and small-caps.
line-height	A relative or absolute value or a number that specifies the amount of vertical space for each line. The excess space is divided equally above and below the font.

How to specify font styles and variants

```
font-style: italic;
font-style: normal;          /* remove style */
font-variant: small-caps;
```

How to specify font weights;

```
font-weight: 700;
font-weight: bold;           /* same as 700 */
font-weight: normal;         /* same as 400 */
font-weight: lighter;        /* relative to the parent element */
```

How to specify line height

```
line-height: 14pt;
line-height: 140%;
line-height: 1.4em;          /* same as 140% */
line-height: 1.4;            /* same as 140% and 1.4em */
```

The syntax for the shorthand font property

```
font: [style] [weight] [variant] size[/line-height] family;
```

How to use the shorthand font property

```
font: italic bold 14px/19px Arial, sans-serif;
font: small-caps 150% "Times New Roman", Times, serif;
font: 90%/120% "Comic Sans MS", Impact, sans-serif;
```

Description

- You can set the font-style, font-weight, and font-variant properties to a value of "normal" to remove any formatting that has been applied to these properties.

- The line-height property determines the spacing between lines within a block element.

- If you specify just a number for the line-height property, the font size is multiplied by that value to determine the line height, and the multiplier is inherited by child elements. If you specify an absolute or relative size for the line-height property, the actual line height is inherited by child elements.

- You can use the *shorthand property* for a font to set all six font properties with a single rule. When you use this property, the font-size and font-family properties are required.

Figure 4-10   How to set the other properties for styling fonts

How to indent and align text

Figure 4-11 presents the properties for indenting and aligning text. You can use the text-indent property to indent the first line of text in a paragraph. When you set this property, it usually makes sense to use a relative unit of measure such as ems. That way, if the size of the current font changes, the indentation will also change.

To align text horizontally, you can use the text-align property. By default, most elements are left-aligned, but you can use the "center", "right", or "justify" values to change that. Note, however, that when you justify text, the spacing between words is adjusted so the text is aligned on both the left and right sides. Since this makes the text more difficult to read, justified text should be avoided.

You can also align inline elements vertically. To illustrate, suppose that you code a span element within a paragraph, and you code a style rule that sets the font size for the text in the span element so it's smaller than the text in the paragraph. Then, the vertical-align property determines how the span element is aligned relative to its parent element. If, for example, you set the vertical-align property to "text-bottom", the bottom of the text in the span element will be aligned with the bottom of the text in the paragraph. Another alternative is to specify a relative or absolute value for this property to determine how far above or below its normal position the element should be displayed.

The example in this figure shows how to use the text-indent and text-align properties. Here, the paragraph below the heading is indented by 2 ems, and the paragraph that contains the copyright information is right-aligned. Because you'll rarely use the vertical-align property, it isn't illustrated here.

Properties for indenting and aligning text

Property	Description
text-indent	A relative or absolute value that determines the indentation for the first line of text. This property is inherited.
text-align	A keyword that determines the horizontal alignment of text. Possible values are left, center, right, and justify. This property is inherited.
vertical-align	A relative or absolute value or a keyword that determines the vertical alignment of text. Possible keywords are baseline, bottom, middle, top, text-bottom, text-top, sub, and super. If you use pixels, points, or ems to specify the value for the vertical-align property, the text is raised if the value is positive and lowered if it's negative. If you specify a percent, the text is raised or lowered based on the percentage of the line height.

The HTML for a web page

```
<div id="page">
    <div id="header">
        <h1>San Joaquin Valley Town Hall</h1>
    </div>
    <div id="main">
        <p>Welcome to San Joaquin Valley Town Hall. We have some
        amazing speakers in store for you this season!</p>
    </div>
    <div id="footer">
        <p>&copy; Copyright 2009 San Joaquin Valley Town Hall.</p>
    </div>
</div>
```

CSS that specifies a text indent and horizontal alignment

```
body {
    font-size: 87.5%;
    margin: 2em; }
h1 {
    font-size: 180%; }
#main p { text-indent: 2em; }
#footer p {
    font-size: 80%;
    text-align: right; }
```

The HTML in a web browser

Description

- The text-indent and text-align properties are commonly used, but you probably won't need the vertical-align property.

Figure 4-11   How to indent and align text

How to transform and decorate text

Figure 4-12 shows two more properties you can use to format text. To start, you can use the text-transform property to display text in all uppercase letters, all lowercase letters, or with the first letter of each word capitalized.

You can use the text-decoration property to display a line under, over, or through text or to make the text blink, but this has limited value for these reasons. First, blinking text is discouraged in modern web sites. Second, you usually shouldn't underline words that aren't links. Third, you can use borders as shown in the next chapter to put lines over and under a block element, and that gives you more control over the lines.

The example in this figure illustrates how the text-transform and text-decoration properties work. Here, the text-transform property for the h1 element is set so the text is displayed in all uppercase letters. In addition, the text-decoration property is set so a line is drawn both above and below the heading. Notice that the heading is also centered using the text-align property.

If you want to remove any text decorations and transformations that have been applied to an element, you can specify a value of "none" for these properties. For example, the text-decoration property of an a element is set to "underline" by default. If that's not what you want, you can set this property to "none".

Properties for transforming and decorating text

Property	Description
text-transform	A keyword that determines how text is capitalized. Possible values are uppercase, lowercase, capitalize, and none. This property is inherited.
text-decoration	A keyword that determines special decorations that are applied to text. Possible values are underline, overline, line-through, blink, and none.

The HTML for a web page

```
<div id="header">
    <h1>San Joaquin Valley Town Hall</h1>
</div>
<div id="main">
    <p>Welcome to San Joaquin Valley Town Hall. We have some
    amazing speakers in store for you this season!</p>
</div>
```

CSS that specifies transforms and decorations

```
h1 {
    font-size: 150%;
    text-align: center;
    text-transform: uppercase;
    text-decoration: underline overline;
}
```

The HTML in a browser

SAN JOAQUIN VALLEY TOWN HALL

Welcome to San Joaquin Valley Town Hall. We have some amazing speakers in store for you this season!

Description

- Although the text-decoration property isn't technically inherited if it is specified for a block element, its value is applied to inline children elements and block descendant elements.

- Internet Explorer doesn't support the blink keyword for the text-decoration property, and blinking is discouraged.

Figure 4-12   How to transform and decorate text

How to format links

Earlier in this chapter, you learned how to code pseudo-class selectors. As you saw there, you can use these selectors to control how links appear when certain conditions occur. If a link contains text, you can control the font styles and color of that text using the properties you've learned about in this chapter. Figure 4-13 illustrates how this works.

To start, this figure lists the three possible states of a link and describes their default appearance. Then, it presents the CSS that's used to format the links in the HTML document. Here, the first rule set indicates that the links should be displayed in a bold font. The next three rule sets specify different colors for the three states of the links. And the last rule set specifies a color for the link when the mouse is hovering over it that is the same as the color for an active link.

The browser display shows how this page is displayed. Here, all three links are displayed differently. That's because the first link has been visited, the second link has not been visited, and the mouse is hovering over the third link. But the third link would be the same color if the user clicked on the link but hadn't yet released the mouse button.

Default appearance of text links

State	Appearance
Unvisited	Blue underlined text.
Visited	Purple underlined text.
Active	Red underlined text.

The HTML for a web page

```
<div id="main">
    <p>Welcome to San Joaquin Valley Town Hall. We have some amazing
    speakers in store for you this season!</p>
    <ul>
        <li>January 20, 2010: <a href="brancaccio.html">
        David Brancaccio</a></li>
        <li>February 17, 2010: <a href="fitzpatrick.html">
        Robert Fitzpatrick</a></li>
        <li>March 17, 2010: <a href="williams.html">Juan Williams</a></li>
    </ul>
    <p>Contact us by phone at (559) 555-1212 for ticket information.</p>
</div>
```

The CSS for text links

```
a { font-weight: bold; }
a:link { color: blue; }
a:visited { color: green; }
a:active { color: fuchsia; }
a:hover { color: fuchsia; }
```

The HTML displayed in a web browser

Welcome to San Joaquin Valley Town Hall. We have some amazing speakers in store for you this season!

- January 20, 2010: **David Brancaccio**
- February 17, 2010: **Robert Fitzpatrick**
- March 17, 2010: **Juan Williams**

Contact us by phone at (559) 555-1212 for ticket information.

Description

- Text links should always be underlined so they are easily recognizable, and text that isn't a link shouldn't be underlined.

- When you hover the mouse over a link, its color doesn't change by default.

- If you use an image for a link, it will appear with a border around it in most browsers. To remove the border, you can set the border-style property of the image to none. See chapter 5 for more information on this property.

Figure 4-13   How to format links

A web page that uses an external style sheet

Now that you've learned how to code selectors and how to format text and links, you're ready to see a web page that uses these skills.

The page layout

Figure 4-14 presents a web page that uses an external style sheet. If you study this web page, you can see that the CSS in the style sheet has been used to change the default font to a sans-serif font, to apply colors to some of the headings and text, to center the headings in the header, to add line height to the items in the unordered list, to apply italics and boldfacing to portions of text, and to right-align the footer. Overall, this formatting makes the page look pretty good.

In terms of typography, though, this web page needs to be improved. In particular, the spacing before and after the headings should be adjusted. For instance, the second heading "Bringing cutting-edge speakers to the valley" should be closer to the main heading so it's clear that this slogan applies to the main heading.

Similarly, there should be less space after the first heading in the body to show that the paragraphs after this heading are related to it. Also, there should be less space or no space between the paragraphs so they are seen as a block of text, not three blocks of text. Last, the line items in the unordered list should be moved up so they're closer to the heading that describes them.

To make these spacing adjustments, though, you need to know how to use the margin and padding properties that are part of the CSS box model. So that's what you'll learn first in the next chapter. Once you learn how to use those properties, you'll be able to get the typography just the way you want it.

A web page that uses some of the styles presented in this chapter

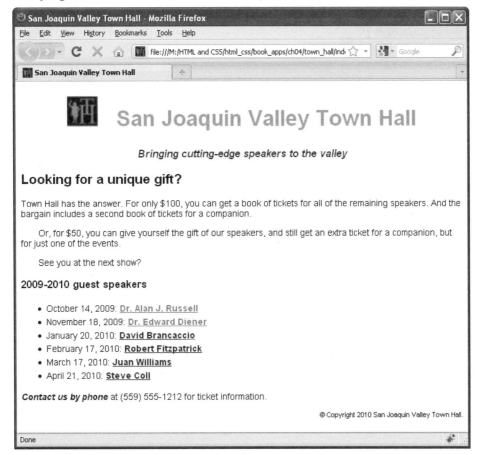

Description

- This web page uses an external style sheet to apply the styles that are illustrated.
- A sans-serif font has been applied to all of the text in this document because that's the most readable type of font for web pages. Also, relative font sizes have been applied to the elements on the page.
- Italics and boldfacing have been applied to portions of the text, the copyright information has been right-aligned, and colors have been applied to two of the headings.
- Colors have also been applied to the a tags in the unordered list. Because the first two lectures have passed, the first two links in the list have the color gray applied to them.

What's wrong with the typography in this web page

- The spacing above and below the block elements should be improved. In the next chapter, you'll learn how to do that by using the margin and padding properties.

Figure 4-14   The page layout for a web page that uses an external style sheet

The HTML file

Figure 4-15 presents the HTML for the web page in figure 4-14. Here, you can see that all of the body code is contained within a div element with "page" as its id. Then, within that element, the code is divided into three div elements with ids of "header", "main", and "footer". This is a typical way to structure a web page.

If you look at the second and third p elements in the main division, you can see that they have class attributes named "indent". This class name will be used in the CSS to indent the first line in these paragraphs. Similarly, the first two line items in the unordered list have "date_passed" as their class name. This name will be used to apply the color gray to those items because this example assumes that the dates for those events have already passed, and the gray color is intended to indicate that to the user.

The HTML file for the web page

```
<!DOCTYPE html PUBLIC "-//W3C//DTD XHTML 1.0 Transitional//EN"
    "http://www.w3.org/TR/xhtml1/DTD/xhtml1-transitional.dtd">
<html xmlns="http://www.w3.org/1999/xhtml">

<head>
    <title>San Joaquin Valley Town Hall</title>
    <link rel="shortcut icon" href="images/favicon.ico" type="favicon/ico" />
    <link rel="stylesheet" type="text/css" href="styles/main.css" />
    <meta http-equiv="content-type" content="text/html; charset=utf-8" />
</head>

<body>
<div id="page">
    <div id="header">
        <h1><img src="images/logo.jpg" alt="Town Hall Logo" width="50px" />
          San Joaquin Valley Town Hall</h1>
        <h3>Bringing cutting-edge speakers to the valley</h3>
    </div>

    <div id="main">
        <h2>Looking for a unique gift?</h2>
        <p>Town Hall has the answer. For only $100, you can get
            a book of tickets for all of the remaining speakers. And the
            bargain includes a second book of tickets for a companion.</p>
        <p class="indent">Or, for $50, you can give yourself the gift of our
            speakers, and still get an extra
            ticket for a companion, but for just one of the events.</p>
        <p class="indent">See you at the next show?</p>
        <h3>2009-2010 guest speakers</h3>
        <ul>
            <li>October 14, 2009: <a class="date_passed"
                href="speakers/russell.html">Dr. Alan J. Russell</a></li>
            <li>November 18, 2009: <a class="date_passed"
                href="speakers/diener.html">Dr. Edward Diener</a></li>
            <li>January 20, 2010: <a href="speakers/brancaccio.html">
                David Brancaccio</a></li>
            <li>February 17, 2010: <a href="speakers/fitzpatrick.html">
                Robert Fitzpatrick</a></li>
            <li>March 17, 2010: <a href="speakers/williams.html">
                Juan Williams</a></li>
            <li>April 21, 2010: <a href="speakers/coll.html">
                Steve Coll</a></li>
        </ul>
        <p><em>Contact us by phone</em> at (559) 555-1212 for ticket
            information.</p>
    </div>

    <div id="footer">
        <p>&copy; Copyright 2010 San Joaquin Valley Town Hall.</p>
    </div>
</div>
</body>
</html>
```

Figure 4-15   The HTML file for the web page

The CSS file

Figure 4-16 shows the CSS file for the web page. To start, note the way that this code is structured. First, the rule sets for specific elements are presented. In effect, this sets the default formatting for these elements. This is followed by rule sets that are grouped by division: header, main, and footer.

This is an efficient way to organize your rule sets because you first see the defaults for specific elements. Then, you see the rule sets within a division that override or enhance those defaults. Also, those rule sets are presented in the same sequence as the elements are presented in the HTML file.

You might also note that many of the rule sets that contain a single rule are coded on a single line. This is illustrated by the rule sets for the h1, h2, and h3 elements. This of course is a valid way to code these rule sets because white space is ignored. For rule sets that require more than one rule, though, each rule should be coded on a single line to make the rules easier to read.

With that as background, you should be able to understand the rule sets in this CSS file without much trouble. But here's a quick review of some of the highlights.

In the rule set for the body element, the two properties specify the font-family and font-size. Because the values of these properties are inherited, they become the defaults for the document. Notice too that the font size is specified as a percent. That means it will be determined by the default font size for the browser, and the user will be able to change this size using the browser. The font sizes for the headings are also specified as percents, so they will be based on the size that's calculated for the body element.

In the rule set for the unordered list, the line-height property is specified. This will increase the spacing between the line items. Similarly, the font weight is specified for the em element. This adds bold to this element, which will also be italicized because that's the normal behavior of this HTML element. To remove the italics, you would have to code a font-style property with normal as its value.

In the rule sets for the header division, you can see that the color blue is applied to all descendent elements. However, this color is overridden by the rule set for the h1 element in this division. Also, the h3 element in this division will be italicized, and both the h1 and h3 elements will be centered.

In the rule sets for the main division, you can see that the elements in the "indent" class will be indented. You can also see that a elements in the "date_passed" class will be gray. Last, in the rule set for the footer section, you can see that the font size for the p elements is reduced to 80% of the base font, and the text is right-aligned.

The CSS file for the web page

```
/* the styles for the elements */
body {
    font-family: Arial, Helvetica, sans-serif;
    font-size: 87.5%;
}
h1 { font-size: 250%; }
h2 { font-size: 150%; }
h3 { font-size: 120%; }

a { font-weight: bold; }
a:link { color: blue; }
a:visited { color: #ef9c00; }
a:active { color: green; }
a:hover { color: green; }

ul {
    line-height: 1.5;
}
em {
    font-weight: bold;
}

/* the styles for the header division */
#header {
    color: blue;
}
#header h1 {
    color: #ef9c00;
    text-align: center;
}
#header h3 {
    font-style: italic;
    text-align: center;
}

/* the styles for the main division */
.indent {
    text-indent: 2em;
}
a.date_passed  {
    color: gray;
}

/* the styles for the footer division */
#footer p {
    font-size: 80%;
    text-align: right;
}
```

Figure 4-16   The CSS file for the web page

Perspective

At this point, you should know how to code all of the types of selectors, and you should know how to code the CSS properties for formatting text and links. That gets you off to a good start with CSS, but there's still a lot to learn.

So, in the next chapter, you'll learn how to use the CSS box model. You use that model to set the margins, borders, and padding for the elements in your pages so your typography looks just the way you want it to. Then, in chapter 6, you'll learn how to use CSS for page layout, which is the modern way to lay out the pages of a web site. When you finish those chapters, you'll have all the skills you need for using CSS at a professional level.

Terms

external style sheet
embedded style sheet
inline style
absolute unit of measure
relative unit of measure
absolute measurement
relative measurement
RGB value
hexadecimal (hex) value
element selector
id selector
class selector
descendant selector
sibling selector
adjacent sibling selector
general sibling selector
universal selector
child selector
attribute selector
pseudo-class
dynamic pseudo-class
pseudo-class selector
pseudo-element
font family
user style sheet
shorthand property

Summary

- The best way to apply CSS to an HTML document is to use the link element to link to an *external style sheet*. However, you can also apply CSS by embedding a style sheet in the HTML or by using the style attribute of an inline element.

- You can use *absolute measurements* like pixels or *relative measurements* like ems or percents to specify the CSS properties for sizes. For fonts, it's better to use relative measurements so the user can change the font sizes by changing the browser's default font size.

- Most graphic designers use *hex* for the *RGB values* that represent the colors that they want because that gives them the most control. However, all modern browsers also support 16 standard color names like red and blue.

- You can code CSS selectors for elements, ids, classes, *descendants*, *adjacent siblings*, and elements with specific attributes. You can also code selectors for combinations of these items.

- A *pseudo-class selector* can be used to apply CSS formatting when certain conditions occur or have occurred, like when the mouse hovers over an element or when a link has been visited.

- If more than one style sheet is applied to an HTML document and two or more rule sets apply to the same element, the *cascade order* determines which rule set takes precedence. The first four levels of this order are: the important rules in a *user style sheet* for the browser; the important rules in a web page; the normal rules in a web page; and the normal rules in a user style sheet.

- If more than one rule set in a cascade level is applied to an element, the rule set with the highest specificity is used. But if the specificity is the same for two or more rule sets in a cascade level, the rule set that's specified last is used.

- The default font for most browsers is a 16-pixel, serif font. However, because sans-serif fonts are easier to read in a browser, you normally change the font family. It's also good to change the font size to a relative measurement like a percent of the default font size.

- The colors and font properties of a parent element are *inherited* by the child elements. But those properties can be overridden by the rule sets for the children.

- The *shorthand property* for fonts can be used to apply all six of the font properties to an element: font-family, font-size, font-style, font-weight, font-variant, and line-height.

- Text properties can be used to indent, align, transform, and decorate the text in a block element like a heading or paragraph.

- The link, visited, active, and hover pseudo-class selectors are commonly used to change the formatting for a elements.

Exercise 4-1   Format the Bait & Tackle Shop web page

In this exercise, you'll format a web page like the one for exercise 3-1 using the skills you learned in this chapter. When you're done, the page should look like this:

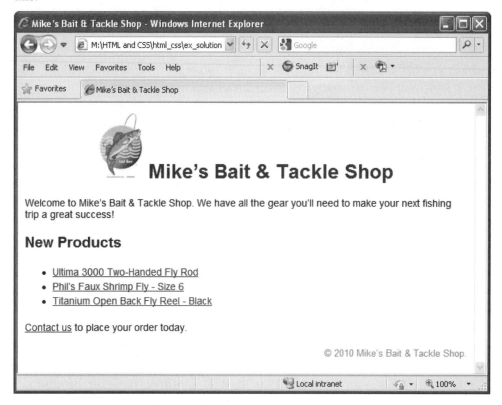

Enter the styles for the body and div elements

1. Use your text editor to open this file:

    `C:\html_css\ch04\bait_shop\index.html`

    Then, display this page in your browser. It should be similar to the one you created in exercise 3-1.

2. Use your text editor to create a CSS file named main.css in this directory:

    `C:\html_css\ch04\bait_shop\styles`

3. In the CSS file, add a rule set for the body element that sets the font-family property so the browser will select the following fonts in sequence: Arial, Helvetica, and sans-serif. Also, set the font size to 87.5 percent of the browser's default size.

4. In the HTML file, add a link element to the head section that includes the main.css file as shown in figure 4-1. Note, however, that the relative URL in this case is styles/main.css (you go down a level, not up).

5. Save both files and switch back to your browser. Now, click the Refresh button in your browser's toolbar to see the styles that are applied by the style sheet. If the display doesn't change, make sure you coded the link element and the styles in the style sheet correctly.

Add more styles to the main style sheet

6. Add rule sets for the h1 and h2 elements. The text for both elements should be displayed using the color blue. The text for the h1 element should be 200% of the body text, and the text for the h2 element should be 150% of the body text. Then, save the file and test this change.

7. Add a rule set for the h1 element that centers it on the page. Then, save the file and test this change.

8. Add a rule set for the ul element that sets the line height to 1.4 times the size of the font. Then, save and test.

9. Add a rule set for the paragraph that's assigned to the class named "copyright". Include rules that set the color of the paragraph text to gray, set the font size to 90% of the body text, and align the text at the right side of the browser window. Then, save and test.

10. Add a rule set for the hover pseudo-class of the a element. This rule set should display a link in boldface when you point to it with a mouse. Then, save the file and test this change.

11. At this point, your page should look like the one at the start of this exercise. If it does, go on to the next exercise. If not, fix the problems.

Exercise 4-2 Add another page to the Bait & Tackle Shop web site

In this exercise, you'll add a page for one of the products sold by the Bait & Tackle Shop. Then, you'll add a second style sheet with two new rule sets for that page. When you're done, the new page will look as shown below.

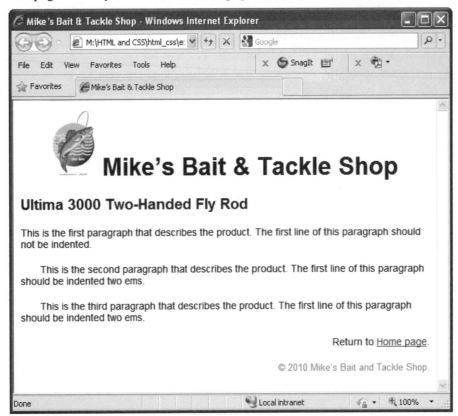

Create the new page

1. If it isn't already open, open this file in your text editor:

   `C:\html_css\ch04\bait_shop\index.html`

   Then, change the href attribute for the first link to products/fly_rod.html, and be sure to save the file. In the rest of this exercise, you'll be creating the fly_rod.html page in the products directory.

2. Save the index.html file as:

   `C:\html_css\ch04\bait_shop\products\fly_rod.html`

   Note that this file goes in the products directory. Then, delete the contents of the main division in the html file.

3. In the fly_rod.html file, check the href properties of the two link elements in the head division to make sure that the URLs for the favicon and main style sheets are correct based on the location of the current page. If they aren't, make the necessary changes. This time, the relative URL has to go up a level before it goes down to the images or style directory.

4. Change the src property of the img element in the header division so it can find the image.

5. Save the changes, and test this page in your browser. You can do that by launching the page from your text editor or from Windows Explorer, but you can also test it by refreshing the index page and then clicking on the link for the fly_rod page. At this point, the styles of the main style sheet should be applied to the header and footer.

6. Add an h2 element to the main division that contains the text "Ultima 3000 Two-Handed Fly Rod". Then, add the four paragraphs with the text shown above. The second and third paragraphs should be assigned to a class named "indent". The fourth paragraph should be given the id "home", and it should contain a link that returns to the home page. When you're done, save and test the page.

Create a style sheet for the new page

7. Use your text editor to create a new style sheet, and save it with the name product.css in this directory:

    `C:\html_css\ch04\bait_shop\styles`

8. Add a rule set that indents the first line of the second and third paragraphs in the main division by 2 ems. To do that, you'll need to use a class selector.

9. Add a rule set for the fourth paragraph in the main division that aligns the paragraph at the right side of the page. To do that, you'll need to refer to the paragraph by its id.

10. Go the fly_rod.html file in your text editor, and add another link element that includes the product.css style sheet. Be sure to add this element after the link element for the main.css style sheet.

11. Save the changes to both the html and css files. Then, test these changes. This illustrates the use of two style sheets for a single file.

Test the pages together and make a final modification

12. Do a final test of the pages to make sure that both pages look right and that the links work. For instance, the first link in the index page should go to the fly_rod page, and the home_page link in the fly_rod page should go back to the home page. Note, however, that the last three links in the home page haven't been implemented.

13. Go to the main.css file in your editor and add a rule for the h1 element that increases its size to 250% of the default size. Then, test this change for both pages. That shows how easy it is to make changes to more than one page when you use CSS.

5

How to use the CSS box model for spacing, borders, and backgrounds

In the last chapter, you learned some basic CSS properties for formatting text. Now, you'll learn the properties for controlling the spacing between elements and for displaying borders and backgrounds. Specifically, you'll learn how to use the CSS box model for those purposes.

An introduction to the box model

When a browser displays a web page, it places each HTML block element in a box. That makes it easy to control the spacing, borders, and other formatting for elements like divisions, headings, and paragraphs. Some inline elements such as links and images are placed in a box as well. To work with these boxes, you use the CSS *box model*.

How the box model works

Figure 5-1 presents a diagram that shows how the box model works. By default, the box for a block element is as wide as the block that contains it and as tall as it needs to be based on its content. However, you can explicitly specify the size of the content area for a block element by using the height and width properties. You can also use other properties to set the borders, margins, and padding for a block element.

If you look at the diagram in this figure, you can see that *padding* is the space between the content area and a border. Similarly, a *margin* is the space between the border and the outside of the box.

If you need to calculate the overall height of a box, you can use the formula in this figure. Here, you start by adding the values for the margin, border width, and padding for the top of the box. Then, you add the height of the content area. Last, you add the values for the padding, border width, and margin for the bottom of the box. The formula for calculating the overall width of a box is similar.

When you set the height and width properties for a block element, you can use any of the units that you learned about in the last chapter. In most cases, though, you'll use pixels so the sizes are fixed. That way, the size of the page won't change if the user changes the size of the browser window. This is referred to as a *fixed* or *frozen layout*.

When you use a fixed layout, you can use either absolute or relative units of measure for margins and padding. If you use a relative unit such as ems, the margins and padding will be adjusted if the font size changes. If you use an absolute unit, the margins and padding will stay the same.

In contrast to a fixed layout, a *liquid layout* is one where the size of the page changes as the user changes the size of the browser window. To create a liquid layout, you can either omit the width property or code it as a percent. In the next chapter, you'll see an example of a web page with a liquid layout.

The CSS box model

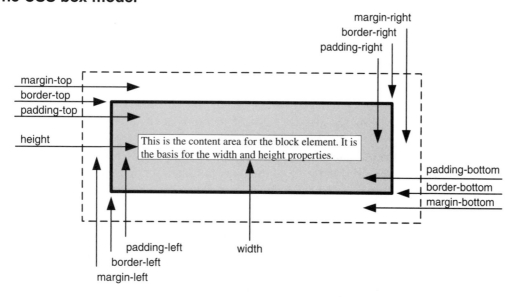

The formula for calculating the height of a box

```
top margin + top border + top padding +
height +
bottom padding + bottom border + bottom margin
```

The formula for calculating the width of a box

```
left margin + left border + left padding +
width +
right padding + right border + right margin
```

Description

- The CSS *box model* lets you work with the boxes that a browser places around each block element as well as some inline elements. This lets you add formatting such as padding, borders, and margins.

- By default, the box for a block element is as wide as the block that contains it and as tall as it needs to be based on its content.

- You can use the height and width properties to specify the size of the content area for a block element explicitly.

- You can use other properties to control the margins, borders, and padding for a block element. Then, these properties are added to the height and width of the content area to determine the height and width of the box.

Figure 5-1   How the box model works

A web page that illustrates the box model

To help you understand how the box model works, figure 5-2 presents the HTML for a simple web page. Then, the CSS adds borders to the four types of elements in the HTML: a dotted 3-pixel border to the body, a solid 2-pixel border to the main division, and dashed 1-pixel borders to the h1 and p elements. If you look at the web page in the browser, you can see how these four borders are rendered. You can also see how the margins and padding for these boxes work.

For the body, the margin on all four sides is set to 10 pixels. You can see that margin on the left, top, and right of the body border, but not on the bottom. That's because the bottom margin for the body is determined by the size of the window.

For the main division, the width is set to 500 pixels, and the margins on the top, right, and left sides of the box are set to 20 pixels. You can see these margins on the left and top of the division box, but not on the right because the width of the division is set to 500 pixels.

The next rule set sets properties for both the h1 and p elements. In this case, the properties set the border and the padding for these elements. Then, the next two rule sets set additional properties for each of these elements.

The rule set for the h1 element sets the top margin to .5 em, the right and left margins to 0, and the bottom margin to .25 em. As a result, there is more space above the h1 element than below it. This rule set also sets the padding on the left side of the element to 15 pixels so space is added between the border of the box and the text.

The rule set for the p element starts by setting all the margins to 0. As a result, all of the space between the h1 and p elements is due to the bottom margin of the h1 element. In addition, the padding on the left side of the element is set to 15 pixels so the text for the h1 and p elements is aligned. Please note that if I had used relative measures for the padding on the left of the h1 and p elements, they wouldn't be aligned because the font sizes for these elements are different.

One more thing you should notice here is that the padding-left properties in the rule sets for the h1 and p elements override the left padding specified by the rule set for both of these elements. Another way to do this would be to specify the padding for each side of these elements on the padding property like this:

```
padding: 10px 10px 10px 15px;
```

Then, you could omit the padding-left properties from the rules sets for the h1 and p elements. This just shows that there is usually more than one way to accomplish the same thing.

This should help you understand how the box model works. Now, it's on to the details for setting the properties for the box model.

The HTML for a page that uses the box model

```
<body>
    <div id="main">
        <h1>San Joaquin Valley Town Hall</h1>
        <p>Welcome to San Joaquin Valley Town Hall.
        We have some amazing speakers in store for you this season!</p>
    </div>
</body>
```

The CSS for the page

```
body {
    border: 3px dotted black;
    margin: 10px;
}
#main {
    border:   2px solid black;
    width:    500px;
    margin:   20px;              /* all four sides */
    padding: 10px;              /* all four sides */
}
h1, p {
    border: 1px dashed black;
    padding: 10px;
}
h1 {
    margin: .5em 0 .25em;   /* .5em top, 0 right and left, .25em bottom */
    padding-left: 15px;
}
p {
    margin: 0;                  /* all four sides */
    padding-left: 15px;
}
```

The web page in a browser

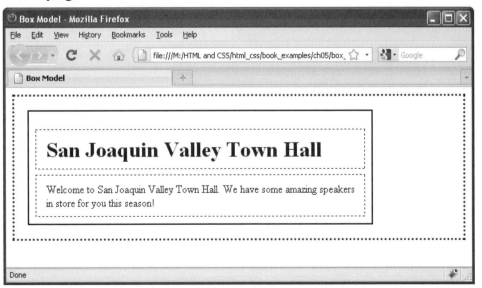

Figure 5-2   A web page that illustrates the box model

How to size and space elements

As you saw in the last figure, you can use several different properties to determine the size of an element and the spacing between the elements on a page. In the topics that follow, you'll learn the details of coding these properties.

How to set heights and widths

Figure 5-3 presents the properties for setting heights and widths. The two properties you'll use most often are width and height. By default, these properties are set to a value of "auto". As a result, the size of the content area for the element is automatically adjusted so it's as wide as the element that contains it and as tall as the content it contains. To change that, you can use the height and width properties.

The first two sets of examples in this figure illustrate how this works. Here, the first example in each set specifies an absolute value using pixels. Then, the second example specifies a relative value using percents. As a result, the width is set to 75% of the *containing block*. Finally, the third example uses the keyword "auto".

In addition to the width and height properties, you can use the min-width, max-width, min-height, and max-height properties to specify the minimum and maximum width and height of the content area. Like the width and height properties, you can specify either a relative or an absolute value for these properties. The last set of examples in this figure, for instance, sets the values of these properties using pixels.

You might want to use the min-width, max-width, min-height, and max-height properties with elements whose size can change. For example, suppose you design a page so the height and width of the page and the elements it contains change depending on the font sizes that are used. Then, you could use these properties to set limits on the widths and heights. Keep in mind, however, that these properties aren't supported by versions of Internet Explorer before version 7.

Properties for setting heights and widths

Property	Description
width	A relative or absolute value that specifies the width of the content area for a block element. You can also specify auto if you want the width of the box calculated for you based on its content. This is the default.
height	A relative or absolute value that specifies the height of the content area for a block element. You can also specify auto if you want the height of the area calculated for you based on its content. This is the default.
min-width	A relative or absolute value that specifies the minimum width of the content area for a block element. The area will always be at least this wide regardless of its content.
max-width	A relative or absolute value that specifies the maximum width of the content area for a block element. You can also specify none to indicate that there is no maximum width.
min-height	A relative or absolute value that specifies the minimum height of the content area for a block element. The area will always be at least this tall regardless of its content.
max-height	A relative or absolute value that specifies the maximum height of the content area for a block element. You can also specify none to indicate that there is no maximum height.

How to set the width of the content area

```
width: 450px;          /* an absolute width */
width: 75%;            /* a relative width */
width: auto;           /* width based on content */
```

How to set the height of the content area

```
height: 125px;
height: 50%;
height: auto;
```

How to set the minimum and maximum width and height

```
min-width: 450px;
max-width: 600px;
min-height: 120px;
max-height: 160px;
```

Description

- If you specify a percent for the width property, the width of the content area for the block element is based on the width of the block that contains it, called the *containing block*. In that case, the width of the containing block must be specified explicitly.

- If you specify a percent for the height property, the height of the content area for the block element is based on the height of the containing block. In that case, the height of the containing block must be specified explicitly, or the block element must be positioned absolutely. Otherwise, "auto" is substituted for the percent.

- The min-width, max-width, min-height, and max-height properties are typically used to accommodate a change in font size. However, these properties aren't supported by versions of Internet Explorer before version 7.

Figure 5-3   How to set heights and widths

How to set margins

Figure 5-4 presents the properties for setting margins. As you can see, you can use individual properties like margin-top or margin-left to set individual margins. This is illustrated in the first set of examples in this figure.

Instead of setting individual margins, you can use the margin property to set the margins for all four sides of a box. When you use a *shorthand property* like this, you can specify one, two, three, or four values. If you specify all four values, they are applied to the sides of the box in a clockwise order: top, right, bottom, and left. To remember this order, you can think of the word *trouble*.

If you specify fewer than four values, this property still sets the margins for all four sides of the box. If, for example, you only specify one value, each margin is set to that value. If you specify two values, the top and bottom margins are set to the first value, and the left and right margins are set to the second value. And if you specify three values, the top margin is set to the first value, the left and right margins are set to the second value, and the bottom margin is set to the third value. This is illustrated in the second set of examples in this figure.

Although it isn't shown here, you can also specify the keyword "auto" for any margin. In most cases, you'll use this keyword to center a page in the browser window. To do that, you specify auto for both the left and right margins. For this to work, you must also set the width of the page. You'll see an example of how that works later in this chapter.

One more thing you should know about margins is that different browsers have different default margins for the page. Because of that, it's a good practice to set the margins of the body element to zero so no space is added outside the body element. In addition, browsers automatically add top and bottom margins to block elements. Because of that, you typically have to specify the amount of space above and below block elements to override any margins that are added by default.

Finally, if you specify a bottom margin for one element and a top margin for the element that follows, the margins are *collapsed*. That means the smaller margin is ignored, and only the larger margin is applied. In that case, there may not be as much space between the two elements as you expected.

One way to solve this problem is to set one of the margins to zero and the other to the total space you want between the two elements. Another way is to use padding instead of margins. The technique you use depends on the situation and your preference. You'll see examples of both of these techniques later in this chapter.

Properties for setting margins

Property	Description
margin-top	A relative or absolute value that defines the space between the top border of an element and the top of the containing block or the bottom of the element above it. You can also specify auto to let the browser calculate the margin for you.
margin-right	A relative or absolute value that defines the space between the right border of an element and the right side of the containing block or the left side of the element to its right. You can also specify auto to let the browser calculate the margin for you.
margin-bottom	A relative or absolute value that defines the space between the bottom border of an element and the bottom of the containing block or the top of the element below it. You can also specify auto to let the browser calculate the margin for you.
margin-left	A relative or absolute value that defines the space between the left border of an element and the left side of the containing block or the right side of the element to its left. You can also specify auto to let the browser calculate the margin for you.
margin	One to four relative or absolute values that specify the size of multiple margins. One value is applied to all four margins. Two values are applied to the top and bottom and right and left margins. Three values are applied to the top, right and left, and bottom margins. And four values are applied to the top, right, bottom, and left margins (think *trouble*).

How to set the margin on a single side of an element

```
margin-top: .5em;
margin-right: 1em;
margin-bottom: 2em;
margin-left: 1em;
```

How to set the margins on multiple sides of an element

```
margin: 1em;               /* all four sides */
margin: 0 1em;             /* top and bottom 0, right and left 1em */
margin: .5em 1em 2em;      /* top .5em, right and left 1em, bottom 2em */
margin: .5em 1em 2em 1em;  /* top .5em, right 1em, bottom 2em, left 1em */
```

Description

- If you specify a bottom margin for one element and a top margin for the following element, the margins are *collapsed*, which means that only the larger margin is applied. The exception is if one margin is negative, in which case the margins are added together. This includes elements that are contained within other elements.

- If you specify a percent for a margin, the margin is based on the width of the containing block.

- You typically use the "auto" keyword to center an element in its containing block. To do that, you must also specify the width of the element.

- Because different browsers have different defaults for margins, it's a good practice to set the margin property of the body element to zero.

- Because browsers automatically add margins above and below block elements, it's a good practice to set these margins explicitly.

Figure 5-4   How to set margins

How to set padding

The properties for setting padding are similar to the properties for setting margins. These properties are presented in figure 5-5. As you can see, you can set the padding for the sides of a box individually, or you can set the padding for all four sides of a box at once using a shorthand property.

Like margins, different browsers can have different defaults for the padding around a page. Because of that, it's a good practice to set the padding for the body element to zero.

Properties for setting padding

Property	Description
`padding-top`	A relative or absolute value that defines the space between the top of an element and its top border.
`padding-right`	A relative or absolute value that defines the space between the right side of an element and its right border.
`padding-bottom`	A relative or absolute value that defines the space between the bottom of an element and its bottom border.
`padding-left`	A relative or absolute value that defines the space between the left side of an element and its left border.
`padding`	One to four relative or absolute values that specify the padding on multiple sides of an element. One value is applied to all four sides. Two values are applied to the top and bottom and right and left. Three values are applied to the top, right and left, and bottom. And four values are applied to the top, right, bottom, and left (think *trouble*).

How to set the padding on a single side of an element

```
padding-top: 0;
padding-right: 1em;
padding-bottom: .5em;
padding-left: 1em;
```

How to set the padding on multiple sides of an element

```
padding: 1em;            /* all four sides */
padding: 0 1em;          /* top and bottom 0, right and left 1em */
padding: 0 1em .5em;     /* top 0em, right and left 1em, bottom .5em */
padding: 0 1em .5em 1em; /* top 0em, right 1em, bottom .5em, left 1em */
```

Description

- If you specify a percent for padding, the padding is based on the width of the containing block.
- Because different browsers have different defaults for padding, it's a good practice to set the padding property of the body element to zero.

Figure 5-5   How to set padding

A web page that illustrates sizing and spacing

To illustrate how you use the properties for sizing and spacing, figure 5-6 presents a web page that uses many of these properties. This web page is similar to the one you saw at the end of the last chapter, although the content has been simplified. In addition, the page has been centered in the browser window, and the spacing between elements has been improved.

The HTML for the web page

The HTML for this web page is also presented in this figure. The only thing to notice here is that   character entities are no longer used to add space between the image and the text that follows it. Instead, CSS is used to add this space, as you'll see in the next figure.

A web page that uses widths, margins, and padding

The HTML for the web page

```
<body>
    <div id="page">
        <div id="header">
            <h1><img src="images/logo.jpg" alt="Town Hall Logo" width="50px" />
            San Joaquin Valley Town Hall</h1>
            <h3>Bringing cutting-edge speakers to the valley</h3>
        </div>
        <div id="main">
            <h2>2009-2010 guest speakers</h2>
            <ul class="speakers">
                <li>October 14, 2009: <a href="speakers/russell.html">
                Dr. Alan J. Russell</a></li>

                    .

                    .
                <li>April 21, 2010: <a href="speakers/coll.html">
                Steve Coll</a></li>
            </ul>
            <p><em>Contact us by phone</em> at (559) 555-1212 for ticket
            information.</p>
        </div>
        <div id="footer">
            <p>&copy; Copyright 2010 San Joaquin Valley Town Hall.</p>
        </div>
    </div>
</body>
```

Figure 5-6   A web page that illustrates sizing and spacing

The CSS for the web page

Figure 5-7 presents the CSS for the web page. Here, I've highlighted all the style rules that affect the size and spacing of the elements on the page. Also, to make this CSS easier to follow, I've coded the rules sets in the same sequence as the related elements in the HTML. Note, however, that you wouldn't normally code the rule sets in this sequence, except maybe for simple web pages.

To start, both the margin and padding properties of the body element are set to zero. That means that no space will appear between the body element and the edge of the browser window. Because of that, the box that contains the div element that's subordinate to the body element (the one with the id "page") will be displayed beginning at this edge.

The rule set for the page division sets the width of the page to 500 pixels, which means the width of the page won't change. Then, the top and bottom margins are set to zero so there's no space between this division and the top and bottom of the browser window. In addition, the left and right margins are set to "auto". Because a width is specified for this division, this value causes the left and right margins to be calculated automatically. In that case, the margins are set to an equal amount so the page is centered.

The next highlighted rule set is for the img element. The single style rule for this element sets the right margin to .25 em. That causes space to be added between the image and the text that follows it.

The remaining highlighted rules set the top and bottom margins for adjacent elements. For example, the rule set for the h1 and h3 elements sets the bottom margin for these elements to zero. Then, the rule set for the h3 element sets the top margin for that element to 1 em. That avoids the problem of collapsing margins between the h1 and h3 elements.

Similarly, the rule set for the h2 element sets the top margin for this element to 1.5 ems. Since the bottom margin of the h3 element that precedes the h2 element is set to zero, this too avoids margin collapse. Note that this is true even if the adjacent elements are in different blocks. In this case, the h3 element is in the block for the header division, and the h2 element is in the block for the main division.

The CSS for the web page

```css
/* the styles for the body element */
body {
    font-family: Verdana, Arial, Helvetica, sans-serif;
    font-size: 84%;
    margin: 0;
    padding: 0; }

/* the styles for the page division */
#page {
    width: 500px;
    margin: 0 auto; }

/* the styles used in the header division */
img { margin-right: .25em; }
h1, h3 {
    color: #ef9c00;
    margin-bottom: 0; }
h1 {
    font-size: 180%;
    margin-top: .7em; }
h3 {
    font-size: 120%;
    font-style: italic;
    margin-top: 1em; }

/* the styles used in the main division */
h2 {
    font-size: 130%;
    margin-top: 1.5em;
    margin-bottom: 0; }
.speakers {
    line-height: 1.5;
    margin-top: .5em; }
a { font-weight: bold; }
a:link { color: #ef9c00; }
a:visited { color: #facd8a; }
a:active { color: green; }
#main p { margin-bottom: 0; }
em { font-weight: bold; }

/* the styles for the footer division */
#footer p {
    font-size: 80%;
    text-align: right;
    margin-top: 2.5em; }
```

Description

- To prevent the margin collapse between adjacent block elements, you can set one of the adjacent margins to zero and the other to the space you want between the two elements.

- To make this code easier to follow, the styles are presented in the same sequence as the related elements in the HTML. Although that's okay for a simple web page like this one, it becomes impractical for complex web pages.

Figure 5-7   The CSS for the web page

Another way to implement spacing

As I mentioned earlier, you can sometimes avoid collapsing margins by using padding to add space between elements instead of using margins. To illustrate how this works, figure 5-8 presents CSS that uses padding to format the web page in figure 5-6. Here, I've highlighted all the style rules that control the spacing between adjacent elements.

Like the CSS in the previous figure, the rule sets for the h1 and h3 elements set the bottom margins for both of these elements to zero. Then, instead of setting the top margin for the h3 element to 1 em, the style rule for the h3 element sets the top margin for this element to zero and sets the top padding to 1 em. This results in the same space between the h1 and h3 elements as the code in figure 5-7.

The remaining rule sets work the same way. For example, instead of setting the top margin for the h2 element to 1.5 ems, the rule set for this element sets the top margin to zero and the top padding to 1.5 ems. Actually, this rule set uses the shorthand margin property to set all the margins to zero. That way, you don't have to set the top and bottom margins separately.

At this point, you may be wondering when you should use the technique shown in this figure and when you should use the technique shown in figure 5-7. The answer is, it depends. For a simple page like this one, you can use whichever technique you prefer. If a page uses borders, however, you may need to use both padding and margins to get the spacing you want.

Another version of the CSS

```css
/* the styles for the body element */
body {
    font-family: Verdana, Arial, Helvetica, sans-serif;
    font-size: 84%;
    margin: 0;
    padding: 0; }

/* the styles for the page division */
#page {
    width: 500px;
    margin: 0 auto; }

/* the styles used in the header division */
img { margin-right: .25em; }
h1, h3 {
    color: #ef9c00;
    margin-bottom: 0; }
h1 {
    font-size: 180%;
    margin-top: .7em; }
h3 {
    font-size: 120%;
    font-style: italic;
    margin-top: 0;
    padding-top: 1em; }

/* the styles used in the main division */
h2 {
    font-size: 130%;
    margin: 0;
    padding-top: 1.5em; }
.speakers {
    line-height: 1.5;
    margin: 0;
    padding-top: .5em; }
a { font-weight: bold; }
a:link { color: #ef9c00; }
a:visited { color: #facd8a; }
a:active { color: green; }
#main p { margin-bottom: 0; }
em { font-weight: bold; }

/* the styles for the footer division */
#footer p {
    font-size: 80%;
    text-align: right;
    margin: 0;
    padding-top: 2.5em; }
```

Description

- Another way to prevent margin collapse is to set both margins for the adjacent elements to zero. Then, you can use padding to set the space between elements.

Figure 5-8   Another way to implement spacing

How to set borders and backgrounds

Now that you know how to size and space elements using the box model, you're ready to learn how to apply other formatting to boxes. That includes adding borders and setting background colors and images.

How to set borders

Figure 5-9 presents the properties for setting *borders* and illustrates how they work. To start, if you want the same border on all four sides of a box, you can use the shorthand border property. This property lets you set the width, style, and color for the borders. This is illustrated in the first set of examples in this figure.

Here, the first example creates a thin, solid, green border. Note that different browsers interpret the thin keyword, as well as the other keywords for width, differently. Because of that, you'll typically set the width of a border to an absolute value as shown in the second and third examples. Notice that the third example doesn't specify a color. In that case, the border will be the same color as the element's text.

If you don't want all four sides of a border to be the same, you can use the other properties shown in this figure to set the border for each side. To set the width for each side of a border, for instance, you can use the shorthand border-width property as shown in the second set of examples. Here, you can see that you can specify one, two, three, or four values on this property. This works just like the shorthand margin and padding properties you learned about earlier in this chapter. That means that the values are applied to the top, right, bottom, and left sides of the border.

The border-style and border-color properties are similar. You can use them to set the border style and color for each side of a border by specifying one to four values. This is illustrated in the third and fourth sets of examples in this figure. Notice in the last example for the border-style property that the left and right borders are set to "none". That way, only top and bottom borders will be displayed.

Finally, if you want to work with the border for just one side of a box, you can use the border-top, border-right, border-bottom, and border-left properties. When you use these properties, you can set all of the properties for the border at once. This is illustrated in the first example in the last set of examples. You can also specify a style, width, and color for an individual side of a border. To do that, you use a property such as border-right-style and border-bottom-width. This is illustrated by the last three examples.

Properties for setting borders

Property	Description
border-width	One to four relative or absolute values (excluding a percent) or keywords that specify the widths for each side of a border. Possible keywords are thin, medium, and thick. In Internet Explorer, thin, medium, and thick borders are 2px, 4px, and 6px. In Firefox, they're 1px, 2px, and 3px.
border-style	One to four keywords that specify the styles for each side of a border. Possible values are dotted, dashed, solid, double, groove, ridge, inset, outset, and none. The default is none.
border-color	One to four color values or keywords that specify the color for each side of a border. The default is the color of the element.
border	A border width, border style, and border color. The values are applied to all sides of the border.
border-side-width	A relative or absolute value (excluding a percent) or a keyword that specifies the width of the indicated side of a border.
border-side-style	A keyword that specifies the style for the indicated side of a border.
border-side-color	A color value or keyword that specifies the color of the indicated side of a border.
border-side	Border width, style, and color values for the specified side of a border.

The syntax for the shorthand border and border-*side* properties

```
border: [width] [style] [color];
border-side: [width] [style] [color];
```

How to set border properties

```
border: thin solid green;
border: 2px dashed #808080;
border: 1px inset;               /* uses the element's color property */
```

How to set the widths of borders

```
border-width: 1px;              /* all four sides */
border-width: 1px 2px;          /* top and bottom 1px, right and left 2px */
border-width: 1px 2px 2px;      /* top 1px, right and left 2px, bottom 2px */
border-width: 1px 2px 2px 3px;  /* top 1px, right 2px, bottom 2px, left 3px */
```

How to set the style of borders

```
border-style: dashed;     /* dashed line all sides */
border-style: solid;      /* solid line all sides */
border-style: solid none; /* solid top and bottom, no border right and left */
```

How to set the color of borders

```
border-color: green;      /* a named color */
border-color: #808080;    /* a hexadecimal value for a color */
border-color: black gray; /* black top and bottom, gray right and left */
```

How to set individual borders

```
border-top: 2px solid black;
border-right-style: dashed;
border-bottom-width: 4px;
border-left-color: gray;
```

Figure 5-9   How to set borders

How to set background colors and images

Figure 5-10 presents the properties you can use to set the *background* for a box. When you set a background, it's displayed behind the content, padding, and border for the box, but it isn't displayed behind the margin.

When you specify a background, you can set a background color, a background image, or both. If you set both, the browser displays the background color behind the image. As a result, you can only see the background color if the image has areas that are transparent or the image doesn't repeat.

As this figure shows, you can set all five properties of a background by using the shorthand background property. When you use this property, you don't have to specify the individual properties in a specific order, but it usually makes sense to use the order that's shown. If you omit one or more properties, the browser uses their default values.

The first set of examples illustrates how this works. Here, the first example sets the background color to blue, the second example sets the background color and specifies the URL for an image, and the third example specifies all five background properties. You can also code each of these properties individually.

By default, the background color for a box is transparent. As a result, you can see through the box to the color that's behind it, which is usually what you want. Otherwise, you need to set the color. The first example in the second set of examples shows how to do that using the background-color property.

If you want to display a background image, you need to specify a URL that points to the file for the image. You can do that using the background-image property as shown in the second example in the second set of examples.

If you add a background image to a box, it will repeat horizontally and vertically to fill the box by default. This works well for small images that are intended to be tiled across or down a box. If you want to change this behavior, you can set the background-repeat property so the image is only repeated horizontally, so it's only repeated vertically, or so it isn't repeated at all. This is illustrated by the first four examples in the last set of examples.

If an image doesn't repeat horizontally and vertically, you may need to set additional properties to determine where the image is positioned and whether it scrolls with the page. By default, an image is positioned in the top left corner of the box. To change that, you use the background-position property. This property lets you specify both a horizontal and a vertical position.

The next three examples illustrate how this works. The first example positions the image at the top left corner of the box, which is the default. The second example centers the image at the top of the box. And the third example positions the image starting 90% of the way from the left side to the right side of the box and 90% of the way from the top to the bottom of the box.

In most cases, you'll want a background image to scroll as you scroll the box that contains it. For example, if you use a background image for an entire page and the page is larger than the browser window, you'll usually want the image to scroll as you scroll through the page. If not, you can set the background-attachment property to "fixed". Then, the image won't scroll with the page.

The properties for setting the background color and image

Property	Description
`background-color`	A color value or keyword that specifies the color of an element's background. You can also specify the transparent keyword if you want elements behind the element to be visible. This is the default.
`background-image`	A relative or absolute URL that points to the image. You can also specify the keyword none if you don't want to display an image. This is the default.
`background-repeat`	A keyword that specifies if and how an image is repeated. Possible values are repeat, repeat-x, repeat-y, no-repeat. The default is repeat, which causes the image to be repeated both horizontally and vertically to fill the background.
`background-position`	One or two relative or absolute values or keywords that specify the initial horizontal and vertical positions of an image. Keywords are left, center, and right; top, center, and bottom. If a vertical position isn't specified, center is the default. If no position is specified, the default is to place the image at the top-left corner of the element.
`background-attachment`	A keyword that specifies whether an image scrolls with the document or remains in a fixed position. Possible values are scroll and fixed. The default is scroll.
`background`	Background color, image, repeat, attachment, and position values.

The syntax for the shorthand background property

```
background: [color] [image] [repeat] [attachment] [position];
```

How to set multiple background properties

```
background: blue;
background: blue url("images/texture.gif");
background: #808080 url("images/header.jpg") repeat-y scroll center top;
```

How to set the background color and image

```
background-color: blue;
background-image: url("images/texture.gif");
```

How to control image repetition, position, and scrolling

```
background-repeat: repeat;          /* repeats both directions */
background-repeat: repeat-x;        /* repeats horizontally */
background-repeat: repeat-y;        /* repeats vertically */
background-repeat: no-repeat;       /* doesn't repeat */

background-position: left top;      /* 0% from left, 0% from top */
background-position: center top;    /* 50% from left, 0% from top */
background-position: 90% 90%;       /* 90% from left, 90% from top */

background-attachment: scroll;      /* image moves as you scroll */
background-attachment: fixed;       /* image does not move as you scroll */
```

Description

- The background for an element applies to its content, padding, and borders, not its margins.

Figure 5-10 How to set background colors and images

A web page that uses borders and backgrounds

Figure 5-11 presents a web page that's similar to the one you saw in figure 5-6. In fact, the HTML for these two pages is identical. As you can see, however, the page in this figure includes some additional formatting. Specifically, the box that contains the page content has a border around it. In addition, the box that contains the header has a border below it, and the box that contains the footer has a border above it.

This page also uses two background colors. First, it uses a background color for the body of the document so that color fills the browser window. It also uses white as the a background color for the box that contains the page content. That way, the background color for the body doesn't show behind the page content.

A warning on the use of background colors and images

When you consider using a background color, remember that a dark font on a white background is easiest to read. As a result, you should avoid the use of colored backgrounds when fonts are displayed over them, especially dark backgrounds.

Similarly, you should avoid the use of background images if fonts are going to be displayed over them. That's especially true if the images are dark or have a texture that makes the fonts more difficult to read.

In this figure, the web page uses a white background for all elements that contain fonts, and it uses a colored background for the part of the body element that doesn't contain fonts. This is a reasonable use of background colors. Also, this web page doesn't use a background image. The result is dark text on a white background, which makes the text easy to read, but it would be even easier to read if the color used for the header fonts and links were darker.

The HTML for the web page

The HTML is identical to the HTML shown in figure 5-6. If necessary, then, you can refer back to that figure as you study the CSS for this web page.

A web page that uses borders and a background color

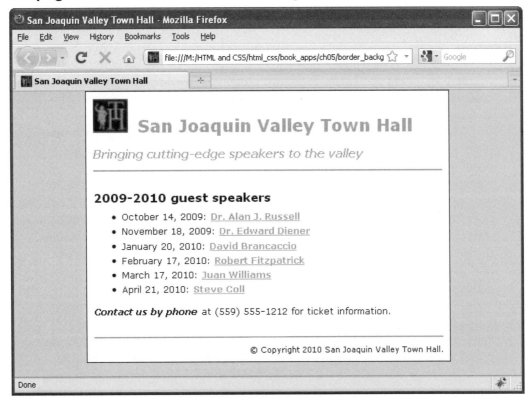

Description

- The HTML for this web page is identical to the HTML shown in figure 5-6.
- The styles for this web page include a border around the page content, a border below the header and above the footer, and background colors for the body element and the page division.

Figure 5-11   A web page that uses borders and a background color

The CSS for the web page

Figure 5-12 presents the CSS for the web page in figure 5-11. In this case, I've highlighted the style rules that are different from the ones in figure 5-7.

To start, the background-color property is used to set the background color for the body of the document. Then, this property is used to set the background color of the page division to white. That way, the contents of the page will be displayed on a white background.

The rule set for the page division also defines padding and a border for the page. In this case, the padding and border properties are used to add 10 pixels of padding inside a solid, black border that's 1 pixel in width.

To add a border below the header, I added a rule set for the header division. This rule set starts by setting the margin-top property of the header to 0. This is done because the padding for the border around the page already adds space above the header. I also set the margin-top property for the first element within the header (h1) to 0 so no additional space is added. Then, I used the border-bottom property to add a two-pixel solid border below the header, and I used the padding-bottom property to add 1 em of space above the border.

To add a border above the footer, I added a rule set for the footer division. This rule set starts by using the margin-top property to add 2 ems of space above the footer. Then, it uses the border-top property to add the border. Finally, it uses the padding-top property to add .7 em of space below the border. Because this adds space above the paragraph within the footer, the margin for this paragraph is set to 0.

The CSS for the web page

```css
/* the styles for the body element */
body {
    font-family: Verdana, Arial, Helvetica, sans-serif;
    font-size: 84%;
    margin: 0;
    padding: 0;
    background-color: #facd8a; }

/* the styles for the page division */
#page {
    width: 500px;
    margin: 0 auto;
    background-color: white;
    padding: 10px;
    border: 1px solid black; }

/* the styles used in the header division */
#header { margin-top: 0;
    padding-bottom: 1em;
    border-bottom: 2px solid #ef9c00; }
img { padding-right: .25em; }
h1, h3 {
    color: #ef9c00;
    margin-bottom: 0; }
h1 {
    font-size: 180%;
    margin-top: 0; }
h3 { font-size: 120%;
    font-style: italic;
    margin-top: 1em; }

/* the styles used in the main division */
h2 {
    font-size: 130%;
    margin-top: 1.5em;
    margin-bottom: 0; }
.speakers {
    line-height: 1.5;
    margin-top: .5em; }
a { font-weight: bold; }
a:link { color: #ef9c00; }
a:visited { color: #facd8a; }
a:active { color: green; }
#main p { margin-bottom: 0; }
em { font-weight: bold; }

/* the styles for the footer division */
#footer {
    margin-top: 2em;
    border-top: 2px solid #ef9c00;
    padding-top: .7em; }
#footer p {
    font-size: 80%;
    text-align: right;
    margin: 0; }
```

Figure 5-12   The CSS for the web page

Perspective

Now that you've completed this chapter, you should understand how the box model is used for margins, padding, borders, backgrounds, and background images. As a result, you should be able to get the spacing, borders, and backgrounds for your web pages just the way you want them. Next, to complete your crash course in HTML and CSS, chapter 6 shows you how to use CSS for laying out the elements on a page in two- and three-column arrangements with both headers and footers.

Terms

box model   liquid layout
padding   containing block
margin   shorthand property
fixed layout   collapsed margins
frozen layout   border

Summary

- The CSS *box model* lets you work with the box that a browser places around each block element as well as some inline elements. Each box includes the content of the element, plus optional padding, borders, and margins. If necessary, you can set the height and width of the content area.

- To set the height and width of a content area, you can use absolute measurements like pixels or relative measurements like percents. If you use a percent, the percent applies to the block that contains the box you're formatting

- You can set the margins for all four sides of a box. Because different browsers have different default values for margins, it's a good practice to set the margins of the body element to zero.

- If you specify a bottom margin for one element and a top margin for the element that follows, the margins are *collapsed* to the size of the largest margin. To avoid that, you can set one of the margins to zero and the other to the size you want.

- Like margins, you can set the padding for all four sides of a box. Also, different browsers have different defaults for the padding around a page. To avoid margin collapse, you can set the margins to zero and use padding for the spacing.

- A *border* can be placed on any of the sides of a box. That border goes on the outside of the padding for the box and inside any margins, and you can set the width, style, and color for a border.

- When you set the *background* for a box, it is displayed behind the content, padding, and border for the box, but not behind the margins. The background can consist of a color, an image, or both a color and image.

Exercise 5-1   Use the box model with the Bait Shop

In this exercise, you'll size and space the elements of a Bait & Tackle Shop web page that you worked on in exercise 4-1. You'll also apply borders and backgrounds. When you're done, the page should look like this:

Size and space the elements on the page

1. Use your text editor to open these files:

   ```
   c:\html_css\ch05\bait_shop\index.html
   c:\html_css\ch05\bait_shop\styles\main.css
   ```

   Then, display the HTML document in both IE and Firefox. In both browsers, the page should look like the one you formatted in exercise 4-1.

2. Set the margins of the body element to zero. Save the changes, and test the page in both browsers. Now, the content of the page should be pushed up against the top and left side of IE, but there might still be space between the top and the content in Firefox. If so, this is a browser variation.

3. To fix this, set the margins for the h1 element to 0. Then, save and test in both browsers. That shows that the extra space in Firefox was coming from the default value for the top margin of the h1 element.

4. Add a rule set for the page division. This rule set should set the width of the page to 500 pixels, the top and bottom margins to zero, and the left and right margins to auto so the page is centered in the browser. Now, save and test in both browsers to make sure this works.

5. Set the bottom margin of the h2 element to zero, and set the top margin of the ul element to .25 em. This should close up some of the space between these two elements. Test the page to make sure it does.

Add borders below the header and above the footer

6. Add a rule set for the header division. This rule set should add a solid gray bottom border that's 2 pixels wide, and it should set the bottom margin to 1.4 ems. Then, test this change.

7. Add a rule set for the footer division. This rule set should set the margin top to .5 em, add a top border like the one below the header division, and set the top padding to .7 em. Then, test this change.

8. Set the margins of the copyright class to zero so no space is added above the copyright paragraph. Then, test this change.

Add a background color behind the page

9. Set the background color of the body element to gray. Then, test this change to see that the background of the page is also gray.

10. Set the background color of the page division to white. Then, test the page again to see that the page content is displayed against a white background. This also shows that there isn't any padding around the contents of the page division.

11. Add 15 pixels of padding around the page division. Then, test the page.

Change the spacing on the fly_rod page

12. In your browser, click on the link for the first new product that's listed. That should take you to the fly_rod page. There, you can see how the changes that you've made to the main CSS file have been applied to that page.

13. Open the product.css file in the styles folder, and add a rule set for the p class that sets the margins to zero and the bottom padding to .5 em. Then, test that change.

14. Add a rule set for h2 elements that sets the bottom padding to .25 em. Then, test that change to see how the spacing after the heading looks.

15. Click on the return to home page link to see that the home page hasn't been changed by the changes to the product.css file. That's because the home page isn't linked to that style sheet.

Experiment on your own

16. Adjust the padding or margins, change colors, try different border styles…that's how you learn. When you're through experimenting, close the files.

6

How to use CSS for page layout

In addition to using CSS to format the elements of a web page and control spacing and borders, you can use it to control the layout of a page. That means that you can control where elements appear on the page.

The two basic techniques for working with page layout are floating and positioning. As you'll see in this chapter, you typically use floating to create pages that consist of two or more columns. Then, you can use positioning to make other adjustments to a layout, such as moving an element to a specific location on a page and aligning a series of values. When you finish this chapter, you should be able to implement sophisticated page layouts.

How to float elements

A page layout technique that's used frequently with web pages is to float elements on top of other page content. This technique is particularly useful for creating pages with columns, as you'll see in the topics that follow.

How floating works

By default, the block elements defined in an HTML document flow from the top of the page to the bottom of the page, and inline elements flow from the left side of the block elements that contain them to the right side. This is illustrated by the first diagram in figure 6-1. Here, you can see that the web page consists of three divisions with the ids "header", "links", and "main". Note that these divisions appear in the same order on the web page as they do in the HTML document that defines them.

For simplicity, each division in this diagram consists of a single block element. For example, the header division consists of an h2 element, and the main division consists of a p element. Both of these elements have simple textual content, and that content flows from left to right within the element.

The links division also contains a single p element. Instead of containing textual content, though, this element contains three a elements. Because these are inline elements, they would be displayed across the page by default. In this case, though, br elements have been added after each a element so each link appears on a separate line. One thing to notice here is that the links division and the paragraph it contains extend the full width of the web page, even though the content only uses part of the width.

When you *float* an element, though, you need to specify its width so it takes up only the space it needs. This is illustrated in the second diagram in this figure. Here, the links division has been floated to the right and is now sitting on top of the main division.

When you float an element, it's taken out of the flow of the document. Because of that, any elements that follow the floated element flow into the space that's left by the floated element. In other words, the document flows just as it would if the floated element wasn't there. The only difference is that the content of the elements that follow the floated element flows around the floated element. In this diagram, for example, you can see that the content of the p element in the main division doesn't flow past the left side of the links division. When the links division ends, though, the content flows below it.

The layout of a web page without floating

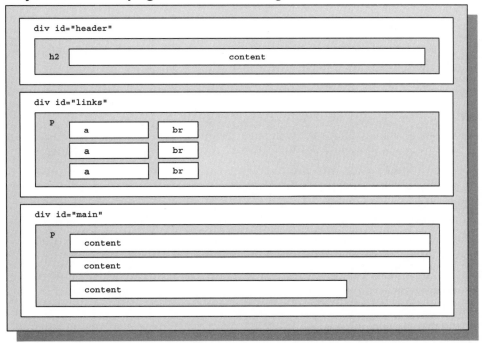

The layout of the web page after the links division is floated to the right

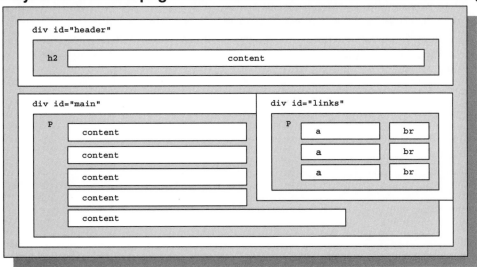

Description

- When you *float* an element, the element is taken out of the normal flow of the document and floats on top of the other content. Then, any elements after the floated element will flow into the space left vacant by the floated element, and the content of the elements will flow around the floated element.

Figure 6-1   How floating works

How to float an element

Figure 6-2 shows how to float an element on a web page. To do that, you use the float property to specify whether you want the element floated to the left or to the right. Then, the element will float above any block elements that follow it in the HTML document.

The example in this figure illustrates how this works. Here, you can see that the division with the id "speakers" is coded before the division with the id "main". Then, in the CSS for the web page, the float property is used to float the speakers division to the right. In addition, the width property is used to set the width of this division, which is a requirement for a floated element.

You can see the result in the web page shown in this figure. Here, I've included borders around each division so you can clearly see the areas they occupy. In particular, you can see that the speakers division now floats on top of the main division. Notice, however, that the last paragraph in the main division flows below the speakers division since the height of the speakers division is less than the height of the main division. In some cases, that won't be a problem. In other cases, though, you won't want content to flow below a floated element.

To prevent content from flowing below a floated element, you can set either the right or left margin of the element or its containing block. For instance, to prevent the last paragraph in this example from flowing below the floated element, you could set the right margin of the main division to the width of the speakers division. You'll see an example of that later in this chapter.

Although you can use the float property with any block element, you can also use it with some inline elements. For instance, images are often floated to the left or right of the text that applies to them. When you float an img element, you don't have to set the width property because an image always has a default size. Later in this chapter, you'll see an application with floated images.

The property for floating elements

Property	Description
float	A keyword that determines how an element is floated. Possible values are left, right, and none. None is the default.

The HTML for a web page

```
<div id="header">
    <h2>San Joaquin Valley Town Hall</h2>
</div>
<div id="speakers">
    <ul>
        <li>January 20, 2010: <a href="brancaccio.html">David
        Brancaccio</a></li>
        <li>February 17, 2010: <a href="fitzpatrick.html">Robert
        Fitzpatrick</a></li>
        <li>March 17, 2010: <a href="williams.html">Juan Williams</a></li>
    </ul>
</div>
<div id="main">
    <p>Welcome to San Joaquin Valley Town Hall.
    We have some amazing speakers in store for you this season!</p>
    <p><a href="contact.html">Contact us</a> to purchase your tickets
    today!</p>
</div>
```

The CSS for the web page

```
div {
    border: 1px solid black;
    padding: 0px 10px; }
#speakers {
    width: 17em;
    float: right; }
li { font-size: 90%; }
```

The web page in a browser

San Joaquin Valley Town Hall

Welcome to San Joaquin Valley Town Hall. We have some amazing speakers in store for you this season!

- January 20, 2010: David Brancaccio
- February 17, 2010: Robert Fitzpatrick
- March 17, 2010: Juan Williams

Contact us by phone at (559) 555-1212 for ticket information.

Description

- You use the float property to float an element in a specified direction. The floated element must also have a width that's either set or implied (like an image width).

- If you don't want content that flows around a floated element to flow below the element, you can set the appropriate margin of the block element that contains the content.

Figure 6-2   How to float an element

How to clear a floated element

By default, any content that follows a floated element in an HTML document will fill in the space to the side of the floated element. That includes block elements as well as inline elements. If that's not what you want, you can use the clear property to indicate whether an element should prohibit floating content to its left, to its right, or both its left and right.

Figure 6-3 illustrates how this property works. In these examples, I put borders around all three divisions to make it easy to see the effect of clearing the footer.

In the first example, the HTML document contains three divisions: speakers, main, and footer. Then, you can see what this HTML looks like in a browser if it is formatted using the CSS in the previous figure. As before, the speakers division is floated to the right. However, because the clear property isn't used for the footer division, this division starts immediately after the main division. And because the main division is shorter than the floated division, the content of the footer division flows to the left of the floated division.

Now, suppose you add a rule set that clears the right side of the footer. Then, the footer won't flow to the left side of the floated element. Instead, it will be moved down so it starts after the floated element as shown in the second browser window. Notice here that the main division still ends in the same place it did before the footer was cleared. However, additional space has been added between the end of the main division and the beginning of the footer division, effectively pushing the footer division down the page.

Incidentally, the clear property could be coded as "both" in this example. However, you only need to clear the side that has the floated element.

The property for clearing a floated element

Property	Description
clear	Determines whether an element is cleared from flowing into the space left by a floated element. Possible values are left, right, both, and none (the default).

Part of the HTML for a web page with a footer

```
<div id="speakers">
    <ul>
        <li>January 20, 2010: <a href="brancaccio.html">David
        Brancaccio</a></li>
        <li>February 17, 2010: <a href="fitzpatrick.html">Robert
        Fitzpatrick</a></li>
        <li>March 17, 2010: <a href="williams.html">Juan Williams</a></li>
        <li>April 21, 2010: <a href="coll.html">Steve Coll</a></li>
    </ul>
</div>
<div id="main">
    <p>Welcome to San Joaquin Valley Town Hall.
    We have some amazing speakers in store for you this season!</p>
</div>
<div id="footer">
    <p>&copy; Copyright 2009 San Joaquin Vally Town Hall.</p>
</div>
```

The HTML in a browser without clearing the footer

Welcome to San Joaquin Valley Town Hall. We have some amazing speakers in store for you this season!	• January 20, 2010: <u>David Brancaccio</u> • February 17, 2010: <u>Robert Fitzpatrick</u> • March 17, 2010: <u>Juan Williams</u> • April 21, 2010: <u>Steve Coll</u>
© Copyright 2009 San Joaquin Valley Town Hall.	

The CSS for the footer

```
#footer { clear: right; }
```

The HTML in a browser after the right side of the footer is cleared

Description

- You can use the clear property to force the placement of an element that follows a floated element. The value you specify indicates the side or sides of the element that a floated element can't occupy.

Figure 6-3   How to clear a floated element

A two-column layout that uses floating

To help you understand how floating works, figure 6-4 presents a web page that uses floating to create a two-column layout with a header and a footer. This is one of the most common types of layouts used by web designers.

In the past, layouts like this one were done by using HTML tables, which you'll learn about in chapter 9. But now that modern browsers support CSS, this type of layout should be done by using CSS because that will make the web page easier to create and maintain.

The page layout

To create a two-column layout, one column, typically called a *sidebar*, is floated to one side of a column that contains the main information for the page. In this figure, the main column contains information about guest speakers, and the sidebar contains other news.

You should notice two things about this layout. First, the content of the main column doesn't flow below the sidebar, even though the sidebar is shorter than the main column. That's because a right margin has been set on the division that contains the main content to maintain the two-column appearance.

Second, the footer appears after both the main content and the sidebar. Because the column that contains the main content is longer than the sidebar, this works without having to clear the footer. Because the content of this page can change, however, you'll want to clear the footer anyway so it appears at the bottom of the page regardless of which column is longer.

A web page with a sidebar floated to the right of the main content

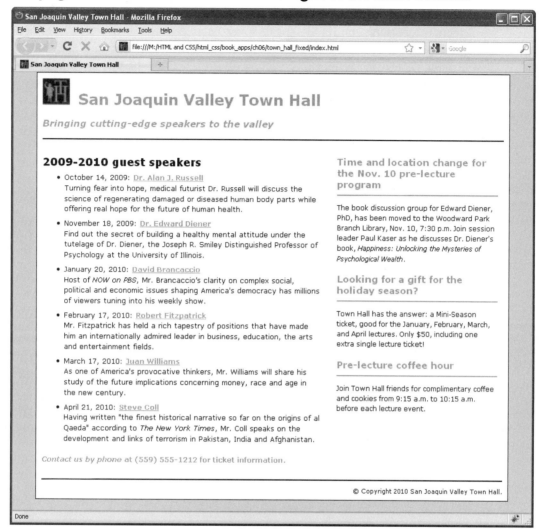

Description

- This web page illustrates a common page layout that consists of a header, two columns, and a footer. The columns are created by floating a division that defines a *sidebar* to the right of a division that defines the main content for the page.

- To keep the main content from flowing below the content of the sidebar, the right margin of the main division has been set to the width of the sidebar, including padding, plus an additional margin for added space between the columns.

- Because the main content extends beyond the content of the sidebar, it isn't necessary to clear the footer. However, it's a good practice to do that in case the content changes.

Figure 6-4   The page layout for a two-column web page that uses floating

The HTML

Figure 6-5 presents the HTML for this web page. As you can see, this HTML consists of four divisions within the division for the entire page. The first division defines the header. The second division defines the news column that's displayed as a sidebar. The third division defines the column that contains the main content for the page. And the fourth division defines the footer.

The most important thing to notice here is the sequence of the divisions in the HTML. Because you want the header to appear at the top of the page, you must code it before any other divisions. Then, because you want to float the news division to the right of the main division, it must be coded before that division. Finally, because you want the footer division to appear at the bottom of the page, you must code it after the other divisions.

The HTML for the web page

```
<body>
    <div id="page">
        <div id="header">
            <h1><img src="images/logo.jpg" alt="Town Hall Logo" width="50px" />
            San Joaquin Valley Town Hall</h1>
            <h3>Bringing cutting-edge speakers to the valley</h3>
        </div>
        <div id="news">
            <h3>Time and location change for the Nov. 10 pre-lecture
            program</h3>
            <p class="news_item">The book discussion group for Edward Diener,
            PhD, has been moved to the Woodward Park Branch Library, Nov. 10,
            7:30 p.m. Join session leader Paul Kaser as he discusses Dr.
            Diener's book, <i>Happiness: Unlocking the Mysteries of
            Psychological Wealth</i>.</p>
            <h3>Looking for a gift for the holiday season?</h3>
            <p class="news_item">Town Hall has the answer: a Mini-Season
            ticket, good for the January, February, March, and April lectures.
            Only $50, including one extra single lecture ticket!</p>
            <h3>Pre-lecture coffee hour</h3>
            <p class="news_item">Join Town Hall friends for complimentary
            coffee and cookies from 9:15 a.m. to 10:15 a.m. before each
            lecture event.</p>
        </div>
        <div id="main">
            <h2>2009-2010 guest speakers</h2>
            <ul class="speakers">
                <li>October 14, 2009: <a href="speakers/russell.html">
                Dr. Alan J. Russell</a><br />
                Turning fear into hope, medical futurist Dr. Russell will
                discuss the science of regenerating damaged or diseased human
                body parts while offering real hope for the future of human
                health.</li>
                    .

                    .

                <li>April 21, 2010: <a href="speakers/coll.html">
                Steve Coll</a><br />
                Having written "the finest historical narrative so far on the
                origins of al Qaeda" according to <i>The New York Times</i>,
                Mr. Coll speaks on the development and links of terrorism in
                Pakistan, India and Afghanistan.</li>
            </ul>
            <p><em>Contact us by phone</em> at (559) 555-1212 for ticket
            information.</p>
        </div>
        <div id="footer">
            <p>&copy; Copyright 2010 San Joaquin Valley Town Hall.</p>
        </div>
    </div>
</body>
```

Figure 6-5   The HTML for the web page

The CSS for a fixed layout

Figure 6-6 presents CSS for this web page that creates a *fixed layout*. That means that the widths of both columns, as well as the width of the page, are fixed. This is the type of layout that you'll see most often.

Before you study the specific styles, notice the way the styles are organized. First, the styles for the elements are listed. You can think of these as the default styles for the document. After that, the styles are grouped by division in the sequence that those divisions appear in the HTML. This is an effective way to organize the styles in your style sheets.

When you use this organization, it's easy to see what happens when a style for a division overrides a default style. For instance, the rule set for the h3 element in the header division applies italics, bottom padding, and a border to the default h3 element. And the p element in the main division has four rules applied to it that change the browser defaults.

On page 2 of this listing, you can see that a class selector is used in both the news and the main division. Because these selectors aren't qualified by the division ids, these rule sets would apply to the classes no matter what division they appear in the HTML. In this case, though, each class is only used within a single division in the HTML so it makes sense to code them with the styles for that division.

With that as background, please note that I've highlighted the style rules that affect the layout of the page. To start, you can see that I've set the width of the page to 850 pixels. That provides plenty of space for both columns, as well as for space between the columns and between the page content and the page border.

The CSS for the web page   **Page 1**

```
/* the default styles for the document */
body {
    font-family: Verdana, Arial, Helvetica, sans-serif;
    font-size: 84%;
    margin: 0;
    padding: 0;
    background-color: #facd8a;
}
h1 {
    font-size: 200%;
    color: #ef9c00;
    margin-top: 0;
    margin-bottom: 0;
}
h2 {
    font-size: 140%;
    margin-top: 1.5em;
    margin-bottom: 0;
}
h3 {
    font-size: 130%;
    color: #ef9c00;
    margin-bottom: 0;
}
img {padding-right: .25em; }
li { margin-top: .5em; }
a { font-weight: bold; }
a:link { color: #ef9c00; }
a:visited { color: #facd8a; }
a:active { color: green; }

/* the styles for the page division */
#page {
    width: 850px;
    margin: 0 auto;
    padding: 10px;
    border: 1px solid black;
    background-color: white;
}

/* the styles for the header division */
#header { margin-top: 0;}
#header h3 {
    font-style: italic;
    padding-bottom: 1em;
    border-bottom: 2px solid black;
}
```

Figure 6-6   The CSS for a fixed layout (part 1 of 2)

At the top of the second page of this listing, you can see the rule set for the news column. Here, I've set the width of the column to 300 pixels, and I've added padding of 10 pixels around the content of the column. In addition, I've floated the column to the right so it appears as shown in figure 6-4.

To keep the content of the main column from flowing below the news column, I set the right margin of the main column to 340 pixels. Because the width of the box that contains the news column is 320 pixels (a 300-pixel width plus 10 pixels of padding on each side), that provides for 20 additional pixels of space between the two columns. Notice here that I didn't specify an overall width for the main column. Because of that, it will take up the remainder of the page width.

The last thing you should notice is the rule set for the footer division. This rule set uses the clear property to clear the right side of the footer. That way, if the content of the page changes so the news column becomes longer than the main column, the footer will still be displayed at the bottom of the page rather than to the left of the news column. Here again, the clear property could be coded as "both", but this illustrates that you only need to clear the side that has the floated element.

The CSS for the web page   **Page 2**

```css
/* the styles for the news division */
#news {
    width: 300px;
    padding: 10px;
    float: right;
}
#news h3 {
    padding-bottom: .5em;
    border-bottom: 2px solid #ef9c00;
}
.news_item {
    font-size: 90%;
    line-height: 1.5;
    margin-top: 1em;
}

/* the styles for the main division */
#main { margin-right: 340px; }
#main p {
    color: #ef9c00;
    font-weight: bold;
    margin-top: 1.5em;
    margin-bottom: 0;
}
.speakers {
    line-height: 1.4;
    margin-top: .5em;
    margin-bottom: 0;
}

/* the styles for the footer division */
#footer { clear: right; }
#footer p {
    font-size: 80%;
    text-align: right;
    margin-top: 2.5em;
    margin-bottom: 0;
    border-top: 2px solid black;
    padding-top: 1em;
}
```

Figure 6-6   The CSS for a fixed layout (part 2 of 2)

The CSS for a liquid layout

Instead of creating a fixed layout like the one in figure 6-6, you can create a *liquid layout*. With a liquid layout, the width of the page changes as the user changes the width of the browser window. In addition, the width of one or more columns within the page changes.

The key to creating a liquid layout is using percents to specify the widths of one or more elements. This is illustrated in the examples in figure 6-7. Notice that, in both of these examples, the width of the page is set to 90%. That means that the page will always occupy 90% of the browser window, no matter how wide the window is. Of course, you can omit the width property entirely if you want the page to occupy 100% of the browser window.

Although the width of the page is specified as a percent in the first example, the width of the news sidebar and the right margin of the main division are still specified using pixels. That means that the widths of these areas won't change if the user changes the size of the browser window. What will change is the width of the main division, since it occupies the rest of the page width.

You can also create a liquid layout that provides for the widths of both columns changing with the width of the browser window. To do that, you use CSS like that shown in the second example in this figure. Here, the width of the news sidebar and the right margin of the main division are specified as percents along with the width of the page. In this case, because the width of the sidebar is specified as 35%, it will always occupy 35% of the page width. Then, the right margin of the main division provides for that 35%, plus an additional 5% for spacing. That leaves 60% for the width of the main division.

As you decide whether to use a fixed or a liquid layout, your main consideration should be the content of the page. If the page consists of a lot of text like the one in figure 6-4, you probably won't want to use a liquid layout. That's because a page becomes more difficult to read as the length of a line of text gets longer. On the other hand, if you want the users to be able to use their browsers to increase the size of the text on a page, you might want to use a liquid layout. Then, the users can adjust the size of their browser windows to get the optimal line length for reading.

CSS that provides for the width of the main column expanding

```
#page {
    width: 90%;
    margin: 0 auto;
    padding: 10px;
    border: 1px solid black;
    background-color: white;
}

#news {
    width: 300px;
    padding: 10px;
    float: right;
}

#main {
    margin-right: 340px;
}
```

CSS that provides for the widths of both columns expanding

```
#page {
    width: 90%;
    margin: 0 auto;
    padding: 10px;
    border: 1px solid black;
    background-color: white;
}

#news {
    width: 35%;
    padding: 10px;
    float: right;
}

#main {
    margin-right: 40%;
}
```

Description

- To change a web page from a *fixed layout* to a *liquid layout*, you can change the width of the page to a percent. You can also omit the page width if you want the page to fill the entire width of the browser window.

- If you want the width of just the main column of a two-column layout to change along with the width of the browser window, you specify the width of the sidebar as an absolute value.

- If you want the width of both the main column and the sidebar to change along with the width of the browser window, you specify the width of the sidebar and the right margin of the main column as a percent.

Figure 6-7   The CSS for a liquid layout

A three-column layout that uses floating

Now that you've seen a web page that uses a two-column layout, you're ready to see a page that uses another common layout. This layout includes a header, three columns, and a footer. Although I'm only going to present the highlights of the HTML and CSS code, you can open the downloaded HTML and CSS files for this application if you want to see all of the code.

Here again, layouts like this used to be done by using HTML tables. With CSS, though, pages like this are much easier to create, format, and maintain.

The page layout

Figure 6-8 shows the layout for a web page with three columns. This page could be seen as a mockup for a new home page. The main area of the page includes information about a new book, as well as information about what we think makes our books the best. Then, the left sidebar contains links to specific books along with our guarantee, and the right sidebar contains an announcement for our eBook offerings as well as some customer testimonials.

The header on this page illustrates the components that are commonly found in the headers of modern web sites. The *tag line* is the line that tries to encapsulate what the site does, as in "Professional programming books since 1974." The *navigation bar* provides the primary links for the site, like Home, Books, Ebooks, Downloads, and Trainers. Above the navigation bar are the *utilities*. These are common links that a site requires, but ones that aren't primary, like About Us, Contact Us, and Privacy Policy. The *logo* is also a common part of a header, and the current practice is to make the logo a link to the Home page.

Although the contents of this page are more complicated than the contents for the page with two columns, you shouldn't have any trouble understanding how to implement this three-column layout. The two main differences are (1) that you must set the margins on both sides of the middle column if you don't want its contents to flow below the contents of the left and right columns, and (2) you must clear both sides of the footer so it always appears below all three columns.

In addition to the two sidebars, the two images in this figure are floated to the left of the elements that follow them. As you'll see when I present the CSS for this page, you can float an image using the same technique that you use to float a block element.

A web page with two sidebars floated to the left and right

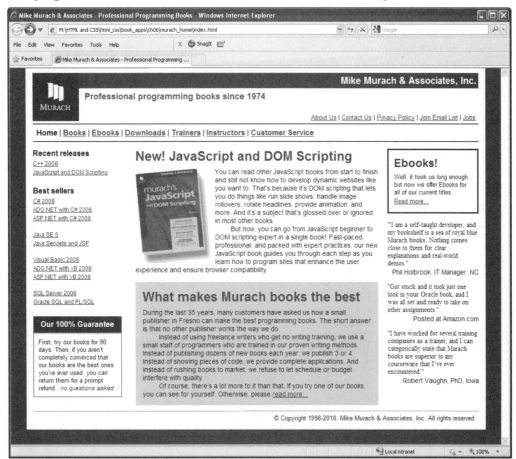

Description

- This web page illustrates a common page layout that includes a header, three columns, and a footer. The columns are created by floating two divisions that define sidebars to the left and right of the division that defines the main content for the page.

- You use the same techniques for a three-column layout as you do for a two-column layout, except you must set the margin on both sides of the main column, and you must clear both sides of the footer.

- The two images in this figure are also floated so they appear to the left of the elements that follow them.

Figure 6-8   The page layout for a three-column web page that uses floating

The structure of the HTML

Because the techniques for creating a three-column layout are basically the same as the techniques for creating a two-column layout, I won't present all of the HTML for the three-column layout. Instead, figure 6-9 shows just the div elements that are defined within the body of the HTML. Since ids are assigned to each of these elements, that will help you understand the corresponding CSS shown in the next figure.

Like the two-column page, the body of this HTML document contains a division that includes the content for the entire page. Within this division are five other divisions that define the main areas of the page. The header division is coded first so it will always appear at the top of the page. It contains two additional divisions that define the utility and navigation links.

The next two divisions are for the sidebars. Remember that these divisions must be coded before the main content because they will be floated to the left and right of this content. Although you can code these sidebars in any sequence, it makes sense to code the left sidebar first.

Both sidebars contain two additional divisions. The first division in the left sidebar defines the links to specific books, and the second division defines the box that contains the guarantee. The first division in the right sidebar defines the box that contains the ebooks announcement, and the second division defines the customer testimonials.

The main division is also divided into two more divisions. The first division defines the content that's displayed for the new JavaScript book, and the second division defines the content that tells what makes our books the best. Finally, the last division defines the footer for the page.

The div elements in the HTML

```
<body>
    <div id="page">
        <div id="header">
            .
            .
            <div id="utilities">
                .
                .
            </div>
            <div id="navigation">
                .
                .
            </div>
        </div>

        <div id="sidebar1">
            <div id="book_links">
                .
                .
            </div>
            <div id="guarantee">
                .
                .
            </div>
        </div>

        <div id="sidebar2">
            <div id="ebooks">
                .
                .
            </div>
            <div id="quotations">
                .
                .
            </div>
        </div>

        <div id="main">
            <div id="new_book">
                .
                .
            </div>
            <div id="best_books">
                .
                .
            </div>
        </div>

        <div id="footer">
            .
            .
        </div>
    </div>
</body>
```

Figure 6-9   The structure of the HTML for the web page

The CSS

Figure 6-10 presents the CSS that implements the floated elements for this web page. To start, you can see that the width of the page division is set to 960 pixels so the page will be wide enough for all three columns. You can also see that the padding provides for 10 pixels above and below the page division and 15 pixels to the right and the left of this division. If you look back to this page in figure 6-8, you can see this padding around the content of the page.

In the rule set for the header division, the bottom margin is set to 1 em. That provides the space after the navigation bar. Also, the rule set for the img element in this division floats the logo to the left with a right margin of 12 pixels. That way, the tagline and utility links appear to the right of the logo. Then, the rule set for the paragraph that contains the navigation links clears the left side of the paragraph so it's displayed below the logo.

Note here that the rule set for the logo image doesn't provide a width, even though a floated element needs to have a width. However, an image always has an implied width, so it can be floated whether or not a width is specified. This is also true for the book image that's floated in the center column.

Next, notice that the rule set for the left sidebar is given a width of 200 pixels with no margins. It is also floated to the left. Similarly, the width of the right sidebar is set to 200 pixels with no margins, and it is floated to the right. Then, in the styles for the main division, you can see that the left and right margins are set to 220 pixels. This provides for the 200 pixels that each sidebar occupies, plus 20 pixels for extra space between the sidebars and the main content.

In the rule set for the paragraphs in the main division, the line height is set to 1.25 and the margins are set to zero. Then, in the rule set for the img element in the new_book division, the image is floated to the left and the right margin is set to 12 pixels. In this case, because the paragraph margins are zero, the paragraphs to the right of this image will flow below the image if the paragraphs are long enough. If you look back to figure 6-8, you can see that's what happened.

The last highlighted style rule is for the footer. This rule clears both the left and right sides of the footer so it is always displayed below the two floated sidebars. It also provides for a top border with 12 pixels of space above it, which you can see in figure 6-8.

The CSS that implements the floated elements

```css
/* the styles for the page */
#page {
    width: 960px;
    background-color: white;
    margin: 0 auto;
    padding: 10px 15px; }

/* some of the the styles for the header */
#header {
    margin-bottom: 1em; }
#header img {
    margin-right: 12px;
    float: left; }
#navigation p {
    font-size: 120%;
    font-weight: bold;
    border-top: 2px solid #004e97;
    border-bottom: 2px solid #004e97;
    margin: 0;
    padding: .5em;
    clear: left; }

/* some of the styles for the left sidebar */
#sidebar1 {
    width: 200px;
    margin: 0;
    float: left; }

/* some of the styles for the right sidebar */
#sidebar2 {
    width: 200px;
    margin: 0;
    float: right; }

/* some of the styles for the center content */
#main {
    margin: 0 220px; }
#main p {
    line-height: 1.25
    margin: 0; }
#new_book img {
    float: left;
    margin-right: 12px; }

/* some of the styles for the footer */
#footer {
    clear: both;
    margin-top: 12px;
    border-top: 1px solid gray }
```

Figure 6-10   The CSS for the web page

How to position elements

Although floating provides an easy way to create pages with two or more columns, you may occasionally need to use other positioning techniques. You'll learn about those techniques in the topics that follow.

Four ways to position an element

To position the elements on a page, you use the properties shown in the first table in figure 6-11. The first property, position, determines the type of positioning that will be used. This property can have four different values as shown in the second table.

The first value, static, is the default, and it causes elements to be placed in the normal flow. The next value, absolute, removes the element from the normal flow and positions it based on the top, bottom, right, and left properties you specify. When you use *absolute positioning*, the element is positioned relative to the closest containing block. If no containing block is positioned, the element is positioned relative to the browser window.

The next value, fixed, works like absolute in that the position of the element is specified using the top, bottom, left, and right properties. Instead of being positioned relative to a containing block, however, an element that uses *fixed positioning* is positioned relative to the browser window. That means that the element doesn't move when you scroll through the window.

The last value, relative, causes an element to be positioned relative to its normal position in the flow. When you use the top, bottom, left, and right properties with *relative positioning*, they specify the element's offset from its normal position.

One more property you can use to position elements is z-index. This property is useful if an element you position overlaps another element. In that case, you can use the z-index property to determine which element is on top.

Properties for positioning elements

Property	Description
position	A keyword that determines how an element is positioned. See the table below for possible values.
top	A relative or absolute value that specifies the position of the top of an element's box for absolute or fixed positioning or the offset of the top of an element's box for relative positioning.
bottom	A relative or absolute value that specifies the position of the bottom of an element's box for absolute or fixed positioning or the offset of the bottom of an element's box for relative positioning.
left	A relative or absolute value that specifies the position of the left side of an element's box for absolute or fixed positioning or the offset of the left side of an element's box for relative positioning.
right	A relative or absolute value that specifies the position of the right side of an element's box for absolute or fixed positioning or the offset of the right side of an element's box for relative positioning.
z-index	An integer that determines the stack level of an element whose position property is set to absolute, relative, or fixed.

Possible values for the position property

Value	Description
static	The element is placed in the normal flow. This is the default.
absolute	The element is removed from the flow and is positioned relative to the closest containing block that is also positioned. The position is determined by the top, bottom, left, and right properties.
fixed	The element is positioned absolutely relative to the browser window. The position is determined by the top, bottom, left, and right properties.
relative	The element is positioned relative to its position in the normal flow. The position is determined by the top, bottom, left, and right properties.

Description

- By default, static positioning is used to position block elements from top to bottom and inline elements from left to right.
- To change the positioning of an element, you can code the position property. In most cases, you also code one or more of the top, bottom, left, and right properties.
- When you use absolute, relative, or fixed positioning for an element, the element can overlap other elements. Then, you can use the z-index property to specify a value that determines the level at which the element is displayed. An element with a higher z-index value is displayed on top of an element with a lower z-index value.
- Fixed positioning isn't supported by versions of Internet Explorer before version 7.

Figure 6-11   Four ways to position an element

How to use absolute positioning

Absolute positioning is occasionally useful. To give you the idea of how it works, figure 6-12 presents a simple example. Here, you can see that the web page is similar to the one in figure 6-2. But that page used floating to place a division with a list of speakers to the right of the main division. In this example, absolute positioning is used so the speakers division doesn't have to be coded before the main division in the HTML.

To make this example easier to follow, all of the divisions have a border, 0 margins, and 5 pixels of padding. That makes it easy to tell where the divisions are.

To start, the position property of the page division is set to absolute, but the top, bottom, left, and right properties aren't set. As a result, the page division is absolutely positioned where it is in the natural flow. In other words, nothing changes. However, because the page division is positioned absolutely, any elements that it contains can be absolutely positioned within it.

Next, the position property for the speakers division is set to absolute. Then, the top property is set so this division is 70 pixels from the top of the containing block, which is the page division. In addition, the left property is set so the speakers division is 20 pixels from the right side of the page division. This works because the page division is positioned absolutely. Otherwise, the top and right properties would be relative to the browser window.

Because an element that uses absolute positioning is taken out of the flow of elements on the web page, the element may overlap other elements on the page. For instance, the speakers division in this example would overlap the main division. Then, to fix that, you can adjust the margins or padding of other elements. In this example, the right padding for the main division is set to 280 pixels so it provides the space needed for the speakers division.

When you use absolute positioning, you typically specify the top or bottom and left or right properties. Then, if you want to specify the width or height of the element, you can use the width or height properties. However, you can also specify all four of the top, bottom, left, and right properties. Then, the height and width are determined by the difference between the top and bottom and left and right properties.

The HTML for a web page

```
<div id="page">
    <div id="header">
        <h2>San Joaquin Valley Town Hall</h2> </div>
    <div id="main">
        <p>Welcome to San Joaquin Valley Town Hall.
        We have some amazing speakers in store for you this season!</p>
    </div>
    <div id="speakers">
        <ul>
            <!-- Three speaker line items are here -->
        </ul> </div>
    <div id="footer">
        <p>&copy; Copyright 2010 San Joaquin Valley Town Hall.</p> </div>
</div>
```

The CSS for the web page

```
body { margin: 0;
       font-size: 82.5%; }
div {
    border: 1px solid black;
    padding: 5px; }
#header { height: 40px; }
#page {
    width: 500px;
    position: absolute; }
#speakers {
    position: absolute;
    top: 70px;
    right: 20px; }
#main {
    height: 100px;
    padding-right: 280px; }
```

The web page in a browser

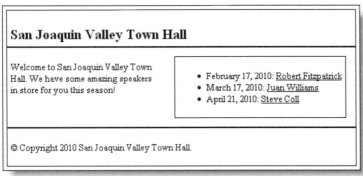

Description

- When you use *absolute positioning* for an element, the remaining elements on the page are positioned as if the element weren't there. Because of that, you may need to make room for the positioned element by setting margins and padding on other elements.

Figure 6-12   How to use absolute positioning

How to use relative positioning

In general, relative positioning is less useful than absolute positioning. To give you an idea of how it works, though, figure 6-13 presents an example. Here again, all of the divisions have a border, 0 margins, and 5 pixels of padding so it's easier to see what's happening.

In this example, the HTML for the web page is the same as the HTML in the previous figure. But this time, relative positioning is used for the main division. First, the top property is set so the main division is 10 pixels below where it would have been in the natural flow. Then, the left property is set so the division is 5 pixels to the right of where it would have been.

Next, relative positioning is used to move the speakers division up 65 pixels. That's done by using a negative value for the top property. Then, the left property is set so the speakers division is moved to the right by 235 pixels.

When you use relative positioning, any elements that follow the relatively positioned element leave space for the positioned element as if it were still there. In other words, no other elements will flow into the space vacated by the positioned element. This is illustrated by the space between the footer division and the main and speaker divisions. The trouble is that you usually don't want space like that.

If you look back to the previous figure, you should now realize that the position property for the page division could be set to either absolute or relative. Either way, that keeps the page division in its normal location. Then, if absolute positioning is used for any of the elements that it contains, the positions will be relative to the page division, not to the browser window.

The CSS for the web page with the HTML that's in figure 6-12

```
body {
    margin: 0;
    font-size: 82.5%; }
#page { width: 500px; }
div {
    border: 1px solid black;
    padding: 5px; }
#header { height: 40px; }
#main {
    width: 200px;
    height: 60px;
    position: relative;
    top: 10px;
    left: 5px;
}
#speakers {
    width: 250px;
    height: 75px;
    position: relative;
    top: -65px;
    left: 235px;
}
```

The web page in a browser

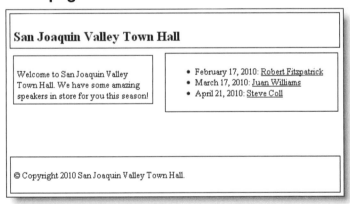

Description

- When you use *relative positioning* for an element, the remaining elements leave space for the moved element as if it were still there.

- If you need to position an element absolutely within a containing block, you can set the position property of the containing block to relative and omit the top, bottom, left, and right properties.

Figure 6-13   How to use relative positioning

How to use fixed positioning

Fixed positioning is the least used of all four types of positioning. In addition, it isn't supported by versions of Internet Explorer before version 7. But if you want to use it, figure 6-14 shows you how.

The example in this figure is for a simple web page that consists of two divisions. As you can see in the HTML, the first division contains a single paragraph with a link, and the second division contains a paragraph and a list. Then, the CSS uses fixed positioning to place the paragraph with the link near the upper right corner of the browser window. To accomplish that, the position property of the paragraph is set to fixed, and the top and right properties are set to 10 pixels.

Notice also that the right padding for the main division is set so plenty of space is available for the positioned element. Like absolute and relative positioning, this is often necessary so elements don't overlap.

You can see the results of this code in the two versions of the browser window at the bottom of this figure. Here, the size of the window has been reduced so you have to scroll to see the whole page. You can see the top of the page in the first window, and you can see the bottom of the page in the second window. Because the fixed element is positioned relative to the browser window, though, it's in the same position in both windows.

The HTML for a web page

```
<div id="win">
    <p><a href="raffle/html">Enter to win a free ticket!</a></p>
</div>
<div id="main">
    <p>Welcome to San Joaquin Valley Town Hall. We have some amazing
    speakers in store for you this season!</p>
    <ul>
        <li>October 14, 2009: <a href="speakers/russell.html">
        Dr. Alan J. Russell</a></li>
           .
           .
        <li>April 21, 2010: <a href="coll.html">Steve Coll</a></li>
    </ul>
</div>
```

The CSS for the web page

```
body { margin: 10px; }
#main { padding-right: 150px; }
#main p {
    text-indent: 2em;
    margin: 0; }
#win p {
    padding: 1em;
    border: 1px solid black;
    background-color: #ef9c00;
    margin: 0;
    width: 80px;
    position: fixed;
    right: 10px;
    top: 10px; }
```

The web page in a browser before and after it's scrolled

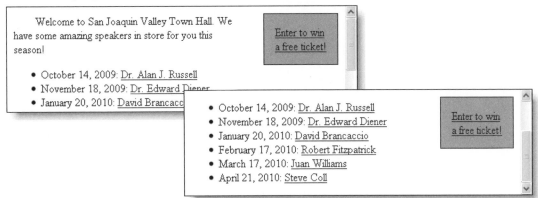

Description

- When you use *fixed positioning* for an element, the element doesn't move in the browser window even when you scroll.

Figure 6-14   How to use fixed positioning

A three-column layout that uses floating and positioning

To complete this chapter, I'll present a web page that uses both floating and positioning. That way, you can see how you can use these skills together in a single web page. Note, however, that I'll only show you the HTML and CSS for implementing the positioned elements since you've already seen how to implement floating. If you want to see all the code, though, you can open the downloaded HTML and CSS files for this application.

The page layout

Figure 6-15 presents the layout for a page that uses both floating and positioning. The main division of the page contains the table of contents for a book, and the sidebars are floated to the left and right of this content. This is done by using the floating techniques that you saw earlier in this chapter.

In the table of contents, though, both relative and absolute positioning are used to provide the alignment of the titles and page numbers. Here, relative positioning is used for each section and chapter heading. Then, absolute positioning is used to align the section and chapter titles and to align the page numbers at the right.

Incidentally, tables are commonly used for alignment problems like this even in modern web sites that use CSS for page layout. As you will see, though, this can be done more effectively by using positioning.

A web page that uses floating and positioning

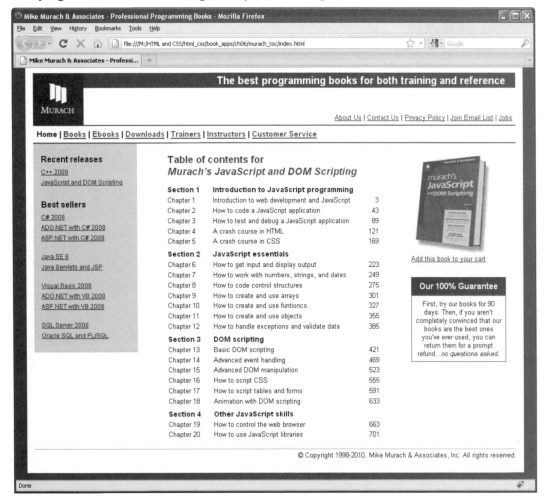

Description

- This web page uses floating to implement a three-column layout just like the page in figure 6-8.

- The section and chapter headings in the main division use relative positioning. Then, the titles and page numbers within those headings are aligned using absolute positioning.

Figure 6-15   The page layout for a web page that uses floating and positioning

The HTML

Figure 6-16 presents the HTML for the web page that's used to position the elements. To start, a span element has been included in each h2 and h3 element to identify the text for each section and chapter title. As you can see, these span elements are assigned to a class named "title". A span element is also included in each h3 element to identify the starting page number for each chapter. These elements are assigned to a class named "number". Because classes are assigned to the span elements, they can be referred to from the CSS for the page.

The HTML for the positioned elements

```
<div id="main">
    <h1>Table of contents for<br />
    <i>Murach&rsquo;s JavaScript and DOM Scripting</i></h1>

    <h2>Section 1<span class="title">Introduction to JavaScript
        programming</span></h2>
    <h3>Chapter 1<span class="title">Introduction to web development and
        JavaScript</span>
        <span class="number">3</span></h3>
    <h3>Chapter 2<span class="title">How to code a JavaScript
        application</span>
        <span class="number">43</span></h3>
    <h3>Chapter 3<span class="title">How to test and debug a JavaScript
        application</span>
        <span class="number">89</span></h3>
    <h3>Chapter 4<span class="title">A crash course in HTML</span>
        <span class="number">121</span></h3>
    <h3>Chapter 5<span class="title">A crash course in CSS</span>
        <span class="number">169</span></h3>

    <h2>Section 2<span class="title">JavaScript essentials</span></h2>
    <h3>Chapter 6<span class="title">How to get input and display output</span>
        <span class="number">223</span></h3>
    <h3>Chapter 7<span class="title">How to work with numbers, strings, and
        dates</span>
        <span class="number">249</span></h3>
    <h3>Chapter 8<span class="title">How to code control structures</span>
        <span class="number">275</span></h3>
    <h3>Chapter 9<span class="title">How to create and use arrays</span>
        <span class="number">301</span></h3>
    <h3>Chapter 10<span class="title">How to create and use funtioncs</span>
        <span class="number">327</span></h3>
    <h3>Chapter 11<span class="title">How to create and use objects</span>
        <span class="number">355</span></h3>
    <h3>Chapter 12<span class="title">How to handle exceptions and validate
        Data
        </span><span class="number">385</span></h3>
        .
        .
        .
    <h2>Section 4<span class="title">Other JavaScript skills</span></h2>
    <h3>Chapter 19<span class="title">How to control the web browser</span>
        <span class="number">663</span></h3>
    <h3>Chapter 20<span class="title">How to use JavaScript libraries</span>
        <span class="number">701</span></h3>
</div>
```

Description

- To implement absolute positioning, span elements are used to identify the text to be positioned at the left and the page numbers to be positioned at the right. Then, classes are assigned to the span elements so they can be referred to from the CSS.

Figure 6-16   The HTML for the web page

The CSS

Figure 6-17 shows the CSS that's used to position the elements on the page. To start, the rule sets for both the h2 and h3 elements in the main division include the position property with a value of "relative". Note, however, that the top, bottom, left, and right properties have been omitted. Because of that, the elements aren't actually offset. However, they are considered positioned for the purpose of positioning any elements they contain. In other words, because relative positioning is used with the h2 and h3 elements, absolute positioning can be used to position the span elements within the h2 and h3 elements relative to the h2 and h3 elements.

To position the span elements, rule sets are included for the two classes they're assigned to. The rule set for the title class positions the section and chapter titles 90 pixels from the left side of the h2 and h3 elements so they're aligned as shown in figure 6-15. Similarly, the rule set for the number class positions the starting page numbers for the chapters at the right side of the h3 elements.

The CSS for the positioned elements

```
#main h2 {
    font-size: 105%;
    margin-top: .6em;
    margin-bottom: 0;
    position: relative;
}

#main h3 {
    font-size: 95%;
    font-weight: normal;
    margin-top: .3em;
    margin-bottom: 0;
    position: relative;
}

.title {
    position: absolute;
    left: 90px;
}

.number {
    position: absolute;
    right: 0;
}
```

Description

- The h2 and h3 elements use relative positioning, but no positions are specified. That way, any elements they contain can be positioned relative to the headings.

- The titles within the h2 and h3 elements are positioned 90 pixels from the left side of the elements using absolute positioning.

- The page numbers within the h3 elements are positioned at the right side of the elements using absolute positioning.

Figure 6-17   The CSS for the web page

Perspective

Now that you've completed this chapter, you should be able to develop web pages that have headers, footers, and two- or three-column layouts. Better yet, you'll be using CSS to do these layouts, which makes these pages easier to create and maintain. In contrast, if you look at the source code for many web sites today, you'll find that they're still using HTML tables to implement page layouts.

This completes the first section of this book, which we think of as a crash course in HTML and CSS. With these skills, you should be able to develop web pages at a professional level. Then, to add to these skills, you can read any of the chapters in the rest of this book in whatever sequence you prefer. In other words, you can learn these skills whenever you need them.

Terms

float an element
sidebar
fixed layout
liquid layout
tag line
navigation bar
utilities
absolute positioning
relative positioning
fixed positioning

Summary

- When you use the float property to *float* an element, the element is taken out of the normal flow and floats on top of the other content. Then, any elements after the floated element will flow into the space left vacant by the floated element. To make this work, the floated element has to have a width.

- To stop an element from flowing into the space left vacant by a floated element, you can use the clear property.

- One of the common ways to lay out a page is with a header, footer, main column, and *sidebar*. To make that layout work, the HTML for the sidebar is coded before the HTML for the main column, and the CSS for the sidebar floats it to the right or left so the main column flows in beside it.

- In a *fixed layout*, the widths of the columns are set. In a *liquid layout*, the width of the page changes as the user changes the width of the browser window. In addition, the width of one or more columns changes. To make that work, the width of the page is set to a percent of the browser size.

- Another common layout for a web site consists of a header, footer, and three columns (a main column and two sidebars). To make that work, one sidebar is floated to the left and the other to the right of the main content.

- When you use *absolute positioning* for an element, the remaining elements on the page are positioned as if the element weren't there. Because of that, you may need to make room for positioned elements by adjusting other elements.

- When you use *relative positioning* for an element, the remaining elements leave space for the moved element as if it were still there.

- When you use *fixed positioning* for an element, the element doesn't move in the browser window, even when you scroll.

Exercise 6-1   Float elements on the Bait Shop page

In this exercise, you'll float an image in the header and float a division to the left of the main division. When you're done, the page should look like this:

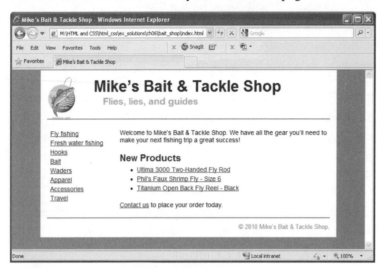

Review the changes in the HTML file

1. Open this file in your text editor:

    `c:\html_css\ch06\bait_shop\index.html`

    Then, launch the file in a browser so you can see that the HTML has been both modified and enhanced, but the CSS hasn't been changed.

2. In the header division of the HTML file, note that the img element precedes the h1 element and that an h2 element for a tag line has been added.

3. In the categories division that has been added to the HTML file, note that eight links are coded within one paragraph element.

Enhance the header division by floating the image

4. Open this file in your text editor:

    `c:\html_css\ch06\bait_shop\styles\main.css`

5. Change the width of the page to 640 pixels so it will accommodate the new column. Then, test this change in both IE and Firefox.

6. Add a rule set for the img element in the header division. That means the selector will be coded like this:

    `#header img { }`

    Then, add rules that float the image to the left. Now, test in both browsers.

7. Add another rule for the header division that sets the height to 90 pixels, the same height as the image. Then, test that change.

8. Delete the text-align property for h1 elements, and add a rule for the h1 element in the header division that sets the left margin to 3 ems. Then, test those changes.

9. Add a rule set for the h2 element in the header division that sets the left margin to 6 ems, the other margins to 0, and the color to #00ced1, which is a shade of aqua. Now, test those changes.

Float the categories division

10. Add a rule set for the categories division. Give this division a width of 150 pixels, and float it to the left. Then, test this change. Because the left margin hasn't been set for the main division, the display isn't quite right.

11. Add a rule set for the main division that sets the left margin to 165 pixels. Then, test the page again. Now, the content in the main division shouldn't flow under the floated division.

12. To improve the formatting of the category links, add a rule set for the p element in the categories division that sets the line height to 1.4, the top margin to zero, the left and right margins to .5 em, and the bottom margin to 1 em. Then, test in both browsers.

13. Because the main division is longer than the categories division, you don't have to clear the footer division. But remember that the fly_rod page also uses the main.css style sheet. To see how that page looks with a categories division and a changed header, click on the first bulleted link on the index page. Then, note that the footer division does need to be cleared for this page.

14. Clear the left side of the footer division, and test again. The two pages should now look the same in both browsers.

Experiment on your own

15. Float the categories division to the right instead of the left. Change widths, padding, margins, colors, or border styles. When you're through experimenting, close the files.

Exercise 6-2   Add a third column to the Bait Shop page

In this exercise, you'll add the start of a third column to the Bait Shop web page. When you're done, the page should look like this:

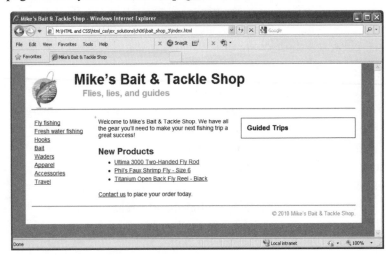

Add a third column to the HTML file

1. Open this file in your text editor:

    `c:\html_css\ch06\bait_shop_3\index.html`

    This is the HTML file for the web page that you developed for exercise 6-1. Note that it is in the bait_shop_3 directory.

2. Add another division to the HTML file so it can be floated to the right of the other two columns in the main portion of the web page. This division should have "trips" as its id, and it should contain one h3 element with "Guided Trips" as its contents. Then, save this file.

Enhance the styles so the third column floats to the right

3. Open this file in your text editor:

    `c:\html_css\ch06\bait_shop_3\styles\main.css`

    Then, change the width of the page to 800 pixels.

4. Add a rule set for the trips division so it is 250 pixels wide, has a 1 pixel black border, and is floated to the right of the main division. Then, test this change in both IE and Firefox.

5. Add a rule set for the h3 element so it is 125% of the default font size and has zero margins. Then, test this change in both browsers.

6. Adjust the margins and padding for the trips division so the third column looks like the one above. Then, test to make sure that this page looks the same in both browsers.

7. Experiment by adding more content to the third column or adjusting any of the styles for the page. When you're through, close the files.

Section 2

Other HTML and CSS skills as you need them

In section 1, you learned a professional subset of HTML and CSS skills that you can use for building most web pages. Now, in this section, you can add to those skills by learning new skills whenever you need them. To make that possible, each chapter in this section is an independent training module. As a result, you can read these chapters in whatever sequence you prefer.

Chapter 7 builds on the skills you learned in chapters 3 and 4 for working with links and lists, and chapter 8 builds on the skills you learned in chapters 3 and 5 for working with images. Then, the remaining chapters present information on new topics.

In chapter 9, you'll learn how to code tables to present tabular data. In chapter 10, you'll learn how to code forms, which are web pages that contain controls. In chapter 11, you'll learn how to add media like audio and video to your web pages. In chapter 12, you'll learn how to create style sheets for printing web pages and how to create web pages for mobile devices. Last, in chapter 13, you'll learn how to use tested JavaScript code to enhance your web pages with features like image rollovers, image swaps, tabs, and slide shows.

7

How to work with links and lists

In chapters 3 and 4, you learned the basic skills for coding links and lists and for using CSS to change the appearance of links. Now, in this chapter, I'll review these skills and present some additional skills for coding and formatting links and lists. When you're done with this chapter, you will be able to create links and lists that look and work just the way you want them to.

How to code links

In chapters 3 and 4, you learn how to code and format simple text links that open another web page in the same window. Now, you'll learn other ways to code and use links.

How to link to another page or start an email message

Figure 7-1 reviews some of the information that you learned earlier about coding a elements that *link* to other pages. To start, you code the href attribute so it identifies the page you want the link to display. Then, you code the content that you want to be displayed for the link. The content can be text, an image, or both text and an image.

The first two examples in this figure illustrate how this works. Here, the first link displays text, and the second link displays an image. Note that this image has a border. Most browsers add this border to identify the image as a link. In that case, the border is the same color as the underline for a text link. However, you can remove the border by using CSS to set the border style to "none".

The third example in this figure shows how you can use a link to open the user's default email program and start an email message. To do that, you code the href attribute as "mailto:" followed by the email address that the message will be sent to. In this example, that address is murachbooks@murach.com. Although this won't work for users who use email services like gmail or yahoo mail instead of the email programs on their computers, those users can at least get the email address from the text that's displayed for the link.

If you want to change the default styles for a link, you can use CSS with the four pseudocode selectors that are shown in this figure. The "link" selector applies to a link that hasn't been visited. The "visited" selector applies to one that has. The "active" selector applies to one that the user has pressed the mouse key down on, but hasn't released. And the "hover" selector refers to a link that the mouse is hovering over. By default, the first three are underlined and displayed in blue, purple, and red, but "hover" doesn't have any special style. In the examples, the fourth rule set changes the font-weight for "hover" to bold.

If you want the user to be able to activate a link with the keyboard, you can include the accesskey attribute. Then, the user can press that key in combination with one or more other keys to activate the link. For example, the accesskey attribute for the text link in this figure is set to the letter "c". Then, if this page is displayed in the Internet Explorer under Windows, the user can activate the link by pressing Alt+C (the Alt key and the C key). If it's displayed in Firefox under Windows, the key combination is Alt+Shift+C. And if it's displayed in a browser under Mac OS, the key combination is typically Ctrl+C.

If you define a shortcut key for a link, the user has no way of knowing what the key is. For the key to be of any use, then, you need to let the user know what

Two attributes of the <a> tag

Attribute	Description
href	Specifies a relative or absolute URL that identifies the document a link will display.
accesskey	Identifies a keyboard key that can be used in combination with other keys to activate the control. The key combination depends on the operating system and browser.

A text link with a shortcut key

```
<a href="/orders/cart.html" accesskey="c"
   title="Keyboard shortcut: C">Shopping cart</a>
```

An image link

```
<a href="/orders/cart.html"><img src="/images/shopping_cart.jpg"
   alt="Shopping cart" /></a>
```

The links in a web browser

A link that starts an email message

```
<a href="mailto:murachbooks@murach.com">murachbooks@murach.com</a>
```

The four CSS pseudo-class selectors for links

```
a:link { color: blue; }
a:visited { color: green; }
a:active { color: fuchsia; }
a:hover { font-weight: bold }
```

Description

- You can use the a element to create a *link* that loads another web page. The href attribute of this element identifies the page to be loaded

- The content of an a element can be text, an image, or text and an image.

- You can also use the a element to open the user's email program and start an email message by coding the href attribute as "mailto:" followed by the email address.

- By default, the text content of a link is underlined. If it hasn't been visited, it's blue. If it has been visited, it's purple. If it's active, it's red. But there's no default for hovering.

- If a link contains an image, most browsers display the image with a border. To remove it, you can use CSS to set the border property to "none".

- To provide a shortcut key that the user can use to activate a link, you can include the accesskey attribute.

- To review the link information in chapters 3 and 4, refer to figures 3-11 and 4-13.

Figure 7-1   How to link to another page or start an email message

the key is. To do that, you can include information about the shortcut key in the text content for the link. Or, you can include a title attribute that identifies the shortcut key as shown in this figure. To display this title, of course, the user must point to the link with the mouse, which defeats the purpose of having a shortcut key. But if the users access a page often enough, they may remember the shortcut key.

How to use a link to open a new browser window

In most cases, you'll want the page that's loaded by a link to be displayed in the same browser window as the current page. If the link loads a page from another web site, however, you may want to display that page in a new browser window. To do that, you set the target attribute of the a element to "_blank" as shown in figure 7-2.

In this figure, a link that displays the home page of the JavaScript web site is coded so it will display the page in a new window. As you can see in the first browser window, this link appears like any other link. When the user activates this link, though, the web page it refers to is displayed in a new window as illustrated by the second browser window.

Although most browsers display a page in a new browser window when you code the target attribute as shown here, Firefox does not. Instead, it displays the page in a new tab by default. The user can change this setting by using the Tools→Options command to display the Options dialog box, displaying the Tabs page, and then removing the check mark from the "Open new windows in a new tab instead" option.

HTML for a link that loads the document in a new window

```
<a href="http://www.javascript.com/"
    target="_blank">official JavaScript web site</a>.</p>
```

The two browser windows

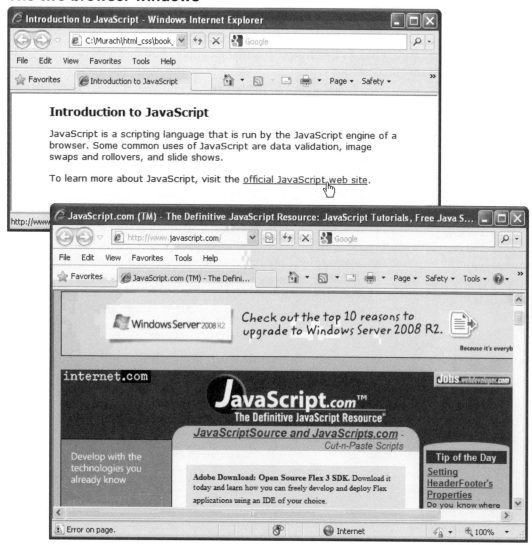

Description

- You can use the target attribute of the <a> tag to specify where the document referred to in a link should be loaded. To load the document in a new browser window, specify "_blank" for this attribute.

- By default, Firefox displays the document in a new tab rather than a new window, but the user can change this setting.

- Although the target attribute has been deprecated, it's still commonly used when a link leads to another web site.

Figure 7-2   How to use a link to open a new browser window

How to create and use an anchor

In addition to coding links that display another page, you can code links that jump to a location on the same page. To do that, you create an *anchor* that identifies the location you want the link to jump to. Then, you code a link that points to that anchor. This is illustrated in figure 7-3.

To create an anchor, you code the id attribute within an a element at the spot where you want the anchor. In this figure, the first example shows an anchor with the id "return" that's coded within an h3 element on the page. Then, the second example shows a link that jumps to that anchor. To do that, it uses the value of the anchor's id attribute preceded by a pound sign (#) as the value of the href attribute. When the user clicks on this link, the page is scrolled so the element that contains the anchor is displayed.

Anchors can make it easier for users to navigate through a long web page. For pages like these, it's common to include an anchor at the top of the page along with navigation links for each section of the page. Then, at the end of each section, it's common to include a link to return to the top of the page.

Although anchors are typically used for navigating within a single page, they can also be used to go to a location on another page. The last example in this figure shows how this works. Here, the name of the page that contains the anchor is coded before the value of the anchor's id attribute. Then, when that page is displayed, it will be positioned at the specified anchor.

A link that jumps to an anchor on the same page

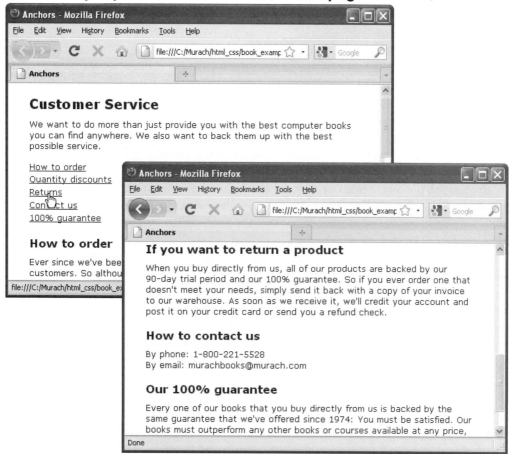

The HTML for the anchor

```
<h3><a id="return">If you want to return a product</a></h3>
```

The HTML for a link that jumps to an anchor on the same page

```
<a href="#return">Returns</a>
```

The HTML for a link that jumps to an anchor on another page

```
<a href="info.html#return">Returns</a>
```

Description

- You can use the id attribute of the <a> tag to create an *anchor* that specifies a location within a web page. Then, you can jump to that anchor by coding a link with its href attribute set to the value of the id attribute, preceded by the pound sign.

- You can also jump to an anchor on another page by coding a URL for the page preceding the id for the anchor.

Figure 7-3   How to create and use an anchor

How to create a navigation bar

Links are commonly used to create the *navigation bars* that provide the primary navigation for a site. This is illustrated by the two navigation bars in figure 7-4. Both of these bars contain links to the four major sections of the web site: Home, Books, Ebooks, and Customer Service. Bars like these are usually displayed at the bottom of a header or just below the header.

Today, a best practice for navigation bars is to indicate which link is current. That reminds the users which section of the web site they're currently in. In this figure, for example, the navigation bars have the Ebooks link highlighted.

In general, it's a best practice to show the default underline for an a element so the user can tell it's a link. In navigation bars, however, the underlines are often removed because users understand that the components of a navigation bar are links. This is illustrated by the second bar in this figure.

If you look at the HTML code for the first navigation bar, you can see that the bar consists of four a elements within a division. Here, each of the first three a elements are followed by a bar (|) character. Those bars are the separators in the navigation bar. Note also that the third a element has a class attribute with "current" as its name. It is used to highlight that link.

The HTML for the second navigation bar is the same as for the first navigation bar, except the bar characters have been removed. Then, CSS is used to provide borders that act as separators.

In the CSS for the first navigation bar, blue borders are added to the top and bottom of the division, and the links are blue because that's their default color. Then, the padding property makes the space above and below the links approximately equal by setting the top padding to 6 pixels and the bottom padding to 9 pixels. Last, the rule set for the current class sets the color to red to indicate that the link is current.

In contrast, the CSS for the second navigation bar sets the background color to blue. It also uses the padding property to set the space above and below the text for the a elements. Note that these values are different than the ones for the first navigation bar because the underlines have been removed from the a elements.

After the rule set for the second navigation bar, the CSS provides a rule set for the a elements in that bar. This calls for a white border to the right of each link and white text in the links. It also calls for padding that provides 10 pixels above and below the text for the links and 20 pixels to the right and left of each link. Note, here, that the top and bottom padding for the links must be the same as the top and bottom padding for the division if you want the right borders to be the same height as the navigation bar. Last, the text-decoration property is set to "none" to remove the underlines for the links.

The last rule set for the second navigation bar applies to the a elements in the current class. Here again, the current link is colored red, but this time the selector only applies to the current class when it's used for a elements in the navigation2 division.

Two navigation bars

A bar that uses bar characters to separate the a elements

Home | Books | Ebooks | Customer Service

A bar that uses right borders to separate the a elements

Home | Books | Ebooks | Customer Service

The HTML for the first navigation bar

```
<div id="navigation1">
    <a href="index.html" >Home</a> |
    <a href="books.html" >Books</a> |
    <a href="ebooks.html" class="current" >Ebooks</a> |
    <a href="custserv/index.html" >Customer Service</a>
</div>
```

The CSS for the first navigation bar

```
#navigation1 {
    font-size: 125%;
    font-weight: bold;
    border-top: 2px solid blue;
    border-bottom: 2px solid blue;
    padding: 6px 10px 9px;
}
.current { color: red; }                    /* current link is red */
```

The CSS for the second navigation bar with no bar separators in the HTML

```
#navigation2 {
    font-size: 125%;
    font-weight: bold;
    background-color: blue;
    padding: 10px 0;
}
#navigation2 a {
    border-right: 2px solid white;
    color: white;
    padding: 10px 20px;                   /* top and bottom padding */
    text-decoration: none;                /* removes underlines */
}
#navigation2 a.current { color: red; } /* current link is red */
```

Description

- The HTML for a *navigation bar* is coded as a series of a elements within a p element. Then, the CSS for those elements gives them the appearance of a bar.

- Often, the underlines for the a elements in a navigation bar are removed by setting the text-decoration property to "none".

- As a best practice, the navigation bar should indicate which of the links is currently in use. To do that, you can apply a different color to the current link.

Figure 7-4   How to create a navigation bar

How to code lists

In the topics that follow, I'll review the basic skills for coding ordered and unordered lists and present some additional examples. Then, I'll show you how to nest one list within another list, and I'll show you how to code a special type of list called a definition list.

How to code unordered lists

Figure 7-5 presents the two elements for coding an *unordered list*. As you know, you use the ul element to create a list, and you use the li element to create each item in a list. This is illustrated in the example in this figure.

In addition to containing text, list items can contain inline elements like links and images. They can also contain block elements like headings, paragraphs, and other lists. For example, the first list item in this figure contains text and a link. The second list item contains only text, but it's divided into two paragraphs. As you can see, the second paragraph is aligned with the first paragraph, but it doesn't have a bullet because it's part of the same list item.

Elements that create unordered lists

Element	Description
ul	Creates an unordered list.
li	Creates a list item for the list.

HTML for an unordered list with text, links, and paragraphs

```
<h3>San Joaquin Valley Town Hall Programs</h3>
<ul>
    <li>
        <p>Join us for a complimentary coffee hour at the
        <a href="saroyan.html">William Saroyan Theatre</a>, 9:15 to 10:15
        a.m. on the day of each lecture. The speakers usually attend this
        very special event.</p>
    </li>
    <li>
        <p>Extend the excitement of Town Hall by purchasing tickets to the
        post-lecture luncheons. This unique opportunity allows you to ask
        more questions of the speakers--plus spend extra time meeting new
        Town Hall friends.</p>
        <p>A limited number of tickets are available. Call (559) 555-1212
        for reservations by the Friday preceding the event.</p>
    </li>
</ul>
```

The list in a web browser

San Joaquin Valley Town Hall Programs

- Join us for a complimentary coffee hour at the William Saroyan
  Theatre, 9:15 to 10:15 a.m. on the day of each lecture. The
  speakers usually attend this very special event.

- Extend the excitement of Town Hall by purchasing tickets to the
  post-lecture luncheons. This unique opportunity allows you to ask
  more questions of the speakers--plus spend extra time meeting new
  Town Hall friends.

  A limited number of tickets are available. Call (559) 555-1212 for
  reservations by the Friday preceding the event.

Description

- By default, an *unordered list* is displayed as a bulleted list, but you can change the
  bullets as shown in figure 7-8.
- An li element typically contains text, but it can also contain other inline elements
  such as links, as well as block elements such as paragraphs and other lists.

Figure 7-5   How to code unordered lists

How to code ordered lists

If you want to indicate that the items in a list have a sequence like the steps in a procedure, you can use an *ordered list*. To create an ordered list, you use the ol and li elements. These elements are presented in figure 7-6.

The only thing new here is the start attribute of the ol element. You can use this attribute to start a list at a value other than the default. You might want to do that if one list continues from a previous list. For example, this figure shows a procedure that's divided into two parts, and each part is coded as a separate list. Because the first list consists of three items, the start attribute of the second list is set to 4.

Keep in mind if you use the start attribute that it doesn't represent the actual value that's displayed. Instead, it represents the position of the item in the list. When you use decimal values to indicate the sequence of the items in a list as shown here, the position and the value are the same. Later in this chapter, though, you'll learn how to number lists using other values like alphabetic characters. In that case, a start value of 4 would represent the letter "D".

Elements that create ordered lists

Element	Description
ol	Creates an ordered list. You can include the start attribute to specify the starting value for the list. The value represents the position in the list. The default is 1.
li	Creates a list item for the list.

HTML for an ordered list that continues from another ordered list

```
<h3>How to use the WinZip Self Extractor program</h3>
<p>Before you start the WinZip Self Extractor</p>
<ol>
    <li>Create a text file that contains the message you want to be
    displayed when the executable starts.</li>
    <li>Create a batch file that copies the exercises starts, and store it
    in the main directory for the files to be zipped.</li>
    <li>Create the zip file.</li>
</ol>
<p>How to create an executable file</p>
<ol start="4">
    <li>Run the WinZip Self Extractor program and click through the first
    three dialog boxes.</li>
        .
        .
        .
    <li>Click the Next button to test the executable.</li>
</ol>
```

The lists in a web browser

How to use the WinZip Self Extractor program

Before you start the WinZip Self Extractor

1. Create a text file that contains the message you want to be displayed when the executable starts.
2. Create a batch file that copies the exercises starts, and store it in the main directory for the files to be zipped.
3. Create the zip file.

How to create an executable file

4. Run the WinZip Self Extractor program and click through the first three dialog boxes.
5. Enter the name of the zip file in the fourth dialog box.

9. Click through the eighth, ninth, and tenth dialog boxes, review the options you've set in the eleventh dialog box, and click the Next button to create the executable.
10. Click the Next button to test the executable.

Description

- By default, an *ordered list* is displayed as a numbered list, but you can change that as shown in figure 7-9.
- The start attribute has been deprecated, but it may be added back to HTML 5. It's most useful for continuing one list from a previous list.

Figure 7-6 How to code ordered lists

How to code nested lists

As I mentioned earlier, a list item can contain block elements, including other lists. When you code a list within another list, the lists are referred to as *nested lists*. Figure 7-7 illustrates how nested lists work.

If you look at the HTML in this figure, you'll see that it consists of three lists. The outer list is an unordered list that contains two list items. The first list item defines the first subheading shown in the web browser, along with the three steps that follow it. Then, the second list item defines the second subheading and the remaining steps.

To define the steps, an ordered list is defined within each list item of the unordered list. These lists are coded just like any other ordered list. Because they're nested within other lists, though, they're indented an additional amount.

HTML for ordered lists nested within an unordered list

```
<h3>How to use the WinZip Self Extractor program</h3>
<ul>
    <li>Before you start the WinZip Self Extractor
        <ol>
            <li>Create a text file that contains the message you want
            to be displayed when the executable starts.</li>
            <li>Create a batch file that copies the exercises starts and
            store it in the main directory for the files to be zipped.</li>
            <li>Create the zip file.</li>
        </ol>
    </li>
    <li>How to create an executable file
        <ol start="4">
            <li>Run the WinZip Self Extractor program and click through the
            first three dialog boxes.</li>
            <li>Enter the name of the zip file in the fourth dialog
            box.</li>
                .
                .
            <li>Click through the eighth, ninth, and tenth dialog boxes,
            review the options you've set in the eleventh dialog box, and
            click the Next button to create the executable.</li>
            <li>Click the Next button to test the executable.</li>
        </ol>
    </li>
</ul>
```

The lists in a web browser

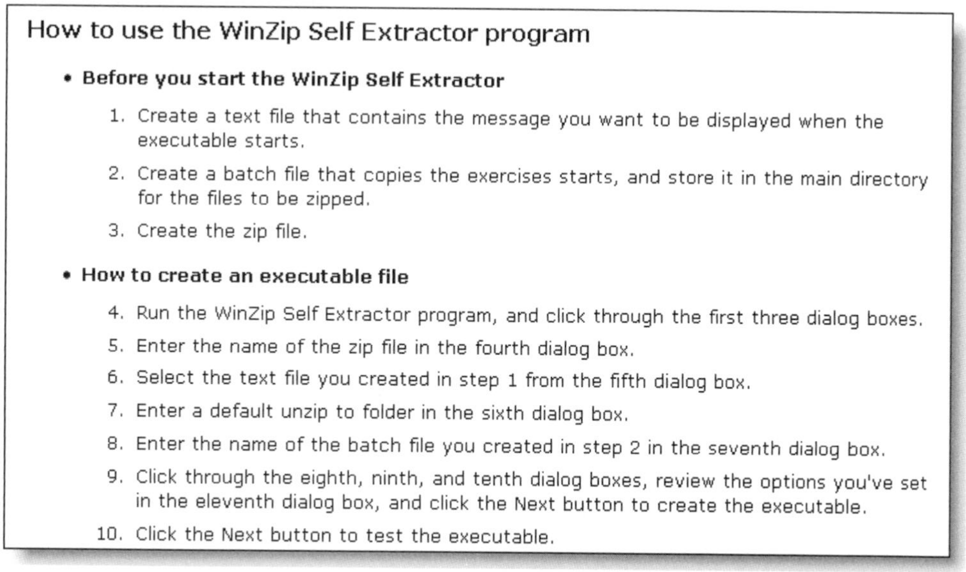

How to use the WinZip Self Extractor program

- **Before you start the WinZip Self Extractor**

  1. Create a text file that contains the message you want to be displayed when the executable starts.
  2. Create a batch file that copies the exercises starts, and store it in the main directory for the files to be zipped.
  3. Create the zip file.

- **How to create an executable file**

  4. Run the WinZip Self Extractor program, and click through the first three dialog boxes.
  5. Enter the name of the zip file in the fourth dialog box.
  6. Select the text file you created in step 1 from the fifth dialog box.
  7. Enter a default unzip to folder in the sixth dialog box.
  8. Enter the name of the batch file you created in step 2 in the seventh dialog box.
  9. Click through the eighth, ninth, and tenth dialog boxes, review the options you've set in the eleventh dialog box, and click the Next button to create the executable.
  10. Click the Next button to test the executable.

Description

- You can nest lists by coding one list as an item for another list.
- When you nest an unordered list within another list, the default bullet is a circle.

Figure 7-7   How to code nested lists

How to code definition lists

In addition to ordered and unordered lists, HTML provides for coding *definition lists*. As the name implies, definition lists are typically used to list terms and their definitions. Figure 7-8 shows how to code definition lists.

To code a definition list, you use the dl, dt, and dd elements. The dl element creates the definition list, the dt element creates the term, and the dd element creates the definition for the term. The example in this figure illustrates how this works. Here, the dt and dd elements are coded within the dl element that defines the list. Notice that the dt and dd elements are coded in pairs so there's a definition for each term.

When you code a definition list, you should know that the dt element can only contain text and inline elements. In contrast, dd elements can also contain block elements. For example, they can contain paragraphs likes the ones shown in the second list item in the unordered list in figure 7-5. And they can contain nested lists like the one shown in figure 7-7.

You should also know that you can code more than one dd element for each dt element. That's useful if you're creating a glossary and a term has more than one meaning. You can also code a single dd element for two or more dt elements. That's useful if you're defining terms that have the same definition.

Although definition lists are used most often to create glossaries like the one shown here, they can also be used for other purposes. In general, you can use them any time you want to create a list that consists of an item and a description. For example, you might want to use a definition list to describe a series of products or upcoming events.

Incidentally, I used some basic CSS formatting for the definition list in this figure. For instance, I applied the bold font-weight to the terms, and I adjusted the space after the heading and after each definition. In most cases, you'll need to do that too.

Elements that create definition lists

Element	Description
dl	Creates a definition list. It contains pairs of dt and dd elements.
dt	Creates a term in a definition list.
dd	Creates a definition in a definition list.

HTML for a definition list

```
<h3>Components of the Internet architecture</h3>
<dl>
    <dt>client</dt>
    <dd>A computer that accesses the web pages of a web application using a
    web browser.</dd>
    <dt>web server</dt>
    <dd>A computer that holds the files for each web application.</dd>
    <dt>local area network (LAN)</dt>
    <dd>A small network of computers that are near each other and can
    communicate with each other over short distances.</dd>
    <dt>wide area network (WAN)</dt>
    <dd>A network that consists of multiple LANs that have been connected
    together over long distances using routers.</dd>
    <dt>Internet exchange point</dt>
    <dd>Large routers that connect WANs together.</dd>
</dl>
```

The list in a web browser

Components of the Internet architecture

client
A computer that accesses the web pages of a web
application using a web browser.

web server
A computer that holds the files for each web application.

local area network (LAN)
A small network of computers that are near each other and
can communicate with each other over short distances.

wide area network (WAN)
A network that consists of multiple LANs that have been
connected together over long distances using routers.

Internet exchange point
Large routers that connect WANs together.

Description

- A *definition list* consists of terms and definitions for those terms.
- The dt element that creates a term in a definition list can only contain text. However, dd elements can contain block elements such as headings and paragraphs.
- You can use one or more dd elements to describe a dt element, and you can describe two or more dt elements with a single dd element.

Figure 7-8   How to code definition lists

How to format lists

Once you have a list coded the way you want it, you can format it so it looks the way you want. In most cases, that just means changing the spacing above and below the list and its items. But you can also change the bullets that are used for an unordered list. You can change the numbering system that's used for an ordered list. And you can change the vertical alignment of the items in a list. You'll learn these skills in the topics that follow.

How to change the bullets for an unordered list

To change the bullets for an unordered list, you can use the list-style-type and list-style-image properties shown in the first table in figure 7-9. In most cases, you'll use the list-style-type property to specify one of the values listed in the second table. By default, a list displays a solid round bullet, but you can specify a value of "circle" to display a circle bullet as shown in the first list in this figure. You can also specify a value of "square" to display a square bullet or "none" if you don't want to display any bullets.

If these predefined bullet types aren't adequate for your needs, you can display a custom image before each item in an unordered list. To do that, you start by getting or creating the image that you want to use. For instance, you can get many images that are appropriate for lists from the Internet. Often, these images are available for free or for a small charge. You'll learn more about how to do that in the next chapter. The other alternative is to use a graphics program to create your own image.

Once you have the image you want to use, you use the list-style-image property to specify the URL for the image file. This is illustrated by the second list in this figure, which uses an image named star.gif. As you can tell from the URL for the image, it's stored in a directory named images that's at the same level as the directory that contains the style sheet.

In most cases, you'll code the list-style-type and list-style-image properties for the ul element as shown in this figure. Then, this property is inherited by all the items in the list. Another way to do this, though, is to code these properties for the li element.

Properties for formatting unordered lists

Property	Description
list-style-type	Determines the type of bullet that's used for the items in the list. See the table below for possible values. The default is disc.
list-style-image	The URL for an image that's used as the bullet.

Values for the list-style-type property of an unordered list

Value	Description
disc	solid circle
circle	hollow circle
square	solid square
none	no bullet

HTML for two unordered lists

```
<p>Popular web browsers include</p>
<ul class="circle">
    <li>Internet Explorer</li>
    <li>Firefox</li>
    <li>Safari</li>
</ul>
<p>We have books on a variety of languages, including</p>
<ul class="star">
    <li><a href="books/javascript.html">JavaScript</a></li>
    <li><a href="books/visual_basic.html">Visual Basic</a></li>
    <li><a href="books/csharp.html">C#</a></li>
</ul>
```

CSS that changes the bullets

```
ul.circle { list-style-type: circle; }
ul.star { list-style-image: url("../images/star.gif"); }
```

The lists in a web browser

Popular web browsers include

o Internet Explorer
o Firefox
o Safari

We have books on a variety of languages, including

★ JavaScript
★ Visual Basic
★ C#

Description

- You can change the bullet that's displayed for an unordered list using the list-style-type property. To display an image for the bullet, use the list-style-image property.

Figure 7-9   How to change the bullets for an unordered list

How to change the numbering system for an ordered list

In addition to changing the bullets that are used for an unordered list, you can use the list-style-type property to change the numbering system that's used for an ordered list. Some of the most common values for this property are listed in the table at the top of figure 7-10, along with examples of the series of numbers or characters they generate.

By default, decimal values are used to number the items in an ordered list. To change that, you code the list-style-type property for the ol or li element. For the list in this figure, for example, you can see that I specified "upper-roman" for this property.

Common values for the list-style-type property of an ordered list

Value	Example
decimal	1, 2, 3, 4, 5 ...
decimal-leading-zero	01, 02, 03, 04, 05 ...
lower-alpha	a, b, c, d, e ...
upper-alpha	A, B, C, D, E ...
lower-roman	i, ii, iii, iv, v ...
upper-roman	I, II, III, IV, V ...

HTML for an ordered list

```
<h3>How to edit a chapter</h3>
<ol>
    <li>Read the printed figures and text, and mark any changes on these
    pages.</li>
    <li>If necessary, analyze the paragraphs for a topic or subtopic.</li>
    <li>Use Word to revise the figures and text based on your marks. Then,
    print the changed pages.</li>
    <li>Proofread just the printed changes and make any corrections.</li>
    <li>Use Word to do some final checking.</li>
    <li>If you&rsquo;ve made extensive changes, proofread the entire chapter
    and make any corrections.</li>
</ol>
```

CSS that formats the list

```
ol { list-style-type: upper-roman; }
```

The list in a web browser

How to edit a chapter

   I. Read the printed figures and text, and mark any changes on these pages.

  II. If necessary, analyze the paragraphs for a topic or subtopic.

 III. Use Word to revise the figures and text based on your marks. Then, print the changed pages.

 IV. Proofread just the printed changes and make any corrections.

  V. Use Word to do some final checking.

 VI. If you've made extensive changes, proofread the entire chapter and make any corrections.

Description

- You can change the numbering system that's used for an ordered list using the list-style-type property. The default is decimal.

Figure 7-10   How to change the numbering system for an ordered list

How to change the alignment of list items

Often, the items in a list will be aligned the way you want them. However, you will usually want to adjust the spacing before and after a list, and you will sometimes want to adjust the spacing before or after the list items. Beyond that, you may want to change the indentation of the items in a list or the amount of space between the bullets or numbers in a list.

In figure 7-11, you can see the HTML and the CSS for a formatted list. In this case, the space between lines has been adjusted. But more important, the list items have been moved left so the bullets are aligned on the left margin instead of being indented. Also, the space between the bullets and the items has been decreased. If you compare this list to the one in figure 7-5, you can clearly see the differences.

In the CSS for the list in this figure, you can see that the margins for the unordered list and its list items have been set to 0. Then, the left padding for the ul element has been set to 1 em. This determines the left alignment of the items in the list. Often, though, you have to experiment with this setting to get the alignment the way you want it.

Similarly, the left padding for the li element is set to .25 ems. This determines the distance between the bullet and the text for an item. Here again, though, you will often have to experiment with this value to get it the way you want it.

For ordered lists, you can use the same techniques to adjust the indentation and to adjust the space between the number and the text in an item. Remember, though, that the numbers in an ordered list are aligned on the right. So if the numbers vary in width as in the ordered list shown in figure 7-10, you have to adjust your values accordingly.

HTML for an unordered list

```
<div id="page">
    <h3>Popular web browsers include</h3>
    <ul>
        <li>Internet Explorer</li>
        <li>Firefox</li>
        <li>Safari</li>
        <li>Opera</li>
        <li>Chrome</li>
    </ul>
</div>
```

CSS that aligns the list items

```
#page {
    margin: 0;
    padding: 2em; }
h3 {
    margin: 0;
    padding: .5em 0 .25em; }
ul {
    margin: 0;
    padding-left: 1em;    /* determines left alignment */}
li {
    margin: 0;
    padding-left: .25em;    /* space between bullet and text */
    padding-bottom: .25em;  /* space after line item */}
```

The list in a web browser

Popular web browsers include

- Internet Explorer
- Firefox
- Safari
- Opera
- Chrome

Description

- You can use margins and padding to control the indentation for the items in an ordered or unordered list, and to control the space between the bullets or numbers and the text that follows.

- You can also use margins and padding to remove the indentation from the items in a list as shown above. However, this doesn't work as well with ordered lists because the numbers or letters are aligned at the right.

- You can remove the indentation from the definitions in a definition list by setting the left margin of the definitions to zero.

- These techniques work best if you specify the padding and margins using ems.

Figure 7-11   How to change the alignment of list items

Perspective

Now that you've completed this chapter, you should have a good perspective on what you can do with links and lists. However, you can't be expected to remember all of the details. Instead, you can use this chapter as a reference whenever you need it.

Terms

link	ordered list
anchor	nested list
navigation bar	definition list
unordered list	

Summary

- You typically code an a element to create a *link* that loads another web page. By default the link is in blue and underlined, and its color changes if it has been visited or if it's active (mouse pressed down on it, but not released).
- You can also use an a element to start an email message by coding the href attribute as "mailto:" followed by the email address.
- You can use pseudocode selectors in CSS to change the defaults for links and to change the styles when the mouse hovers over a link.
- You can use the accesskey attribute of an a element to provide a shortcut key for activating the link, and you can use the target attribute to load the linked page in a new browser window.
- An *anchor* is a location on a page that can be linked to. To create an anchor, you use the id attribute of an a element. To go to the anchor, you specify that id in the href attribute of another a element.
- A *navigation bar* can be created by coding a series of elements within a block element like a division or paragraph. Often, the underlines for the links are removed because users understand that the components of a navigation bar are links.
- An *unordered list* is displayed as a bulleted list, but you can change the bullets with CSS.
- An *ordered list* is displayed as a numbered list, but you can change the types of numbers that are used with CSS.
- A *definition list* consists of terms and definitions.
- In most cases, you need to use CSS to change some of the spacing before, after, or within a list. In some cases, you may also want to change the indentation of the list items or the space between the bullet or number and the list item.

Exercise 7-1   Lists, links, and navigation bars

This exercise will give you a chance to work with lists, links, and navigation bars. When you're through, your web page should look like the one below.

Review the starting files for this web page

1. Open these files in your text editor:

   ```
   c:\html_css\ch07\bait_shop\lists.html
   c:\html_css\ch07\bait_shop\styles\lists.css
   ```

   Then, launch the HTML file in a browser so you can see what this page looks like and how much work you have to do with it.

2. In the CSS file, note that comments are included that show you where you can code the rule sets that you will need for the lists and the navigation bar.

Adjust the formatting and alignment of the bulleted lists

3. In the CSS, create a rule set for ul elements that sets the margins to 0 and the left padding to 1 em. That should close the spacing before and after each list and move the lists left.

4. Create a rule set for li elements that sets the margins to 0 and the bottom padding to .25 em. That should improve the spacing of the list items.

Add anchors to the lists and link to them

5. In the HTML, add an anchor named "top" to the heading for the first list in the main division. Then, add anchors named "list2", "list3", "list4", and "list5" to the headings for the next four lists.

6. Within the p elements that "Return to top", code a elements that return to the "top" anchor. Next, finish the href attributes in the links in the first column so they go to the anchors for the five lists. Then, test these changes.

Change the bullets in the first three lists

7. Change the bullets in the first list to circles. To do that, use the class attribute named "circle" that's coded for this list as the selector for your CSS.

8. Change the third list to an ordered list. To do that, change the list from a ul element to an ol element. Then, test to see that this changes the formatting. To fix that, create a rule set for ol elements that sets the margins to zero and the left padding to 2 ems.

9. Change the bullets in the second list to the fish favicon that's in the images directory. To do that, use the id attribute called "fish_list" that's coded for this ul element as the selector for a rule set that changes the bullets to the favicon. Test this in both IE and Firefox, and you'll see that it's going to take some adjustments to get this to look right in both browsers.

10. To fix this, set the margins for the fish list to zero and the left padding to 2 ems. Then, create a rule set for the li elements within the fish_list element that sets the margins to zero and the left padding to .5 em. This padding is used to set the space between the favicons and the text. When you test this in both browsers, you'll see that this works pretty good but not great. In the next chapter, though, you'll learn other ways to get the same effect.

Add the navigation bar

11. Add the navigation bar to the web page using figure 7-4 as a guide. First, code the HTML for the bar in a division named "navigation_bar" that comes after the header division. Then, add the CSS for the division and for its a elements. To make that work, put a 2 pixel blue border around the navigation bar, but just a right border on the a elements. Also, remove the underlines from the a elements.

12. Add a "current" class to the a element for the current page (Lists). Then, code a rule set for that class that changes the font color to the same one that's used for the tag line in the header. To make this work, you may have to qualify the class name as in: #navigation_bar a.current.

Make the image in the header a link that goes to the index page

13. In the HTML, put an a element around the image in the header so when you click on it the index page is displayed. Then, add a rule to the rule set for that image so the border around the link isn't displayed.

Test, adjust, and experiment

14. Test to make sure all of the available links work and that the margins and padding look the way they ought to. Then, experiment to make sure you understand everything. When you're through, close all of the files.

8

How to work with images

In chapter 3, you learned about the three types of images you can use on a web page, and you learned the basic skills for including images on a web page. Now, this chapter will expand upon those skills. It will also show you how to use an image editor to work with the images for your web pages. When you finish this chapter, you should have all the skills you need for working with images.

Basic skills for working with images

In the topics that follow, you'll learn the basic skills for working with images. This information will review and expand upon the skills you learned in chapter 3.

Types of images for the Web

Figure 8-1 presents the three types of images you can use on a web page. To start, *JPEG files* are commonly used for photographs and scanned images, because these files can represent millions of colors and they use a type of compression that can display complex images with a small file size.

Although JPEG files lose information when they're compressed, they typically contain high quality images to begin with so this loss of information isn't noticeable on a web page. Similarly, although JPEG files don't support transparency, it usually doesn't make sense for any of the colors in a photograph to be transparent.

In contrast, *GIF files* are typically used for simple illustrations or logos that require a limited number of colors. Two advantages of storing images in this format are (1) that they can be compressed without losing any information, and (2) that one of the colors in the image can be transparent. You'll learn more about transparency later in this chapter.

A GIF file can also contain an *animated image*. An animated image consists of a series of images called *frames*. When you display an animated image, each frame is displayed for a preset amount of time, usually fractions of a second. Because of that, the image appears to be moving. For example, the two globes in this figure are actually two of 30 frames that are stored in the same GIF file. When this file is displayed, the globe appears to be rotating.

Unlike the GIF and JPEG formats, which have been used for years in print materials, *PNG files* were developed specifically for the Web. In particular, this format was developed as a replacement for the GIF format. The PNG advantages over the GIF format include better compression, support for millions of colors, and support for variable transparency.

Image types

Type	Description
JPEG	Typically used for photographs and scanned images because it uses a type of compression that can display complex images with a small file size. A JPEG file can represent millions of colors, loses information when compressed, and doesn't support transparency.
GIF	Typically used for logos, small illustrations such as clip art, and animated images. A GIF file can represent up to 256 colors, doesn't lose information when compressed, and supports transparency on a single color.
PNG	Typically used as a replacement for still GIF images. Compressed PNG files are typically smaller than GIF compressed files, although no information is lost. This format can represent millions of colors and supports transparency on multiple colors. Although PNG files are supported by most modern browsers, they aren't supported by older browsers including IE 6 and earlier and they have limited support on mobile devices.

Typical JPEG images

Typical GIF images

Description

- *JPEG* (Joint Photographic Experts Group) images are commonly used for the photographs and images of a web page. Although information is lost when you compress a JPEG file, the reduced quality of the image usually isn't noticeable.

- *GIF* (Graphic Interchange Format) images are commonly used for logos and small illustrations. They can also be used for animated images.

- The *PNG* (Portable Network Graphics) format was developed specifically for the web as a replacement for GIF files. Although this format can also be used for photographs, JPEG is the preferred format for photographs because it results in smaller file sizes.

Figure 8-1   Types of images for the Web

How to include an image on a page

To include an image on a web page, you use the img element. Figure 8-2 presents the most common attributes of this element. Because you saw these attributes in chapter 3, you shouldn't have any trouble understanding how they work.

The HTML shown in this figure contains two img elements. Although they both display the same image, the first element includes height and width attributes. These attributes can be used to indicate the actual size of the image. That way, the browser can reserve the correct amount of space for the image on the page as the page is being loaded. Without these properties, the flow of the page will change each time an image is displayed. This can lead to a poor user experience, particularly if the images are large and the Internet connection is slow.

One drawback of specifying the size of an image is that if the size changes, you'll need to change the HTML. If the image is only used on one page, that's probably not a problem. If it's used on many pages, though, you may want to omit the height and width attributes if you think the size of the image will change.

How to resize an image

Figure 8-2 also shows how to resize an image. Although you might think that you would use the height and width attributes of the img element to do that, that's not the best approach. That's because, even if you specify a size that's smaller than the full size of the image, the image still has to be downloaded at its full size before it's reduced. The best way to resize an image, then, is to use an image editor to create an image that's the size you need. You'll learn how to do that later in this chapter.

If you do need to resize an image after it's downloaded, you should do that using the CSS height and width properties. Although the full image must still be downloaded when you use this technique, this separates the formatting of the image from its definition in the HTML. In the CSS in this figure, I resized the second image (the one with the id "small") so it's half of its original size. Note that although I specified both the height and width in this example, that's not necessary. Instead, you can specify the height or width and the other value will be calculated automatically based on the original proportions of the image.

Attributes of the <img> tag

Attribute	Description
src	Specifies the relative or absolute URL of the image to display. It is required.
alt	Specifies alternate text to display in place of the image. It is required for XHTML, and it is recommended whenever it can help the visually impaired.
longdesc	Specifies a long description of the image.
height	Specifies the height of the image in pixels.
width	Specifies the width of the image in pixels.

Properties for sizing an image

Property	Description
height	A relative or absolute value that specifies the height of the image if the height is different from its original size.
width	A relative or absolute value that specifies the width of the image if the width is different from its original size.

The HTML for two images

```
<p><img src="images/lilies.jpg" alt="lilies"
        height="150px" width="200px" />  
    <img id="small" src="images/lilies.jpg" alt="lilies" /></p>
```

CSS for resizing the second image

```
#small {
    height: 75px;
    width: 100px; }
```

The images in a web browser

Description

- You should use the height and width attributes of the <img> tag only to specify the size of the existing image. That way, the browser can reserve the right amount of space for the image and continue rendering the page even if the image is still being loaded.

- If you need to display an image at a size other than its full size, you can use the CSS height and width properties. A better solution, though, is to use an image editor to create an image that's the right size.

Figure 8-2   How to include and resize an image

How to align an image vertically

When you include an image on a web page, you may want to align it with the in-line elements that surround it. If an image is preceded or followed by text, for example, you may want to align the image with the top, middle, or bottom of the text. To do that, you use the vertical-align property shown in figure 8-3.

To indicate the alignment you want to use, you typically specify one of the keywords listed in this figure. If you specify text-bottom, for example, the image is aligned with the bottom of the surrounding text. In contrast, if you specify bottom, the image is aligned with the bottom of the box that contains the surrounding text. In most cases, the bottom of the text and the bottom of the box are the same. The exception is if a line height is specified for the box. In that case, the text is centered in the box. Then, if you specify bottom for the image alignment, the image will be aligned at the bottom of the box, which is below the bottom of the text. The top and text-top keywords work the same way.

The middle keyword is useful because it lets you center an image with the surrounding text. This is illustrated in the example in this figure. Here, the HTML includes three paragraphs, each with an image followed by some text. When I didn't specify the vertical alignment for the images, the bottom of each image was aligned with the bottom of the text. When I specified middle for the vertical alignment, though, the center of each image was aligned with the center of the text.

Note that I specified a right margin for the images for both the aligned and unaligned examples to create space between the images and the text. In addition to margins, you can use padding and borders with images. This works just like it does for block elements.

The property for aligning images vertically

Property	Description
vertical-align	A relative or absolute value or a keyword that determines the vertical alignment of an image. See the table below for common keywords.

Common keywords for the vertical-align property

Keyword	Description
bottom	Aligns the bottom of the image box with the bottom of the box that contains the surrounding in-line elements.
middle	Aligns the midpoint of the image box with the midpoint of the containing block.
top	Aligns the top of the image box with the top of the box that contains the surrounding in-line elements.
text-bottom	Aligns the bottom of the image box with the bottom of the text in the containing block.
text-top	Aligns the top of the image box with the top of the text in the containing block.

The HTML for a web page with three images

```
<h2>To order now:</h2>
<p><img src="images/computer.gif" alt="computer" /><b>Web:</b>
www.murach.com</p>
<p><img src="images/telephone.gif" alt="phone" /><b>Phone:</b>
1-800-221-5528</p>
<p><img src="images/fax.gif" alt="fax" /><b>Fax:</b> 1-559-440-0963</p>
```

CSS that aligns the images in the middle of the text

```
img {
    vertical-align: middle;
    margin-right: 10px; }
```

The images in a web browser before and after they're aligned

Description

- If you use pixels, points, or ems to specify the value for the vertical-align property, the image is raised if the value is positive and lowered if it's negative. If you specify a percent, the image is raised or lowered based on the percentage of the line height.

- You can use margins, padding, and borders with images just like you can with block elements. The result is a box that contains the image.

Figure 8-3   How to align an image vertically

How to float an image

In chapter 6, you learned how to float block elements on top of other page content. You also saw a web page in that chapter that contained two floated images. Now, figure 8-4 reinforces what you learned in that chapter.

At the top of this figure, you can see the two properties for floating images: float and clear. These properties work just like they do for block elements. You use the float property to determine whether the image should be floated to the right or to the left. And you use the clear property to determine whether an element that follows a floated image allows the floated image to its left or right. This figure illustrates how these properties work.

In the HTML in this figure, you can see that the first element defines an image. This image is followed by an unordered list and a paragraph. In the CSS that follows, you can see that the image is floated to the left. In addition, top and bottom margins are specified for the image to create space between the image and the text that precedes and follows it. Note that it's not necessary to specify a right margin for the image because the items in the list are indented by default. Also note that it's not necessary to specify a width when you float an image. That's because the width can be determined from the actual width of the image.

Finally, notice that the clear property with a value of "left" is specified for the paragraph that follows the list. Because of that, this paragraph won't flow into the space to the right of the image. Instead, the text starts below the image.

The properties for floating images

Property	Description
float	A keyword that determines how an image is floated. Possible values are left, right, and none. None is the default.
clear	A keyword that determines if an element that follows a floated element flows into the space left by the floated element. Possible values are left, right, both, and none. None is the default.

Some of the HTML for a web page

```
<img src="images/students.jpg" alt="students" width="256px"
    height="171px" />
<ul>
    <li>in college and university MIS programs that focus on providing
    students with practical, real-world experience</li>
    <li>by technical institutes and community colleges that focus on the
    skills that employers are looking for</li>
    <li>in Continuing Ed and Extension programs where the students are
    professionals who are expanding their skills</li>
</ul>
<p id="last">So if your program fits one of those profiles, please take
a look at our books. I&rsquo;m confident you&rsquo;ll discover a new level
of structure, clarity, and relevance that will benefit both you and your
students.</p>
```

CSS that floats the image and clears the last paragraph

```
img {
    float: left;
    margin-top: 15px;
    margin-bottom: 10px; }
#last { clear: left; }
```

The HTML in a web browser

College instructors:
Teach your students using the books the professionals use

Although our books are written for professional programmers who need to master new job skills, there have always been instructors teaching job-oriented curricula who've adopted our books. For example, our books are used:

- in college and university MIS programs that focus on providing students with practical, real-world experience
- by technical institutes and community colleges that focus on the skills that employers are looking for
- in Continuing Ed and Extension programs where the students are professionals who are expanding their skills

So if your program fits one of those profiles, please take a look at our books. I'm confident you'll discover a new level of structure, clarity, and relevance that will benefit both you and your students.

Description

- You can use the same techniques to float an image as you use to float a block element. See chapter 6 for more information.

Figure 8-4   How to float an image

How to use an image editor

Even if you have the images that you want to use on a web page, they may not be formatted or sized properly. In that case, you can use an image editor to make the necessary modifications. Many image editors are available, from those that are free to those that cost several hundred dollars. One of the most popular with professional web developers and one of the most expensive is Adobe Photoshop.

In the topics that follow, I'll show you how to use a moderately-priced consumer product from Adobe called Photoshop Elements. This product illustrates the basic features that your image editor should provide. If you would like to try using it, you can download a 30-day free trial from the Adobe web site.

As you read the topics that follow, keep in mind that the larger the image files are and the more images a web page contains, the slower the page is loaded. But web site users like web pages that load quickly. As a result, one of the goals of using an image editor is to keep the image files as small as possible without losing too much image quality.

An introduction to Photoshop Elements

Photoshop Elements is designed to be used for both organizing and editing images. To edit images, you click on the Edit button from the welcome screen that's displayed when you start the program. Then, the main screen for editing images shown in figure 8-5 is displayed.

To locate and open an image for editing, you use the Open dialog box shown here. When you open an image for editing, you should realize that Photoshop Elements supports only the RGB (red, green, blue) format, which is the format that's used to display color images. It doesn't support the CMYK (cyan, magenta, yellow, black) format that's used by most printers to print color images. Because of that, you'll need to be sure that your images are in RGB format before you open them in Photoshop Elements. If they aren't, you'll need a product such as Adobe Photoshop Creative Suite to convert them from CMYK format to RGB format.

Once you open an image, you can use a variety of features to modify it. In this chapter, I'll focus on the features for modifying images so they're appropriate for the Web. These features are available from the Save For Web dialog box shown in the next four figures.

Note that when you save an image for the Web using Photoshop Elements, it's always saved with a resolution of 72 ppi (points per inch). That's because this is the resolution that most monitors support. In addition, a lower resolution means a smaller file size and faster loading.

The main Photoshop Elements screen for editing images

Description

- When you start Photoshop Elements, a welcome screen is displayed. From this screen, you can click the Edit button to use the image editor.

- To open an image in Photoshop Elements, use the File→Open command to display the Open dialog box. Then, locate and select the file you want to open. You can also use the File→Open Recently Edited File command to select the file you want to open from a list of recently opened files.

- To modify an image so it's appropriate for use on a web page, use the File→Save for Web command to display the Save For Web dialog box. See figures 8-6 though 8-9 for details.

Figure 8-5   An introduction to Photoshop Elements

How to size an image

Figure 8-6 shows the Save for Web dialog box that you use to modify images for the Web. This dialog box displays the original image in the left window and the image with any changes you make in the right window. That way, you can see how the changes affect the original image.

In this figure, I've outlined the controls for working with the size of an image. To start, you can see the current width and height of the image in pixels in the Original Size group box. In this case, the image is 800 pixels wide and 600 pixels high.

Below the Original Size group box is the New Size group box. Here, you can enter a new width and height, or you can enter a percent to have the new width and height calculated for you. In this example, I've entered 50 for the percent so the image will be reduced to half its original size. As you can see, the width and height values have been changed accordingly.

By default, the Constrain Proportions option is checked so the original proportions of the image will be maintained. Then, if you enter a width or height value, the other value will be changed automatically. If you remove the check mark from this option, it's possible to distort the image by entering width and height values that aren't proportionate to the original values. Since that's usually not what you want, you'll typically leave this option checked.

After you enter the appropriate size, you can click the Apply button to apply it to the image. When you do, both the original image and the new image are displayed at the new size. That way, you can compare how they appear when you change other settings. Note, however, that the new image hasn't been saved at this point. To do that, you have to click the OK button and then complete the dialog box that's displayed.

By the way, you might notice in this figure that even though the original image is a JPEG file, the resized image is displayed as a GIF file. That's the default the first time you display this dialog box. If you change this setting or any of the other settings, though, the new settings will be used the next time you display this dialog box.

The controls for working with the size of an image

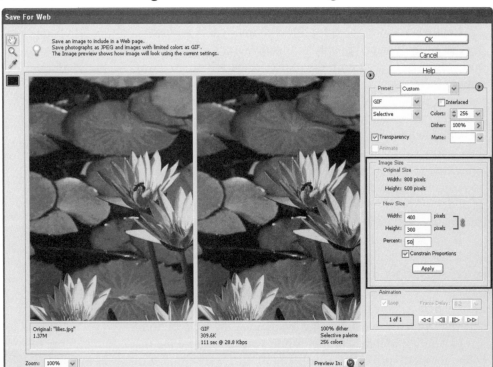

Description

- The Image Size group at the right side of the Save For Web dialog box displays the current width and height of the image in pixels along with controls for changing the width and height.

- To change the size of an image, you can enter new values in the Width and Height text boxes, or you can enter a value in the Percent text box to resize the image to a percent of its original size. If you enter a percent, the width and height values are changed automatically.

- The Constrain Proportions option determines if the original proportions of the image are maintained. If this option is selected, you can enter just a height or width and the other value will be calculated automatically. This is usually what you want.

- To apply the new size to the image, click the Apply button. Then, the image is redisplayed at the new size.

- To save the image at its new size, click the OK button. Then, enter a name for the file and select the location where you want to save it in the Save Optimized As dialog box that's displayed.

Figure 8-6   How to size an image

How to change the image type and quality

Figure 8-7 shows the Save For Web dialog box with the controls for changing the image type and quality outlined. Here, I selected the JPEG Medium option from the Preset drop-down list. When I did that, the JPEG and Medium options were selected from the next two drop-down lists, and the Quality value was changed to 30. Although you can't see it here, these values were also applied to the image in the right window.

The Medium option indicates that medium compression will be used, and the Quality value indicates the actual compression amount. To specify a custom value for the compression, you can enter any value between zero and 100. Or, you can click the arrow at the right side of the Quality control and use the pop-up slider to specify a value. Note that the higher the compression value, the less information will be lost and the larger the file will be.

If you select GIF or PNG-8 for the file format, the controls that are available change as shown in this figure. Here, the drop-down list below the format specifies the algorithm that's used to create the color table for the image. Selective is the default, and it's the value you'll use most often. For more information on how the algorithms work, see the online documentation for this software, which you can display by clicking the Help button.

In addition to the color algorithm, you can choose the maximum number of colors for a GIF or PNG-8 file. Like GIF images, an image that uses the PNG-8 format can have a maximum of 256 characters. In most cases, you'll use this format only if you need the variable transparency it provides. Whichever format you choose, you typically won't change the maximum number of colors.

Another option that's available for GIF and PNG-8 files controls the amount of dithering that's used. *Dithering* is a technique that's used to make it appear as if an image has more colors than it actually does. To do that, pixels of different colors are placed side-by-side so they appear to blend into another color. For example, red and blue pixels may be arranged so they appear to be a purple color that doesn't exist in the color palette. By default, GIF and PNG-8 images are dithered 100% so as many colors as possible can be represented. However, because dithering leads to larger file sizes, you may want to reduce this percent if an image doesn't require as much dithering.

The PNG-24 format is similar to the JPEG format in that it can support millions of colors. Because of that, you can't select the maximum number of colors for this type of image like you can for a PNG-8 file, you can't select a color algorithm, and you can't select the amount of dithering. In addition, you can't select the amount of compression like you can for a JPEG file because the compression algorithm is fixed.

By default, an image is displayed on a page only after the entire file has been loaded. In many cases, that's okay. If a page contains large images, however, or the user has a slow Internet connection, it can make viewing the page unpleasant. One way to improve the user experience is to create a *progressive JPEG*, an *interlaced GIF*, or an *interlaced PNG*. To do that, you can select the Progressive or Interlaced option. Then, the image will fade into view as the file is loaded.

The controls for changing the image type and quality of a JPEG file

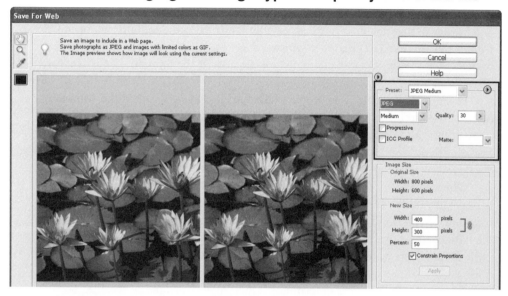

The controls for GIF, PNG-8, and PNG-24 files

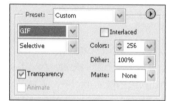  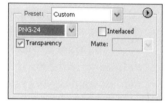

Description

- The first group of controls at the right side of the Save For Web dialog box lets you select the type of image and other values related to the quality of an image. The available controls depend on the type of image you choose.

- To change the file type and quality, you can select one of the values from the Preset drop-down list. Or, you can select a file type and then set the other values manually.

- The default values for GIF and PNG-8 files of 256 colors and 100% dither are usually what you want. If you select the PNG-24 file type, the color and dither options aren't available since this file type provides for millions of colors just like JPEG files.

- You can select a predefined quality for JPEG files from the drop-down list, or you can use the Quality control to select a specific quality. The lower the quality, the better the compression.

- You can also create a *progressive JPEG* or an *interlaced GIF* or *PNG* by selecting the appropriate option. These images fade into view as the image file is loaded rather than waiting to be displayed until after the entire file is loaded. This can improve the experience for users who have slow Internet connections.

Figure 8-7   How to change the image type and quality

How to work with animated images

Earlier in this chapter, you learned that a GIF file can contain two or more *frames* that are used to create an *animated image*. When you save an animated image for the Web, you can control some aspects of the animation. Figure 8-8 shows you how.

To start, if you want to animate a GIF file, you need to select the Animate option. This option is in the same group as the controls for setting the image type, colors, and dither, and it's available only if the file contains multiple frames. If you don't select the Animate option, only the first frame will be displayed.

When you select the Animate option, the controls in the Animation group become available. The first option, Loop, determines if the frames in the file are repeated. If you don't select this option, each frame is displayed only once. In the case of the globe shown in this figure, that means that the globe will rotate only once. If you want it to rotate continuously, you should select the Loop option.

The Frame Delay value determines how long each frame in the file is displayed. The default is .2 seconds, but you can change that value if you want the animation to appear to move faster or slower. To change the Frame Delay value, you can either enter a new value in the control or select a predefined value from the drop-down list.

If you want to view the different frames in a file, you can use the buttons with the arrowheads on them. These buttons display the first, previous, next, and last frames. As you move from one frame to another, the number of the current frame is displayed to the left of the buttons along with the total number of frames.

The controls for working with an animated image

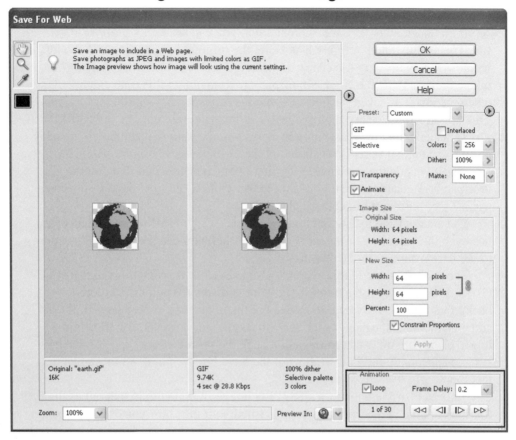

Description

- If a GIF file contains two or more frames, you can cause the frames to be displayed in sequence by selecting the Animate option.

- To control how an animated image works, you can use the controls in the Animation group. The Loop option determines whether the frames are repeated continuously, and the Frame Delay drop-down list lets you select how many seconds each frame is displayed.

- The controls at the bottom of this group indicate which frame is displayed and the total number of frames. They also let you move to the first, previous, next, and last frames.

Figure 8-8   How to work with animated images

How to work with transparency and mattes

If an image includes a transparent color, you can save it as a GIF or PNG file. This is illustrated in figure 8-9. Here, the original image, shown in the left window, is a Photoshop file. The checkerboard around the starburst in this image indicates that the color is transparent. To maintain this transparent color when the image is saved, just be sure that the Transparency option is selected. This option will also save multiple levels of transparent colors in a PNG file.

To understand how *transparency* works, you need to realize that an image is always rectangular. This is illustrated in the example in this figure. Here, the area that's outside the starburst in the first image is white, and that color is not transparent. Because of that, you can see the white when the image is displayed against a background of another color.

The area outside the starburst in the second image is also white. In this case, however, the color is transparent. Because of that, you can see through the color to the background color behind it.

The second image in this example also uses a *matte*. A matte is useful if a GIF or PNG image with a transparent color is displayed against a colored background. Without a matte, the edges of the image can appear jagged. If you add a matte that's the same color as the background, however, it will help the image blend into the background and reduce the jagged edges. You can see how a matte appears in the right window of the Save For Web dialog box shown in this figure.

You can also use a matte with a JPEG image. When you do that, all of the transparent area in the original image is filled with the color you choose. Then, that area appears to be transparent when the image is displayed against a background that's the same color as the matte.

An image with a transparent color and a matte

An image without transparency and with transparency and a matte

Description

- GIF and PNG files support *transparency*. Then, the transparent color is represented by a checkerboard pattern as illustrated above.

- To save a Photoshop file with a transparent color as a GIF or PNG file, just select the Transparency option.

- If you will be displaying an image against a color background, you use a *matte* to help the image blend into the background color. To do that, select that color from the Matte drop-down list or the Choose a Color dialog box that's available from that list.

- You can also use a matte with a JPEG file. Then, the entire transparent area is filled in with the matte color.

Figure 8-9   How to work with transparency and mattes

Four more skills for working with images

In addition to the skills you've already learned for working with images, there are some other skills you should be familiar with. You'll use some of these skills with most of the web sites you develop.

How to get images and icons

For most web sites, most of the photographs that you use will be your own, and you may also create most the graphic images that you use. But even then, you may want to get some images and icons from another source. The easiest way to do that is to copy or download them from another web site.

Figure 8-10 lists several of the most popular web sites you can use to get and search for images and icons. For example, www.freefoto.com, openphoto.com, and www.sxc.hu are three of the most popular web sites for getting images. Similarly, www.smashingmagazine.com is a popular site for finding sets of icons.

Although you can use many of the images and icons that are available on the Web for free, most require a Creative Commons license. The types of licenses that are available and the conditions required by these licenses are summarized in this figure. As you can see, all of the licenses require attribution, which means that you must give credit to the author of the image or the web site that provided the image. The other license conditions determine how an image can be shared, whether it can be used for commercial purposes, and whether you can derive new images from the existing image.

Stock photos are special images that are typically produced in a studio. For example, the JPEG file that you saw in figure 8-4 is a stock photo. You must pay for these types of images, and they can be quite expensive.

Incidentally, you can also get an image or the link to an image from another site by right-clicking on the image and selecting the appropriate command from the shortcut menu. Then, if you save the link to the image in the href attribute of an <image> tag, your web page will display the image that's actually stored on the other site. This is known as "hot linking" and it is highly discouraged unless you have an agreement with the other site. If, for example, you agree to provide a link to another site and that site agrees to provide a link to your site, this is a quick way to get the images and URLs that you will need.

Creative Commons license conditions for images and icons

Conditions	Description
Attribution	You can use the image and images derived from it as long as you give credit as requested by the author or web site providing the image.
Share Alike	You can distribute the image based on the license that governs the original work.
Non-Commercial	You can use the image and images derived from it for non-commercial purposes only.
No Derivative Works	You can use only the original image and not images derived from it.

Creative Commons licenses

- Attribution
- Attribution No Derivatives
- Attribution Non-Commercial Share Alike
- Attribution Share Alike
- Attribution Non-Commercial
- Attribution Non-Commercial No Derivatives

Popular web sites for images

- www.freefoto.com
- openphoto.net
- www.sxc.hu

Popular web sites for stock photos

- www.istockphoto.com
- us.fotolia.com
- www.gettyimages.com

Popular search engines for stock photos

- search.creativecommons.org
- everystockphoto.com

Popular web site for finding icons

- www.smashingmagazine.com

Description

- Many of the images and icons that are available from the Web are licensed under a Creative Commons license. The license can restrict the use of an image to one or more of the conditions listed above. The most common condition is attribution.
- Stock photos are typically produced in studios and can be purchased for a one-time fee of one dollar to several hundred dollars.
- The Smashing Magazine web site provides information on web related topics. From the Graphics section of this site, you can find links to a variety of icon sets.
- You can also search for specific images and icons from a generic search engine such as Google.

Figure 8-10   How to get images and icons

How to create and work with thumbnails

Because large images can make loading a page inefficient, you may want to display the images at a smaller size initially. Then, you can provide a way for the user to display the larger image if necessary. For example, many e-commerce sites will display a small image of each product by default. Then, the user can click on a link to see a larger image.

Smaller images are also useful if a page contains several images. That can save space on the page and make viewing the page easier. Regardless of why you use smaller images, they're typically referred to as *thumbnails*. Although this name implies that an image is about the size of your thumbnail, it can be used to refer to any small image.

Figure 8-11 presents an example that uses thumbnails. At the top of this figure, you can see part of a web page with six thumbnails. If you look at the HTML for this page, you can see that the thumbnail images are coded within a elements. That way, when the user clicks on an image, the page specified on the href attribute of the a element will be displayed. In this case, the page displays a description of the photo along with a larger image.

To create thumbnails, you can use the techniques you learned in figure 8-6 for sizing an image. Then, when you save the thumbnail, I recommend you store it in a subdirectory of the directory that contains the full-sized images. That way, you can use the same name for both images. To keep it simple, though, the example in this figure doesn't do that.

In the example in this figure, the thumbnails are displayed on one web page and the full photos are displayed on separate pages. In other words, a new web page is displayed with a full photo each time a thumbnail is clicked. By using JavaScript, though, you can display the full photos on the same page as the thumbnails by replacing the current photo with a new one each time a thumbnail is clicked. That way, you can greatly reduce the number of web pages that are needed to display a series of photos. In chapter 13, you'll learn more about this JavaScript capability.

Thumbnails in a web page

The photo that's displayed when the fifth thumbnail is clicked

The HTML for the page that contains the thumbnails

```
<h3>Ram Tap Combined Test</h3>
<p>
    <a href="p1.html"><img src="thumbnails/t1.jpg" alt="Photo 1" /></a>
    <a href="p2.html"><img src="thumbnails/t2.jpg" alt="Photo 2" /></a>
    <a href="p3.html"><img src="thumbnails/t3.jpg" alt="Photo 3" /></a>
    <a href="p4.html"><img src="thumbnails/t4.jpg" alt="Photo 4" /></a>
    <a href="p5.html"><img src="thumbnails/t5.jpg" alt="Photo 5" /></a>
    <a href="p6.html"><img src="thumbnails/t6.jpg" alt="Photo 6" /></a>
</p>
```

Description

- A *thumbnail* is a small version of an image that can be used to make downloading the image faster and to save space on a web page that contains multiple images.
- To create a thumbnail, you can use the techniques in figure 8-6 for sizing an image.
- A thumbnail can be used as the image for a link that displays a page with a larger version of the image.
- A larger version of a thumbnail can also be displayed on the same page using a client-side scripting language such as JavaScript. See chapter 13 for more information.

Figure 8-11   How to create and work with thumbnails

How to create favicons

In chapter 3, you learned how to add a favicon to a web page. Now, figure 8-12 shows you how to create a favicon.

To start, you should know that a favicon is just a special-purpose icon. Like other icons, a favicon should always be stored in a file with the ico extension. That's because this is the only extension Internet Explorer supports for favicons.

To create a favicon, you can use a program or tool like the ones described in this figure. If you want to create your own icons from scratch, you can purchase a program like Axialis Icon Workshop. Otherwise, you can get one of the free products listed here.

If you're using Photoshop, for example, you can get the free plug-in that's available for that program. You can also download a free image converter such as IrfanView from the Internet. Or, you can use an online image converter such as FavIcon from Pics.

Although they can be larger, most favicons are 16 pixels wide and tall. In fact, some image converters will automatically convert the image you specify to 16 x 16 pixels. That's the case with FavIcon from Pics. Other image converters will maintain the original size of the image when they create the favicon. When the favicon is displayed on the web page, however, it will be cropped so it's square. That's the case with IrfanView. To make sure a favicon is displayed the way you want, then, you should make sure the original image is square before you convert it to a favicon.

A web page with a favicon displayed

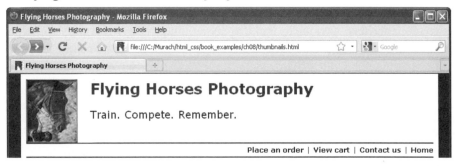

Popular programs and tools for creating favicons

Program/tool	Description
Axialis Icon Workshop	A software product that lets you create, edit, and convert icons. For more information, go to www.axialis.com/iconworkshop/.
Photoshop plug-in	Free software that you can use with Photoshop. To download, go to www.telegraphics.com.au/sw/.
IrfanView	A free image converter that you can download from www.irfanview.com.
FavIcon from Pics	A free image converter that you can run online at: www.html-kit.com/favicon/.

Description

- A *favicon* is a small image that appears to the left of the URL in the browser's address bar. It may also appear to the left of the title in a browser tab, and it may be used by the browser for a favorite or bookmark.

- A favicon is typically 16 pixels wide and tall and typically has the extension ico since that's the only extension currently supported by Internet Explorer for icons.

- You can create an ico file by using an icon editor, a program that converts an image to an ico file, or a web-based converter.

- You may be able to find icons you can use by searching the Internet as described in figure 8-10.

Figure 8-12   How to create favicons

How to create image maps

You've probably seen web pages that display an image and perform a function depending on where you click in the image. If you're using a store locator, for example, the United States map might be displayed so you can select a state by clicking on it. To create this type of image, you use an *image map*.

Figure 8-13 shows how image maps work. Here, the image consists of pictures of two books. When the C++ 2008 book is clicked, one page should be displayed. When the JavaScript book is clicked, a different page should be displayed. Within the image map, each clickable area is called a *hotspot*.

To define an image map, you use the map, area, and img elements. On the map element, you specify the name of the map. Then, within the map element, you code one or more area elements that define the different areas of the map. Finally, you use the usemap attribute of the img element to identify the map that should be used for the image.

The key to defining an area map is coding the area elements. To start, you code the href attribute to specify what page you want to display when the area is clicked. Then, you code the shape attribute to identify the type of shape you want to use for the region. In this example, I used two polygons.

To identify the actual shape and location of an area, you code the coords attribute. The values you code for this attribute depend on the shape of the area. For rectangular areas, four values are specified for the coords attribute. The first two identify the x, y coordinates in pixels of the upper left corner of the area relative to the upper left corner of the image. The second two identify the x, y coordinates in pixels of the lower right corner of the area.

To define a circular region, you specify "circle" for the value of the shape attribute. Then, you specify three values for the coords attribute. The first two values are x, y coordinates for the center of the circle. The third value is the radius of the circle in pixels.

If you want to define a more complex shape than a rectangle or circle, you can specify "poly" for the value of the shape attribute as shown in this figure. Then, the coords attribute will consist of a series of x, y coordinates that identify the shape. To identify the shape for the C++ 2008 book, for example, I included six sets of x, y coordinates. To identify the shape for the JavaScript book, I only used four sets of coordinates.

Note that you can get the coordinates you need for an image map from most image editors. To do that, just point to a location in the image. In Photoshop Elements, the coordinates are displayed in the Info window. If this window isn't open, you can display it using the Window→Info command.

You may also need to set the unit of measure to pixels in Photoshop Elements to get the correct coordinates. To do that, use the Edit→Preferences→Units & Rulers command to display the Units & Rulers tab of the Preferences dialog box. Then, select the pixels option from the Rulers drop-down list.

The attribute of the map element for creating image maps

Attribute	Description
name	Provides a name for the image map.

The attributes of the area element for creating image maps

Attribute	Description
href	Specifies a relative or absolute URL that identifies the page that will be displayed when the area is clicked.
shape	A keyword that indicates the type of shape the area represents. Possible keywords are rect, circle, poly, and default, which is the same as rect.
coords	Values that indicate the shape and location of the area. Two sets of x, y coordinates are required for a rectangle to identify the upper left and lower right corners. Three values are required for a circle to identify the x, y coordinates of the center and the radius. Polygonal shapes require a series of x, y coordinates.
alt	Text that's displayed in place of the area if the image can't be displayed.

The attribute of the img element for creating image maps

Attribute	Description
usemap	Identifies the map the image is associated with. The value of this attribute is the value of the name attribute of the map element, preceded by a pound sign (#).

An image that consists of two overlapping books

HTML for an image map that uses the image

```
<img src="images/new_books_2009.jpg" alt="New books" usemap="#books" />
<map name="books">
    <area href="pls8.html" shape="poly"  alt="C++ 2008" title="C++ 2008"
          coords="1, 19, 114, 0, 122, 53, 106, 143, 26, 158, 24, 149" />
    <area href="mdom.html" shape="poly" alt="JavaScript" title="JavaScript"
          coords="128, 21, 241, 42, 218, 178, 103, 159" />
</map>
```

Description

- You can use the map and area elements to define an *image map* that provides clickable areas for the image called *hotspots*.
- The coordinates for an area are relative to the upper left corner of the image and are measured in pixels.

Figure 8-13   How to create image maps

Perspective

Because you'll include images on almost every web page you develop, it's important for you to know how to work with them. Now that you've finished this chapter, you should have all the skills you need. Your next step, then, should be to get an image editor that provides the functionality you need. At the least, the image editor you choose should provide for sizing images and changing the image type and quality.

If you're developing web pages for personal use, you may be able to get by with one of the free image editors that are available. If you want something more sophisticated, though, you can purchase a program like Photoshop Elements. Programs like this typically run under $100. Finally, if you want a program for professional use, you can purchase an advanced image-editing program like Photoshop. Programs like this sell for several hundred dollars and up.

Terms

GIF file
animated image
frame
JPEG file
PNG file
dithering
progressive JPEG
interlaced GIF
interlaced PNG
transparency
matte
thumbnail
image map
hotspot

Summary

- The three common formats for images are *JPEG* (for photographs and scanned images), *GIF* (for small illustrations, logos, and animated images), and *PNG* (typically used as a replacement for still GIF images).

- You should use the height and width attributes of an <img> tag only to specify the size of the image, not to resize it. Then, the browser can reserve the right amount of space for the image and continue rendering the page, even if the image is still being loaded.

- You can use CSS to vertically align an image within the block element that contains it. You can also use CSS to float an image, just as you can to float a block element.

- To resize an image so it's the right size for a web page, you can use an image editor like Photoshop or Photoshop Elements.

- To reduce the loading time for an image, you can use an image editor to change the image type or quality. To improve the user experience as images load, you can create *progressive JPEGs*, *interlaced GIFs*, and *interlaced PNGs*.

- A GIF file with two or more *frames* is an *animated image*. Then, you can use an image editor to control how that animation works.

- GIF and PNG files support *transparency*. Then, the background color that's behind the image shows through the transparent color.

- If you use an image editor to specify a *matte* for an image, the transparent area for the image is filled with the matte color. If you set this color to the same one that's used for the background color, the image will blend in better with the background.

- The Internet has many sites that offer images, stock photos, and icons that you may want to use for your site.

- A *thumbnail* is a small version of an image that is often used as a link to a page that displays a larger version of the image.

- A *favicon* is a small image that appears to the left of the URL in the browser's address bar. It is typically 16 pixels wide and has ico as its extension.

- An *image map* defines the clickable *hotspots* for an image. To define these hotspots, you code map and name elements in the HTML for the image.

Exercise 8-1 Size and float an image

This is quick exercise that will refresh your memory on how to size and float an image. When you're through, your web page should look like this:

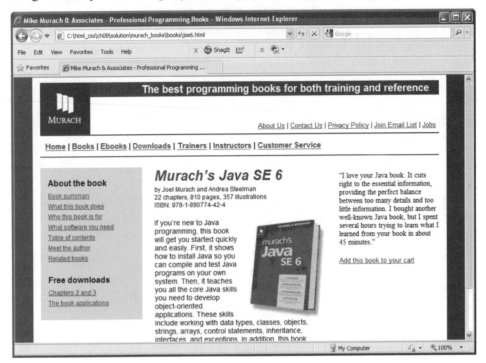

Add and size the image

1. Use your text editor to open these files:

   ```
   c:\html_css\ch08\murach_books\books\jse6.html
   c:\html_css\ch08\murach_books\styles\book.css
   ```

   Then, display the HTML document in a browser to see how it looks.

2. Add an img element to the HTML file that displays the image named jse6.jpg that's in the murach_book\images directory. This img element should be coded right before the second p element in the main division. Then, refresh the page in the browser to see how this looks.

3. Add width and height attributes to the img element so they specify the size of the image (159 pixels wide by 192 pixels tall). Then, refresh the browser again to see that this doesn't change the image. But remember that this lets the browser render the page before all of the images are loaded.

Float the image

4. Add the necessary CSS to float the image to the right of the paragraph that describes the book. Next, add margins to the image to provide more space between the image and the text. Then, refresh the page to make sure it looks like the one above.

Exercise 8-2   Create and use thumbnails

In this exercise, if you have an image editor, you'll create thumbnails from larger images. Then, you'll add them to a web page (or you'll add our thumbnails). When you're done, the web page should look like this:

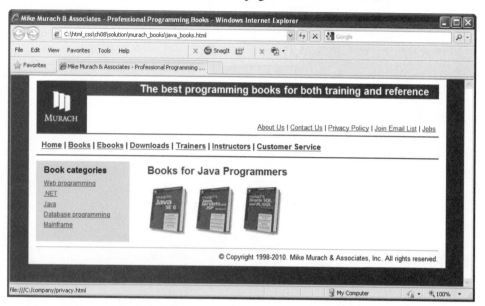

Create and use thumbnails

1. If you have an image editor, use it to reduce three of the image files in this directory:

    `c:\html_css\ch08\murach_books\images`

    These files are named jse6.jpg, jsp2.jpg, and osql.jpg, and they should be reduced to 50% of their original size. Save them as JPEG files with medium compression in this directory, but don't change the file names:

    `c:\html_css\ch08\murach_books\images\thumbnails`

2. Open this file in your text editor

    `c:\html_css\ch08\murach_books\java_books.html`

    Then, add img elements for the three thumbnails that you created in step 1 within the three a elements in the main division. Or, if you didn't create your own thumbnails, add img elements for the three thumbnails in the our_thumbnails directory. Now, refresh the page in the browser to see how the images look.

3. Open the category.css file in the styles directory. Then, add a rule set for the images that removes the border around the images and adds space between the images so the page looks like the one above. Then, test this change.

4. Click the first thumbnail on the page. This should display the page you created in exercise 8-1. Then, click the Back button to return to the page above.

Exercise 8-3   Create and use a favicon

In this exercise, you'll create and use a favicon. When you're done, the web page will look like this:

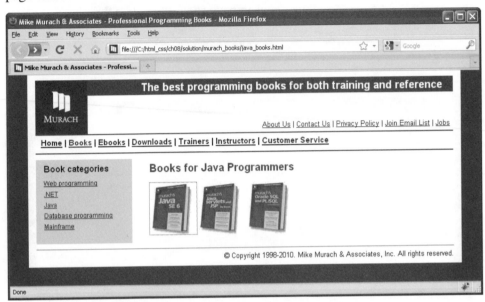

Create and use a favicon

1. If you have an icon editor, use it to create a favicon from the murach_logo.gif file in this directory and then save the favicon in this directory:

    `c:\html_css\ch08\murach_books\images`

    Otherwise, use the image converter at www.html-kit.com/favicon/ to upload the logo from the images directory, create the favicon from the image, download the Favicon Package that's created (a zip file), and unzip the favicon into the images directory.

2. Use your text editor to open the java_books.html file in the murach_books directory. Then, display this page in Firefox. (Remember that IE won't display a favicon if a page is displayed from your local file system.)

3. Add a link element that identifies the favicon that you created in step 1. (Refer to figure 3-2 in chapter 3 if you don't remember how to code this element.) Then, refresh the page in the browser to make sure that the favicon is displayed in the address bar and on the tab.

9

How to work with tables

If you look at the HTML for some of the web pages that are available today, you'll see that many of them use tables to control the page layout. As you saw in chapter 6, however, you can now use CSS to lay out your pages. Because of that, you should use tables only to display tabular data. That's what you'll learn in this chapter.

How to code and format simple tables

In the topics that follow, you'll learn the basic skills for coding and formatting tables. But first, I want to introduce you to the structure of a table in HTML.

An introduction to tables

Figure 9-1 presents a simple table and points out its various components. To start, a table consists of one or more *rows* and *columns*. As you'll see in the next figure, you define a table by defining its rows. Then, within each row, you define a *cell* for each column.

A table can contain two different kinds of cells. *Header cells* identify what's in the columns and rows of a table, and *data cells* contain the actual data of the table. For example, the three cells in the first row of the table in this figure are header cells. In contrast, the cells in the next four rows are data cells. The last row consists of two header cells that have been merged into a single cell, along with one data cell. You'll learn how to merge cells like this later in this chapter.

If a table includes one or more rows that contain header cells, you can group those rows into a *table header*. Similarly, you can group one or more rows at the end of a table into a *table footer*. When you do that, you'll usually want to group the rows between the header and footer into the *table body*, as shown in figure 9-5. Grouping rows like this can make it easier to apply styles to all the rows in a group.

Finally, a table can contain a caption. The caption simply describes the contents of the table.

A simple table with basic formatting

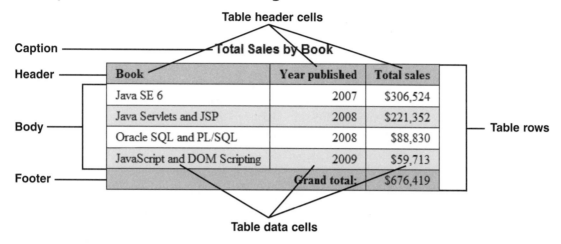

Description

- A *table* consists of *rows* and *columns* that intersect at *cells*. Cells that contain the data of the table are called *data cells*. Cells that identify the data in a column or row are called *header cells*.

- You can group one or more table rows that contain header cells into a *table header*. You can also group one or more rows at the end of a table into a *table footer*. A table footer typically provides summary information for the data in the table.

- If you define a table header and a table footer, you may also want to group the rows between the header and footer into a *table body*, as shown in figure 9-5.

- A table can also include a caption above the table that describes the contents of the table.

- You should use tables only for tabular data. You should not use them to define the layout of a page. Instead, you should use CSS.

Figure 9-1   An introduction to tables

How to code a table

Figure 9-2 presents the four most common elements for coding tables. The table element defines the table itself. Then, you code the other elements within this element.

To define each row in a table, you use the tr (Table Row) element. Within this element, you code one th (Table Header) or td (Table Data) element for each cell in the row. You can see how this works in the table in this figure. This is the same table that's in figure 9-1, but without the last row and without formatting.

Note that, by default, the content of a header cell is boldfaced and centered in the cell. In contrast, the content of a data cell is left-aligned by default. The width of the cells themselves is determined by the data they contain, with each cell in a column being as wide as the widest cell. Of course, you can change these and other styles for a table using CSS. You'll see how to do that in the next figure.

Before I go on, you should notice the cellspacing attribute for the table element in this figure. This attribute specifies the amount of space in pixels that's added around the cells in the table. Although you might think that you could set this spacing using CSS, the border-spacing property that provides for this isn't supported by versions of Internet Explorer before version 8. So if you want the cells in a table spaced consistently across browsers, you'll need to use the cellspacing attribute. Keep in mind, though, that it isn't always necessary to set the cell spacing. You'll see why in the next figure.

Common elements for coding tables

Element	Description
table	Defines a table. The other elements for the table are coded within this element.
tr	Defines a row.
th	Defines a header cell within a row.
td	Defines a data cell within a row.

The HTML for a simple table

```
<table cellspacing="5">
    <tr>
        <th class="left">Book</th>
        <th>Year published</th>
        <th>Total sales</th>
    </tr>
    <tr>
        <td class="left">Java SE 6</td>
        <td>2007</td>
        <td>$306,524</td>
    </tr>
    <tr class="aqua">
        <td class="left">Java Servlets and JSP</td>
        <td>2008</td>
        <td>$221,352</td>
    </tr>
    .
    .
    .
</table>
```

The table in a web browser

Book	Year published	Total sales
Java SE 6	2007	$306,524
Java Servlets and JSP	2008	$221,352
Oracle SQL and PL/SQL	2008	$88,830
JavaScript and DOM Scripting	2009	$59,713

Description

- By default, the width of each column in a table is determined automatically based on its contents.

- The content of a th element is boldfaced and centered by default, and the content of a td element is left-aligned.

- The cellspacing attribute of the table element determines the amount of space around the cells of a table in pixels. Although you can also use the CSS border-spacing property to add spacing between cells as shown in the next figure, this property isn't supported by Internet Explorer version 7 and earlier.

Figure 9-2   How to code a table

How to use CSS to format a table

Figure 9-3 presents some of the most common CSS properties for formatting tables. If you review these properties, you'll see that many of them are the same properties you use to format the other elements of a web page. Because of that, I'll focus on just the most important ones for formatting tables.

As you saw in the last figure, a table doesn't include borders by default. (I added the border around the table in that figure when I captured the screen for that table. It isn't part of the table.) In many cases, though, you'll want to add a border around a table to make it stand out on the page. In addition, you may want to add borders around the cells or rows in a table to help identify the columns and rows. To do that, you can use any of the border properties you learned about in chapter 5. In the CSS in this figure, for example, I used the shorthand border property to add a solid black border around the table and around each cell in the table.

As I've already mentioned, the border-spacing property isn't supported by versions of Internet Explorer before version 8. Because of that, you should use the cellspacing attribute when you want to add spacing between cells. If you look at the second table in this figure, for example, you can see the space that was added by the cellspacing attribute I coded on the table element in figure 9-2.

In most cases, you won't want space between the cells when you use borders. Although you might think that you could remove the space by omitting the cellspacing attribute, that's not the case. That's because a small amount of space is included between the cells by default. One way to remove the space is to set the cellspacing attribute to 0. If you do that, though, the borders will be displayed next to each other. That means that if you define borders that are one pixel wide as shown in this figure, it will appear as if you added two-pixel borders.

A better way to remove the space between borders is to use the border-collapse property. To do that, just set this property to a value of "collapse". Then, the borders between adjacent cells will be collapsed to a single border as shown in the first table in this figure. Note that when you use this technique, you can omit the cellspacing attribute. Also note that if two adjacent cells have different borders, the most dominant border will be displayed. If one border is wider than the other, for example, the wider border will be displayed.

The last property I want to mention here is padding. This property works similarly to the way it works with the box model. That is, it specifies the amount of space between the contents of a cell and the outer edge of the cell. In this figure, for example, you can see that I added .2 em of space above and below the contents of each cell, and I added .7 em of space to the left and right of the contents.

Common properties for formatting tables

Property	Description
border	A shorthand property for specifying the border width, style, and color. You can also use individual border properties, and you can specify borders for individual sides.
border-collapse	A keyword that determines whether space exists between the borders of adjacent cells or the borders are collapsed so a single border is displayed between cells. Possible values are collapse and separate. The default is separate.
border-spacing	A relative or absolute value that specifies the space between cells when the borders aren't collapsed. Not supported by Internet Explorer version 7 and earlier.
padding	The space between the cell contents and the outer edge of the cell.
text-align	The horizontal alignment of text.
vertical-align	The vertical alignment of text.
background-color	The background color.
font	A shorthand property for specifying the font style, weight, variant, size, line height, and family. You can also use individual font properties.

CSS for the table in figure 9-2

```
table {
    border: 1px solid black;
    border-collapse: collapse; }
th { background-color: #40e0d0; }
td, th {
    border: 1px solid black;
    padding: .2em .7em;
    text-align: right; }
.left { text-align: left; }
.aqua { background-color: #afeeee; }
```

The table in a web browser

Book	Year published	Total sales
Java SE 6	2007	$306,524
Java Servlets and JSP	2008	$221,352
Oracle SQL and PL/SQL	2008	$88,830
JavaScript and DOM Scripting	2009	$59,713

The table without collapsed borders

Book	Year published	Total sales
Java SE 6	2007	$306,524
Java Servlets and JSP	2008	$221,352
Oracle SQL and PL/SQL	2008	$88,830
JavaScript and DOM Scripting	2009	$59,713

Description

- You can use the properties listed above with table, tr, td, or th elements.

Figure 9-3   How use CSS to format a table

How to add a caption

To add a caption to a table, you use the caption element as shown in figure 9-4. As you can see, you code this element immediately after the opening tag for the table. The content of this element is simply the text you want to display.

Although the caption element makes it easy to add a caption to a table, many developers prefer to use a heading instead. That's because a heading indicates a position in a hierarchy, but a caption does not. A heading can also make it easier for a user of an assistive device such as a screen reader to scan the contents of a web page.

The element for adding a caption

Element	Description
caption	Contains a description of a table. Must be coded immediately after the opening tag for the table element.

The HTML for a table with a caption

```
<table>
    <caption>Total Sales by Book</caption>
    <tr>
        <th class="book">Book</th>
        <th>Year published</th>
        <th>Total sales</th>
    </tr>
    <tr>
        <td class="book">Java SE 6</td>
        <td>2007</td>
        <td>$306,524</td>
    </tr>
    .
    .
    .
</table>
```

The CSS for the caption

```
caption {
    font-family: Arial, Helvetica, sans-serif;
    font-weight: bold;
    margin-bottom: .5em;
}
```

The table in a web browser

Total Sales by Book		
Book	**Year published**	**Total sales**
Java SE 6	2007	$306,524
Java Servlets and JSP	2008	$221,352
Oracle SQL and PL/SQL	2008	$88,830
JavaScript and DOM Scripting	2009	$59,713

Description

- By default, a caption is centered above the table and is not boldfaced.
- You can use the caption-side property with the caption element to specify whether the caption is displayed at the top or bottom of the table. However, this property isn't supported by Internet Explorer version 7 and earlier.
- Many developers prefer to code a heading outside the table rather than use the caption element. That's because headings indicate a hierarchy in the document.

Figure 9-4   How to add a caption

How to add a header and footer

Figure 9-5 presents the elements for grouping rows into headers and footers. It also presents the element for grouping rows in the table body, which you'll typically do when you use a header and footer.

To code a header, you simply code the rows that make up the header between the opening and closing tags of the thead element. Similarly, you code a footer by coding rows within a tfoot element. And you code a body by coding rows within a tbody element.

The example in this figure illustrates how this works. Here, the first row of the table is coded within a thead element, the last row of the table is coded within a tfoot element, and the remaining rows are coded within a tbody element. Then, the CSS for this page applies a background color to the header and footer using a selector that includes the thead and tfoot elements. In addition, instead of adding a border around each cell in the table, the CSS adds a border around the header and footer. You can see the result in the table shown here.

Because the header and footer in this example each consist of a single row, it's debatable whether it makes sense to add them. Another option would be to assign a class to the header and footer rows and then apply styles to that class. If a header or footer consists of two or more rows, though, it can be easier to group the rows so you can apply styles to all the rows in the group at once rather than having to assign a class to each row.

Elements for coding headers and footers

Element	Description
thead	Groups one or more rows into a table header.
tfoot	Groups one or more rows into a table footer.
tbody	Groups the rows between the header and footer into a table body.

The HTML for a table with a header and a footer

```
<table>
    <thead>
        <tr>
            <th class="book">Book</th>
            <th>Year published</th>
            <th>Total sales</th>
        </tr>
    </thead>
    <tbody>
        <tr>
            <td class="book">Java SE 6</td>
            <td>2007</td>
            <td>$306,524</td>
        </tr>
        .
        .
    </tbody>
    <tfoot>
        <tr>
            <td></td>
            <td id="total">Grand total:</td>
            <td>$676,419</td>
        </tr>
    </tfoot>
</table>
```

The CSS for the header and footer

```
thead, tfoot {
    background-color: #40e0d0;
    border: 1px solid black; }
```

The table in a web browser

Book	Year published	Total sales
Java SE 6	2007	$306,524
Java Servlets and JSP	2008	$221,352
Oracle SQL and PL/SQL	2008	$88,830
JavaScript and DOM Scripting	2009	$59,713
	Grand total:	$676,419

Description

- The thead, tfoot, and tbody elements can make it easier to style a table with CSS. You can code these elements in any sequence, although we recommend the sequence shown above.

Figure 9-5   How to add a header and footer

Advanced skills for working with tables

For some tables, the skills you've just learned will be all you need. But other tables will require some of the skills that are presented next.

How to merge cells in a column or row

When I presented the table in figure 9-1, I mentioned that the first two cells in the last row had been merged into a single cell. Now, figure 9-6 presents the two attributes of the th and td elements that you can use to *merge* cells. You use the colspan attribute to merge cells so a cell in a row spans two or more columns, and you use the rowspan attribute to merge cells so a cell in a column spans two or more rows. The value you code on these attributes indicates the number of cells that will be merged.

The example in this figure illustrates how these attributes work. Here, you can see that the table header consists of two rows and five columns. However, the first header cell spans two rows. As a result, the second row doesn't include a th element for the first column.

Notice here that the content of the merged cells is aligned at the bottom of the cell. To accomplish that, I had to set the vertical-align property for this cell to "bottom". The default is to center the content vertically in the cell.

Now, take a look at the second header cell in the first row of the header. This cell spans the remaining four columns of the row. As a result, this row includes only two th elements: the one that defines the cell that contains the "Book" heading, and the one that defines the cell that contains the "Sales" heading.

Although this is a relatively simple example of merged cells, it should help you understand how merging works. Then, if you need to merge cells in a more complex table, you can simply extend the skills presented here.

Attributes of the <th> and <td> tags for merging cells

Attribute	Description
colspan	Identifies the number of columns that a cell will span. The default is 1.
rowspan	Identifies the number of rows that a cell will span. The default is 1.

A table with merged cells

Book	Sales			
	Retail	College	Trade	Total
Java SE 6	$55,174	$73,566	$177,784	$306,524
Java Servlets and JSP	$28,775	$24,349	$168,228	$221,352
Visual Basic 2008	$27,688	$39,995	$239,968	$307,651
ASP.NET 3.5 with VB 2008	$23,082	$24,858	$129,619	$177,559
ADO.NET 3.5 with VB 2008	$6,056	$2,782	$47,195	$56,033
Grand totals:	$140,775	$165,550	$762,794	$1,069,119

The HTML for the table

```
<table>
    <thead>
        <tr>
            <th class="left bottom" rowspan="2">Book</th>
            <th class="center" colspan="4">Sales</th>
        </tr>
        <tr>
            <th>Retail</th>
            <th>College</th>
            <th>Trade</th>
            <th>Total</th>
        </tr>
    </thead>
    <tbody>
        <tr>
            <td class="left">Java SE 6</td>
            <td>$55,174</td>
            <td>$73,566</td>
            <td>$177,784</td>
            <td>$306,524</td>
        </tr>
        .
        .
        .
    </tbody>
    <tfoot>
        <tr>
            <td id="total">Grand totals:</td>
            <td>$140,775</td>
            <td>$165,550</td>
            <td>$762,794</td>
            <td>$1,069,119</td>
        </tr>
    </tfoot>
</table>
```

Figure 9-6   How to merge cells in a column or row

How to nest tables

In the past, when tables were used for laying out pages, it was common to nest one table within another table. Although *nested tables* aren't used as often for displaying tabular data, they can occasionally be useful. Figure 9-7 shows how nested tables work.

The table at the top of this figure is a simple table that lists the year-to-date sales by region. For the West and East regions, a single sales amount is displayed. For the Central region, however, two sales amounts for two different regional managers are displayed. To accomplish that, the cell for this region contains another table.

To code a table within another table, you simply code a table element within a td element. Then, you code the other elements of the table within the table element just like you would any other table. In this case, the table consists of two rows, each with two cells.

Because the table shown here is so simple, using a nested table probably wasn't the best solution. Instead, I could have inserted another column between the two columns shown here with the name of the manager for each region. Then, I could have included a separate row for each manager, and I could have coded the cell that contains the "Central" heading so it spanned the two rows with the two sales managers. If you're working with a more complex table, though, using nested tables may be the best solution.

A table with another table nested within it

```
YTD Sales by Region
┌────────┬──────────────────────────┐
│ Region │        YTD sales         │
├────────┼──────────────────────────┤
│ West   │        $68,684.34        │
├────────┼──────────┬───────────────┤
│        │ Williams │  $21,223.08   │
│ Central├──────────┼───────────────┤
│        │ Andrews  │  $41,274.06   │
├────────┼──────────┴───────────────┤
│ East   │        $72,741.06        │
└────────┴──────────────────────────┘
```

The HTML for the table

```html
<table id="outer">
    <caption>YTD Sales by Region</caption>
    <tr>
        <th class="left">Region</th>
        <th class="right margin">YTD sales</th>
    </tr>
    <tr>
        <th class="left">West</th>
        <td class="right margin">$68,684.34</td>
    </tr>
    <tr>
        <th class="left">Central</th>
        <td>
            <table id="inner">
                <tr>
                    <th class="left">Williams</th>
                    <td class="right">$21,223.08</td>
                </tr>
                <tr>
                    <th class="left">Andrews</th>
                    <td class="right">$41,274.06</td>
                </tr>
            </table>
        </td>
    </tr>
    <tr>
        <th class="left">East</th>
        <td class="right margin">$72,741.06</td>
    </tr>
</table>
```

Description

- You can *nest* one table within another table by coding a table element within a td element.
- Nested tables were used frequently when tables were used to lay out pages. But now that CSS is available on all major browsers, tables shouldn't be used for page layout, and nested tables are rarely needed.

Figure 9-7   How to nest tables

How to control wrapping

By default, the content of the cells in a table will *wrap* to two or more lines if you size the browser window so the content can't be displayed on a single line. This is illustrated by the table shown at the top of figure 9-8. Here, you can see that the headings in the second and third columns as well as the data in the first column have wrapped onto two lines.

In some cases, though, you won't want the headings and data to wrap. Then, you can use the white-space property to prevent that from happening. In the CSS in this figure, for example, I coded this property with a value of "nowrap" for the table element. Then, the table appears as in the second browser window. Here, you can see that because wrapping isn't allowed, the table is too wide for the window. Because of that, a horizontal scroll bar is displayed so the user can scroll to see the rest of the table.

Although I changed the wrapping for the entire table in this example, you should know that you can also change the wrapping for individual cells. For this table, for example, it might be acceptable to let the headings wrap. On the other hand, you might not want the names of the books to wrap.

A table with wrapping

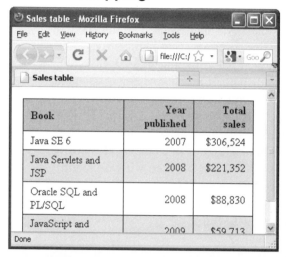

A table without wrapping

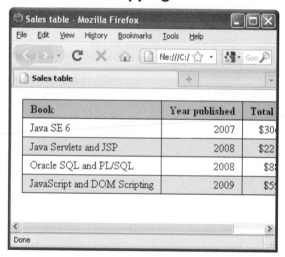

The CSS for the table without wrapping

```
table {
    border: 1px solid black;
    border-collapse: collapse;
    margin: 10px;
    white-space: nowrap;
}
```

Description

- You can use the white-space property to keep table data from wrapping if the table doesn't fit in the browser window. To do that, code the value "nowrap" for this property.

- You can code the white-space property for an entire table or individual cells.

Figure 9-8   How to control wrapping

How to provide for accessibility

Because tables can be difficult for visually impaired users to understand, HTML provides a number of attributes that improve accessibility. These attributes can be read by screen readers and are described in figure 9-9.

To start, you can use the summary attribute of the table element to include descriptive information about a table's content. You can also include a brief description of a cell's content using the abbr attribute of the td or th element. These attributes are typically read aloud by screen readers.

You can also code the headers attribute on a td or th element. This attribute identifies one or more header cells that the cell is associated with. To identify a header cell, you code the value of the cell's id attribute.

To illustrate how this works, take a look at the HTML in this figure. This is the HTML for the table you saw in figure 9-1 with some accessibility attributes added. Here, you can see that an id attribute is coded for each of the three th elements in the table header as well as the th element in the table footer. Then, each of the td elements in the table body includes a headers attribute that names the associated th element. For example, the headers attribute for the first td element in each row names the header cell that contains the header "Book" because the content of these cells are book names. In addition, the td element in the table footer includes a headers attribute that names two th elements. The first one is for the header cell in the third column of the first row (the one with the heading "Total sales"), and the second one is for the header cell in the first column of the last row (the one with the heading "Grand total:").

The last attribute you can use for accessibility is scope. Although you can code this attribute on either the td or th element, it's used most often with the th element. The scope attribute indicates if a cell is associated with a column, a row, or a group of merged cells in a column. In this figure, for example, I used this attribute to indicate that each of the three th elements in the header row is associated with a column.

By the way, you should know that you won't typically code all the attributes shown here on a simple table like this. The more complex your tables are, however, the more useful these attributes become.

Attributes that can be used for accessibility

Element	Attribute	Description
table	summary	Provides information about a table's content.
td/th	abbr	Provides a brief description of the cell content.
	headers	Identifies one or more header cells that describe the content of the cell.
	scope	A keyword that indicates if a cell is associated with a column or row. Common keywords are col and row. You can also use the keyword rowgroup to refer to merged cells.

The HTML for a table that provides for accessibility

```html
<table summary="Total sales for books published from 2007 to 2009">
    <caption>Total Sales by Book</caption>
    <thead>
        <tr>
            <th id="hdr_book" class="book" scope="col">Book</th>
            <th id="hdr_year" scope="col">Year published</th>
            <th id="hdr_sales" scope="col">Total sales</th>
        </tr>
    </thead>
    <tbody>
        <tr>
            <td class="book" abbr="Java" headers="hdr_book">Java SE 6</td>
            <td headers="hdr_year">2007</td>
            <td headers="hdr_sales">$306,524</td>
        </tr>
        <tr class="aqua">
            <td class="book" abbr="Servlets" headers="hdr_book">Java
                Servlets and JSP</td>
            <td headers="hdr_year">2008</td>
            <td headers="hdr_sales">$221,352</td>
        </tr>
        .
        .
    </tbody>
    <tfoot>
        <tr>
            <th id="hdr_total" colspan="2">Grand total:</th>
            <td headers="hdr_sales hdr_total">$676,419</td>
        </tr>
    </tfoot>
</table>
```

Description

- You can use the attributes listed above to make a table more accessible to visually-impaired users who use screen readers.

Figure 9-9   How to provide for accessibility

Perspective

As you've seen in this chapter, it's relative easy to create and format tables. The most difficult part of working with tables is merging cells so they span two or more columns or rows. Remember, though, that you should only use tables when you're trying to present tabular data. You should be using CSS, not tables, to lay out the components of your web pages.

Terms

table
row
column
cell
data cell
header cell
table header
table footer
table body
merged cells
nested tables
wrapped rows

Summary

- A *table* consists of *rows* and *columns* that intersect at *cells*. *Data cells* contain the data of a table. *Header cells* identify the data in a column or row.
- The rows in a table can be grouped into a *table header*, a *table body*, and a *table footer*.
- To define a table in HTML, you use the table, tr, th, and td elements. Then, you can use CSS to apply borders, spacing, fonts, and background colors to these elements.
- If you use the thead, tfoot, and tbody elements to group the rows in a table, it's usually easier to style the table with CSS.
- You will often want to *merge* two or more cells in a column or row, and you may occasionally want to *nest* one table within another.
- If a table doesn't fit in the browser window, the browser will wrap the data so it does fit. If you don't want that, you can use CSS to turn the wrapping off.
- To make tables more accessible to visually impaired users, you can use the HTML attributes that can be read by screen readers.

Exercise 9-1   Create and format a simple table

In this exercise, you'll create and format a table that contains employee contact information. When you're done, the table should look something like this:

Employee Contact Information

Name	E-mail	Phone
Mike Murach	mike@murach.com	559.440.9071 x15
Anne Boehm	anne@murach.com	559.440.9071 x16
Judy Taylor	judy@murach.com	559.440.9071 x17
Cyndi Vasquez	cyndi@murach.com	559.440.9071 x18
Kelly Slivkoff	kelly@murach.com	559.440.9071 x12

Create the HTML table

1. Use your text editor to open the employee.html file in the c:\html_css\ch09 directory.

2. Enter opening and closing tags for the table element within the body of the document. Set the cellspacing attribute for the table to 5 pixels.

3. Enter opening and closing tags for the first tr element. Then, enter a th element for each header cell in the row. Use the table above to determine the content of each cell.

4. Enter opening and closing tags for the next tr element. Then, enter a td element for each data cell with the content in the table above. Repeat for each of the remaining rows in the table.

5. Add a caption element with the text shown above. Then, display the table in a browser to see how it looks. Notice that the table doesn't have any borders and the column headings are boldfaced and centered over each column. Also notice that the caption is centered over the table but it's not boldfaced.

Format the table

6. Create a style sheet named employee.css in the c:\html_css\ch09\styles directory.

7. Add a one-pixel, solid black border around the table and around each cell in the table.

8. Add a link element to the html file that links to the style sheet you just created. Then, save the changes to the html and css files and refresh the browser window. Notice that there's space around the border of each cell.

9. Remove the cellspacing attribute from the table element and refresh the browser window again. Notice that there's still a small amount of space around the border of each cell.

10. Add the border-collapse property to the table and set its value to "collapse". Refresh the browser window again to see that there's no longer space between the cell borders.

11. To make the table more readable, add some padding between the content of each cell and the cell border. In addition, align the column headers at the left side of the column. Finally, use a sans-serif font for the caption, make the caption boldfaced, and add some space below it. Refresh the browser window to see how this looks.

12. Add a background color to each header cell. Then, add a different background color to every other row in the table. The easiest way to do that is to assign a class to each row you want to have a colored background.

13. Refresh the browser window one more time. If the table looks like the one above, close the browser and then close the HTML and CSS files.

Exercise 9-2   Enhance the Employee table

In this exercise, you'll enhance the table you created in exercise 9-1 so it uses merged cells and doesn't allow wrapping. When you're done, the table should look like this:

Employee Contact Information

Department	Name	E-mail	Phone
Editorial	Mike Murach	mike@murach.com	559.440.9071 x15
	Anne Boehm	anne@murach.com	559.440.9071 x16
Marketing	Judy Taylor	judy@murach.com	559.440.9071 x17
	Cyndi Vasquez	cyndi@murach.com	559.440.9071 x18
Customer Service	Kelly Slivkoff	kelly@murach.com	559.440.9071 x12

Add another column to the Employee table

1. Use your text editor to open the department.html file in the c:\html_css\ch09 directory.

2. Add another th element at the beginning of the first row of the table for the "Department" heading.

3. Add a td element at the beginning of the second row of the table for the "Editorial" department. This element should span two rows. Add a similar element for the "Marketing" department to the fourth row.

4. Add a td element at the beginning of the last row for the "Customer Service" department. Then, display the page in a browser to see how it looks.

Modify the table so the data doesn't wrap

5. Reduce the width of the browser window so the table doesn't fit, and notice how the data in some of the columns wraps.

6. Open the department.css file in the c:\html_css\ch09\styles directory. Then, add the white-space property with a value of "nowrap" to the table. Refresh the browser to see that the data no longer wraps.

7. Close the browser and then close the HTML and CSS files.

10

How to work with forms

When you create dynamic web pages, you use HTML to code forms that provide for user interaction. Then, the data in the form can be submitted to a web server for processing, or it can be processed on the client with a client-side script. In many cases, the two approaches are combined so a client-side script is used to validate the form data on the client before it sends the valid data to the server.

In this chapter, you'll learn how to code forms and the controls they contain. Then, in chapter 13, you'll learn about JavaScript and how you can use it to process the form data on the client.

How to code forms

A *form* contains one or more *controls* such as text boxes and buttons. In the topics that follow, you'll learn how to code the various controls that you can add to a form. But first, you need to know how to create the form itself.

How to create a form

Figure 10-1 shows how to code a form that contains three controls: a label, a text box, and a button. To start, you code the form element. On the opening tag for this element, you code the action and method attributes. The action attribute specifies the file on the web server that should be used to process the data when the form is submitted. The method attribute specifies the HTTP method that should be used for sending the form to the web server.

In the example, the form will be submitted to the server using the HTTP "post" method when the user clicks the Subscribe button. Then, the data in the form will be processed by the code that's in the file named subscribe.php.

When you use the post method, the form data is packaged as part of an HTTP transaction and isn't visible in the browser. Because of that, the submission is more secure than it is when you use the "get" method, but the resulting page can't be bookmarked. When you use the get method, the form data is sent as part of the URL for the HTTP request. That means that the data is visible in the browser and the page can be bookmarked. Note that browsers and servers limit the amount of data you can include in a URL. So if a page contains a lot of data, you may be forced to use the post method.

Within the opening and closing tags of the form element, you code the controls for the form. In this example, the label element provides a label for the text box that follows. The first input element is for the text box that will receive the user's email address. And the second input element displays a button. You'll learn how to code these controls in the next two figures.

But first, this figure summarizes five attributes that are common to most of the controls. To start, the name attribute specifies a name that can be used by client-side or server-side code to refer to the control. This attribute is similar to the id attribute, which can be used by client-side code to refer to the control. Because of that, it usually makes sense to use the same values for these attributes. By the way, you can also code these attributes on the form element.

The value attribute provides the value that's stored in a control. How this works depends on the control. For example, the value attribute of a text box stores the text that's in the text box. In contrast, the value attribute for a button specifies the text that's displayed on the button.

The disabled attribute disables a control so the user can't interact with it. The readonly attribute is similar. It makes a control read-only, which prevents the user from modifying the value of the control. Unlike the disabled attribute, though, the readonly attribute doesn't prevent the user from moving the focus to the control or even copying and pasting its contents.

Attributes of the form element

Attribute	Description
action	Specifies the URL of the page or server-side script that will process the data in the form.
method	Specifies the HTTP method to use to submit the form data. It's set to either "get" or "post". The default value is "get".

Attributes common to most controls

Attribute	Description
name	Specifies a name that can be referred to by client-side or server-side code. Except for radio buttons, the id attribute should be set to the same value. Required for all controls except submit and reset buttons.
id	Specifies a unique identifier that can be referred to by CSS or client-side code.
value	Sets the value stored in the control.
disabled	A Boolean attribute that disables and grays out the control so the user can't interact with it.
readonly	A Boolean attribute that prevents a user from changing the value of the control.

The HTML for a simple form

```
<form action="subscribe.php" method="post">
    <p>Please enter your e-mail address to subscribe to our newsletter.</p>
    <p><label for="email">E-Mail:</label>
        <input type="text" name="email" id="email" />
    </p>
    <p><input type="submit" value="Subscribe" /></p>
</form>
```

The form in a web browser

Description

- A *form* contains one or more *controls* like text boxes, radio buttons, or check boxes that can receive data.

- When a form is submitted to the server for processing, the data in the controls is sent along with the HTTP request. When the get method is used, the data is sent as part of the URL for the next web page. When the post method is used, the data is hidden.

Figure 10-1   How to create a form

How to code buttons

Figure 10-2 shows four different types of *buttons*: "submit", "reset", "button", and "image". To code these buttons, you can use the input element as shown in the HTML in this figure. Here, the first two buttons are *submit buttons*. When you click on one of these buttons, its name/value pair is sent to the server. This lets the server perform different actions depending on which button is clicked.

The type attribute of the third button in this figure is set to "button". This type of button can be used to run client-side code, such as a script that validates the data on the form. Then, if the data is valid, the script can submit the data to the server.

The type attribute of the fourth button is set to "reset". When you click a *reset button*, the values in all of the controls on the form are reset to their default values.

The type attribute of the last button is set to "image". Like a submit button, an *image button* submits the form to the server when the user clicks on it. The difference is that an image button displays an image rather than text. You code the URL for the image on the src attribute. In addition, you code the text you want to be displayed on the button if the image can't be displayed on the alt attribute.

By the way, if you don't specify a value attribute for a button, the web browser supplies a default value depending on the button type. For example, the text for a submit button is usually "Submit", and the text for a reset button is usually "Reset".

Although it's not shown here, you should know that you can also code a button using the button element. When you use the button element, you can format the text that's displayed on the button, and you can include elements other than text. Because the button element doesn't work well with Internet Explorer, though, you should avoid using it.

Attributes of the input element for buttons

Attribute	Description
type	Specifies the type of button. Valid values include "submit", "reset", "button", or "image". The "submit" and "image" types submit the form to the server, the "reset" type resets all fields to their default values, and the "button" type is used to run a client-side script.
value	Specifies the text that's displayed on the button and submitted to the server when the button is clicked.
src	For an image button, specifies the relative or absolute URL of the image to display.
alt	For an image button, specifies alternate text to display in place of the image.

The HTML for four buttons

```
<p>
    <input type="submit" name="order" id="order" value="Place Order" />
    <input type="submit" name="wish" id="wish" value="Save as Wish List" />
</p>
<p>
    <input type="button" id="validate" value="Validate" />
    <input type="reset" />
</p>
<p>
    <input type="image" id="submit" src="images/submit.jpg"
        alt="Submit page" />
</p>
```

The buttons in a web browser

Description

- When you click on a *submit button* for a form, the form data is sent to the server as part of an HTTP request. When you click on a *reset button*, the data in all of the fields are reset to their default values.

- You can use the button type if you need to perform some processing on the client before the form is submitted to the server. For example, you might want to validate the data the user entered. To do that, you use a client-side script. Then, if the data is valid, the script can submit the form to the server.

- You can also use the button element to create a button. The main difference between the input and button elements is that the input element only allows a button to contain plain text, while the button element allows a button to contain formatted text as well as other HTML elements such as images. The button element doesn't work well with Internet Explorer.

Figure 10-2   How to code buttons

How to code labels and text fields

Figure 10-3 shows how to use the input element to create three types of *text fields*, also referred to as *text boxes*. It also shows how to use the label element to provide *labels* that describe text fields.

The first input element in the example in this figure displays a text field that accepts input from a user. To do that, the type attribute is set to "text". In addition, the name and id attributes are set to "quantity", and the value attribute is set to 1. As a result, when the browser displays this text field for the first time, it will contain a default value of 1.

The label element that precedes the input element displays the value "Quantity:" to the left of the text field. This value is coded as the content of the label element. The label element also includes a for attribute that identifies the text field that's associated with the label. For this attribute to work correctly, it must match the id attribute of the text field.

Most of the attributes that are used to code the first label and text field work the same for the other examples. For the second input element, though, the disabled attribute is set to "disabled". As a result, the browser grays out the text field and prevents the user from interacting with it.

The third input element creates a *password field* that works much like the first two text fields. However, the value in the field is displayed as bullets or asterisks. This improves the security of an application by preventing others from reading a password when a user enters it.

This password field also shows how to use the maxlength attribute. Here, this attribute is set to 6. As a result, the user can enter a maximum of six characters into this field. This is particularly useful if you're working with a database that limits the number of characters that can be stored in a field.

The fourth input element creates a *hidden field* that works much like the other three text fields. However, this field isn't displayed by the browser. Nevertheless, you can use client-side or server-side code to work with the value that's stored in this field. Note that because the user can't enter text into a hidden field, you usually code a value attribute for a hidden field.

In these examples, all of the text boxes are displayed at their default width. One way to change that is to include the size attribute. A better way, though, is to use CSS. You can also use CSS to align controls. You'll see how to format and align controls later in this chapter.

Attributes of the label element

Attribute	Description
for	Specifies the name of the control that the label is associated with.

Attributes of the input element for text fields

Attribute	Description
type	Specifies the type of text field. Valid values include "text", "password", and "hidden". The default value is "text".
value	Specifies the default value for the field, but the user can change this value. If a reset button is clicked, the field will revert to this value.
maxlength	Specifies the maximum number of characters that the user may enter in the field.
size	Specifies the width of the field in characters based on the average character width of the font. Instead of setting this attribute, you should use CSS to set the size of a field.

The HTML for labels and text fields

```
<label for="quantity">Quantity:</label>
<input type="text" name="quantity" id="quantity" value="1" /><br /><br />

<label for="future_value">Future Value:</label>
<input type="text" name="future_value" id="future_value"
       value="$16,256.32" disabled="disabled" /><br /><br />

<label for="pin_code">Pin Code:</label>
<input type="password" name="pin_code" id="pin_code" maxlength="6"
       value="sesame" /><br /><br />

<input type="hidden" name="product_id" id="product_id" value="Q36" />
```

The labels and text fields in a web browser

Quantity: 1

Future Value: $16,256.32

Pin Code: ••••••

Description

- A *label* is commonly used to identify a related field, and a *text field* (or *text box*) is used to get data from the user.

- A *hidden field* has name and value attributes that are sent to the server when the form is submitted, but the field isn't displayed in the browser. However, if you view the source code for the web page, you can see the data for the hidden field.

- The data for a *password field* is obscured by bullets or asterisks, but the name and value attributes are passed to the server when the form is submitted.

Figure 10-3   How to code labels and text fields

How to code radio buttons and check boxes

Figure 10-4 shows how to use the input element to code *checkbox fields* and *radio fields*, commonly referred to as *check boxes* and *radio buttons*. Although check boxes work independently of each other, radio buttons are typically set up so the user can select only one radio button from a group of buttons. In the example in this figure, for instance, you can select only one of the three radio buttons. However, you can select or deselect any combination of check boxes.

To create a radio button, you set the type attribute of the input element to "radio". Then, to create a group, you set the name attribute for all of the radio buttons in the group to the same value. In this figure, all three radio buttons have "crust" as their name attribute. That way, the user will only be able to select one of these radio buttons at a time. Note, however, that each of these buttons has different id and value attributes. That way, your client-side or server-side code can refer to each individual radio button.

To create a check box, you set the type attribute of the input element to "checkbox". Then, you can set the name and id attributes so you can access the control from your client-side and server-side code. When you submit the form to the server, a name/value pair for the check box is submitted to the server only if it's selected. However, an indication of whether the control is selected is always sent to the server. The same is true of radio buttons.

If you want a check box or radio button to be selected by default, you can code the checked attribute. In this figure, for example, the second radio button has been selected by default. If you're using XHTML, you code any Boolean attribute with the attribute name as the value, like this:

```
checked="checked"
```

If you're using HTML, you can code just the attribute name, like this:

```
checked
```

On most browsers, this will work in XHTML too, but you won't be able to validate the page. If a Boolean attribute isn't coded, it is treated as false or off.

Attributes of the input element for radio buttons and check boxes

Attribute	Description
`type`	Specifies the type of control. It's set to "radio" or "checkbox".
`value`	Specifies the value to submit to the server when the control is checked.
`checked`	A Boolean attribute that causes the control to be checked when the page is loaded. If a reset button is clicked, the control reverts to the checked state.

The HTML for radio buttons and check boxes

```
<label>Crust:</label><br />
<input type="radio" name="crust" id="crust1" value="thin" />
    Thin Crust<br />
<input type="radio" name="crust" id="crust2" value="deep"
        checked="checked" />
    Deep Dish<br />
<input type="radio" name="crust" id="crust3" value="hand" />
    Hand Tossed<br /><br />

<label>Toppings:</label><br />
<input type="checkbox" name="topping1" id="topping1" value="pepperoni" />
    Pepperoni<br />
<input type="checkbox" name="topping2" id="topping2" value="mushrooms" />
    Mushrooms<br />
<input type="checkbox" name="topping3" id="topping3" value="olives" />
    Black Olives
```

The radio buttons and check boxes in a web browser

Description

- Only one *radio button* in a group can be selected at one time. The radio buttons in a group must have the same name attribute, but different ids and values.

- *Check boxes* are unrelated, so more than one check box can be checked at the same time. The id and name attributes of a check box are set to the same value.

- When a form is submitted to the server, the state of the radio buttons and check boxes on the form is sent along with the other data. The state of a radio button or check box indicates whether it is selected.

- To turn on a Boolean attribute with XHTML, you code the attribute name, an equal sign, and the attribute name in quotes. With HTML, you can code just the attribute name.

Figure 10-4   How to code radio buttons and check boxes

How to code drop-down lists

Figure 10-5 shows how to code a *drop-down list*, which is one type of *select list*. With a drop-down list, the user can select one option from a list of options. To display the list of options, the user must click the arrow at the right side of the control. In this figure, for example, you can see a drop-down list of sizes before and after the list is displayed.

To code a drop-down list, you use a select element. On this element, you code the name and id attributes. Then, between the opening and closing tags, you code two or more option elements that supply the options that are available for the list. On each option element, you code a value attribute. In addition, you supply the text that's displayed in the list for the content of the element. This text is often the same as or similar to the value for the option.

If you want to group the options in a drop-down list, you can code one or more optgroup elements. In this figure, for example, two optgroup elements are used to divide the options that are available into two groups: Juniors and Misses. To do that, the label attribute specifies the label for each group. Note that when you use groups, the user can't select a group, only the options it contains.

When a drop-down list is first displayed, the first option in the list is selected by default. If that's not what you want, you can include the selected attribute with a value of "selected" on the option you want to be selected. You'll see how that works when I present another type of select list in the next figure.

An attribute of the option element

Attribute	Description
selected	A Boolean attribute that causes the option to be selected when the page is loaded.

An attribute of the optgroup element

Attribute	Description
label	Specifies the text that's used to identify a group of options.

The HTML for a drop-down list

```
<label>Size:</label><br />
<select name="size" id="size">
    <optgroup label="Juniors">
        <option value="5">5</option>
        <option value="7">7</option>
        <option value="9">9</option>
        <option value="11">11</option>
    </optgroup>
    <optgroup label="Misses">
        <option value="6">6</option>
        <option value="8">8</option>
        <option value="10">10</option>
        <option value="12">12</option>
    </optgroup>
</select>
```

The drop-down list in a web browser before and after the list is displayed

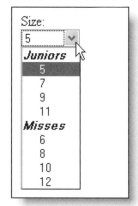

Description

- To use a *drop-down list*, you click the arrow at the right side of the field to display the list. Then, you can click on an option to select it.
- By default, the first option in the list is selected when the page is loaded. To change the default option, include the selected attribute on the option you want to be selected.
- It can sometimes be helpful to group the options in a list to make them easier to work with. To do that, you code the options in a group within an optgroup element.

Figure 10-5   How to code drop-down lists

How to code list boxes

In addition to drop-down lists, you can code another type of select list called a *list box*. A list box differs from a drop-down list in that two or more of its options are always displayed. In addition, you can define a list box so that two or more options can be selected at the same time.

Figure 10-6 shows how to code list boxes. To start, you code a select element with name and id attributes. In addition, you include the size attribute to indicate the number of options that are displayed at a time. In the example in this figure, the size attribute is set to 5. Because the list contains seven options, however, a scroll bar has been added to the list.

By default, the user can select only one option from a list box. In some cases, though, it makes sense to let the user select two or more options. To do that, you code the multiple attribute with the value "multiple". Then, the user can select multiple options by holding down the Ctrl key in Windows or the Command key in Mac OS and clicking on the options.

Notice in the example in this figure that the first option includes the selected attribute. As I explained in the previous topic, you use this attribute to select a default option. Unlike a drop-down list, none of the options are selected by default from a list box. If a list box provides for multiple selections, you can code the selected attribute on as many options as you want.

Attributes of the select element for list boxes

Attribute	Description
size	Specifies the number of items to display in the control. If the value is 1, the control will be a drop-down list. The default value is 1.
multiple	A Boolean attribute that determines whether multiple items can be selected. It is only valid if size is greater than 1.

The HTML for a list box

```
<label>Toppings:</label><br />
<select name="toppings" id="toppings" size="5" multiple="multiple" >
    <option value="pepperoni" selected="selected">Pepperoni</option>
    <option value="sausage">Sausage</option>
    <option value="mushrooms">Mushrooms</option>
    <option value="olives">Black olives</option>
    <option value="onions">Onions</option>
    <option value="bacon">Canadian bacon</option>
    <option value="pineapple">Pineapple</option>
</select>
```

The list box in a web browser

Description

- A *list box* displays the number of options you specify on the size attribute. If the list contains more options than can be displayed at once, a scroll bar is added to the list box.

- By default, only one option can be selected from a list box. To allow two or more selections, include the multiple attribute.

- You use the option element to define the options in a list box, and you use the optgroup element to define option groups. See figure 10-5 for details.

Figure 10-6   How to code list boxes

How to code text areas

Figure 10-7 shows how to code a *textarea field*, or just *text area*. Although a text area is similar to a text field, a text area can display multiple lines of text. As the user enters text into a text area, the text is automatically wrapped to the next line when necessary. The user can also start a new line manually by pressing the Enter key. If the user enters more lines than can be displayed at one time, a scroll bar is automatically added to the text area.

To code a text area, you use a textarea element. Within the opening tag, you code the name and id attributes just as you do for other controls. You also code the rows attribute to specify the approximate number of visible rows the text area will contain, and you code the cols attribute to specify the approximate number of columns. In this figure, for example, the rows attribute is set to 4, but five lines of text are displayed. Although the rows and cols attributes are required, you can override them with CSS if you need more precise control over the size of the text area.

You can also include default text that will be displayed in a text area by coding the text as content of the textarea element. If you do that, you should know that any whitespace you include in the text is displayed in the text area. That includes spaces, tabs, and carriage returns. In this figure, for example, you can see that carriage returns have been used to start new paragraphs.

Attributes of the textarea element

Attribute	Description
rows	Specifies the approximate number of rows in the text area. It is required.
cols	Specifies the approximate number of columns in the text area. It is required.

The HTML for a text area with default text

```
<label>Comments:</label><br />
<textarea name="comments" id="comments" rows="4" cols="50">
If you have any comments, we would be delighted to hear from you.

Just delete this text and enter your own.
</textarea>
```

The text area in a web browser

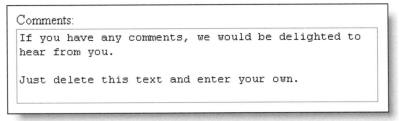

The text area after text has been entered into it

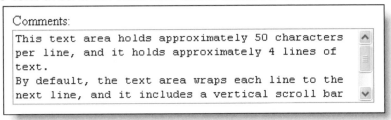

Description

- A *textarea field* (or just *text area*) can be used to get multi-line text entries from the user.
- Any whitespace you include in the HTML for the content of a text area is reflected in the value that's displayed in the browser.
- Although the rows and cols attributes are required, you can override these attributes using the CSS height and width properties.

Figure 10-7   How to code text areas

How to group controls

In many cases, you'll want to group related controls on a form to make it easy for users to see that they're related. To group controls, you use the fieldset and legend elements as shown in figure 10-8.

To start, you code the fieldset element. Then, between the opening and closing tags for this element, you code the legend element. The content of this element determines the text that's displayed for the group. Note that this element must be coded right after the opening tag of the fieldset element. Then, the controls in the group follow the legend element.

The example in this figure illustrates how this works. Here, two groups are defined: one that contains radio buttons and one that contains check boxes. Notice the thin gray border that's placed around the groups by default. You can use CSS to change the appearance of this border if you want to.

HTML that uses fieldset and legend elements

```
<fieldset>
    <legend>Crust</legend>
    <input type="radio" name="crust" id="crust1" value="thin" />
        Thin Crust<br />
    <input type="radio" name="crust" id="crust2" value="deep"
            checked="checked" />
        Deep Dish<br />
    <input type="radio" name="crust" id="crust3" value="hand" />
        Hand Tossed
</fieldset>

<fieldset>
    <legend>Toppings</legend>
    <input type="checkbox" name="topping1" id="topping1"
            value="pepperoni" />
        Pepperoni<br />
    <input type="checkbox" name="topping2" id="topping2"
            value="mushrooms" />
        Mushrooms<br />
    <input type="checkbox" name="topping3" id="topping3" value="olives" />
        Black Olives
</fieldset>
```

The elements in a web browser

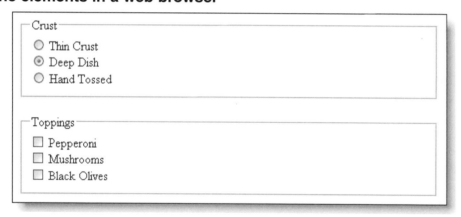

Description

- The fieldset element is used to group controls like radio buttons or check boxes.
- The legend element is coded within a fieldset element. It is used to label the grouped controls.

Figure 10-8   How to group controls

Other skills for working with forms

Now that you know how to code forms, you're ready to learn some other skills for working with forms and controls. In particular, you should know how to use CSS to align and format controls. You should also know how to set the tab order of the controls on a form, and you should know how to assign access keys to the controls on a form. Finally, you should know how to add a search function to a form.

How to align controls

As you saw in figure 10-3, if you code a series of labels followed by text fields, the text fields won't be aligned by default. That's because the labels are different widths. Although you might think that you could just set the width property for a series of labels so they all have the same width, that's not the case. That's because labels are inline elements, and you can't set the width or height of an inline element.

The best way to align controls is to use the technique shown in figure 10-9. Here, the rule set for the labels starts by floating the labels to the left. That causes the labels to be treated like block elements. Then, the rule set can set the width property so all the labels are the same width. The text-align property is also included so the labels are aligned at the right. This can often make the form more readable.

In addition to the rule set for the labels, a rule set is included for the input controls in the data division (the text boxes). The first property in this rule set increases the space between the labels and text boxes to 2 ems. The second property in this rule set sets the space between the text boxes to .5 em.

The last rule set aligns the buttons on the form. To start, padding is added above the buttons to increase the space between the last text box and the buttons. Then, the left margin is set so the left side of the first button is aligned with the text boxes.

Label, text box, and button controls aligned on a form

The HTML for the form

```
<form action="register.html" method="post">
    <div id="data">
        <label for="first_name">First name:</label>
        <input type="text" name="first_name" id="first_name" /><br />
        <label for="last_name">Last name:</label>
        <input type="text" name="last_name" id="last_name" /><br />
            .
            .
            .
        <label for="zip_code">Zip code:</label>
        <input type="text" name="zip_code" id="zip_code" /><br />
    </div>
    <div id="buttons">
        <input type="button" name="register" id="register"
            value="Register" />
        <input type="reset" name="reset" id="reset" value="Reset" />
    </div>
</form>
```

The CSS for the controls

```
label {
    float: left;
    width: 5em;
    text-align: right; }
#data input {
    margin-left: 1em;
    margin-bottom: .5em; }
#buttons {
    padding-top: .5em;
    margin-left: 6em; }
```

Description

- If a form includes a series of controls and labels that identify them, you can align the labels by floating them to the left of the controls and setting a width that provides enough space for all the labels. Then, you can set a left margin for the controls to add space between the labels and the controls.

- A series of labels is typically more readable if the labels are aligned at the right, particularly if there is a sizable variance in length.

Figure 10-9   How to align controls

How to format controls

In the last topic, you saw how to use a few of the CSS properties to align the controls on a form. But you can also use CSS properties to format controls. Figure 10-10 illustrates how this works.

The form shown here is the same form you saw in the previous figure, but with some additional formatting. To start, I set the font family and font size for the entire form. Note, however, that this does not affect the text on the buttons. In addition, I set the color for the labels to navy.

Next, I used the focus: pseudo-class to change the appearance of a text box when it has the focus. In this case, I added a two-pixel wide solid navy border around the text box. In this example, you can see that the first text box has the focus.

I also changed the widths of three of the text boxes so they are more appropriate for the data the user will enter. Specifically, I increased the widths of the Last name and Address text boxes to 20 ems, and I reduced the width of the State text box to 2 ems.

Finally, I changed the appearance of the two buttons on the form. First, I set the width property so both of the buttons have the same width. (By default, the width is determined by the text that's displayed on the button.) Then, I changed the font color to navy, and I changed the background color to silver. Note that when I changed the background color, the shape of the buttons changed so the corners are square rather than rounded. In addition, the buttons appear three-dimensional.

The form in figure 10-9 with some additional formatting

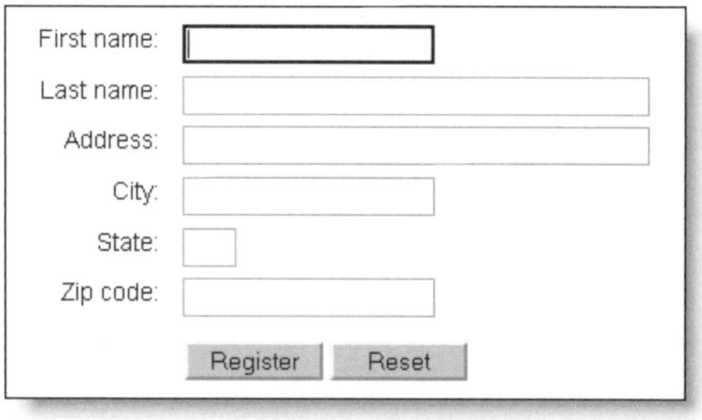

The CSS for the form

```
body {
    font-family: Arial, Helvetica, sans-serif;
    font-size: 90%;
    margin: 0;
    padding: 20px;
}
label {
    color: navy;
    float: left;
    width: 5em;
    text-align: right;
}
#data input {
    margin-left: 1em;
    margin-bottom: .5em;
}
#data input:focus {
    border: 2px solid navy;
}
#lastname, #address { width: 20em; }
#state { width: 2em; }
#buttons {
    padding-top: .5em;
    margin-left: 6em;
}
#buttons input {
    width: 6em;
    color: navy;
    background-color: silver;
}
```

Description

- You can use many of the properties you learned about in chapters 4 and 5 to format controls.

- You can use the :focus pseudo-class to change the appearance of a control when it has the focus. This class also applies to a link if the user moves the focus to the link using the keyboard. This class is not supported by Internet Explorer version 7 and earlier.

Figure 10-10   How to format controls

How to set the tab order for controls

Figure 10-11 presents a form that contains many of the controls that you've just learned about in this chapter, including labels, text boxes, radio boxes, a check box, a drop-down list, and a button. By default, when the user presses the Tab key on a page like this, the focus moves from one control to another in the sequence that the controls appear in the HTML, not including labels. This sequence is referred to as the *tab order* of the controls. Often, the default tab order is acceptable, so you don't need to change it.

If the default tab order isn't what you want, though, you can use the tabindex attribute to change the tab order or to leave some controls out of the tab order. To remove a control from the tab order, you assign a negative number to its tabindex attribute. This is illustrated by the example in this figure. Here, the second and third radio buttons are removed from the tab order. Then, the rest of the controls retain the default tab order. Often, a change like this is all you'll want to make.

To change the default tab order, you assign values to the tabindex attributes of the controls that indicate the sequence in which you want the controls to receive the focus. The value of the tabindex attribute can start at zero or any positive number and can be incremented by any amount. You can also code the same tabindex value for more than one control. Then, within those controls, the tab order will be the sequence that the controls appear in the HTML.

Controls that aren't assigned a tabindex value will also receive the focus in the sequence that the controls appear in the HTML. These controls will receive the focus after all the controls that are assigned tabindex values. As a result, you usually assign tabindex values to all of the controls on a form if you assign values to any of the controls.

When you work with the tab order, you should be aware of one browser variation. That is, when you press the Tab key right after a page is loaded, the focus may move to a browser control like the address bar instead of the first control on the page. In fact, you may have to press the Tab key several times before the focus is moved to the first control. To get around this problem, you can use JavaScript to move the focus to a control when the page is loaded.

Something else you should be aware of is that most browsers include links in the tab order. So, if you include links on a web page that has one or more controls, you'll need to make sure that the tab order still works the way you want it to. If you want to remove the links from the tab order, for example, you can set their tabindex attributes to a negative number.

The attribute that's used to control the tab order

Attribute	Description
tabindex	To set the tab order for a control, use a value of 0 or more. To take a control out of the tab order, use a negative value.

A form for a survey

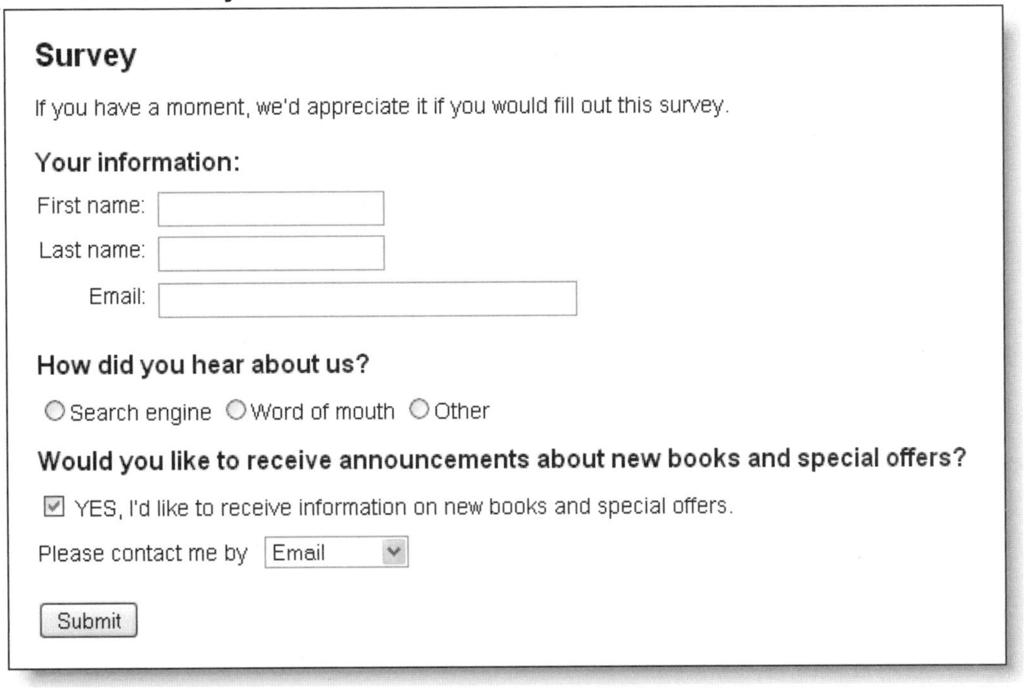

Survey

If you have a moment, we'd appreciate it if you would fill out this survey.

Your information:

First name: [   ]

Last name: [   ]

Email: [   ]

How did you hear about us?

○ Search engine   ○ Word of mouth   ○ Other

Would you like to receive announcements about new books and special offers?

☑ YES, I'd like to receive information on new books and special offers.

Please contact me by [Email   ▾]

[Submit]

Code that takes two controls out of the tab order

```
<input type="radio" name="heardFrom" id="heardFrom2" value="Friend"
    tabindex="-1" />Word of mouth
<input type="radio" name="heardFrom" id="heardFrom3" value="Other"
    tabindex="-1" />Other
```

Description

- The *tab order* of a form is the sequence that the controls receive the focus when the Tab key is pressed. By default, the tab order is the order of the controls in the HTML, not including labels. You can change the tab order by using the tabindex attribute.

- When you press the Tab key after a page is loaded, it may move the focus to browser controls before it moves it to the controls on the form. To fix that, you can use a client-side script to set the focus to a form control when the page is loaded.

- Most browsers include links in the default tab order.

- If you code the tabindex attribute for some, but not all, of the controls on a form, the controls without a tabindex attribute will come last in the tab order.

Figure 10-11   How to set the tab order for controls

How to assign access keys

In the last topic, you learned that you can use the Tab key to move the focus from one control to another using the keyboard. You can also move the focus directly to a control with the keyboard by using an *access key*. An access key is simply a key on the keyboard that you can press in combination with one or more other keys to move the focus to a control.

If the page is displayed in Internet Explorer under Windows, for example, the user can move the focus to a control by pressing the Alt key and the access key. If it's displayed in Firefox under Windows, the key combination is the Alt and Shift keys plus the access key. And if it's displayed in a browser under Mac OS, the key combination is typically the Ctrl key plus the access key.

To define an access key for a control, you code the accesskey attribute as shown in figure 10-12. The value of this attribute is the keyboard key you want to use to move the focus to the control. In the first example in this figure, you can see that the accesskey attribute is coded for the three text boxes on the form. The access key for the First name text box is "F", the access key for the Last name text box is "L", and the access key for the Email text box is "E". Notice that the letters that are used for the access keys are underlined in the labels that are associated with the controls. This is a common way to identify the access key for a control.

The second example in this figure shows another way to code access keys for controls that have labels associated with them. Here, the accesskey attribute is coded for each of the labels instead of for the text boxes. Then, when the user activates one of these access keys, the focus is moved to the associated text box (the one specified by the for attribute) because labels can't receive the focus.

The attribute that's used to specify an access key

Attribute	Description
accesskey	Identifies a keyboard key that can be used in combination with other keys to move the focus to the control. The key combination depends on the operating system and browser.

Three labels with access keys

First name:
Last name:
Email:

The HTML for the controls

```
<label for="first_name"><u>F</u>irst name:</label>
<input type="text" name="first_name" id="first_name" accesskey="F" /><br />
<label for="last_name"><u>L</u>ast name:</label>
<input type="text" name="last_name" id="last_name" accesskey="L" /><br />
<label for="email"><u>E</u>mail:</label>
<input type="text" name="email" id="email" accesskey="E" /><br />
```

Another way to define the access keys

```
<label for="first_name" accesskey="F"><u>F</u>irst name:</label>
<input type="text" name="first_name" id="first_name" /><br />
<label for="last_name" accesskey="L"><u>L</u>ast name:</label>
<input type="text" name="last_name" id="last_name" /><br />
<label for="email" accesskey="E"><u>E</u>mail:</label>
<input type="text" name="email" id="email" /><br />
```

Description

- *Access keys* are shortcut keys that the user can press to move the focus to specific controls on a form. To assign an access key to a control, you code the accesskey attribute.

- The accesskey attribute can be used with any form element except for form, optgroup, and option.

- The easiest way to let the user know that an access key is available for a control is to underline the access key in the label or text that identifies the control.

- If you assign an access key to a label, the focus is moved to the control that's associated with the label since labels can't receive the focus.

Figure 10-12   How to assign access keys

How to add a search function to a web site

Now that you know how to use forms, you have the skills that you need for adding a search function to a web site. To do that, you use HTML to create a form that submits the search data to a search engine. This is illustrated in figure 10-13.

At the top of this figure, you can see the two controls that are needed for a search function: a text box for the search entry and a Search button that submits the search entry to the search engine. This is the standard way to set up the controls for a search entry, and this mimics the way that Google uses these controls. If you want to vary from this at all, you can use Go instead of Search on the button, but users expect all search functions to look this way. You should also make the text box large enough for a typical entry.

If you look at the HTML code for this function, you can see that the form is submitted to www.google.com, which is the Google search engine. That's why the results of the search are displayed on the standard Google results page. To limit the search to www.murach.com, this HTML uses two hidden fields that pass the required data to the Google search engine. To use this HTML for a Google search of your site, you just need to change the value attribute in the two hidden fields to the URL for your web site.

The trouble with the standard Google search engine is that sponsored links will be displayed. That's why it's better to use a search engine that can be customized so it returns results that are appropriate for users of your site. To find a search engine like this, you can search the web for "add search function to web site." Some of these search engines are free, and some like Google Site Search charge a nominal fee like $100 a year for a small site.

The controls for a search function

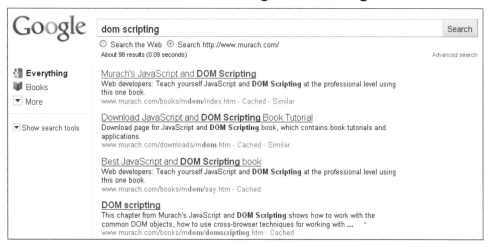

The results of a search when the Google search engine is used

The HTML for using the Google search engine

```html
<form method="get" action="http://www.google.com/search">
    <div id="search">
        <input id="q" name="q" size="30" maxlength="255" value=""
            type="text" />
        <input name="domains" value="http://www.murach.com/"
            type="hidden" />
        <input name="sitesearch" value="http://www.murach.com/"
            type="hidden" />
        <input name="search" value="Search" type="submit" />
    </div>
</form>
```

Description

- To implement a search function, you use an HTML form to submit the search text and other required data to the search engine.

- A search function should consist of a text box where users can enter the search text, followed by either a Search or a Go button. In addition, it must include two hidden fields that specify the domain for the search and that only that domain should be searched.

- If you use a generic search engine such as Google, you have no control over the results of the searches. If you want to customize search results, you can use a search engine such as Google Site Search.

- Search engines like Google Site Search are designed to be used on and customized for a single web site. Some search engines like this are free, and some charge a nominal fee for a small web site.

Figure 10-13   How to add a search function to a web site

Perspective

Now that you've completed this chapter, you should have all the skills you need for creating forms. Then, the data in your forms can be processed on the client by using a client-side language like JavaScript. Or, the data in your forms can also be processed on the server by using a language like JSP or PHP. In practice, JavaScript is often used to validate the form data on the client before it is submitted to the web server for processing.

In chapter 13, you'll be introduced to JavaScript so you'll get a better idea of what JavaScript can do. Then, if you want to learn more, you can get *Murach's JavaScript and DOM Scripting*. Similarly, to learn how to process form data on a web server, please check our web site for our latest books on server-side programming, including our books on ASP.NET, Java Servlets and JSP, and PHP and MySQL.

Terms

form
control
button
submit button
reset button
image button
label
text field
text box
hidden field
password field
check box field
check box
radio field
radio button
drop-down list
select list
list box
textarea field
text area
tab order
access key

Summary

- A *form* contains one or more *controls* like text boxes, radio buttons, or check boxes that can receive data. When a form is submitted to the server for processing, the data in the controls is sent along with the HTTP request.

- When the get method is used to submit a form, the data is sent as part of the URL for the next web page. When the post method is used, the data is hidden.

- A *submit button* submits the form data to the server when the button is clicked. A *reset button* resets all the data in the form when it is clicked. Buttons can also be used to start client-side scripts when they are clicked.

- The controls that are commonly used within a form are *labels*, *text fields* (or *text boxes*), *radio buttons*, *check boxes*, *drop-down lists*, *list boxes*, and *text areas*.

- A label is commonly used to identify a related control. You use its for attribute to specify the id of the related control.

- A *hidden field* contains data that is sent to the server, but the field isn't displayed on the form. A *password field* also contains data that is sent to the server, but its data is obscured on the form by bullets or asterisks.

- You can use CSS to align controls by floating the labels to the left of the controls. You can also use CSS to format the controls.

- The *tab order* of a form is the order in which the controls receive the focus when the Tab key is pressed. By default, this is the sequence in which the controls are coded in the HTML. But you can change that by using the tabindex attribute for the controls.

- *Access keys* are shortcut keys that the user can press to move the focus to specific controls on a form. To assign an access key to a control, you use its accesskey attribute. To let the user know that an access key is available, you can underline the access key in the label for the control.

Exercise 10-1   Create a Payment form

In this exercise, you'll create a form that uses many of the controls you learned about in this chapter. This form accepts billing information from a customer as shown below. Note that because the code that processes the form isn't provided, this form won't be fully functional.

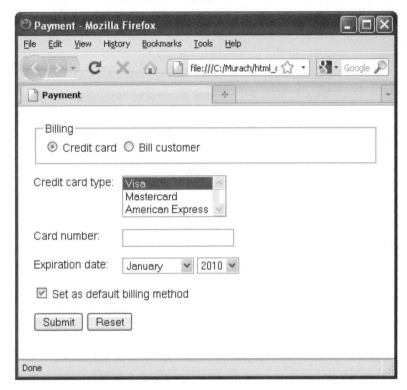

Enter the code for the form controls

1.   Use your editor to open this file:

   `c:\html_css\ch10\payment.html`

   This file contains a form element with four divisions.

2.   Add the HTML code for the two radio buttons and the group that contains them to the first division. Code the Credit card option so it's selected when the form is first displayed.

3.   Add three paragraphs to the second division. The first one should contain the list box and its associated label, the second one should contain the text box and its associated label, and the third one should contain the two drop-down lists and their associated label. The list box should display three options at a time, and the first option should be selected by default. The drop-down list for the expiration month should contain one option for each of the twelve months of the year. The drop-down list for the expiration year should contain an option for the current year plus the next four years.

4. Add a paragraph that contains the code for the check box to the third division. This box should be checked when the form is first displayed.

5. Add a paragraph that contains the code for the two buttons to the fourth division. Code the first button as a submit button so the data on the form will be submitted when this button is clicked. Code the second button so it will reset the controls on the form when it's clicked.

Format the form

6. Display the form in a browser to make sure all the controls are displayed. Then, use your text editor to open the payment.css file in the c:\html_css\ch10\styles directory.

7. Add properties to the rule set for the body of the page so the text on the form is displayed in a sans-serif font at 90% of the default size.

8. Add a rule set for the three labels on the form. This rule set should float the labels to the left and set the width of the labels to 8 ems.

9. Display the form in a browser, and make sure the controls are formatted like the ones shown above. If you want to make any additional changes to the formatting, do that now.

Test the form

10. In the browser, click on the Bill customer option to select it, and notice that the Credit card option is no longer selected. Then, select a credit card type other than the one that's selected by default, enter a credit card number, and select an expiration month and year. Also, remove the check mark from the check box.

11. Click the Reset button to return the controls to their default values. Then, enter more data.

12. Click the Submit button. This should send the data to the web page that's specified in the form element: payment_summary.html. Because the form was submitted via the "get" method, you should be able to see the data that's submitted at the end of the URL for that page. This page also uses JavaScript to get the data from the URL and display it in the body of the page. If this doesn't work, make sure that your submit button is coded with its type attribute set to "submit". To return to the payment page, click the Back button.

13. Change the submit method in the form element from "get" to "post". Then, refresh the page, enter more data, and click the Submit button. This time, the payment_summary page will be displayed, but you won't be able to see the data at the end of the URL because that data is hidden. As a result, the JavaScript for the page can't display the data.

14. Change the submit method in the form element back to "get". Then, test again, and close the files.

11

How to add audio, video, and other media to your web site

Earlier in this book, you learned how to add images to your web pages. Images are a type of media, and they're the type that you'll use the most. In some cases, though, you'll want to include other types of media in your web pages such as audio and video. In this chapter, you'll learn how to do that. You'll also learn how to work with some common media players.

An introduction to media

Before I show you how to include media files in a web page, you need to be familiar with the various media types and formats. In addition, you should be familiar with some of the most popular media players that you can use to display media content. Finally, you should know how to use a link to display a media file on a separate page.

Media types and formats

The first table in figure 11-1 lists the most common types of media. If you've read chapter 8, you're already familiar with still and animated images. The other four media types listed here are documents, which can contain text, images, and graphics; audio files, which contain only sound; video files, which can contain just video or video and sound; and Flash files, which can contain animated images, video, and other Flash components.

The second table in this figure lists some of the formats that a media file can be stored in and describes each format. For example, ShockWave Flash files are stored in the SWF format, which means that the file has an extension of .swf. Audio and video files can be stored in a variety of formats. Two of the most popular formats are MP3 for audio and MPG (or MPEG) for video. These formats were developed based on standards designed by the *Moving Picture Experts Groups*, and files that use these formats can be played in most media players. The most popular document format on the Web is PDF.

The second table also lists the *MIME types* that you'll be using for the media formats in the type attributes of your HTML code. For instance, "audio/x-wave" is the MIME type for WAV audio files. You'll see how these types are used starting in figure 11-3. By the way, MIME is an organization that sets the Internet standards for content types.

Media types

Type	Description
Image	A still picture that's stored in a GIF, JPEG, or PNG file. See chapter 8 for details.
Animated image	A visual animation that consists of a series of images called frames. This type of image is stored in a GIF file. See chapter 8 for details.
Document	A file with a fixed layout that can include text, images, and graphics.
Audio file	A file that contains only sound.
Video file	A file that can contain video and sound.
Flash file	A file that can contain animation, video, and other Flash components. Unlike other types of media files, the user can interact with Flash files.

Common media formats and MIME types

Format	Description	MIME type
PDF	Portable Document Format file	application/pdf
WAV	Waveform audio file	audio/x-wave
MP3	MPEG audio file	audio/mpeg or audio/x-mpeg
MPG/MPEG	MPEG video file	video/mpeg
WMA	Windows Media Audio file	audio/x-ms-wma
WMV	Windows Media Video file	video/x-ms-wmv
RA	RealPlayer Audio file	audio/vnd.rn-realaudio
RV	RealPlayer Video file	video/vnd.rn-realvideo
RM	RealMedia file (audio or video)	audio/x-pn-realaudio-plugin
MOV	QuickTime movie file	video/quicktime
SWF	ShockWave Flash file	application/x-shockwave-flash

Description

- PDF is the most common document type for the Internet, and all major browsers recognize it.

- Two of the most popular formats for storing audio and video files are MP3 and MPG/MPEG, which are based on standards developed by the *Moving Picture Experts Group*.

- The MIME types describe the contents of a file and can assist browsers in determining what player to use to open a file.

Figure 11-1   Media types and formats

Media players

To display a document or to play a Flash, audio, or video file, you use a *media player*. At the top of figure 11-2, for example, you can see a video file that's being displayed in a media player called RealPlayer.

The table in this figure lists some popular media players and describes the types of files they can display. The first player in this table is Adobe Reader, the player that's commonly used for displaying PDF files.

The second player is Adobe Flash Player, the player that is commonly used for playing Flash animations as well as Flash videos. In fact, YouTube and other popular video sites use Flash Player to play their video files. These files are actually in FLV (Flash Video) or FL4 format, but the video files are embedded in SWF files. Although you can also play Flash files in some other media players, those players don't always provide all of the required features. That's particularly true if the Flash file provides for user interaction.

On Windows systems, Windows Media Player is the default player so it is widely used. It can play most audio and video files as well as Flash files.

RealPlayer and QuickTime Player are available for both Windows and Mac OS X. These players support their own proprietary media formats, as well as most other audio and video formats.

To get a media player, the user typically downloads it from the manufacturer's web site for free. Then, when the user installs the media player, a *plug-in* for the player is added to any browsers the user has installed. The plug-in makes it possible to use the media player to display or play a file within a web page.

Some plug-ins can also be installed without downloading the media player. That's the case with Adobe Flash Player and QuickTime Player. In fact, Adobe Flash Player is only available as a plug-in; it's not available as a standalone media player.

The RealPlayer interface in Firefox

Some popular media players

Player	Description
Adobe Reader	Used to display PDF files.
Adobe Flash Player	Commonly used to display Flash animation and videos (SWF).
Windows Media Player	Comes with Windows operating systems and provides for playing files in a variety of formats (SWF, WAV, MP3, MPG, WMA, WMV, and MOV). It was originally available for Mac OS X as well, but has been discontinued. Windows Media (WMV and WMA) can still be played with QuickTime Player under Mac OS X by installing the WMV player plug-in developed by Flip4Mac.
RealPlayer	Provides for playing audio and video in all of the formats listed in figure 11-1. Available for Windows and Mac OS X.
QuickTime Player	Provides for displaying animated images (GIF) and flash files (SWF) and for playing audio (WAV and MP3) and video (MPEG and MOV) files. Available for Windows and Mac OS X.

Description

- Special *media players* may be required to play a media file in a browser.
- Most media players come with *plug-ins* that provide browsers with features for playing specific types of files.
- The media players listed above will only play MPEG movies in MPEG-1 format (the format used for video CDs), not MPEG-2 (the format for DVDs). You may be able to purchase plug-ins that support the MPEG-2 format, however.

Figure 11-2   Media players

How to link to a media file

The easiest way to display or play a media file is to use the a element to create a link to the file. This is illustrated in figure 11-3. Here a PDF file is displayed by Adobe Reader within a browser window. Notice here that the file is displayed in its own web page, which is what you would expect when you use the a element.

Because the a element is presented in detail in chapter 7, I won't repeat the information from that chapter. Note that when you use this tag to link to media files, though, you don't specify the URL of another page on the href attribute. Instead, you specify the URL of the media file. Then, when you click the link, a new page is opened for the file.

In addition to the href attribute, you typically include a type attribute on the a element. This attribute identifies the MIME type of the file, which can help the browser determine what media player to use. For instance, the first HTML example in this figure uses "application/pdf" as the MIME type. Because all the major browsers recognize the PDF format, though, it's probably safe to omit this attribute.

Before I go on, you should realize that the MIME type doesn't identify a specific player. Because of that, the browser will use the default player that's associated with the MIME type or, if the MIME type is omitted, the file format.

If you use the target element as shown in the first example in this figure, the page for the media file is opened in a new tab or a new browser window, depending on your browser settings. Then, the user can switch between the media file and the page that linked to it by clicking on the tab or browser window. In the browser in this figure, you can see two tabs: one for the PDF document and the other for the page that provided the link that opened the document. If you don't code the target attribute, the media file is opened in the same tab or window, so you need to click on the Back button to return to the window that linked to the file.

As the first technical note in this figure points out, if you're using IE, you may see a message at the top of the page when you try to open a media file. This message indicates that IE has restricted the web page from running scripts or ActiveX controls that could access your computer. If you see this message, click on it, select Allow Blocked Content from the menu that's displayed, and click Yes in the message box that asks if you're sure you want to let the file run active content.

Microsoft added this security message to Internet Explorer 7 due to an ongoing patent infringement case. To stop this message from being displayed, you can use the Tools→Internet Options command to display the Internet Options dialog box. Then, you can display the Advanced tab, scroll down to the Security group, and select the "Allow active content to run in files on My Computer" option. After you restart Internet Explorer, you will no longer see the security message.

A PDF file displayed in a browser

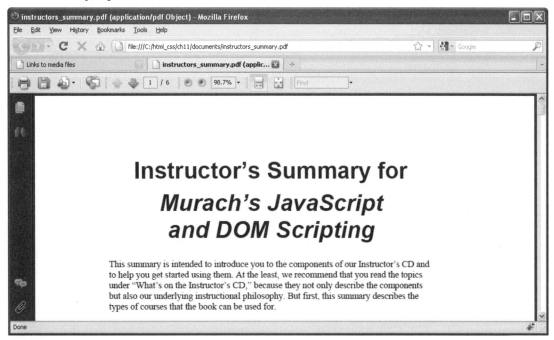

An HTML link that displays a PDF file in a new window

```
<a href="documents/instructors_summary.pdf"
   type="application/pdf"
   target="_blank">Read the Instructor's Summary<a>
```

An HTML link that plays an MP3 file

```
<a href="music/twist_away.mp3" type="audio/mpeg">MP3 file</a>
```

Description

- When you use the a element to display a media file, the file is typically displayed in its own web page and opened in the default player associated with the file type.
- To help the browser determine which player to use, you can include a type attribute on the a element. The type attribute specifies a *MIME type*, which identifies the type of content the file contains. For a list of common MIME types, see figure 11-1.

Technical notes for IE users

- When you use IE to open a media player, a bar may appear at the top of the page that indicates that IE has restricted the page from running scripts or ActiveX controls. To get past this restriction once, click on the bar and then on Allow Blocked Content and Yes.
- To stop this message from appearing, use the Tools→Internet Options command, click on the Advanced tab, scroll down to "Allow active content to run files on My Computer" in the Security group, click on its check box to check it, and restart IE.

Figure 11-3   How to link to a media file

How to embed media players and files

Now that you know about media types, formats, and players and you know how to open a media file in its own page, you're ready to learn how to embed media players and files in your web pages.

How to use the object and param elements

Figure 11-4 shows how you can use the object and param elements to embed a media player or file in a web page. The object element is the standard element for embedding media files. When you use this element, you can include one or more param elements to provide values to the media player that's being used. This is one of the advantages of using an object element rather than a link.

When you code the object element, you usually code the four attributes listed in this figure. The type attribute specifies the MIME type. The data attribute specifies the URL of the file you want to play. And the width and height attributes specify the width and height of either the media file or the player. For a Flash file, these attributes apply to the file. For other types of files, they apply to the media player. Also, if a file doesn't have a visual element, you can omit the width and height attributes or set their values to 0. You can use this technique, for example, to play an audio file in the background.

This figure also presents the two attributes of the param element you're most likely to use. For the name attribute, you specify the name of a parameter for a specific media player, and you specify the parameter's value on the value attribute.

In the example in this figure, you can see how this works for the filename, volume, autostart, and autoplay parameters. Here, the filename parameter provides the URL of the media file, the volume parameter provides a starting value for volume, and the autostart and autoplay parameters tell the player to start playing the file automatically. In this case, both the autostart and autoplay parameters are coded because some players support one parameter and some support the other.

At this point, you may be wondering why the URL of the file is specified on both the data attribute of the object element and on a parameter element. The answer is that some browsers, most notably Internet Explorer, require an extra push to play a file. So if you're having trouble getting Internet Explorer to play a file, you should include a parameter element that specifies the URL of the file.

Of note in this example is that the object element doesn't explicitly specify what player to use. In some cases, that's what you want. Then, the file will be played in the player that's specified in the user's browser as the default for the MIME type. In this case, that's the Windows Media Player.

The object and param elements

Element	Description
object	Embeds a media file into a web page.
param	Provides parameters to the media player that's used to open a file.

Attributes of the object element

Attribute	Description
type	The MIME type of the file. See figure 11-1 for common MIME types.
data	The URL of the file.
width	The width of a Flash file or the media player that's used.
height	The height of a Flash file or the media player that's used.

Attributes of the param element

Attribute	Description
name	The name of the parameter. Each media player has its own parameters.
value	The value of the parameter.

An object element for playing a Windows Media Player video file

```
<object type="video/x-ms-wmv"
        data="videos/surfing.wmv"
        width="400" height="300">
    <param name="filename" value="videos/surfing.wmv" />
    <param name="volume" value="10" />
    <param name="autostart" value="false" />
    <param name="autoplay" value="false" />
</object>
```

Description

- When you use the object element, you can control the appearance and operation of the media player by coding parameter elements. These elements are standard HTML.

- If you don't specify the MIME type for a file, the file will be opened in the browser's default media player for the media format.

- Because different players accept different parameters, you typically specify the parameters for all the players you want to provide for. Then, if a player doesn't support a parameter, it will ignore it.

- If you don't want to display the interface for a media player, you can omit the width and height attributes or set them to 0.

- Some browsers require a param element that specifies the URL of the file even if the file is identified in the object element.

Figure 11-4   How to use the object and param elements

How to use the embed element

Another element you can use to embed a media file is the embed element. Although this element isn't supported by the current HTML standards, it is supported by all major browsers; it will be included in the HTML 5 standards that are under development; and it is commonly used in existing sites. As a result, you should feel free to use it, especially if you're having trouble getting the object and param elements to work right.

Figure 11-5 presents some of the most useful attributes of the embed element. Except for the alt attribute, all of these are the same or similar to the attributes you code on the object element. You use the alt attribute to specify text that's displayed if the media file can't be opened.

In addition to the basic attributes, you can code the parameters for media players as attributes. For instance, the first example in this figure uses the loop, autostart, and autoplay attributes to pass parameters to the default player for an MP3 file. Here, the loop attribute tells the player to keep playing the file, and the autostart and autoplay parameters tell the player to start playing the file automatically. Here again, both the autostart and autoplay parameters are coded because some players support one of these parameters and some support the other.

When you use the embed element, you should realize that your HTML editor won't recognize its attributes, so they won't be color-coded like other attributes. That's because this element is non-standard. Nevertheless, these attributes will be recognized by the media player. You should also realize that an HTML file that uses the non-standard embed element can't be validated.

Attributes of the embed element

Attribute	Description
type	The MIME type of the file to be played.
src	The URL of the file to be played.
width	The width of a Flash file or the media player that's used.
height	The height of a Flash file or the media player that's used.
alt	The text to display if the media file can't be opened.

An embed element for playing an MP3 file

```
<embed type="audio/mpeg"
       src="music/twist_away.mp3"
       width="300" height="16"
       loop="true"
       autostart="true"
       autoplay="true">
</embed>
```

An embed element that displays a Flash file

```
<embed type="application/x-shockwave-flash"
       src="flash/3dballcube.swf"
       width="250" height="250">
</embed>
```

An embed element that plays a MOV file

```
<embed type="video/quicktime"
       src="videos/baja.mov"
       width="400" height="265"
       autostart="false"
       autoplay="false" >
</embed>
```

Description

- When you use the embed element, you code all parameters as attributes, not as param elements.

- Although the embed element isn't part of the current HTML standards, this element is supported by all major browsers, and it will be included in the HTML 5 standards.

- Often, an embed element is easier to code and works better than a comparable object element. That's why the embed element is currently in use on many web sites.

- If you don't specify a MIME type for a file, the file will be opened in the browser's default media player for the media format.

- Because different players accept different parameters, you typically specify the parameters for all the players you want to provide for. Then, if a player doesn't support a parameter, it will ignore it.

Figure 11-5   How to use the embed element

When and how to nest object and embed elements

If you want to tell Internet Explorer to use a specific player, you need to use the classid and codebase attributes that are summarized in figure 11-6. The classid attribute identifies a media player by referring to the ActiveX control that's associated with that player. The codebase attribute indicates where the ActiveX control can be downloaded from. These attributes also tell IE to stream the data in the file so the file can start playing as it's being downloaded.

The trouble is that other browsers don't recognize these attributes. One way to get around that problem, though, is to *nest* an embed element within an object element. Then, if a browser can't process the object element, it will try to process the embed element.

The first example in figure 11-6 illustrates how this works. Here, the outer object element uses the classid and codebase attributes to identify the QuickTime media player and the location from which it can be downloaded. Then, to provide for the other browsers, an embed element is nested within the object element.

The second example shows how to get the same result with one object element nested within another object element. Unfortunately, though, IE versions 6 and earlier will try to display both object elements. Then, to prevent those versions of IE from processing the inner object element, you need to use *conditional comments* like the shaded lines in this figure. Here, the first comment says that the inner object element should be processed only by browsers other than IE. ("!IE" means "not Internet Explorer".) Because conditional comments are an IE feature, they are ignored by other browsers.

Note here that you don't need to use conditional comments when you nest an embed element within an object element. That's because all versions of Internet Explorer ignore nested embed elements. This is one advantage of using the embed element rather than the object element.

In practice, many web sites use nested embed elements within object elements to provide for specific players. That way, they don't need to use conditional comments. In addition, the embed element sometimes works when a nested object element doesn't. In fact, that's the case with the examples in this figure. Here, the code in the second example doesn't work consistently with the current release of Firefox, but the code in the first example does.

Internet Explorer attributes of the object element for specific players

Attribute	Description
classid	Identifies the media player to use. The class id refers to an ActiveX control that must be installed before the file can be opened in the player.
codebase	Identifies the location at which the ActiveX control can be downloaded.

An object element for a QuickTime Player with a nested embed element

```
<object classid="clsid:02BF25D5-8C17-4B23-BC80-D3488ABDDC6B"
        codebase="http://www.apple.com/qtactivex/qtplugin.cab"
        width="400" height="265">
    <param name="src" value="videos/baja.mov" />
    <param name="autoplay" value="false" />
        <embed type="video/quicktime"
               src="videos/baja.mov"
               width="400" height="265"
               autoplay="false" >
        </embed>
</object>
```

Nested object elements with conditional comments

```
<object classid="clsid:02BF25D5-8C17-4B23-BC80-D3488ABDDC6B"
        codebase="http://www.apple.com/qtactivex/qtplugin.cab"
        width="400" height="265">
    <param name="src" value="videos/baja.mov" />
    <param name="autoplay" value="false" />
    <!--[if !IE]>-->
        <object type="video/quicktime"
                data="videos/baja.mov"
                width="400" height="265">
            <param name="autoplay" value="false" />
        </object>
    <!--<![endif]-->
</object>
```

Description

- To tell Internet Explorer what player or plug-in is needed, you code the classid and codebase attributes on the object element. These attributes are also required to stream data in IE so the file will start playing before the entire file is loaded.

- Because some browsers don't recognize the classid and codebase attributes, you need to *nest* an object or embed element that provides for those browsers within the object element that uses the classid and codebase attributes.

- When you nest elements, most browsers ignore the inner element if the outer element works. Otherwise, the browsers try to process the inner element.

- IE 6 and earlier tries to process the inner object element in a nest. To prevent that, you can code *conditional comments* around the nested element. These comments are an IE feature.

Figure 11-6   When and how to nest elements

How to work with media players

In the topics that follow, you'll learn how to work with some of the most popular media players. If you want to provide for players other than the ones presented here, you can search the Internet for a list of their parameters and for their classid and codebase values.

How to work with Adobe Flash Player

Figure 11-7 presents some of the parameters you can use with Adobe Flash Player. This figure also presents an example that uses nested object elements with conditional comments to display a flash file in all browsers. In this example, the value for the codebase attribute must be coded with no intervening spaces. That's why it has rolled over to the left margin.

In the parameter list, you can see that the movie parameter can be used to specify the URL of the file to be played, but you can also use the data attribute for this purpose. To illustrate, the movie parameter is used in the outer object element in the example, and the data attribute is used in the inner object element.

The play, loop, and quality parameters for Flash Player should be self-explanatory, but the wmode parameter requires some explanation. This parameter sets the Window Mode property of the Flash file. This property is set to "window" by default, which causes the Flash file to be displayed in its own window on top of the main browser window. Because it's in its own window, you can't see anything behind the file, and you can't place anything on top of it. This is the most efficient way to display a Flash file.

If you want to be able to see what's behind a Flash file, you can set the wmode parameter to "transparent" as shown in the example in this figure. Then, the Flash file will appear like the first image in this figure. In this case, the background of the file is transparent so you can see behind it. In contrast, the second image shows what happens if you set the wmode parameter to "opaque". In that case, the background of the file is visible and you can't see behind it.

Note in these examples that there isn't any content behind the Flash file. However, when the file is transparent, you can see through to the page background, which is white. When the file is opaque, you can't see this background.

If you want to display other elements on top of a Flash file, you can set the wmode parameter to either "opaque" or "transparent". Then, if you position the other elements so they overlap the Flash file, the elements will appear on top of the Flash file.

Before I go on, you should realize that Flash files can be interactive. That means that they can be programmed to respond to user actions. For example, a Flash file can be programmed so it changes in some way when the user clicks on it. To provide for this functionality, Flash includes a scripting language called ActionScript, but you don't need to know how to code ActionScript to use interactive Flash files.

Common parameters for working with Adobe Flash Player

Parameter	Description
movie	The URL of the file to be played. Can also be coded as src.
play	A Boolean value that determines if a file starts playing automatically. The default is true.
loop	A Boolean value that determines if a file repeats. The default is true.
quality	A keyword that controls the appearance and playback speed. Possible values are low, autolow, autohigh, medium, high, and best.
wmode	A keyword that sets the Window Mode property of the Flash file. Possible values are window, which causes the file to be displayed in its own window on top of the main browser window; opaque, which keeps content behind the file from showing through; and transparent, which lets the content behind the file show through transparent areas of the file. The default is window.

HTML that plays a Flash animation in Adobe Flash Player

```
<object classid="clsid:D27CDB6E-AE6D-11cf-96B8-444553540000"
        codebase="http://download.macromedia.com/pub/shockwave/cabs/
flash/swflash/cab#version=6,0,0,0"
        width="150" height="150">
    <param name="movie" value="flash/globe.swf" />
    <param name="wmode" value="transparent" />
    <param name="quality" value="high" />
    <!--[if !IE]>-->
        <object type="application/x-shockwave-flash"
                data="flash/globe.swf"
                width="150" height="150">
            <param name="wmode" value="transparent" />
            <param name="quality" value="high" />
        </object>
    <!--<![endif]-->
</object>
```

The animation in a web browser with and without transparency

Description

- Unlike animated images and video files in other formats, Flash files can be interactive. That means that they can be programmed to respond to user actions.

- To add interactivity to a Flash file, you use the Flash scripting language, called ActionScript.

Figure 11-7   How to work with Adobe Flash Player

How to work with Windows Media Player

Figure 11-8 presents some common parameters for working with Windows Media Player. If you read the descriptions of these parameters, you shouldn't have any trouble understanding how they work.

Four of these parameters determine what controls are displayed in the media player. By default, all of the controls, including the Play/Pause and Stop buttons, the Sound/Mute button and the volume control, the Rewind, Previous, Fast Forward, and Next buttons, and the Seek slider are displayed. If that's not what you want, you can set the appropriate parameters to false.

The last two parameters let you display additional information about a file. If you set the showdisplay parameter to true, the name of the playlist, the name of the file, the author, and the copyright date are displayed. If you set the showstatusbar parameter to true, the status of the media player is displayed (stopped, playing, or paused), along with the playlist name, file name, author, copyright date, and streaming speed.

Unlike the information that's displayed when you set the showdisplay parameter to true, the status bar displays only one item of information at a time. This status bar also displays the current position in the file and the total length of the file. If you include additional information, you'll need to provide space for it by increasing the height attribute. Otherwise, the video will be distorted.

Notice in the code in this figure that it isn't necessary to include a separate object element for Internet Explorer when you use Windows Media Player to play a Windows Media file (WMA or WMV). That's because Windows Media Player is installed with the Windows operating system, which is the only operating system Internet Explorer runs on. Because of that, you don't need to identify the ActiveX control.

If you want to use Windows Media Player to play another type of file, though, you can use the classid value shown in this figure. Or, as an alternative, you can use the application/x-mplayer2 MIME type. This MIME type is specific to Windows Media Player and works for any browser.

You should also realize that a parameter like showpositioncontrols will only work with Internet Explorer. That's because this parameter is only supported by the ActiveX control that's used by Internet Explorer. In fact, only the filename, playcount, and volume parameters are supported by the plug-in that's used by other browsers.

Common parameters for working with Windows Media Player

Parameter	Description
filename	The URL of the file to be played. Can also be coded as src.
autostart	A Boolean value that determines if the file starts playing automatically. The default is true.
loop	A Boolean value that determines if the file repeats. The default is true.
playcount	A number that determines how many times the file is played. The default is 1.
mute	A Boolean value that determines if the sound is turned off. The default is false.
volume	A number from 0 to 100 that determines the starting volume for the file.
showcontrols	A Boolean value that determines if the player controls are displayed. The default is true.
showaudiocontrols	A Boolean value that determines if the Mute/Sound button and the volume control are displayed. The default is true.
showpositioncontrols	A Boolean value that determines if the Previous, Rewind, Fast Forward, and Next buttons are displayed. The default is true.
showtracker	A Boolean value that determines if the slider that shows the current position in the file is displayed. The default is true.
showdisplay	A Boolean value that determines if information about the file is displayed. The default is false.
showstatusbar	A Boolean value that determines if the status bar is displayed. The default is false.

HTML that plays a WMV file in Windows Media Player

```
<object type="video/x-ms-wmv"
        data="videos/surfing.wmv"
        width="320" height="280">
    <param name="filename" value="videos/surfing.wmv" />
    <param name="volume" value="10" />
</object>
```

The classid value for Windows Media Player

```
clsid:6BF52A52-394A-11D3-B153-00C04F79FAA6
```

Description

- Because Windows Media Player is installed with Windows, you don't need to include the classid or codebase attributes on the object element.

- Except for the filename, playcount, and volume parameters, the parameters shown above work only with Internet Explorer. That's because the other parameters aren't supported by the plug-in that's used by the other browsers.

- The plug-in for Windows Media Player doesn't support WAV or MP3 files. Because of that, these files will only play under Windows Media Player in Internet Explorer.

- If you want to force a file with a generic format such as MPEG to play in Windows Media Player rather than the default player, you can use application/x-mplayer2 for the MIME type.

Figure 11-8   How to work with Windows Media Player

How to work with RealPlayer

Figure 11-9 presents some of the parameters you can use with RealPlayer. One parameter you'll usually set is maintainaspect. By default, this parameter is set to false, which means that the aspect ratio of a video isn't maintained when it's sized to fit the image window within the player. Because of that, the video can be distorted. To avoid that, you can set the maintainaspect parameter to true. Then, the video is sized so it maintains its original aspect ratio of height to width.

When you use RealPlayer, you don't set individual parameters to determine the controls and information that are displayed like you do when you use Windows Media Player. Instead, you set the controls parameter to one of the values listed in this figure. For example, if you only want the Play/Pause button to be displayed, you can set this parameter to "PlayButton". Or, if you don't want any of the controls displayed, you can set this parameter to "ImageWindow". The default value for this parameter is "All", which displays the player with all of its controls.

The example in this figure uses standard HTML code with one object element nested within another. Note, however, that the outer object element doesn't include the codebase attribute. That's because you can't download just the plug-in for RealPlayer. The only way you can get the plug-in is by downloading the RealPlayer application. So if you embed a RealPlayer file on a web page using an object element with the classid attribute, you'll also want to include a link that lets users download RealPlayer if they don't already have it.

Common parameters for working with RealPlayer

Parameter	Description
`src`	The URL of the file to be played.
`autostart`	A Boolean value that determines if the file will start playing automatically. The default is false.
`controls`	One of the values listed below that determines the appearance of the player.
`loop`	A Boolean value that determines if the playback of the file repeats. The default is false.
`maintainaspect`	A Boolean value that determines if a video maintains its aspect ratio when it's sized to fit the image window. The default is false.
`numloop`	A number that determines how many times the file is played. The default is 1.

Values for the controls parameter

Value	Description
`All`	Displays the full player with all controls. This is the default.
`InfoVolumePanel`	Displays the title, author, and copyright information and the volume slider.
`InfoPanel`	Displays the title, author, and copyright information.
`ControlPanel`	Displays the position and volume sliders and the Play, Pause, and Stop buttons.
`StatusPanel`	Displays messages, the current time position, and the clip length.
`PlayButton`	Displays the Play and Pause buttons.
`StopButton`	Displays the Stop button.
`VolumeSlider`	Displays the volume slider.
`PositionField`	Displays the current time position and clip length.
`StatusField`	Displays messages.
`ImageWindow`	Displays the video image.
`StatusBar`	Displays the status bar with status, position, and channel information.

HTML that plays an RM file in RealPlayer

```
<object classid="clsid:CFCDAA03-8BE4-11cf-B84B-0020AFBBCCFA"
        width="600" height="420">
    <param name="src" value="videos/edinburgh.rm" />
    <param name="autostart" value="true" />
    <param name="maintainaspect" value="true" />
    <!--[if !IE]>-->
        <object type="audio/x-pn-realaudio-plugin"
                data="videos/edinburgh.rm"
                width="600" height="420">
            <param name="autostart" value="true" />
            <param name="maintainaspect" value="true" />
        </object>
    <!--<![endif]-->
</object>
```

Description

- The plug-in for RealPlayer is only available with the RealPlayer download. Because of that, you can omit the codebase attribute from the object element.

Figure 11-9   How to work with RealPlayer

How to work with QuickTime Player

The last media player I'll present is QuickTime Player. This is an Apple product that is commonly used on Macs. However, there are known problems when you use a nested object element to embed a QuickTime Player with Firefox on a Windows system. To avoid that problem, the example in figure 11-10 uses the embed element.

This figure presents the most common parameters for the QuickTime Player. You should already understand how the src, autoplay, loop, and volume parameters work. However, you should notice that the autoplay and loop parameters can have values other than true or false.

The autoplay parameter can also specify a time code. This code represents a position in the movie timeline. For example, if a movie is 10 minutes long, you could set the time code to "@00:03:26:00" to start playing the movie when the download reaches the three minute and 26 second mark.

The loop parameter can also have a value of "palindrome". If you use this value, the movie will play forward as usual, but then it will play backward. You probably won't come across many situations where you'll want to use this value.

You can also specify where in a movie's timeline playback begins and ends. To do that, you use the starttime and endtime parameters. Note that when you use these parameters, you don't code an at sign (@) at the beginning of the time value like you do when you code a time for the autoplay parameter. It's required for autoplay only because this parameter can also be set to a Boolean value.

When you use QuickTime Player, you don't have much control over the controls that are displayed. The default is to display all the controls. To remove the controls, you set the controller parameter to false.

By default, when you play a movie in QuickTime Player, the QuickTime logo is displayed as the movie is being downloaded until it starts playing. Similarly, a broken QuickTime logo is displayed if the browser doesn't have the QuickTime plug-in installed when it tries to load the player. If for some reason you don't want these default behaviors, you can set the showlogo parameter to false.

Common parameters for working with QuickTime Player

Parameter	Description
src	The URL of the file to be played.
autoplay	A Boolean value that determines if the file will start playing automatically. You can also code a time code in the format "@HH:MM:SS:FF". Then, the file will start playing when the download reaches the specified position in the movie timeline. The default is true.
loop	A Boolean value that determines if the playback of the file repeats. You can also code the value "palindrome" to cause the file to loop so it displays forward and then backward. The default is false.
volume	A value from 0 to 300 that specifies the volume based on a percent of the sound setting of the user's system. Not typically set above 100.
starttime	A time in the format "HH:MM:SS:FF" that specifies a position in the movie timeline when the movie will start playing.
endtime	A time in the format "HH:MM:SS:FF" that specifies a position in the movie timeline when the movie will stop playing.
controller	A Boolean value that determines if the controls are displayed. The default is true.
showlogo	A Boolean value that determines if the QuickTime logo is displayed while the file is being downloaded. The default is true.

HTML that plays a MOV file in QuickTime Player

```
<object classid="clsid:02BF25D5-8C17-4B23-BC80-D3488ABDDC6B"
        codebase="http://www.apple.com/qtactivex/qtplugin.cab"
        width="600" height="400">
    <param name="src" value="videos/baja.mov" />
    <param name="autoplay" value="true" />
    <param name="showlogo" value="false" />
        <embed type="video/quicktime"
               src="videos/baja.mov"
               width="400" height="265"
               autostart="false"
               showlogo="false" >
        </embed>
</object>
```

Description

- When you code the value of the autoplay, starttime, or endtime parameters as "HH:MM:SS:FF", it represents the hours, minutes, seconds, and thirtieths of a second.

- For the QuickTime Player, we recommend that you nest an embed element instead of a second object element, because a nested object element doesn't work in some browsers.

Figure 11-10   How to work with QuickTime Player

Perspective

Now that you know how to link to media files and embed them in your web pages, here's a caution about overusing them. In general, you should only use media files when they serve the purposes of your web site. For instance, a banner that scrolls across the top of a page or a rotating Flash file in the corner of a web page can distract your users from the main purpose of the page. The same can be true for a slide show that cycles through a series of photos.

Keep in mind too that media files are often large. Because of that, web pages that embed media files are likely to load slowly, particularly on systems that have slow Internet connections. So before you use media files, you should be sure that they support the goals of your web site and enhance the user experience.

Terms

MPEG (Moving Picture Experts Group)	MIME type
media player	nested elements
plug-in	conditional comment

Summary

- A browser uses a *media player* to play an audio or video file. Adobe Flash Player is used for Flash files. Windows Media Player is commonly used on Windows systems for both audio and video files. RealPlayer and Apple's QuickTime Player can be used on both Windows and Mac systems for audio and video files.

- Audio and video files use a variety of media formats. The MP3, MPG, and MPEG formats were designed by the *Moving Picture Experts Group* (*MPEG*), and MP3 is the audio layer of the MPEG format.

- The easiest way to start a media file in a new web page is to code an a element with an href attribute that points to the file. To help the browser determine which player to use, you can also code a type attribute that identifies the *MIME type*.

- To embed media players in a web page, you can either use the object and param elements or the embed element.

- If you want IE to tell users to download a specific media player, you need to code the classid and codebase attributes of the object element. Then, to provide for browsers that don't recognize those attributes, you can *nest* one object element within another and use IE's *conditional comments*.

- Although the embed element is non-standard, it is supported by all major browsers; it will be in the HTML 5 standards; it doesn't require conditional comments when you nest an embed element within an object element, and it sometimes works when an object element doesn't.

Exercise 11-1   Link to and embed media files

This exercise will give you a chance to play media files by linking to them and also to embed media players and files within a web page. When you're through, your web page should look something like this:

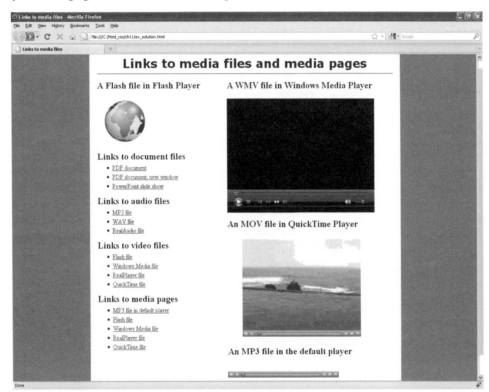

Review the starting files for this web page

1. Open this file in your text editor:

    `c:\html_css\ch11\index.html`

    Then, launch the HTML file in Firefox so you can see what this page looks like and how much work you have to do with it.

2. Review the code in the html file. There, you'll see that all of the links to the media files and pages are already coded.

Test the links to the document, audio, and video files

3. In the browser, click on the first link to a PDF document. It will open in the same window or tab. Then, click on the Back button to return to the index page.

4. Click on the second link to a PDF document. This time, it opens in a new window or tab. If you look at the HTML code for this link, you can see that's because the target attribute is coded for this link.

5. Click on the other links to the documents, audio files, and video files. All of them should play in the default player for that type of file as long as the player is installed on your system. The third link, for example, should run a

PowerPoint slide show, but only if PowerPoint is installed on your system. This is a good way to find out what media players or plug-ins your system is missing. To return to the index page after each file is played, click the Back button.

6. Test the links again using Internet Explorer. If a bar is displayed that stops the page from using active content, click on the bar, select the Allow Blocked Content command, and click on the OK button in the next dialog box. If you want to stop IE from displaying this bar, use the technique that's summarized at the bottom of figure 11-3.

Test the links to the media pages

7. Click on the links to the media pages in both IE and Firefox. Here again, the media files will only run if you have the right media player for it.

8. If your browsers don't have the QuickTime Player installed, install it. To help with that, Firefox will display a bar that includes an Install Missing Plugins button when you open a page that requires a specific plug-in. Then, you can click on that button to start the installation process.

Embed some of the media files in the index page

9. Embed the Flash file into the index page as shown above. The easiest way to do that is to copy the code from the page with the Flash file that you linked to in step 7, and paste it into the index file right below the Flash file heading at the top of the first column. Then, test this change in both IE and Firefox.

10. Repeat step 9 for the Windows Media file, but paste the code below the first heading in the second column of the index file. Also, set the width to 400, the height to 300, and autostart to false. Then, test this change in both IE and Firefox. If you're using a Windows system, this should work because Windows Media Player is installed on all Windows systems. If you're using a Mac, this won't work.

11. Repeat step 9 for the QuickTime file. This time, paste the code below the second heading in the second column, set the width to 400, the height to 266, and autoplay to false. If QuickTime is installed on your system, this should work in both IE and Firefox.

12. Repeat step 9 for playing an MP3 file in the default player. This time, paste the code below the third heading in the second column, and set autostart to false. This should work in both IE and Firefox.

Experiment

13. This exercise is likely to raise a few questions because different browsers and operating systems will produce different results. The best way to answer those questions is to experiment until you can answer them yourself.

12

How to work with print media and mobile devices

Up until this point, you've learned how to create and format web pages that will be displayed on a computer screen. Now, in this chapter, you'll learn how to create and use a style sheet for printing a web page. You'll also learn how to create and work with web pages that are displayed on mobile devices like cell phones and PDAs.

How to define style sheets for different media types

When you specify a style sheet that's used with a document, you can identify the media type that it should be used for. Within a style sheet, you can identify a media type for a specific rule set.

How to identify the media type for a style sheet

The first example in figure 12-1 shows how to use the HTML link element to include a style sheet file that applies to a specific media type. To do that, you code the media attribute. Although this is considered the best way to do that, you can use a style element to get the same result as in the second example.

The third example shows how you can specify the media type in a style element that's embedded within the HTML for a file. From the start, though, we've recommended that you avoid this technique because it mixes content with presentation. And that in turn makes it more difficult for you to create and maintain the web site.

The table at the top of this figure lists some of the values you can code for the media type. The most common values are "all", "screen", and "print". If you use a specific media type like screen or print, the style sheet is used only for that media type. That's the case for the first example in this figure. Here, the first style sheet is used when the page is displayed on a screen, and the second style sheet is used when the page is printed. This makes the CSS files easier to create and maintain.

Note, however, that you can use a single style sheet for one or more specific media types. To do that, you code a comma-separated list of media types in the link or style element. For example, if you want to use the same style sheet for screen and projection media, you can code a link element like this:

```
<link rel="stylesheet" type="text/css" href="styles/main.css"
    media="screen, projection" />
```

Although this might be okay for some simple applications, it's usually best to provide one style sheet for each media type.

How to identify the media type for a rule set

If you use one style sheet for more than one media type, you can specify the media type for specific rule sets. To do that, you use the @media rule as in the last example in figure 12-1. Here, the @media rule indicates that the rule set that it contains should be applied only when the page is printed.

In this case, the @media rule contains a rule set for just the body element, but you can include as many rule sets as you like within a single @media rule. Here again, this might be okay in some simple cases, but it's usually best to provide one style sheet for each media type so you won't need @media rules.

Possible values for the media type

Value	Device types
`all`	All device types
`screen`	Computer screens
`print`	Printed pages and Print Preview mode
`handheld`	Handheld devices such as mobile phones and PDAs
`braille`	Braille tactile feedback devices
`embossed`	Paged Braille printers
`speech`	Speech synthesizers
`projection`	Projection devices such as projectors

Link elements that include style sheets for screen and print media

```
<link rel="stylesheet" type="text/css" href="styles/main.css"
    media="screen" />
<link rel="stylesheet" type="text/css" href="styles/print.css"
    media="print" />
```

A style element that includes a style sheet for print media

```
<style type="text/css">
    @import "styles/print.css" print;
</style>
```

A style element in the HTML that provides rules for printing

```
<style type="text/css" media="print">
    font-family: "Times New Roman", Times, serif;
    background-color: white;
</style>
```

A @media rule in a style sheet that specifies styles just for printing

```
@media print {
    body {
        font-family: "Times New Roman", Times, serif;
        background-color: white;
    }
}
```

Description

- To provide for more than one media type, you can use link or style elements to include one style sheet for each type.
- Within the HTML for a page, you can embed a style element that provides rules for a specific media type.
- Within a style sheet, you can specify that a rule set or a group of rule sets is for a specific media type using the @media rule.
- All of the major browsers support the "screen", "print", and "all" values for the media attribute, but support for the other values is unreliable.

Figure 12-1   How to define style sheets for different media types

How to work with print media

If a web page contains information that a user might want to print, you should provide a way to do that. For example, if you're developing a web site that lets users place orders, you'll want them to be able to print the invoice information. Although you can use a browser's built-in printing function to print a page just as it appears on the screen, it usually makes sense to format the page so it's more appropriate for printing.

Recommendations for formatting printed pages

When you create a style sheet for printing a page, you should consider any changes that will make the page more readable. Some basic recommendations for formatting printed pages are listed at the top of figure 12-2. As you can see, the first three recommendations have to do with changing the fonts so they're more readable.

The fourth recommendation is to remove site navigation. That makes sense because navigation can't be used when the page is printed. Note, however, that you don't typically remove other types of navigation. That's because you want the user to know when a page contains links to other topics.

The last recommendation is to remove any images that aren't needed to understand the content of the page. That will make the page print more quickly and will save on ink.

CSS properties for controlling printed pages

Figure 12-2 also shows the CSS properties you can use to control printing. The one you'll probably use most often is display. Although you can use it to display an inline element as a block element and vice versa, you're most likely to use it to exclude an element such as an image from a page when it's printed. To do that, you set this property to "none".

You can also use the visibility property to hide an element when a page is printed. When you use this property, though, the space occupied by the element is still included on the page. If that's not what you want, you should use the display property instead.

The remaining properties let you control page breaks. The page-break-before and page-break-after properties let you specify if a page break always occurs before or after an element, may occur before or after an element, or shouldn't occur before or after an element if possible. The page-break-inside property is similar, but it specifies whether a page break can occur within an element.

When a page break occurs within an element, the orphans and widows properties specify the minimum number of lines that can be printed at the bottom of the current page and the top of the next page. In most cases, you'll want at least two lines on each page. Unfortunately, these properties aren't supported by most browsers.

Recommendations for formatting printed pages

- Change the text color to black and the background color to white.
- Change text other than headings to a serif font to make text easier to read when printed.
- Use a base font size that's easy to read when printed.
- Remove site navigation since it can't be used from a printed page.
- Remove as many images as possible, particularly Flash and animated images.

CSS properties for printing

Property	Description
display	A keyword that determines how an element is displayed. Common keywords are block, inline, and none.
visibility	A keyword that determines if an element is visible. Common keywords are visible and hidden.
page-break-before	A keyword that determines when a page break is allowed before an element's box. Common keywords are always, auto, and avoid.
page-break-after	A keyword that determines when a page break is allowed after an element's box. Common keywords are always, auto, and avoid.
page-break-inside	A keyword that determines when a page break is allowed within an element's box. Possible keywords are auto and avoid. Not supported by most browsers.
widows	An integer that determines the minimum number of lines within an element that can be printed on the next page when a page break occurs within the element. Not supported by most browsers.
orphans	An integer that determines the minimum number of lines within an element that can be printed at the bottom of a page when a page break occurs within the element. Not supported by most browsers.

CSS that uses two of the properties for printing

```
img {
    display: none;
}
h1, h2, h3 {
    page-break-after: avoid;
}
```

Description

- If you don't want an element to be included when a page is printed, you can set its display property to none. Then, no space is allocated for the element's box.
- If you don't want an element to be included when a page is printed but you want to allocate space for the element's box, you can set the visibility property to hidden.
- The auto keyword for the page-break properties indicates that a break may occur, but doesn't have to occur, like it does when you use the always keyword.
- The avoid keyword for the page-break properties tells the browser to avoid a page break if it can. This keyword isn't supported by Firefox.

Figure 12-2   Formatting recommendations and CSS properties for printed pages

The screen layout for a two-column web page

To illustrate the use of style sheets for a printed page, I'll use a web page that contains two columns. The screen layout for this page is presented in figure 12-3. This is an enhanced version of the web page you saw back in figure 6-4 of chapter 6. In addition to the enhancements, this web page has been coded so that the main content of the page will appear before the information in the sidebar when the page is printed. You'll see how that's done in the next two figures, which present the HTML and CSS for the page.

The HTML for the web page

Figure 12-4 presents the HTML for the web page in figure 12-3. The first thing you should notice here are the two link elements in the document head. The first one indicates that a style sheet named main.css should be used when the page is displayed on the screen. The second one indicates that a style sheet named print.css should be used when the page is printed.

The other thing you should notice here is that, unlike the two-column page that you saw in chapter 6, the main division is coded before the sidebar. That way, the main content can be printed before the content of the sidebar, which is usually what you want. This illustrates that when you code the HTML for a web page that you know will be printed, you need to keep in mind the sequence in which the content will be printed as well as how the content will be displayed.

A web page with two columns

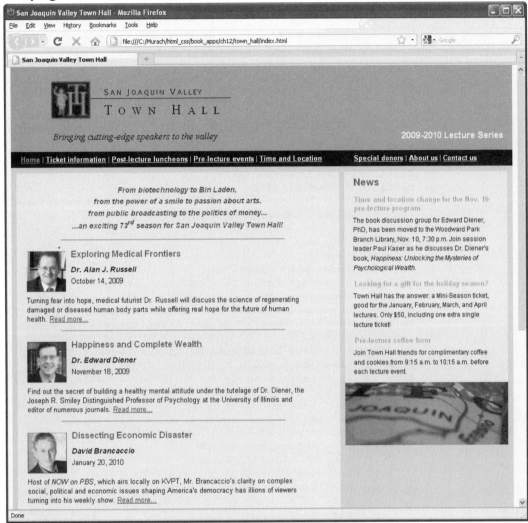

Description

- This web page uses a two-column layout like the one that was presented in figure 6-4 of chapter 6. In this case, though, the columns are created by floating the main division to the left of the sidebar instead of floating the sidebar to the right of the main division. That way, the main division will appear before the sidebar when the page is printed.

Figure 12-3   The screen layout for a two-column web page

The HTML for the web page   **Page 1**

```html
<head>
    <title>San Joaquin Valley Town Hall</title>
    <meta http-equiv="content-type" content="text/html; charset=utf-8" />
    <link rel="stylesheet" type="text/css" href="styles/main.css"
        media="screen" />
    <link rel="stylesheet" type="text/css" href="styles/print.css"
        media="print" />
</head>
<body>
    <div id="page">
        <div id="header">
            <img src="images/logo_black.jpg" alt="Town Hall Logo" />
            <p id="title1">San Joaquin Valley</p>
            <p id="title2">Town Hall</p>
            <p id="tagline">Bringing cutting-edge speakers to the valley
                <span>2009-2010 Lecture Series</span></p>
        </div>
        <div id="main">
            <p id="navigation">
                <a href="index.html">Home</a> |
                <a href="tickets.html">Ticket information</a> |
                <a href="luncheons.html">Post-lecture luncheons</a> |
                <a href="pre-lecture.html">Pre-lecture events</a> |
                <a href="location.html">Time and Location</a></p>
            <div id="speakers">
                <p id="intro">From biotechnology to Bin Laden,<br />
                from the power of a smile to passion about arts,<br />
                from public broadcasting to the politics of money...<br />
                ...an exciting 73<sup>rd</sup> season for San Joaquin
                Valley Town Hall!</p>
                <div class="speaker">
                    <p class="divider"></p>
                    <img src="images/russell_bw.jpg"
                        alt="Dr. Alan J. Russell" />
                    <h1>Exploring Medical Frontiers</h1>
                    <p class="name">Dr. Alan J. Russell</p>
                    <p class="date">October 14, 2009</p>
                    <p class="description">Turning fear into hope, medical
                        futurist Dr. Russell will discuss the science of
                        regenerating damaged or diseased human body parts
                        while offering real hope for the future of human health.
                    <a href="speakers/russell.html">Read more...</a></p>
                </div>
                .
                .
```

Figure 12-4   The HTML for the web page (part 1 of 2)

The HTML for the web page   **Page 2**

```
            <div class="speaker">
                <p class="divider"></p>
                <img src="images/coll_bw.jpg" alt="Steve Coll" />
                <h1>The Changing World of Terrorism</h1>
                <p class="name">Steve Coll</p>
                <p class="date">April 21, 2010</p>
                <p class="description">Having written "the finest
                    historical narrative so far on the origins of al
                    Qaeda" according to <i>The New York Times</i>,
                    Mr. Coll speaks on the development and links of
                    terrorism in Pakistan, India and Afghanistan.
                <a href="speakers/coll.html">Read more...</a></p>
            </div>
        </div>
    </div>
    <div id="sidebar">
        <p id="utilities">
            <a href="donors.html">Special donors</a> |
            <a href="about.html">About us</a> |
            <a href="contact.html">Contact us</a>
        </p>
        <div id="news">
            <h1>News</h1>
            <h2>Time and location change for the Nov. 10 pre-lecture
            program</h2>
            <p class="news_item">The book discussion group for Edward
                Diener, PhD, has been moved to the Woodward Park Branch
                Library, Nov. 10, 7:30 p.m. Join session leader Paul
                Kaser as he discusses Dr. Diener's book, <i>Happiness:
                Unlocking the Mysteries of Psychological Wealth</i>.</p>
            <h2>Looking for a gift for the holiday season?</h2>
            <p class="news_item">Town Hall has the answer: a Mini-
                Season ticket, good for the January, February, March,
                and April lectures. Only $50, including one extra
                single lecture ticket!</p>
            <h2>Pre-lecture coffee hour</h2>
            <p class="news_item">Join Town Hall friends for
                complimentary coffee and cookies from 9:15 a.m. to
                10:15 a.m. before each lecture event.</p>
            <img src="images/map.jpg" alt="California Map" />
        </div>
    </div>
    <div id="footer">
        <p>&copy; Copyright 2009 San Joaquin Valley Town Hall.</p>
    </div>
  </div>
</body>
```

Figure 12-4   The HTML for the web page (part 2 of 2)

The CSS for the screen layout

Figure 12-5 presents the CSS for displaying the web page. Since you've seen code like this throughout this book, you shouldn't have any trouble understanding how it works. So I'll just point out one thing here. Then, when I show you the CSS for printing the page, you can compare it to the code shown in this figure to see how it differs.

Because the main division of the page is coded before the sidebar in the HTML, the main division must be floated to the left of the sidebar. You can see the style rule that accomplishes that at the bottom of page 1 of this figure. Here, the width property of the division is set to 635 pixels and the float property is set to "left".

At the top of page 3, you can see the style rule for the sidebar. It simply sets the left margin of the sidebar to the width of the main division so the content of the main division won't flow below the sidebar. In other words, this works just the opposite of the page in chapter 6.

The CSS for the displayed web page   **Page 1**

```css
/* styles for the elements */
body {
    font: 81.25% Arial, Helvetica, sans-serif;
    margin: 0;
    padding: 0;
    background-color: white;
}

/* styles for the page */
#page {
    width: 960px;
    margin: 0 auto;
    background-color: #facd8a;
}

/* styles for the header */
#header { background-color: #ef9c00; }
#header img {
    width: 75px;
    padding: 2em .8em .8em 6em;
    float: left;
}
#title1 {
    font: small-caps 115% "Lucida Sans", Arial, Helvetica, sans-serif;
    letter-spacing: .2em;
    margin: 0 540px 0 150px;
    padding: 2.5em 0 .2em 2em;
    border-bottom: 1px solid black;
}
#title2 {
    font: small-caps 190% "Times New Roman", Times, serif;
    letter-spacing: .5em;
    margin: .2em 0 0 180px;
}
#tagline {
    font: italic normal 130% "Times New Roman", Times, serif;
    margin: 1.5em 0 0 4.8em;
    padding-bottom: 1em;
    clear: left;
    position: relative;
}
#tagline span {
    font: normal bold 100% Arial, Helvetica, sans-serif;
    color: white;
    position: absolute;
    right: 1em;
}

/* styles for the main division */
#main {
    width: 635px;
    float: left; }
```

Figure 12-5   The CSS for the screen layout (part 1 of 3)

The CSS for the displayed web page   **Page 2**

```
#navigation {
    background-color: black;
    font-weight: bold;
    color: white;
    padding: .5em 1.5em;
    margin: 0; }
#navigation a:link { color: white; }
#navigation a:visited { color: #ef9c00; }
#speakers {
    background-color: #fdebcf;
    padding-bottom: 2em;
    margin: 10px; }
#intro {
    font-size: 110%;
    font-style: italic;
    font-weight: bold;
    line-height: 1.5;
    padding-top: 1.5em;
    margin-top: 0;
    color: #363636;
    text-align: center; }
.divider {
    padding-left: 1.5em;
    border: 1px solid #ef9c00;
    margin: 1em 8em 0 6.5em; }
#speakers img {
    width: 75px;
    height: 75px;
    float: left;
    margin: 1.5em .8em .5em 1.5em; }
#speakers h1 {
    font-size: 120%;
    color: green;
    margin-top: 1em;
    margin-bottom: 0; }
.name {
    font-size: 110%;
    font-weight: bold;
    font-style: italic;
    margin-top: .7em;
    margin-bottom: 0; }
.date {
    margin-top: .4em;
    margin-bottom: 0; }
.description {
    line-height: 130%;
    padding-right: 5em;
    padding-left: 1.5em;
    margin-top: 1.5em;
    margin-bottom: 0;
    clear: left; }
```

Figure 12-5   The CSS for the screen layout (part 2 of 3)

The CSS for the displayed web page

```css
/* styles for the right sidebar */
#sidebar { margin-left: 635px; }
#utilities {
    background-color: black;
    font-weight: bold;
    color: white;
    padding: .5em 1em .5em 1.5em;
    margin: 0; }
#utilities a:link { color: white; }
#utilities a:visited { color: #ef9c00; }
#news {
    background-color: #fdebcf;
    margin-top: 10px;
    margin-right: 10px; }
#sidebar h1 {
    font-size: 140%;
    font-weight: bold;
    color: green;
    padding: .5em 0 0 1em;
    margin: 0; }
#sidebar img { width: 315px; }
#sidebar h2 {
    font-size: 100%;
    font-weight: bold;
    color: #ef9c00;
    padding: 0 1.5em;
    margin-top: 1em;
    margin-bottom: 0; }
.news_item {
    font-size: 90%;
    line-height: 150%;
    padding: 0 1.5em;
    margin-top: .5em; }

/* styles for the footer */
#footer { clear: both; }
#footer p {
    font-size: 90%;
    background-color: #ef9c00;
    margin: 0;
    padding: .5em 1em;
    text-align: right; }
```

Figure 12-5   The CSS for the screen layout (part 3 of 3)

The print layout for the web page

Figure 12-6 shows the print layout for the web page in figure 12-3. If you compare these two layouts, you'll notice a number of differences. First, the print layout consists of a single column that contains both the main content and the content of the sidebar. (Although you can't see the sidebar content in this figure, it appears after the main content.)

Second, I removed all the color from the page so it's printed in black text on a white background. This will make the page more readable when it's printed. I also changed most of the text to a serif font to improve readability.

Third, I omitted all the images except for the logo in the top left corner of the page since they aren't necessary for understanding the content of the page. I also removed the border above the information for each speaker because I felt they weren't necessary on the printed page.

Finally, I removed the navigation bar at the bottom of the header since the user can't use the links in this bar when the page is printed. In contrast, I left the link at the end of the description for each speaker. That way, the user will know that additional information is available for each speaker on the web site.

By the way, the page in this figure is displayed in Print Preview mode. This mode is helpful when you're designing a style sheet for printed output because it lets you see the layout without having to print the page. Of course, once you have a page laid out the way you want it, you should print it to do a final check.

This figure presents the techniques for displaying a page in Print Preview mode and for printing a page using the browser commands and buttons. Note, however, that you can also provide a Print button on the web page that prints the page. Then, you can use JavaScript to print the page when the button is clicked. No matter how the page is printed, though, the style sheet for print media is used if one is available.

Although it isn't presented in this figure, you can also provide for printing a web page by including a link to a separate, printer-friendly page. When you do that, the printer-friendly page is displayed in a separate window using the style sheet specified by the HTML for the page. Then, the user can print the page from that window. The drawback to using this technique is that you have to code two pages: one for displaying on the screen and one for printing.

The layout for the web page in Print Preview mode

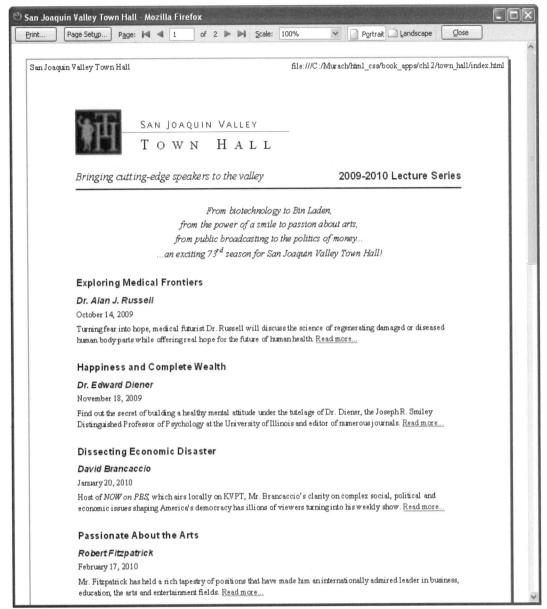

Description

- To display a page in Print Preview mode, choose the File➔Print Preview command from the browser's menu.
- To print a page, you can click the Print button in the browser's toolbar, choose the File➔Print command from the menu, or click the Print button from Print Preview mode.
- You can also include a Print button on a page and use JavaScript to print the page when the button is clicked.

Figure 12-6   The print layout for the web page

The CSS for the print layout

Figure 12-7 presents the CSS for the printed web page. If you compare these styles to the styles in figure 12-5 for the screen layout, you'll notice a number of differences. Many of those differences provide for changes in the fonts, colors, spacing, and the size of the printed page. Because you should be able to figure out how these styles work, I won't focus on them here.

One property that's used for spacing that I do want to point out is the margin property of the body element. Notice that the value for this property provides a measurement in inches. Although you don't typically use this measurement for screen layouts, it makes sense to use it for print layouts. Here, the margin is set to .25 inch. Note, however, that this value doesn't replace the default margin provided by a browser for printed output. Instead, this value is added to the default margin.

Unfortunately, different browsers can have different default margins. For example, the default margins for Firefox, Internet Explorer, and Safari are .5 inch, .75 inch, and 1 inch respectively. Because of that, you may want to specify a small margin or no margin at all.

Although I specified the margins for the document in inches, the other measurements are in pixels, ems, and percents just like the style sheet for the screen layout. That's because I created this style sheet by copying the style sheet for the screen layout and then making the necessary modifications. This is the easiest way to create a style sheet for printing.

Next, notice that I omitted the style rule for the main division. That makes sense because this division isn't floated in the printed layout. Then, I set the display property of the navigation division, the divider class, and the img elements in the speakers division to "none" so they don't appear in the printed layout. I also set the page-break-after property of the h1 element in the speakers division to "avoid" to keep these elements together if possible.

The CSS for the printed web page   **Page 1**

```
/* styles for the elements */
body {
    font: 81.25% Arial, Helvetica, sans-serif;
    margin: .25in; }

/* styles for the header */
#header img {
    width: 75px;
    padding: 0 .8em .8em 0;
    float: left; }
#title1 {
    font: small-caps 115% "Lucida Sans", Arial, Helvetica, sans-serif;
    letter-spacing: .2em;
    margin: 0 280px 0 75px;
    padding: 1em 0 .2em 2em;
    border-bottom: 1px solid black; }
#title2 {
    font: small-caps 180% "Times New Roman", Times, serif;
    letter-spacing: .5em;
    margin: .2em 0 0 105px; }
#tagline {
    font: italic normal 130% "Times New Roman", Times, serif;
    margin: 1.5em 0 0;
    padding-bottom: .5em;
    border-bottom: 2px solid black;
    clear: left;
    position: relative; }
#tagline span {
    font: normal bold 100% Arial, Helvetica, sans-serif;
    position: absolute;
    right: 0; }

/* styles for the main division */
#navigation { display: none; }
#intro {
    font-family: "Times New Roman", Times, serif;
    font-size: 112%;
    font-style: italic;
    line-height: 150%;
    padding-top: 1.5em;
    margin-top: 0;
    text-align: center; }
.divider { display: none; }
#speakers img { display: none; }
#speakers h1 {
    font-size: 120%;
    font-weight: bold;
    margin-top: 1.5em;
    margin-bottom: 0;
    page-break-after: avoid; }
```

Figure 12-7   The CSS for the print layout (part 1 of 2)

On page 2, you can see more of the same. First, I set the display property of the utilities division and the img element in the sidebar division to "none" so these elements won't be displayed. Second, I set the page-break-after property for two of the classes to "avoid" to keep these elements together if possible.

At this point, you may want to consider what would happen if you tried to use one style sheet for both the screen and print media. Then, you would have to use @media rules to apply the various rule sets to the right selectors for the right media. Or, consider what would happen if you used one style sheet for all media and a second style sheet for print. Then, you would have to carefully override any style rules in the primary style sheet that you don't want applied to print media.

In either case, the coding would get complicated for all but the simplest applications. That in turn would mean that the files would be more difficult to create, test, and maintain. In general, the simplest way is usually the best way. And that means that you use one style sheet for each media type.

The CSS for the printed web page   **Page 2**

```
.name {
    font-size: 110%;
    font-weight: bold;
    font-style: italic;
    margin-top: .7em;
    margin-bottom: 0;
    page-break-after: avoid; }
.date {
    font-family: "Times New Roman", Times, serif;
    margin-top: .4em;
    margin-bottom: 0;
    page-break-after: avoid; }
.description {
    font-family: "Times New Roman", Times, serif;
    line-height: 1.3;
    margin-top: .5em;
    margin-bottom: 0; }

/* styles for the right sidebar */
#utilities { display: none; }
#sidebar h1 {
    font-size: 140%;
    font-weight: bold;
    padding-top: .5em;
    margin-top: 1.5em;
    margin-bottom: 0; }
#sidebar img { display: none; }
#sidebar h2 {
    font-size: 100%;
    font-weight: bold;
    margin-top: 1em;
    margin-bottom: 0; }
.news_item {
    font: 105%/1.3 "Times New Roman", Times, serif;
    margin-top: .5em; }

/* styles for the footer */
#footer p {
    font-size: 90%;
    margin-top: 3em;
    margin-bottom: 0;
    padding: .75em;
    border-top: 1px solid black;
    text-align: center; }
```

Figure 12-7   The CSS for the print layout (part 2 of 2)

How to work with mobile devices

Many different types of mobile devices are in use today, and these devices are frequently used to access web sites. Because the screens on these devices are much smaller than standard computer screens, a web site that's designed to be used on the desktop can be difficult to work with on a mobile device. To accommodate mobile users, then, web developers typically provide pages that are designed specifically for mobile devices.

How to provide pages for mobile devices

Figure 12-8 presents five ways to provide web pages for mobile devices. To start, you can use a style sheet for the handheld media type. But the problem here is that not all mobile browsers recognize the handheld media type. That includes the Safari browser used by Apple's iPhone, current versions of the Opera Mobile and Opera Mini browsers that can be used by many mobile devices, and the S60 web browser used by Nokia S60 mobile phones. These browsers only recognize style sheets for the screen media type.

On the other hand, iPhone's Safari and Opera's Mobile and Mini browsers do support a new feature of CSS 3 called *media queries*. These queries let you use a conditional expression for a media type. If, for example, the maximum screen width for a mobile device is 480 pixels, you can code a link element like this if you want to use a different style sheet for those devices:

```
<link rel="stylesheet" type="text/css" href="styles/mobile.css"
      media="only screen and (max-device-width: 480px)" />
```

Then, you can code another link element for screen media with a minimum screen width of 481 pixels. The style sheet for this element would then be used for standard computer screens. To learn more about media queries, you can see the documentation for CSS 3, but most browsers don't support this feature.

The next four techniques in this figure require that you develop a separate web site for mobile devices. When you use the first of these techniques, you include a link on the home page that lets the user switch to the mobile version of the site. The trouble with this is that users don't always enter a site at the home page, so you may need to provide links to the mobile site on other pages.

When you use the last three techniques in this figure, the web site detects when a mobile device is being used and then redirects the user to the mobile version of the site automatically. This is the way this is done on commercial web sites that service many mobile device users. For these sites, one common convention for the mobile site name is to precede the domain name for the main site with m and a period as in m.yahoo.com.

To detect the mobile device, a web site can use JavaScript on the client, a scripting language on the server, or *WURFL* on the server. Because this book isn't about JavaScript or server-side programming, though, these techniques aren't presented in this book.

Define a style sheet for the handheld media type

- When you use this technique, you don't have to maintain a separate version of the web site for mobile devices. However, many mobile browsers don't recognize the handheld media type.

- Although CSS 3 provides a feature called *media queries* that gives you more control over the style sheet for a web page, most browsers don't support this feature yet. For more information, see http://www.w3.org/TR/css3-mediaqueries/.

Include a link to a mobile version of the web site

- When you use this technique, you display the desktop version of the web site no matter what device accesses it. Then, you include a link to a mobile version of the site near the top of the home page.

Use JavaScript to detect mobile devices and redirect

- When you use this technique, you use JavaScript to detect mobile devices. Then, if a mobile device is detected, the user is redirected to the mobile version of the web site.

- The problem with this is that there are so many different mobile devices that it's difficult to detect them all. Also, some mobile devices don't support JavaScript.

Use a server-side scripting language to detect and redirect

- With this technique, you use a server-side scripting language such as PHP or ColdFusion to detect mobile devices. To do that, the script looks at the web browser that made the request. Then, if a mobile device is detected, the user is redirected to the mobile version of the web site.

- The problem with this is that there are so many different mobile browsers that it's difficult to detect them all.

Use the WURFL to detect mobile devices

- The *WURFL* (*Wireless Universal Resource File*) is an XML configuration file that contains information about a variety of mobile devices, including the features and capabilities they support. This file is updated frequently with new devices.

- To use the WURFL, you implement the API (Application Programming Interface) using languages such as Java, PHP, C++, or .NET. Among other things, the API lets you determine the browser that's being used and then retrieve information about that browser from the XML file. When you use this technique, you have to download the XML configuration file periodically so it's up-to-date.

Description

- At present, the best way to provide for mobile devices is to redirect the user to a mobile version of the main web site. That can be done by providing a link to the mobile version or by automatically detecting mobile devices and redirecting them.

- To detect mobile devices, you can use one of the last three techniques above.

Figure 12-8   How to provide pages for mobile devices

How to set viewport properties

In the rest of this chapter, I'll assume that you're creating a separate web site for mobile devices. In that case, you can use a special meta element that lets you configure a device's *viewport*. This meta element is presented in figure 12-9.

To start, you should know that the viewport on a mobile device works differently from the viewport on a computer screen. On a computer screen, the viewport is the visible area of the web page. The user can change the size of the viewport by changing the size of the browser window.

In contrast, the viewport on a mobile device can be larger or smaller than the visible area and determines how the page content appears in that area. In this figure, for example, you can see that the first web page is displayed so the entire width of the page is visible. In contrast, the second web page extends beyond the visible area of the screen. Because this page is larger, however, it's easier to work with. In many cases, you'll want to configure the viewport so a web page is easy to use when it's first displayed.

To configure the viewport, you use a meta element with the name attribute set to "viewport". Then, for the content attribute, you can specify any of the properties listed in this figure. Note, however, that this meta element isn't supported by all browsers, and some of the browsers that do support it don't support all of the properties shown here. Even so, you should code this meta element for those browsers that do support it.

The three examples in this figure illustrate how this meta element works. The first example sets the viewport width to the width of the web page. This is useful if the page width is less than the device width. For example, the device width for the iPhone in this figure is 320 pixels, and the default width for the viewport is 980 pixels. That means that a page that's 980 pixels wide can be displayed in the visible area. Then, if the width of the page is 290 pixels, you can set the viewport to this width so the page fills the entire visible area. You'll see an example of how this works in the next figure.

The second example sets the width of the viewport to the width of the mobile device. You're most likely to use this setting if a page is wider than the device width but narrower than the default viewport width. Then, the page will be enlarged so it fills the visible area. Notice that this example also sets the user-scalable property to "no". Because of that, the user can't zoom in or out of the page.

Of course, the device width and default viewport width vary from one device to another. If you use one of these techniques to set the viewport width, then, you'll need to decide which technique works best for a particular page.

The third example in this figure shows how to set the initial zoom factor, or *scale*, for the viewport. In this case, I changed the initial scale to .5 to zoom in to the first web page shown in this figure so it looks like the second web page. To understand how this works, you need to realize that if you don't set the width or height of the viewport, they're inferred from the initial scale. For example, if you set the initial scale to 1, the viewport width would be set to the width of the device. For the iPhone, that means the viewport width would be set

A web page on an iPhone before and after scaling

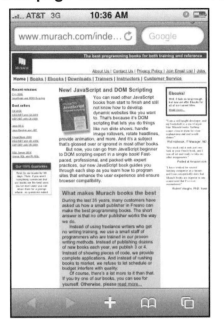 

Content properties for viewport metadata

Property	Description
`width`	The logical width of the viewport specified in pixels. You can also use the device-width keyword to indicate that the viewport should be as wide as the screen.
`height`	The logical height of the viewport specified in pixels. You can also use the device-height keyword to indicate that the viewport should be as tall as the screen.
`initial-scale`	A number that indicates the initial zoom factor that's used to display the page.
`minimum-scale`	A number that indicates the minimum zoom factor for the page.
`maximum-scale`	A number that indicates the maximum zoom factor for the page.
`user-scalable`	Indicates whether the user can zoom in and out of the viewport. Possible values are yes and no.

Meta elements that set viewport properties

```
<meta name="viewport" content="width=290" />
<meta name="viewport" content="width=device-width, user-scalable=no" />
<meta name="viewport" content="initial-scale=.5" />
```

Description

- The *viewport* on a mobile device determines the content that's displayed on the page and how text wraps on the page. It can be larger or smaller than the actual visible area of the screen.

- If you don't set the width, height, and initial-scale properties, the mobile device will determine the values of the properties that aren't set from the properties that are set.

Figure 12-9   How to set viewport properties

to 320 pixels. Since the page in this example is 980 pixels wide, that means that less than a third of the page width would be displayed. Because I set the initial scale to .5, though, the viewport is zoomed in so that 640 pixels are displayed.

In practice, it is difficult to figure out what values to use as you configure the viewport. In particular, the relationship between the device width, viewport width, and zoom factor can be confusing. As a result, you often need to experiment with a variety of values before you determine which ones to use.

Guidelines for designing mobile web pages

If you create web pages specifically for mobile devices, you should follow some general guidelines so it's easy for users to work with those pages. Figure 12-10 presents these guidelines.

In general, you want to simplify the layout and content of your pages. To simplify the web page shown in figure 12-9, for example, I removed all of the content from the main section of the page except for the first heading and the book image. Although the other content is important, it can easily be displayed on other pages.

I also removed the information in the right sidebar, and I removed the guarantee information from the bottom of the left sidebar. Then, I modified the tagline at the top of the page so it would fit in a smaller viewport; I removed the links for the utilities; I left only the most important links in the navigation bar; and I put the remaining links at the bottom of the page along with a link to the utilities. What's left is a page with a header, links to the products on the site, and a footer.

You can see this web page at the top of this figure. Here, the first screen shows how the page looks on an iPhone if you don't configure the viewport. Then, the second screen shows how the page looks if you set the width of the viewport to the width of the page. As you can see, the page now fills the visible area of the screen, making it easier to use.

How to test mobile web pages

Because there are so many different mobile devices, it's important to test a mobile web page on as many devices and in as many browsers as possible. Although the best way to test a mobile web page is to publish the page and then display it on a variety of devices, that's not always possible. In that case, you may want to use the device emulators and browser simulators that are available for many of the most popular mobile devices and browsers.

In most cases, you need to download the required emulator or simulator from the manufacturer's web site so you can run it on your desktop. In a few cases, though, you can run the emulator or simulator online. To do that, you first need to deploy the web page so it can be accessed online. Keep in mind, though, that emulators and simulators may not always provide accurate results. However, they should at least approximate what a page will look like.

A web page on an iPhone before and after the width is set

Guidelines for designing mobile web pages

- Keep your layout simple so the focus is on the content. One-column layouts typically work best.
- Include only essential content, and divide that content into smaller pages.
- Keep images small and to a minimum.
- Avoid using Flash. Most mobile devices don't support it.
- Include only essential navigation at the top of the page. Additional navigation should follow the main content.
- Make links and other elements large enough that the user can manipulate them easily.
- Use relative measurements so the page looks good regardless of the scale.

Description

- If you're designing a separate web site for mobile devices, you can include just the content you need for that site in your HTML document.
- If you're using a single HTML document for both standard and mobile devices, you can use a different style sheet for mobile devices to control what's displayed.

Figure 12-10   Guidelines for designing mobile web pages

The HTML for the mobile web page

Figure 12-11 presents the HTML for the web page you saw in the previous figure. Except for the meta element, this code is just like the code for any other web page. In this case, the meta element sets the viewport width to 275 pixels, which is the width of the page. That causes the page to fill the visible area of the screen.

Although you can't tell from the code shown here, I also reduced the size of the two images on the page. That way, these images will download more quickly and will take up less space on the screen.

The CSS for the mobile web page

Figure 12-12 presents the CSS for the mobile web page. Like the HTML for this page, the CSS is similar to the CSS for most any page. So I'll just point out a couple of things here.

First, you should notice that I set the default font size for the page to 8 points. That way, the font size won't vary based on the browser that's being used. So if you want your pages to be displayed consistently across browser and mobile devices, you should use an absolute value for the default font size rather than a relative value. You should still use relative values for other measurements, though.

Second, you should notice that the width of the page is set to 275 pixels, which is just wide enough to accommodate the page contents. This is the value you use in the meta element to set the width of the viewport if you want the page to fill the visible area of the screen.

The HTML for the web page

```
<html xmlns="http://www.w3.org/1999/xhtml">
    <head>
        <title>Mike Murach & Associates</title>
        <link rel="stylesheet" type="text/css" href="styles/mobile.css" />
        <meta name="viewport" content="width=275" />
    </head>
    <body>
        <div id="page">
            <div id="header">
                <img src="images/murach_50_square.jpg" alt="Murach Logo" />
                <p id="tagline">Professional programming books</p>
                <div id="navigation">
                    <p><a href="index.html" class="black">Home</a> |
                        <a href="books.html" class="blue">Books</a> |
                        <a href="ebooks.html" class="blue">Ebooks</a> |
                        <a href="downloads/index.html" class="blue">
                        Downloads</a></p>
                </div>
            </div>
            <div id="main">
                <div id="new_book">
                    <h1>New! JavaScript and DOM Scripting</h1>
                    <a href="books/mdom/index.html">
                        <img src="images/javascriptbook_60.jpg"
                            alt="JavaScript book" /></a>
                </div>
                <div id="book_links">
                    <h2>Other recent releases</h2>
                    <p><a href="books/pls8/index.html">C++ 2008</a></p>
                    <h2>Best sellers</h2>
                    <p><a href="books/cs08/index.html">C# 2008</a></p>
                    <p><a href="books/dcs8/index.html">
                        ADO.NET with C# 2008</a></p>
                    <p><a href="books/acs8/index.html">
                        ASP.NET with C# 2008</a></p><br />
                        .
                        .
                    <p><a href="books/osql/index.html">
                        Oracle SQL and PL/SQL</a></p>
                </div>
                <div id="utilities">
                    <p><a href="trainers/index.html">Trainers</a> |
                        <a href="instructors/index.html">Instructors</a><br />
                    </p>
                    <p><a href="custserv/index.html">Customer Service</a> |
                        <a href="company/index.html">Company Information</a>
                    </p>
                </div>
            </div>
            <div id="footer">
                <p>&copy; Copyright 1998-2009. Mike Murach & Associates,
                Inc.</p>
            </div>
        </div>
    </body>
</html>
```

Figure 12-11   The HTML for the mobile web page

The CSS for the web page

```css
/* the default styles for the document */
body {
    font-family: Arial, Helvetica, sans-serif;
    font-size: 8pt;
    margin: 0;
    padding: 0;
}
h1 {
    font-size: 130%;
    color: #004e97;
    margin: 0;
}
h2 {
    font-size: 120%;
    margin-top: 1.2em;
    margin-bottom: .6em;
}
/* the styles for the page */
#page { width: 275px; }

/* the styles for the header */
#header img {
    height: 50px;
    width: 50px;
    float: left;
}
#tagline {
    font-size: 115%;
    font-weight: bold;
    color: white;
    background-color: #004e97;
    text-align: right;
    margin: 0;
    padding: .3em 1em;
}
#navigation p {
    font-size: 110%;
    font-weight: bold;
    border-top: 2px solid #004e97;
    border-bottom: 2px solid #004e97;
    margin: 0;
    padding: .3em 1em;
    clear: left;
}
.black {
    color: black;
    text-decoration: none;
}
.blue { color: #004e97; }
```

Figure 12-12   The CSS for the mobile web page (part 1 of 2)

The CSS for the web page   **Page 2**

```css
/* the styles for the main content */
#main { margin: 0 1em; }
#new_book {
    text-align: center;
    margin-top: 1.6em;
}
#new_book img {
    margin-top: 1em;
    border-style: none;
}
#book_links { padding-top: .5em; }
#book_links p {
    margin-top: 0;
    margin-bottom: 0;
    padding-bottom: 1em;
}
#book_links a {
    color: #004e97;
    font-weight: bold;
}
#utilities {
    margin: 2em 0 0;
    text-align: center;
}
#utilities a { color: #004e97; }

/* the styles for the footer */
#footer p {
    font-size: 90%;
    border-top: 1px solid gray;
    padding: .25em .5 0;
    margin-top: 2.5em;
    margin-bottom: 0;
}
```

Figure 12-12   The CSS for the mobile web page (part 2 of 2)

Perspective

The use of mobile devices has increased dramatically over the past few years. Because of that, it has become increasingly important to design web sites that are easy to use from these devices. Although that often means developing a separate web site, this can be a critical aspect of maintaining your presence in the business world.

It's also important to provide a readable layout for web pages that a user is likely to print. You probably know from experience how frustrating it can be to print a page and have part of the content cut off or have it print so small that you can barely read it. So if the information on a page is important enough to print, be sure to provide a style sheet that will make it easy to read when printed.

Terms

media query
WURFL (Wireless Universal Resource File)
viewport
scale

Summary

- If a web page is going to be used for more than one media type, you can use a link or style element to include a separate style sheet for each type.

- CSS provides several properties for printing, including the display property for hiding an element and several page-break properties for controlling where page breaks occur.

- When you code the HTML for a page that's going to be printed, you need to code the elements in the same sequence that you want them printed.

- When you code the CSS for a page that's going to be printed, you should remove site navigation and unnecessary images, use dark print on a white background, and use a serif font in a size that's easy to read for the text of the page.

- Since many mobile devices don't recognize the handheld media type, style sheets usually aren't used for mobile devices. Instead, a separate web site is used for mobile devices that provides a simple layout with the focus on the content.

- One way to let a mobile device user access the mobile web site is to provide a link at the top of the home page for the main site. A better way is to use JavaScript or server-side programming on the main site to detect mobile devices and automatically redirect the users to the mobile web site.

- The viewport on a mobile device determines the content that's displayed and how text wraps on the page. It can be larger or smaller than the visible area of the page.

Exercise 12-1   Create a style sheet for printing

In this exercise, you'll create a style sheet for printing. When you're done, the Print Preview for the printed page should look like this:

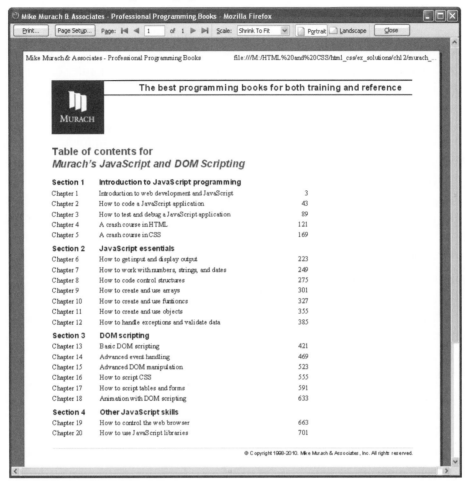

Review the existing web page and create a style sheet for printing

1. Open these files in your text editor:

    ```
    c:\html_css\ch12\murach_print\index.html
    c:\html_css\ch12\murach_print\styles\main.css
    ```

2. Display the page in your browser so you can see how it looks. This is the page you saw in figure 6-15 of chapter 6 that displays a table of contents.

3. Use the browser's Print Preview command to see how the page will look when it's printed. Depending on the defaults for your browser, the right side of the page may be cut off or the content may be reduced in size so it fits on the page.

4. Save the main.css style sheet as print.css in the styles directory. Then, add a link to this style sheet in the index.html file and set the media type to "print". Last, add a media attribute to the link element for the main.css file that specifies "screen."

Modify the print style sheet so it prints the page as shown above

At this point, the print.css file contains all of the rule sets for screen display. Now, you need to delete the rules sets that you don't need for printing, add the rule sets that you do need, and modify the other rule sets so they're right for printing.

5. Delete the rule sets that you don't need for printing. That includes the rule sets for the page, utilities, navigation, sidebar1, sidebar2, cart_link, guarantee, guarantee_head, and guarantee_text ids. That also includes the rule sets for the blue and black classes.

6. Set the display property for the utilities, navigation, sidebar1, and sidebar2 divisions to "none". Then, delete the background-color rule for the body element. Now, test these changes by displaying the web page in print preview. This will not only test the CSS changes that you made but also the link elements that you coded in step 4.

7. Modify the rule set for the main division so it sets the margins to zero, sets the top padding to 1.5 ems, and clears the floated image in the header. Now, test these changes. At this point, the print preview should start to look like the one above.

Make the final adjustments

8. Delete the color and background-color properties from the rule set for the tagline, change its the font-size to 125%, and add a 2-pixel solid black border above and below the tagline.

9. Set the right padding for the main division to 200 pixels, and set the left padding to zero.

10. Change the font-family for the h3 element in the main division so it uses a serif font with a font size of 100%, and change the font size for the footer to 75%.

11. Test these changes in both IE and Firefox, and make any final adjustments so the page prints the same in both browsers.

Exercise 12-2   Create a web page for mobile devices

In this exercise, you'll create a mobile web page from the Town Hall page you saw in figure 12-3. When you're done, the page should look like this:

Review the existing web page

1. Open these files in your text editor:

    ```
    c:\html_css\ch12\town_hall_mobile\index.html
    c:\html_css\ch12\town_hall_mobile\styles\mobile.css
    ```

2. Modify the first link element in the index.html file so it will use the mobile.css style sheet, and delete the link element for the print style sheet. Then, display the web page in your browser to see how it looks.

Simplify the page contents in the HTML so it's like the content above

3.   Move the utilities division from the sidebar division to the end of the main division. Then, delete the rest of the sidebar division.

4.   Delete the beginning of the text from the last paragraph in the header division (the one with the id "tagline") so all that's left is the text that's in the span element.

5.   Delete the paragraph with the id "intro" from the speakers division. Then, for each speaker, delete the first paragraph (the one that's assigned to the class named "divider") and the image.

6.   Enclose the h1 paragraph for each speaker in an a element that displays the page for the speaker. This should be the same page that's referred to in the link in the last paragraph for the speaker. Then, delete the last paragraph.

7.   Code each link in the utilities division so it's in its own paragraph. Then, add a new link at the beginning of this division with the text "News" that will display a page named news.html.

8.   Display the page in your browser to see how it looks. Although the content is now more manageable, the formatting still needs to be simplified and the sizes need to be reduced.

Simplify the formatting in the CSS and reduce the sizes

9.   Change the font size for the body element to 8 points, change the width of the page to 530 pixels, and change all the page margins to 0.

10. Remove the background colors from the page, speakers, and navigation divisions, remove the color from the h1 elements in the speakers division, and change the color of the link pseudo-class for the a elements in the utilities division to #ef9c00.

11. Delete the style rule for the main division since it is no longer floated. You may also want to delete the style rules for any HTML content you deleted.

12. Reduce the width of the logo to 50 pixels. Then, adjust the margins and padding for the elements in the header division so it looks like the one shown above. In particular, you'll need to change the right margin for the title1 element since it's currently based on a page width of 960 pixels.

13. Refresh the page in your browser. It should now look more like the one above, but some spacing adjustments are still needed. Make and test those adjustments now.

Deploy and test the page on mobile devices

14. If you can deploy the page on an Internet server, you can test it with any mobile devices that are available to you. Before you do that, though, add a meta element to the HTML file that sets the viewport width to 275.

13

How to use JavaScript to enhance your web pages

In this chapter, you'll learn how you can use JavaScript to enhance your web pages, even though you won't learn how to code JavaScript. Instead, you'll first learn the concepts and terms that you need for understanding how JavaScript works. Then, you'll learn how you can use tested JavaScript code in your web pages to get the results you want.

Introduction to JavaScript and DOM scripting

In this introduction, you'll learn how JavaScript and DOM scripting work together. You'll also learn how you can include JavaScript in your HTML documents.

How JavaScript works

Figure 13-1 presents a diagram that shows how JavaScript fits into the client/server architecture. Here, you can see that the *JavaScript* code is executed in the web browser by the browser's *JavaScript engine*. This is referred to as *client-side processing,* in contrast to the *server-side processing* that's done on the web server. This takes some of the processing burden off the server and makes the application run faster. Today, almost all web browsers have JavaScript enabled so JavaScript applications will run on them.

To illustrate the use of JavaScript code, the example in this figure gets the current date and the current year and inserts both into an HTML document. To do that, the JavaScript code is embedded within script elements in the body of the document. This code is executed when the page is loaded.

You can see the results in the web browser that follows the code. In this case, the JavaScript code in the first script element writes the first line into the web page, which includes the current date. And the JavaScript code in the second script element writes the copyright line into the web page, which includes the current year.

How JavaScript fits into the client/server architecture

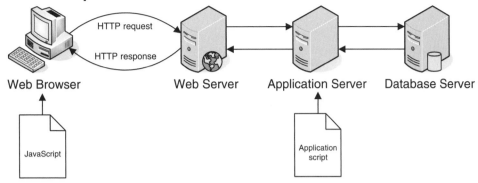

JavaScript in an HTML document that gets the current date and year

```
<div id="main">
    <p>
        <script type="text/javascript" >
            var today = new Date();
            document.write( "Current date: " );
            document.write( today.toDateString() );
        </script>
    </p>
    <p><em>Contact us by phone</em> at (559) 555-1212 for ticket
        information.</p>
</div>
<div id="footer">
    <p>
        <script type="text/javascript" >
            var today = new Date();
            document.write( "&copy; " );
            document.write( today.getFullYear() );
            document.write( ", San Joaquin Valley Town Hall" );
        </script>
    </p>
</div>
```

The JavaScript in a web browser

Current date: Mon May 3 2010

Contact us by phone at (559) 555-1212 for ticket information.

© 2010, San Joaquin Valley Town Hall

Description

- *JavaScript* is a scripting language that is run by the *JavaScript engine* of a browser. As a result, the work is done on the client, not the server.

- JavaScript can modify the contents of a web page when the page is loaded or in response to a user action. In this example, JavaScript inserts the current date and later the current year into the web page when the page is loaded.

Figure 13-1   How JavaScript works

How the DOM (Document Object Model) works

The *document object model* (*DOM*) is an internal representation of the HTML elements in a web page. As an HTML page is loaded by the web browser, the DOM for that page is created in the browser's memory. In figure 13-2, you can see a simple HTML document and the structure of the DOM for that document.

Each element of the web page is represented by a *node* in the DOM. The nodes in the DOM have a hierarchical structure based on how the HTML elements are nested inside each other. The DOM starts with the html element and follows the nesting of the elements down to the text that is in each element.

Within the DOM, several types of nodes are used to represent the contents of the web page. HTML elements are stored in *element nodes*, and text is stored in *text nodes*. In this figure, element nodes are shown as ovals, and text nodes are shown as rectangles. Other common node types are *attribute nodes* and *comment nodes*.

The nodes that make up the DOM can be modified by JavaScript. This allows the web page to be modified after it is displayed by the web browser. Whenever a change is made to the DOM, the web browser displays the updated page in the browser window.

The code for a web page

```
<!DOCTYPE html PUBLIC "-//W3C//DTD XHTML 1.0 Transitional//EN"
    "http://www.w3.org/TR/xhtml1/DTD/xhtml1-transitional.dtd">
<html xmlns="http://www.w3.org/1999/xhtml">
<head>
<title>Mike's Bait and Tackle Shop</title>
</head>
<body>
    <h1>Mike's Bait and Tackle Shop</h1>
    <p>Welcome to Mike's Bait and Tackle Shop. We have all the gear you'll
    need to make your next fishing trip a great success!</p>
    <h2>New Products</h2>
    <ul>
        <li>Ultima 3000 Two-handed fly rod</li>
        <li>Phil's Faux Shrimp Fly - Size 6</li>
        <li>Titanium Open Back Fly Reel - Black</li>
    </ul>
    <p>Contact us by phone at 559-555-6624 to place your order today.</p>
</body>
</html>
```

The DOM for the web page

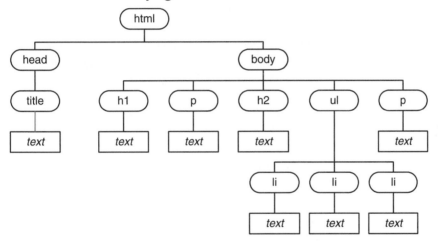

Description

- The *document object model* (DOM) is a hierarchical collection of *nodes* in the web browser's memory that represents the current web page.
- The DOM for a web page is built as the page is loaded by the web browser.
- JavaScript can modify the web page in the browser by modifying the DOM. Whenever the DOM is changed, the web browser displays the results of the change.
- Many JavaScript applications manipulate the DOM based on user actions.

Figure 13-2   How the DOM (Document Object Model) works

How DOM scripting works

DOM scripting lets you use JavaScript to update a web page in response to user actions that are called *events*. An event is typically an action the user performs with the mouse or keyboard. The JavaScript code that is executed in response to an event is called an *event handler*.

The diagram at the start of figure 13-3 describes the event cycle that drives DOM scripting. First, the page is loaded and the event handlers are attached to the events that will be processed. Next, when an event occurs, the appropriate event handler is executed. Then, if this event handler modifies the DOM, the page is immediately updated.

The example in this figure illustrates the event cycle. It shows how DOM scripting can be used to print a web page when the Print button is clicked. In contrast to the JavaScript code in figure 13-1, the code in this example is embedded in the head section of the HTML document. That's because this code doesn't generate any output.

Although this chapter isn't going to teach you how to code JavaScript code, here's a quick idea of what's going on in this example. The JavaScript comments in this example, which start with //, divide the code into three functions. The first function, named $, gets an element from the DOM based on the id that's passed to it. The second function is the event handler that runs when the Print button is clicked. And the third function is an event handler that runs when the page is loaded.

When the page is loaded, the third function does two tasks. First, it assigns the click event of the Print button to the event handler named print_click. That's the second function in this example. Then, the third function moves the focus to the Print button. This is how JavaScript can be used to move the focus to the appropriate control when a page is loaded. Both of the statements in this third function use the $ function at the start of the page to get the element with "print" as its id.

In this example, the $ function gets the "print" element from the DOM, but it doesn't actually modify the DOM. However, you'll soon see examples that do modify the DOM.

A web page that uses a JavaScript button for printing

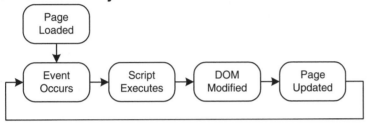

The DOM event cycle

```
Page
Loaded
  │
  ▼
Event  ──►  Script  ──►  DOM  ──►  Page
Occurs      Executes     Modified   Updated
```

The HTML code for the button in the body section

```html
<input type="button" id="print" value="Print the TOC" />
```

The JavaScript in the head section

```javascript
<script type="text/javascript" >
    // this $ function gets the element with the specified id
    var $ = function (id) {
        return document.getElementById(id);
    }
    // this event handler runs when the print button is clicked
    var print_click = function () {
        window.print();                    // prints the page
    }
    // this function runs when the page is loaded
    window.onload = function () {
        $("print").onclick = print_click;  // attaches the event handler
                                           // to the click event of the print button
        $("print").focus();               // moves the focus to the print button
    }
</script>
```

Description

- *DOM scripting* is the process of manipulating the DOM by using JavaScript.
- An *event* is an action the user performs like clicking a mouse button. When the event occurs, JavaScript is used to process it. This code is called an *event handler*.
- As an event handler executes, it has full access to the DOM so it can read the elements on the page, and it can change their attributes and contents. When the DOM is modified, the web browser immediately updates the web page.
- When the event handler is finished, the web browser waits for another event to occur and the cycle starts over again until another page is loaded.

Figure 13-3   How DOM scripting works

How to include JavaScript in an HTML document

Figure 13-4 shows three ways to use the script element to include JavaScript code in an HTML document. To start, this figure describes two attributes that can be used with the script element. The type attribute identifies the JavaScript language. The src attribute specifies the location of the external JavaScript file that should be included in the document.

In the examples in this figure, you can see how the script tag is used for external files and embedded scripts. In the first example, the src attribute is used to specify an external file named future_value.js. This assumes that the external file is in the same folder as the HTML page. If it isn't, you can code the path to the file along with the file name.

In the second example, a script tag that contains JavaScript code is embedded in the head of an HTML document. As you saw in figure 13-3, JavaScript code in the head section is typically used to define functions and event handlers.

In the third example, a script is embedded in the body of an HTML document. As you saw in figure 13-1, a script element like this is replaced by the output of the JavaScript code when the application is loaded.

In the last example, you can see how the noscript element can be used. It is usually coded after a script element in the body of a document. Then, if JavaScript is disabled in a user's browser, the content of the noscript tag is displayed. But if JavaScript is enabled, the script element is replaced by the output of the JavaScript code and the noscript tag is ignored. This way some output will be displayed whether or not JavaScript is enabled.

Two attributes of the script element

Attribute	Description
type	Use "text/javascript" when you use JavaScript as the scripting language.
src	Specifies the location and name of an external JavaScript file.

How to load JavaScript from an external file

```
<script type="text/javascript" src="future_value.js"></script>
```

How to embed JavaScript in the head of an HTML document

```
<head>
    ...
    <script type="text/javascript">
        var $ = function (id) { return document.getElementById(id); }
    </script>
    ...
</head>
```

How to embed JavaScript in the body of an HTML document

```
<p>&copy;
    <script type="text/javascript">
        var today = new Date();
        document.writeln( today.getFullYear() );
    </script>
</p>
```

How to use the noscript tag in the body of an HTML document

```
<script type="text/javascript">
    var today = new Date();
    document.writeln( today.getFullYear() );
</script>
<noscript>2010</noscript>
```

Description

- You can have more than one script element in a web page. These elements are executed in the order that they appear in the document.
- If a script element in the head section includes an external JavaScript file, the JavaScript in the file runs as if it were coded in the script element.
- If a script element is coded in the body of a document, it is replaced by the output of the JavaScript code.
- The noscript element is used to display content when JavaScript is disabled in a user's browser.
- The HTML document must be valid before and after all scripts have been executed.

Figure 13-4   How to include JavaScript in an HTML document

A standalone JavaScript application

A standalone JavaScript application runs in its own web page. This is illustrated by the Future Value application in figure 13-5. Standalone JavaScript applications are often used for games and calculations that don't require data from the database server.

The Future Value application is a simple standalone application that calculates the future value of a monthly investment. To use it, the user types values into the first three text boxes and clicks the Calculate button. Then, the application validates the entries and either displays an error message in a dialog box or displays the result of the calculation in the Future Value text box.

In this figure, an error message is displayed because the user has entered an invalid investment amount ($100). This is invalid because a number can't contain special characters like the dollar sign.

The HTML for the Future Value application

In the head section of the HTML code for this application, you can see a link element for a CSS file named future_value.css. Although the CSS isn't shown in this chapter, it is available in the downloadable application.

In the head section, you can also see the script element for the JavaScript that's used by this application. It is stored in a file named future_value.js that is included when the page is loaded.

In the body section, you can see the HTML code for the labels, text boxes, and button that this application uses. If you've read chapter 10, you should understand what this code does. Of note, though, are the id attributes because those ids are used by the JavaScript code.

The Future Value application in a web browser

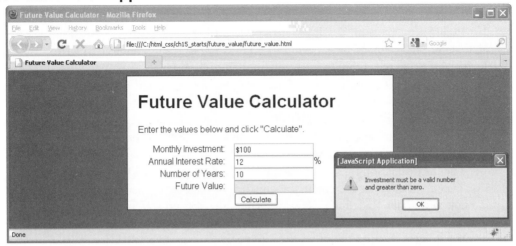

The HTML file

```
<!DOCTYPE html PUBLIC "-//W3C//DTD XHTML 1.0 Transitional//EN"
    "http://www.w3.org/TR/xhtml1/DTD/xhtml1-transitional.dtd">
<html xmlns="http://www.w3.org/1999/xhtml">
<head>
    <title>Future Value Calculator</title>
    <link rel="stylesheet" type="text/css" href="future_value.css" />
    <script type="text/javascript" src="future_value.js"></script>
</head>

<body>
    <div id="content">
        <h1>Future Value Calculator</h1>
        <p>Enter the values below and click "Calculate".</p>

        <label for="investment">Monthly Investment:</label>
        <input type="text" id="investment" /><br />

        <label for="rate">Annual Interest Rate:</label>
        <input type="text" id="rate" />%<br />

        <label for="years">Number of Years:</label>
        <input type="text" id="years" /><br />

        <label for="futureValue">Future Value:</label>
        <input type="text" id="futureValue" disabled="disabled" /><br />

        <label> </label>
        <input type="button" id="calculate" value="Calculate" /><br />
    </div>
</body>
</html>
```

Figure 13-5   The HTML for the Future Value application

The JavaScript for the Future Value application

Figure 13-6 presents the JavaScript code for the Future Value application. Here again, the point of presenting this code is *not* to teach you how to write JavaScript code, but rather to give you an idea of how JavaScript code works.

This application defines three functions that are identified by the highlighted comments that precede them. The first function is the $ function that's used to get elements based on their ids. The second function is the event handler that will run when the Calculate button is clicked. The third function is the event handler for the onload event.

The third function runs after the page is loaded and the DOM is built. Its first statement attaches the calculate_click event handler to the click event of the button that has "calculate" as its id. Then, the second statement uses the focus method to move the focus to the text box that has "investment" as its id.

When the user clicks the Calculate button, the calculate_click function is executed. This function starts by using the $ function to get the contents of the three text boxes with "investment", "rate", and "years" as their ids. After it gets their contents, it stores those values in three variables named investment, annualRate, and years. Then, this function uses the $ function to move an empty string into the box that has "futureValue" as its id. That clears any value that was displayed by a previous calculation.

Next, this function uses an if statement to check each of the three user entries to see whether it is not numeric or it is less than or equal to zero. If one of these conditions is true, the alert method is used to display an appropriate error message and the if statement ends.

However, if all three user entries are valid, the last else clause is executed. The code in this clause first converts the annual interest rate to a monthly rate and the years to months. Then, it uses those values in a for statement that calculates the future value. When the for statement ends, the future value is rounded to two decimal places and displayed in the text box that has "futureValue" as its id.

If you have any programming experience, you can probably follow this code. In particular, you should see how the if statements are used to check the validity of the user's entries. You should also see how a "for loop" is used to do the calculation that derives the future value from the three variables.

If you don't have any programming experience, you should at least get a general idea of how JavaScript programming works. In brief, event handlers are used to respond to events like the loading of a web page or the click of a button. These event handlers can get the values that users have entered into input controls, test to see whether those values are valid, perform calculations with the values, and display the results in other controls. But as you will soon see, these event handlers can also use DOM scripting to produce some dramatic results.

The JavaScript file

```javascript
// the $ function that gets an HTML element based on its id
var $ = function (id) {
    return document.getElementById(id);
}


// The calculate_click function that does the future_value calculation
var calculate_click = function () {

    // Get the user entries from the first three text boxes.
    var investment = parseFloat( $("investment").value );
    var annualRate = parseFloat( $("rate").value );
    var years = parseInt( $("years").value );

    // Set the value of the fourth text box to an empty string.
    $("futureValue").value = "";

    // Test the three input values for validity.
    if (isNaN(investment) || investment <= 0) {
        alert("Investment must be a valid number\nand greater than zero.");
    } else if(isNaN(annualRate) || annualRate <= 0) {
        alert("Annual rate must be a valid number\nand greater than zero.");
    } else if(isNaN(years) || years <= 0) {
        alert("Years must be a valid number\nand greater than zero.");

    // If all input values are valid, calculate the future value.
    } else {
        var monthlyRate = annualRate / 12 / 100;
        var months = years * 12;
        var futureValue = 0;

        for ( i = 1; i <= months; i++ ) {
            futureValue = ( futureValue + investment ) *
                (1 + monthlyRate);
        }

        // Set the value of the fourth text box to the future value
        // but round it to two decimal places.
        $("futureValue").value = futureValue.toFixed(2);
    }
}


// the event handler for the onload event
window.onload = function () {
    $("calculate").onclick = calculate_click;
    $("investment").focus();
}
```

Figure 13-6   The JavaScript for the Future Value application

How to use JavaScript in your web pages

This topic shows you how to use tested JavaScript code in your own web pages, even though you didn't write it and don't know how it works. To start, it presents five JavaScript applications that are included in the downloads for this book, and it shows you how you can use the JavaScript for these applications in your own web pages.

If these applications are hard to follow as you read about them, you will get a chance to experiment with them in the exercises for this chapter. That should resolve any questions that you have.

JavaScript for image rollovers

Figure 13-7 presents an application that does image rollovers. An *image rollover* occurs when the user moves the mouse pointer over one image and that image is temporarily replaced by another image. Then, when the user moves the mouse pointer off the image, the rollover ends.

In this example, the top image and the bottom image are set up for image rollovers. When you use an image rollover, you often replace the current image with a close-up of it or with the same image shot from another angle.

To use the JavaScript code for this application for your own image rollovers, you need to code the two script elements in the head section of your HTML. You also need to copy the file named rollover_library.js into the directory for your application.

Then, in the body of the document, you need to code one img element for each image that is going to be rolled over. If you're going to use two images, the ids for these elements should be "image1" and "image2" so they match the ids that are used in the JavaScript code. If you're going to use more images, you can continue this id pattern.

Now, back to the JavaScript code that's embedded in the document. For each image rollover, you need to code one JavaScript statement like this:

```
rollover1 = new Rollover("image1", "images/h4.jpg");
```

Here, "rollover1" is a name used by the JavaScript in the rollover library; "image1" is the id of the image; and "images/h4.jpg" is the path and file name for the rollover image.

If you're going to use just one image rollover on a page, you can delete the statement that starts with rollover2. If you're going to use more than one rollover, you can continue with rollover3 and image3. In this application, you're actually changing the embedded JavaScript code, but as you will see, you don't always need to do that.

By the way, this is an example of DOM scripting. When the mouse pointer hovers over an image, that event triggers a JavaScript event handler that changes the DOM so the src attribute in the img element points to the rollover image.

A web page with two images that can be rolled over

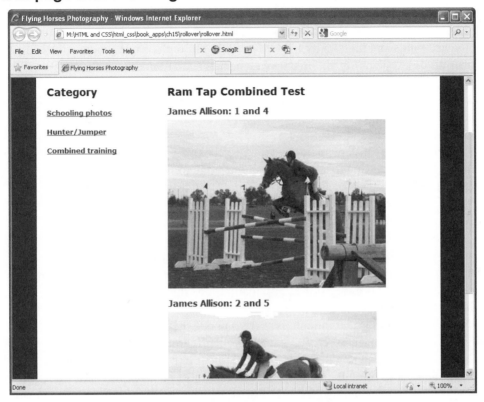

The HTML for using the JavaScript for two rollovers

```
<script type="text/javascript" src="rollover_library.js"></script>
<script type="text/javascript" >
    var $ = function (id) { return document.getElementById(id); }
    var rollover;
        window.onload = function () {
        // You need to provide one statement for each rollover here
        rollover1 = new Rollover("image1", "images/h4.jpg");
        rollover2 = new Rollover("image2", "images/h5.jpg");
        }
</script>
```

The HTML for the img elements that get rolled over

```
<p><img src="images/h1.jpg" alt="" id="image1" /></p>
<p><img src="images/h2.jpg" alt="" id="image2" /></p>
```

How to use this JavaScript

- Code one img element for each image that you want rolled over.
- In the embedded JavaScript, provide one statement for each rollover. For these statements, you can use rollover1, rollover2, and so on as the names before the equal signs. Then, within the parentheses for each statement, you code (1) the id of the image to be rolled over, and (2) the location of the rollover image.

Figure 13-7   JavaScript for image rollovers

JavaScript for image swaps

Figure 13-8 presents an application that does image swaps. An *image swap* occurs when an event handler uses DOM scripting to replace one image with another. In this application, an image swap occurs each time the user clicks on one of the thumbnail images at the top of the web page. Here, the user has clicked on the fourth thumbnail so the caption and image in the body of the document have been replaced with the caption and image that correspond to that thumbnail image.

The benefit of image swapping is that you use one web page to present more than one image. In this case, you use one page to present six different images. If you didn't use image swapping, that would require six different web pages. That's the case with the application that's shown in figure 8-11 of chapter 8.

To use the JavaScript for this application for your own image swaps, you start by copying the two JavaScript files into the directory for your application. Then, you code two script elements in the head section of the HTML document that include those two files. For this application, you don't have to modify any of the JavaScript code.

What's most important, though, is that you code the HTML for the thumbnails, caption, and image exactly as shown in this figure. For the caption, you must code a span element within any block element like the h3 element in this example, and the id attribute for the span element must be "caption". For the image, you must code an img element with "image" as its id, and its src attribute must locate the first image that will be used for the page.

For the thumbnails, you code an unordered list with "image_list" as its id. Then, you code one li element for each item swap. Within each li element, you code an a element that uses the href attribute to identify the image and the title attribute to identify the caption. Last, you code an img element for the thumbnail as the content for the a element within each li element.

When the page is loaded, the JavaScript code uses the attributes in the unordered list to build a list of the captions and images that are going to be swapped when the thumbnails are clicked. Then, a new image is swapped in each time a thumbnail is clicked.

This is another example that illustrates the power of DOM scripting. Each time the click event occurs, the related event handler changes the DOM so the contents of the span tag and the src attribute in the img element display the swapped caption and image.

Incidentally, to get the thumbnails displayed in a row the way they are in this example, you need a CSS file that does that formatting. You can review that file when you do the exercises for this chapter.

A web page with thumbnails that are used to swap the main image

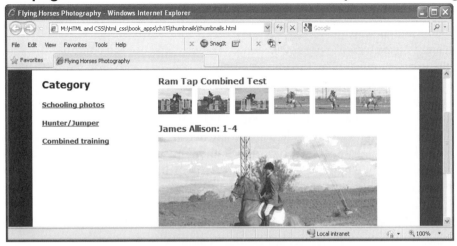

The script elements for the two JavaScript files

```
<script type="text/javascript" src="image_swap_library.js"></script>
<script type="text/javascript" src="image_swap.js"></script>
```

The HTML for the images, captions, and thumbnails

```
<ul id="image_list">
    <li><a href="images/h1.jpg" title="James Allison: 1-1" >
        <img src="thumbnails/t1.jpg" alt="" /></a></li>
    <li><a href="images/h2.jpg" title="James Allison: 1-2" >
        <img src="thumbnails/t2.jpg" alt="" /></a></li>
    <li><a href="images/h3.jpg" title="James Allison: 1-3" >
        <img src="thumbnails/t3.jpg" alt="" /></a></li>
    <li><a href="images/h4.jpg" title="James Allison: 1-4" >
        <img src="thumbnails/t4.jpg" alt="" /></a></li>
    <li><a href="images/h5.jpg" title="James Allison: 1-5" >
        <img src="thumbnails/t5.jpg" alt="" /></a></li>
    <li><a href="images/h6.jpg" title="James Allison: 1-6" >
        <img src="thumbnails/t6.jpg" alt="" /></a></li>
</ul>
```

The HTML for the caption and image that get swapped

```
<h3><span id="caption">James Allison 1-1</span></h3>
<p><img id="image" src="images/h1.jpg" alt="" /></p>
```

How to use this JavaScript

- Code an unordered list with "image_list" as its id. Then, within each list item, code an a element. In each a element, the href attribute should locate the image to be swapped, and the title attribute should provide the caption for the swapped image.
- As the contents for the a elements, code the img elements for the thumbnails.
- For the caption, code a span element within any block element with "caption" as its id.
- For the main image, code an img element with "image" as its id.

Figure 13-8   JavaScript for image swaps

JavaScript for slide shows

Figure 13-9 presents an application that does a slide show. In this case, the caption and image change every few seconds. You can also use the controls above the image to change the time between image changes or to stop the slide show and move manually forward or backward through the images.

To use the JavaScript code for this application for your own slide show, you set up the slide show in a way that's similar to using the JavaScript for image swaps. First, you code two script elements in the head section that include the required JavaScript files. Second, you code an unordered list that contains a elements that identify the images and captions for the slide show. Third, you include the HTML for the controls. Last, you code a span element for the slide caption and an img element for the slide.

To make this work, you must also copy the JavaScript files and control images into the directory for your application. In addition, you must use a CSS file that provides the right formatting for the controls. Here again, you can review the CSS file for this application when you do the exercises.

A web page with a slide show that's running

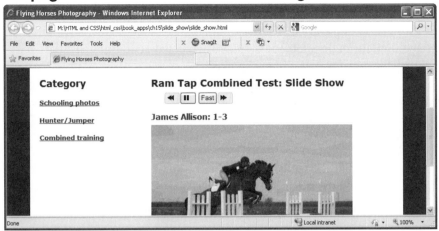

The script elements for the two JavaScript files

```
<script type="text/javascript" src="slide_show_library.js"></script>
<script type="text/javascript" src="slide_show.js"></script>
```

The HTML for the slides and captions

```
<ul id="image_list">
    <li><a href="images/h1.jpg" title="James Allison: 1-1" ></a></li>
    <li><a href="images/h2.jpg" title="James Allison: 1-2" ></a></li>
    <li><a href="images/h3.jpg" title="James Allison: 1-3" ></a></li>
    <li><a href="images/h4.jpg" title="James Allison: 1-4" ></a></li>
    <li><a href="images/h5.jpg" title="James Allison: 1-5" ></a></li>
    <li><a href="images/h6.jpg" title="James Allison: 1-6" ></a></li>
</ul>
```

The HTML for the controls

```
<p id="controls">
    <button id="btn_previous" disabled="disabled" >
        <img src="prev.gif" alt="Previous Image" /></button>
    <button id="btn_play">
        <img src="pause.gif" alt="Play or Pause" id="img_play_pause" />
    </button>
    <input type="button" id="btn_speed" value="Fast" />
    <button id="btn_next" disabled="disabled">
        <img src="next.gif" alt="Next Image" /></button>
</p>
```

The HTML for the caption and image area

```
<h3><span id="caption">James Allison 1-1</span></h3>
<p><img src="images/h1.jpg" alt="" id="image" /></p>
```

How to use this JavaScript

- The HTML is similar to the HTML for image swaps, but you don't code img elements within the a elements, and you do need to add the HTML for the controls.

Figure 13-9   JavaScript for slide shows

JavaScript for tabbed data

Figure 13-10 shows how *tabs*, or *tabbed data*, can be used in a web application. When the user clicks on a tab, the display is changed so it looks like the tab is active and the data for that tab is displayed.

This is an interface that users are familiar with so it's easy for them to use. However, the current "best practices" for the use of tabbed data include these guidelines:

- Tabs should be used for secondary data, not the primary data on a page.

- The graphics should clearly indicate which tab is active, usually by showing a border below the inactive tabs and no border below the active tab.

- The text on each tab should be short and clearly indicate what type of data the tab holds.

- The data for each tab should be independent of the other tabs so the users aren't forced to switch back and forth between tabs to see related data

- The data for each tab should be part of a single HTML page so clicking on a tab doesn't load a new page.

To implement that last guideline, of course, you need to use a client-side scripting language like JavaScript.

To use the JavaScript for the tabs in this figure, you code the HTML the way it's illustrated. First, you code the two script elements for the JavaScript files. Second, you code one div element for the tabs. That div element must contain an unordered list that will be converted into the tabs. Third, you code another div element that contains one div element for the contents of each tab.

The keys here are that the ul element must have "tab_list" as its id, and the div element for the tab contents must have "tab_contents" as its id. Also, the a element for the active tab when the page is loaded should have "active" as its class attribute, and the div elements for the tab contents that aren't active when the page is loaded should have "hide" as their class attributes. Note here that you don't need to code id attributes for the content divisions, but you do need to code them in the same sequence as the related list items.

When the user clicks on a tab after the page is loaded, the JavaScript applies the "active" class to the corresponding a element, and it sets the class attribute for the other a elements to an empty string. Then, the JavaScript sets the class attribute for the contents div that corresponds to the active tab to an empty string, and it sets the class attribute for the other div elements to "hide".

The key to this application, then, is the CSS that creates the tabs, shows which one is active, and shows the contents for that tab. That CSS is on the next page.

Tabbed data with the first tab active

The script elements for the two JavaScript files

```
<script type="text/javascript" src="tabs_library.js"></script>
<script type="text/javascript" src="tabs.js"></script>
```

The HTML for the tabs and tab contents

```
<div id="tabs" >
    <ul id="tab_list" >
        <li><a href="" id="tab1" class="active">Contents</a></li>
        <li><a href="" id="tab2" class="">Author</a></li>
        <li><a href="" id="tab3" class="">Downloads</a></li>
    </ul>
</div>
<div id="tab_contents" >
    <div class="" >
        <h2>The table of contents</h2>
        <p>The descriptive text for this tab.</p>
    </div>
    <div class="hide">
        <h2>About the author</h2>
    </div>
    <div class="hide" >
        <h2>About the downloads</h2>
    </div>
</div>
```

How to code the HTML that is processed by the JavaScript

- For the tabs, code an unordered list with "tab_list" as its id. Then, within each list item, code an a element with an empty href attribute.

- For the tab that you want to be active when the page is loaded, code a class attribute for the a element with "active" as its value.

- For the tab contents, code a division with "tab_contents" as its id. Within this division, code one division for each tab. These divisions don't need id attributes, but they should be in the same sequence as the related list items.

- For each division that isn't going to be active when the page is loaded, code a class attribute with "hide" as it's value.

- Within the division for a tab, code whatever content you want.

Figure 13-10   JavaScript for tabbed data

The CSS for the tabbed data in figure 13-11 is interesting because it shows how easy it is to create simple, but effective tabs. In fact, another guideline for using tabs is to keep the graphics simple.

To some extent, you need to experiment with this CSS to see how easily you can change the size of the tabs, the spacing between the tabs, the background colors of the tabs and contents, and so on. But here are some of the key points that you should be aware of.

First, the rule set for the unordered list (#tab_list) sets the border below the tabs. Second, the rule set for the li elements in the tab list removes the bullets and displays the list items in-line. Third, the rule set for the a elements in the tab list sets the background color for the inactive tabs to yellow. More important, this rule set sets the left, top, and right borders that define the tabs, but doesn't set a bottom border. Remember that the bottom border comes from the rule set for the tab list.

How then does that bottom border get removed for the active tab? The rule set for the active class of an a element sets the bottom border to white. Then, this border overlays the black border for that portion of the tab list, so it looks like the tab is active.

Last, the rule set for the hide class turns the display of the related element off. That's what hides the contents for the tabs that aren't active. Because the CSS works this way, all the JavaScript has to do is turn on the "active" class for the active tab and the "hide" class for the content elements that aren't active.

The CSS for the tabbed data

```css
#tabs {
    margin-top: 1em;
}
#tab_list {
    margin:0;
    padding: 3px 6px;
    border-bottom: 1px solid black;
}
#tab_list li {
    list-style: none;
    display: inline;
}
#tab_list li a {
    padding: 3px 1em;
    margin-left: 3px;
    text-decoration: none;
    font-weight: bold;
    color: black;
    background: yellow;
    border: 1px solid black;
    border-bottom: none;
}
#tab_list li a:hover {
    background: white;
    border-color: black;
}
#tab_list li a.active {
    background-color: white;
    border-bottom: 1px solid white;
}
#tab_contents div {
    padding: 5px 10px 10px;
    border: 1px solid black;
    border-top: 0;
    height: 100px;
}
.hide { display: none; }
```

Description

- The rule set for the ul element (#tab_list) puts a black border at the bottom of all the tabs.

- The rule set for the li elements displays them inline with no bullets.

- The rule set for the a elements within the li elements displays them with a top, left, and right border, but no bottom border.

- The rule set for the a element with the "active" class applies a white bottom border, which overlays the black border for the ul element. That shows which tab is selected.

- The "hide" class doesn't display any element that it is coded for.

- When the user clicks on a tab, the JavaScript applies the "active" class to the underlying a element and removes it from the other a elements. It also removes the "hide" class from the related contents division and applies the "hide" class to the other contents divisions.

Figure 13-11   The CSS for the tabbed data

JavaScript for data validation

Figure 13-12 presents an application that provides *data validation* before the form data is sent to the server for processing. When data is validated, it is checked to make sure it is valid. For instance, a required field can be checked to make sure the user has made an entry in it. A phone number can be checked to make sure it has been entered in the right format. A numeric field can be checked to make sure it is within a valid range. In short, thorough data validation means that all of the fields have been checked for all conditions that would make them invalid.

In this example, the user entered some valid data and some invalid data. Then, when he clicked on the Register button, an error message was displayed in a dialog box, and error messages were displayed to the right of the invalid fields. In contrast, if all of the data is valid when the user clicks on the Register button, the form is submitted to the web server for processing, and all of the data is sent along with the HTTP request. To reset all of the fields in the form to what they were when the web page was loaded, the user can click on the Reset button.

To use the JavaScript for this application in your own web page, you must code the form element and the elements for the Register and Reset buttons just as they are in the HTML in figure 13-13. You must also use the same field ids that this application uses. If you look at the HTML, for example, you can see that you must use "email", "password", and "verify" for the first three fields on the form. Last, you must code span elements for the error messages after the fields using the same ids that this application uses. For instance, you must use "email_error", "password_error", and "verify_error" for the span elements that follow the first three fields on this form.

If you use all of the fields in this application and only those fields, that's all you have to do. But if you don't want to use all of the fields, you must modify the code in the register_library.js file that's shown in figure 13-14. Specifically, you must delete any of the lines of code that refer to a field that you're not using. If, for example, you aren't going to use the card_type, card_number, and exp_date fields, you must delete the last three lines of code in the array of field objects, the last two lines of code in the starting field messages, and the last six lines of code in the field error messages.

What if you want to add fields that aren't included in this application? What if you want to change the rules for what a valid field is? That would require changes to the JavaScript code, and that would mean that you would have to know how to modify the code. That's why every serious web developer should eventually learn how to develop JavaScript and DOM scripting applications.

The user interface

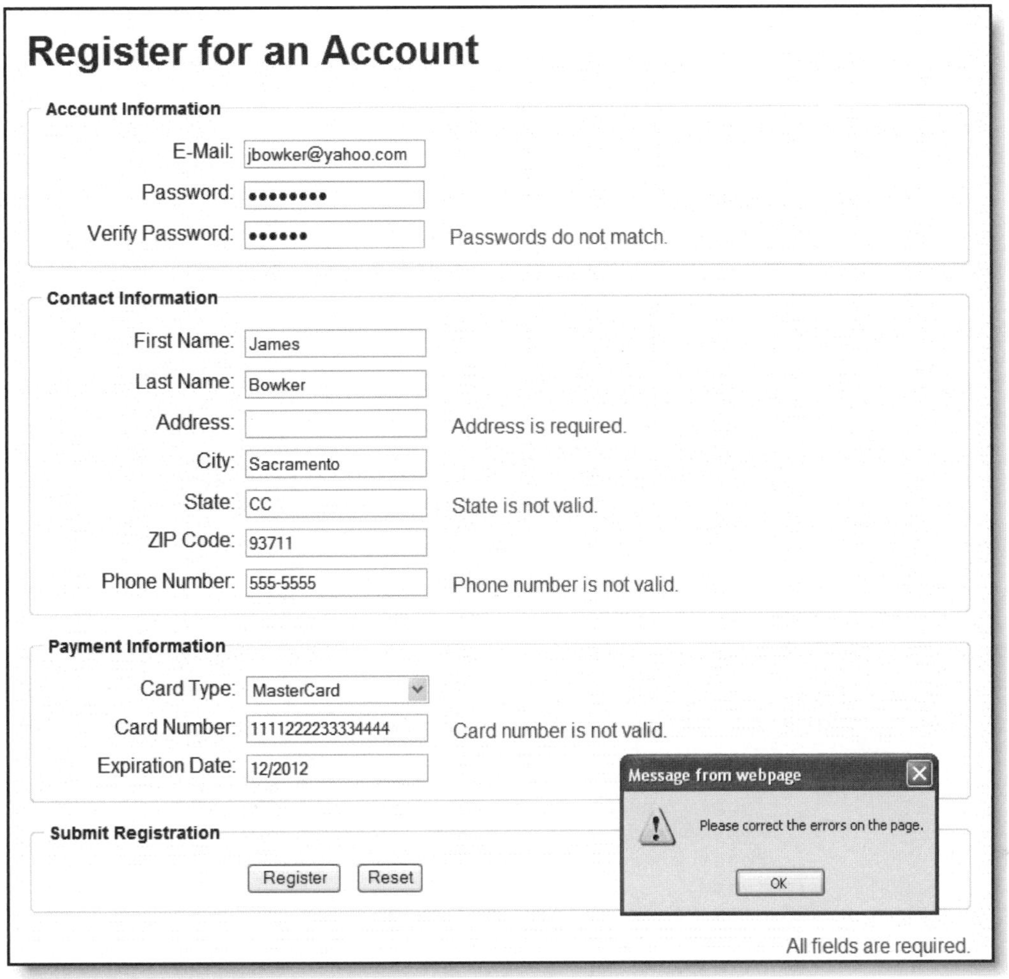

Register for an Account

Account Information

E-Mail: jbowker@yahoo.com

Password: ••••••••

Verify Password: ••••••   Passwords do not match.

Contact Information

First Name: James

Last Name: Bowker

Address: Address is required.

City: Sacramento

State: CC   State is not valid.

ZIP Code: 93711

Phone Number: 555-5555   Phone number is not valid.

Payment Information

Card Type: MasterCard

Card Number: 1111222233334444   Card number is not valid.

Expiration Date: 12/2012

Message from webpage ☒

⚠ Please correct the errors on the page.

OK

Submit Registration

Register   Reset

All fields are required.

Description

- The JavaScript for this application validates the data in the form before the data is submitted to the server for processing. If the data isn't valid, the form isn't submitted to the server, red error messages are displayed, and a dialog box is displayed.

How to use the JavaScript for this application in your own application

- In the HTML for your application, use the same ids for the fields that this application uses. Note, however, that your form doesn't have to include all of the fields shown above, and they don't have to be in the same sequence.
- If you don't include all of the fields shown above, you must modify the first page of the register_library.js file. To do that, delete all lines of code that refer to the fields that you haven't included in your HTML.
- Code the form element and the Register and Reset buttons the same way they're coded for this application. However, you can change the value properties of the buttons.

Figure 13-12   The user interface for the data validation application

Some of the HTML for the body of the document

```
<body>
<div id="content">
    <h1>Enter and Submit Data</h1>
    <form action="register_account.html" method="get"
        name="registration_form" id="registration_form">
    <fieldset>
        <legend>Account Information</legend>
        <div class="formLayout">
            <label for="email">E-Mail:</label>
                <input type="text" name="email" id="email" />
                <span id="email_error">Must be a valid
                    email address.</span><br />
            <label for="password">Password:</label>
                <input type="password" name="password" id="password" />
                <span id="password_error">Must be at least 6 characters.
                    </span><br />
            <label for="verify">Verify Password:</label>
                <input type="password" name="verify" id="verify" />
                <span id="verify_error"> </span><br />
        </div>
    </fieldset>

    /* Missing fieldset elements */

    <fieldset>
        <legend>Payment Information</legend>
        <div class="formLayout">
            <label for="card_type">Card Type:</label>
                <select name="card_type" id="card_type">
                    <option value="">Select One:</option>
                    <option value="m">MasterCard</option>
                    <option value="v">Visa</option>
                </select>
                <span id="card_type_error"> </span><br />
            <label for="card_number">Card Number:</label>
                <input type="text" name="card_number" id="card_number" />
                <span id="card_number_error">
                    Use 1111-2222-3333-4444 format.</span><br />
            <label for="exp_date">Expiration Date:</label>
                <input type="text" name="exp_date" id="exp_date" />
                <span id="exp_date_error">Use mm/yyyy format.</span><br />
        </div>
    </fieldset>
    <fieldset>
        <legend>Submit Data</legend>
        <div class="formLayout">
            <label> </label>
                <input type="button" id="register" value="Register" />
                <input type="button" id="reset_form" value="Reset" /><br />
        </div>
    </fieldset>
    </form>
    <p class="notice">All fields are required.</p>
</body>
</html>
```

Figure 13-13   The HTML for the data validation application

The first page of the register_library.js file

```
var $ = function (id) { return document.getElementById(id); }

var RegisterForm = function () {
    // The array of field objects with the required ids
    this.fields = [];
    this.fields["email"] = {};
    this.fields["password"] = {};
    this.fields["verify"] = {};
    this.fields["first_name"] = {};
    this.fields["last_name"] = {};
    this.fields["address"] = {};
    this.fields["city"] = {};
    this.fields["state"] = {};
    this.fields["zip"] = {};
    this.fields["phone"] = {};
    this.fields["card_type"] = {};
    this.fields["card_number"] = {};
    this.fields["exp_date"] = {};

    // Starting field messages
    this.fields["email"].message = "Must be a valid email address.";
    this.fields["password"].message = "Must be at least 6 characters.";
    this.fields["state"].message = "Use 2 letter abbreviation.";
    this.fields["zip"].message = "Use 5 or 9 digit ZIP code.";
    this.fields["phone"].message = "Use 999-999-9999 format.";
    this.fields["card_number"].message = "Use 1111-2222-3333-4444 format.";
    this.fields["exp_date"].message = "Use mm/yyyy format.";

    // Field error messages
    this.fields["email"].required = "Email is required.";
    this.fields["email"].isEmail = "Email is not valid.";
    this.fields["password"].required = "Password is required.";
    this.fields["password"].tooShort = ["Password is too short.", 6];
    this.fields["verify"].required = "Please retype your password.";
    this.fields["verify"].noMatch = ["Passwords do not match.", "password"];
    this.fields["first_name"].required = "First name is required.";
    this.fields["last_name"].required = "Last name is required.";
    this.fields["address"].required = "Address is required.";
    this.fields["city"].required = "City is required.";
    this.fields["state"].required = "State is required.";
    this.fields["state"].isState = "State is not valid.";
    this.fields["zip"].required = "ZIP Code is required.";
    this.fields["zip"].isZip = "ZIP Code is not valid.";
    this.fields["phone"].required = "Phone number is required.";
    this.fields["phone"].isPhone = "Phone number is not valid.";
    this.fields["card_type"].required = "Please select a card type.";
    this.fields["card_number"].required = "Card number is required.";
    this.fields["card_number"].isCC = "Card number is not valid.";
    this.fields["exp_date"].required = "Expiration date is required.";
    this.fields["exp_date"].isDate = "Expiration date is not valid.";
    this.fields["exp_date"].expired = "Card has expired.";
}
```

Figure 13-14   The JavaScript for the first page of the register_library.js file

Web sites for JavaScript code

You can, of course, use any of the JavaScript code in the applications that you've just reviewed because the code is available in the downloadable applications for this book. But you should also know that many web sites provide JavaScript code that you can use in your programs, and much of it is free. In figure 13-15, for example, you can see a web page that offers free JavaScript code for doing what we call "image rollovers," and what they call "image swaps."

To find sites like this, you can search for "free javascript code" or "javascript code examples". Often, these sites provide JavaScript for games and special effects that you can easily add to your site. Remember, though, that you don't want to distract the users of your site from the doing what you see as the primary goals of your site.

One of the problems with the code that you get from web sites like this is that it can be difficult to figure out how to use, especially if you don't understand JavaScript. How, for example, do you use the code in this figure in one of your web pages? Since the instructions aren't that clear, you would probably need to do some experimenting before you could get this code to work right in your own application.

Another problem is that web sites like this often provide code that you embed in your HTML, instead of code that's in separate JavaScript files. For instance, you're supposed to embed all of the code in this figure in the body of your document. That, however, just makes your code more difficult to create, test, and maintain.

With these problems in mind, it still makes sense to search for free JavaScript code, especially if you're looking for code that does a specific function. Eventually, though, you should learn how to do your own JavaScript coding. Then, you can develop the perfect solution for each of your presentation problems.

A web site that offers free JavaScript code

Description

- Many web sites provide JavaScript code that you can download or cut-and-paste into your web pages. Most of these sites also provide instructions for using that code.

- To find sites that provide JavaScript code, you can search for terms like "free javascript code" or "javascript code examples".

- These sites often provide JavaScript code that provides special effects or games that you can add to your site. Remember, though, to keep your focus on the goals of your web site.

- One of the problems with the code that you get from these sites is that it is often hard to figure out how to use it. Another problem is that these sites often provide code that you embed in your HTML, but that makes your code more difficult to create and maintain.

Figure 13-15   Web sites for JavaScript code

How to test and debug a JavaScript application

Whenever you use JavaScript, errors can occur. Then, you need to debug the application by finding the errors and correcting them. When you're using tested JavaScript code, however, the errors aren't likely to be in the JavaScript code. More likely, they'll be in the HTML code that is used by the JavaScript code.

For instance, figure 13-16 shows a web page in Internet Explorer that has encountered a JavaScript error. In this case, an error message is displayed in a dialog box, but that depends upon the browser and how the browser is set up. For some browsers, no message is displayed when an error occurs. Then, you have to guess that a JavaScript error has occurred when the JavaScript functions don't work.

One way to tell for sure that a JavaScript error has occurred is to use Firefox to test the web page. Then, when the page doesn't work the way it is supposed to, you can display the Error Console and see whether an error message is displayed. If one is, you can click on the link to go to the line of JavaScript code that has caused the error. Although this won't help much if you don't know JavaScript, it may give you a clue that will help you fix the problem.

If Firefox has already detected other JavaScript errors when you first display the Error Console, the dialog box may contain many errors. To clear those messages, you can click the Clear button at the top of the dialog box. Then, when you reload the page and display the Error Console, it will display only the current error.

When you use tested JavaScript code, one common error is not providing the script elements that include the required JavaScript files. In this case, though, a JavaScript error won't occur unless embedded JavaScript code refers to code in a missing JavaScript file.

Another common error is coding the wrong ids for elements that are used by the JavaScript code. For instance, the error in this figure was caused by an incorrect id for the unordered list. As a result, the JavaScript code is looking for a node in the DOM that isn't there.

Perhaps the best debugging advice when you're using JavaScript code that you don't understand is to be especially careful when you code the HTML that the JavaScript code is going to use. If you code all of the attributes right in the first place, that's easier than looking for problems later on.

A web page in Internet Explorer that has encountered a JavaScript error

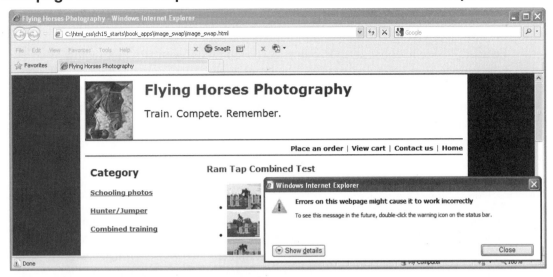

The Error Console in Firefox

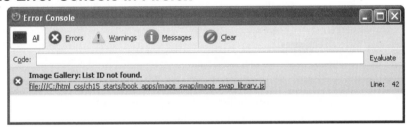

How to display the Firefox Error Console

- Use the Tools→Error Console command or press Ctrl+Shift+J.

How to tell when a JavaScript error has occurred

- The JavaScript for the web page doesn't do anything
- An error message is displayed

Common HTML errors when using tested JavaScript code

- Not providing the script elements that include the required JavaScript files
- Coding the wrong ids for the HTML elements that are used in the DOM scripting

Description

- Some browsers will display an error message when a JavaScript error occurs, but some won't. To some extent, that depends on how the browser is set up.
- One way to tell that a JavaScript error has occurred is to load the page in Firefox and then display the Error Console. That may also give you a clue about what you've done wrong.

Figure 13-16   How to test and debug a JavaScript application

Perspective

Now that you've completed this chapter, you should be able to use tested JavaScript code to enhance your web pages, even though you still don't know how to code JavaScript applications. The trouble with that approach, though, is that you won't be able to modify the code you're using so it does exactly what you want it to do. That's why we recommend that you learn how to develop your own JavaScript applications, and for that we recommend *Murach's JavaScript and DOM Scripting*.

Terms

JavaScript	element node	event handler
JavaScript engine	text node	image rollover
client-side processing	attribute node	image swap
server-side processing	comment node	tabs
DOM (Document Object Model)	DOM scripting	tabbed data
node	event	data validation

Summary

- *JavaScript* is a scripting language that is run by the *JavaScript engine* of a browser. As a result, the work is done on the client, not the server, and that takes some of the processing burden off the server.

- The *DOM* (*Document Object Model*) is a hierarchical collection of *nodes* in the web browser's memory that represents the current web page. The DOM for each page is built as the page is loaded.

- *DOM scripting* is the process of changing the DOM by using JavaScript. When the DOM changes, the browser immediately displays the results of the change.

- An *event* is an action the user performs, like clicking on a button. When an event occurs, it can be handled by JavaScript code known as an *event handler*.

- To embed JavaScript code or to include JavaScript files in an HTML document, you code a script element.

- If a script element is coded in the body of a document, it is replaced by the output of the JavaScript code. This element can be followed by a noscript element that displays content if JavaScript isn't enabled in the user's browser.

- JavaScript can be used for standalone applications that run in their own web pages, like those for games and calculations.

- Four common uses of JavaScript that can be copied into your own pages are *image rollovers*, *image swaps*, slide shows, *tabs*, and *data validation*.

Exercise 13-1   Review and modify the chapter applications

In this exercise, you'll review the chapter applications. Then, you'll make some minor modifications to these applications.

Review the chapter applications

1. You'll find copies of the chapter applications in this directory:

   `c:\html_css\ch13\book_apps`

   To start any of these applications, you either open the index.html file or the html file that has the same name as the directory. For instance, the index.html file in the validation directory will start the validation application, and the rollover.html file in the rollover directory will start the rollover application.

2. Start the future_value application, enter values, and click the Calculate button to see how this standalone application works. As part of your testing, enter invalid data to see how that is handled.

   Note: If you're using Internet Explorer, a bar may appear at the top of the page that says the page is restricted from running scripts. To get past that, click on the bar, and then click on Allow Blocked Content. Otherwise, use Firefox for testing your JavaScript applications.

3. Run the image rollover, image swap, slide show, tabs, and validation applications to see how they work. You can also open any of the files for these applications in your text editor to review the code.

Add another set of images to the image rollover application

4. Using figure 13-7 as a guide, add a third set of image rollovers to the rollover application. This third set should be below the second set, and it should use the files named h3.jpg and h6.jpg for the main image and the rollover.

Delete one of the image swaps in the image swap application

5. Using figure 13-8 as a guide, delete the third thumbnail and swap from the image_swap application. To do that, you just need to delete one line of HTML. This shows how easy it is to modify an application when it's coded this way.

Reduce the number of fields in the register application

6. Using figure 13-12 as a guide, modify the HTML for the validation application so it doesn't include the three fields for payment information.

7. In the portion of the register_library.js file that's shown in figure 13-14, carefully delete (or comment out) all of the statements that refer to the card_type, card_number, and exp_date fields. Then, test these changes.

8. In the HTML file for the form, move the first_name and last_name fields to the top of the fields in the Account Information group. Then, test these changes. This shows how the JavaScript code can be adapted to other forms.

Exercise 13-2 Apply JavaScript to the Bait Shop

In this exercise, you'll apply some of the JavaScript that you've seen in this chapter to the Bait Shop application.

Automatically update the date on the fly_rod page

1. Open this file in your text editor and browser:

   `c:\html_css\ch13\bait_shop\products\fly_rod.html`

2. Using figure 13-1 as a guide, use JavaScript to get the current year and put it into the copyright line at the bottom of the page. Then, test this change, and be sure that the content and spacing hasn't been changed by your use of JavaScript.

Add a button for printing the fly_rod page

3. Using figure 13-3 as a guide, add a Print button to the top of the first column on this page. Test this change, and then modify the product.css file so there's more space between the button and the link that follows it.

4. Add the JavaScript for printing the page when this button is clicked to the head section of the file. Then, test to make sure this works.

Run a slide show

5. Open this file in your text editor and browser:

   `c:\html_css\ch13\bait_shop\slide_show.html`

6. Using figure 13-9 as a guide, add a slide show to the main division of the slide_show.html file. To make this easier for you, all the files that you need have already been copied from the chapter application into the appropriate bait_shop directories.

   The easiest way to add the slide show is to first copy the required code from the slide_show book application of exercise 13-1 into your web page. Then, you can modify that code so it uses the jpg files in the images directory for the slides. For the captions, you can use Fishing 1-1, Fishing 1-2, and so on. Also, be sure that you've provided the script elements for the two JavaScript files.

7. Test your slide show. Although it should work, the formatting should be messy. Note, however, how photos of different sizes are handled. To fix that, you would need to resize the photos, but you don't need to do that for this exercise.

8. To fix the formatting, code a link element in the head section that includes the slide_show.css file. Be sure to code this element after the link element for the main.css file. Then, test that change. This should work, but it should completely change the look of the page.

9. To fix that, open the slide_show.css file in your text editor and delete all of the styles that override the ones in the main.css file. Then, test to make sure this works. When you've got everything the way you want it, close the files.

Section 3

How to design and deploy a web site

In section 1, you learned a professional subset of HTML and CSS that you can use for building web pages. Now, in the two chapters of this section, you can learn how to design and deploy a web site. You can read these chapters anytime after you complete the chapters in section 1, and you can read these chapters in whichever sequence you prefer.

In chapter 14, you'll learn how to design all of the pages for a web site and how to design the navigation between those pages. You'll also learn the guidelines that will help you create an effective web site. Then, in chapter 15, you'll learn how to deploy your web site from your local computer or server to a web server that has Internet access. You'll also learn how to get your web site into the major search engines and directories.

14

How to design a web site

If you've read section 1, you know how to use HTML and CSS to develop web pages. Now, in this chapter, you'll learn the guidelines, methods, and procedures that you need for designing a web site. When you complete this chapter, you should be able to design and develop an effective web site.

Users, usability, and accessability

Before you design a web site, you need to think about who your users are going to be and what they are going to expect. After all, it is your users who are going to determine the success of your web site.

What users want is usability

What do users want when they reach a web site? They want to find what they're looking for as quickly and easily as possible. And when they find it, they want to extract the information or do the task as quickly and easily as possible.

How do users use a web page? They don't read it in an orderly way, and they don't like to scroll. Instead, they scan the page to see if they can find what they're looking for or a link to what they're looking for. Often, they click quickly on a link to see if it gives them what they want, and if it doesn't, they click on the Back button to return to where they were. In fact, users click on the Back button more than 30% of the time when they reach a new page.

If the users can't find what they're looking for or get too frustrated, they leave the site. It's that simple. For some web sites, more than 50% of first-time visitors to the home page leave without ever going to another page.

In web development terms, what the users want is *usability*. This term refers to how easy it is to use a web site, and usability is one of the key factors that determines the effectiveness of a web site. If a site is easy to use, it has a chance to be effective. If it isn't easy to use, it probably won't be effective.

Figure 14-1 presents one page of a web site that has a high degree of usability, and it presents three guidelines for improving usability. First, you should try to present all of the essential information "above the fold." This term refers to what's shown on the screen when a new page is displayed, which is analogous to the top half of a newspaper. This reduces the need for scrolling, and gives the page a better chance for success.

Second, you should try to group related items into separate components, and limit the number of components on each page. That will make the page look more manageable and will help people find what they're looking for.

Third, you should adhere to the current conventions for web site usability. For instance, clickable links should look like they're clickable and items that aren't clickable shouldn't fool users by looking like they are clickable.

If you look at the web site in this figure, you can see that it has implemented these guidelines. All of the critical information is presented above the fold. The page is divided into a header and six other well-defined components, including a set of tabs near the bottom of the page. It's also easy to tell where to click.

Of course, it's relatively easy to build a web site like this because it has a small number of products. In contrast, building usability into a large web site with dozens of product categories and hundreds of products is a serious challenge.

A web site that is easy to use

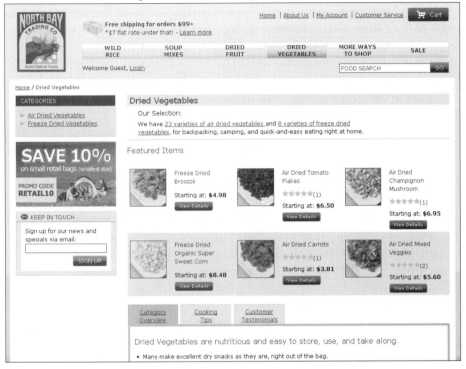

What web site users want

- To find what they're looking for as quickly and easily as possible
- To get the information or do the task that they want to do as quickly and easily as possible

How web site users use a web page

- They scan the page to find what they're looking for or a link to what they're looking for, and they don't like to scroll. If they get frustrated, they leave.
- They often click on links and buttons with the hope of finding what they're looking for, and they frequently click on the Back button when they don't find it.

Three guidelines for improving usability

- Present all of the critical information "above the fold" so the user doesn't have to scroll.
- Group related items into separate components, and limit the number of components on each page.
- Adhere to the current conventions for web site usability (see the next figure).

Description

- *Usability* refers to how easy it is to use a web site, and usability is the critical requirement for an effective web site.

Figure 14-1   What web users want is usability

The current conventions for usability

If you've been using web sites for a while, you know that you expect certain aspects of each web site to work the same way. For example, you expect underlined text to be a link to another web page, and you expect that something will happen if you click on a button. These are web site conventions that make a web site easier to use because they work the same on almost all sites.

Figure 14-2 summarizes some of the other conventions that lead to improved usability. By following these conventions, you give the users what they expect, and that makes your web site easier to use.

To start, a header usually consists of a logo, tag line, utilities, navigation bar, and search function. As a result, the users look for these items in the header. In the example in this figure, this tag line is below the logo: "Powered by Service." The utilities are in the top border, including "Logout", "My Account", "My Favorites", and "Help". The navigation bar contains links that divide the web site into sections. And the search function consists of a text box that's large enough for long entries followed by a Search button. All of these are web site conventions, and that's where experienced users look for these components.

The navigation conventions are also critical to the usability of a web site. In brief, clickable items should look like they're clickable, and items that aren't clickable shouldn't look like they're clickable. In other words, don't trick the users. In addition, the last navigation convention says that clicking on the logo in the header should take you back to the home page. This is a more recent convention that isn't widely implemented right now.

If you implement all of these conventions on your site, you will be on your way to web usability. But that's just a start. In the rest of this chapter, you'll learn many other ways to improve the usability of a site.

A web page that illustrates some of the current web site conventions

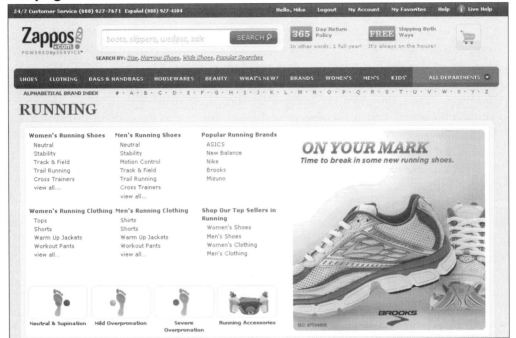

Header conventions

- The header consists of a logo, tag line, utilities, and a navigation bar.
- The tag line identifies what's unique about the web site.
- The navigation bar provides links that divide the site into sections.
- The utilities consist of links to useful but not primary information.
- If your site requires a search function, it should be in the header, and it should consist of a large text box for the text followed by a button that's labeled either "Go" or "Search."

Navigation conventions

- Underlined text is always a link.
- Images that are close to short text phrases are clickable.
- A small symbol in front of a text phrase is clickable.
- Clickable buttons should look like they're 3D.
- Short text phrases in columns are clickable.
- If you click on a cart symbol, you go to your shopping cart.
- If you click on the logo in header, you go to the home page.

Description

- If your web site implements the current web site conventions, your users will be able to use the same techniques on your site that they use on other sites.

Figure 14-2   The current conventions for web site usability

The importance of accessibility

Accessibility refers to how accessible your web site is to all types of users, especially to disabled users. To make your site as accessible as possible, you need to implement the guidelines that are presented in figure 14-3.

For the visually impaired, the most important guideline is to use relative font sizes. Then, the users can increase the font sizes by using the Zoom feature of their browsers. This is illustrated by the web site in this figure, which is especially for the blind. If you click on the plus sign at the top of the header, the font sizes are increased. Of course, you should also start with a font size that's large enough to work well with the zoom feature. The other guideline is to use the alt attribute for images. That way, if a user is using a screen reader, the alt attributes will be read aloud so the user can tell what each image represents.

For the hearing impaired, you need to make sure that none of the essentials of your web site depend on audio. For the motor impaired, you need to make sure that all of the features can be accessed through keystrokes.

How important is it to provide access for the disabled? To some extent, that depends on who you work for. If you work for a government agency, you have to follow the guidelines in Section 508 that are required by federal law. If you work for a large company, it may have guidelines for accessibility. But even if you aren't forced to build accessibility into your web site, it's the right thing to do.

The web site for the American Foundation for the Blind

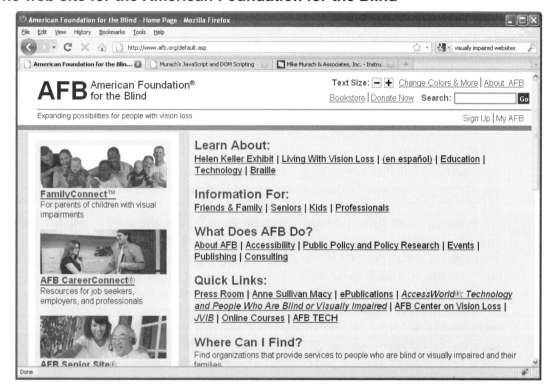

Guidelines for the visually impaired

- Most important is to use relative font sizing so the user can increase the font sizes by using the View→Zoom command or by holding the Ctrl key and pressing the + sign.
- Use the alt attribute with img elements so screen readers will be able to indicate what the images represent.

Guidelines for the hearing impaired

- Present all of the essentials without using audio.

Guidelines for the motor impaired

- Make sure that all of the essential features are available through keystrokes.

Description

- *Accessibility* refers to the qualities that make a web site accessible to users, especially disabled users.
- If you work for a government agency, you have to follow the accessibility guidelines in Section 508 that are required by federal law. For more on this, go to http://www.section508.gov.

Figure 14-3   The importance of accessibility

Design guidelines

Did you ever think about what makes a good web site? Well, a lot of experts have. What follows, then, is a distillation of some of the best thinking on the subject.

Use the home page to sell the site

Figure 14-4 presents 10 guidelines for the design of a home page. Most important is the first one, which says to emphasize what's different about your site and why it's valuable from the user's point of view. In other words, sell the site to your visitors.

If you're a well-known company with a successful site, this isn't as important. That's why the web sites for most large companies don't make any special efforts to sell their sites. But if you're developing the web site for a small company that still needs to develop a customer base, by all means use the home page to sell the site. That may determine whether or not the site is successful.

The other nine guidelines should be self-explanatory. For instance, you don't need to welcome users to your site because that space should be used to sell the site. You don't want to include an active link to the home page on the home page because it would just reload the page. You do want to limit the use of drop-down menus (which aren't presented in this book) because the users can't tell that the menus are there until they drop down. You do want to limit the length of the page title to 8 words and 64 characters because it's used in bookmarks. And you do want to use a different design for the home page to set it off from the other pages of the site.

If you look at the home page in this figure, you can see that it tries to sell the site. It's tag line says: "Genuine software at wholesale prices." The three links at the top of the center column lead to text that helps sell the site. And the component at the bottom of the right column also summarizes the site's advantages. On the other hand, the site has a "Welcome" component in the middle of the page, which is space that probably could be put to better use.

A home page that tries to sell the site

10 guidelines for developing an effective home page

1. Emphasize what your site offers that's valuable and how your site differs from competing sites.

2. Emphasize the highest priority tasks of your site so users have a clear idea of what they can do.

3. Don't welcome users to your site because that's a waste of space.

4. Group items in the navigation areas so similar items are next to each other, and don't provide multiple navigation areas for the same types of links.

5. Only use icons for navigation if the users will readily recognize them.

6. Use drop-down menus sparingly, especially if the items aren't self-explanatory.

7. Design the home page so it is different from the other pages of the site.

8. Don't include an active link to the home page on the home page.

9. Code the title for the home page as the organization name, followed by a short description, and limit the title to 8 or fewer words and 64 or fewer characters.

10. If your site provides shopping, include a link to the shopping cart on your home page.

Description

*   *Homepage Usability* by Jakob Nielsen and Marie Tahir presents 113 guidelines for home pages, plus an analysis of the home pages for 50 web sites. Though somewhat dated, it is still worth reading.

Figure 14-4   Use the home page to sell the site

Let the users know where they are

As users navigate through a site, they like to know where they are. That's why letting the users know where they are is one of the current conventions for web site use. Remember too that many users will reach your site via search engines so they won't arrive at the home page. They have a special need to find out where they are.

As figure 14-5 shows, there are three primary ways to let the users know where they are. First, you should highlight the links that led the user to the current page. Second, the heading for the page should be the same as the link that led to it.

This is illustrated by the first web page in this figure. Here, the Fly Fishing link is highlighted in the navigation bar, which means that the user started there. Then, the Fly Rods and Freshwater Helios Rods are highlighted in the links of the left sidebar (they're red), which means the user first clicked the Fly Rods link followed by the Freshwater Helios Rods link. Last, the heading for the page is "Freshwater Helios Rods", which is the same as the link that led to the page.

The third way to let the users know where they are is to provide *breadcrumbs* that show the path to the page. This is illustrated by the second page in this figure. When you use breadcrumbs, the current convention is to do it just as this web site did it, with a greater than sign (>) to mark each step in the path.

A product page with the active links highlighted

A product page that provides breadcrumbs

How to let the users know where they are

- Highlight the active links.
- The heading for the page should be the same as the link that led to the page.
- Provide breadcrumbs in this format: Homepage > Men > Shoes & Sandals.

Description

- As your site gets more complex, the users are likely to lose track of where they are in the site. But even simple sites should let the users know where they are.

Figure 14-5   Let the users know where they are

Make the best use of web page space

As you design a web page, remember that the part of the page that's above the fold is the most valuable space. As a result, you want to put the most important components of the page in that space. That's why many of the most successful web sites have relatively small headers. That way, they have more space for the components that make each page effective. In fact, the home pages of many of the best web sites have all of the components above the fold.

To emphasize this point, figure 14-6 presents an extreme example of a web page that doesn't get the most out of the space above the fold. In fact, none of the text of the page can be seen above the fold. You have to scroll down for all of the information. Granted that the photos are beautiful (if you're a fly fisher), but does the fish have to show on every page that relates to Bob Cusack's Alaska Lodge? This is a case where the graphics got out of control and diminished the usability of the page.

As you design your pages, then, remember the three guidelines in this figure. Keep your header relatively small. Prioritize the components that are going to go on the page. And then give the best space to the most important components.

Wasted space on a primary page

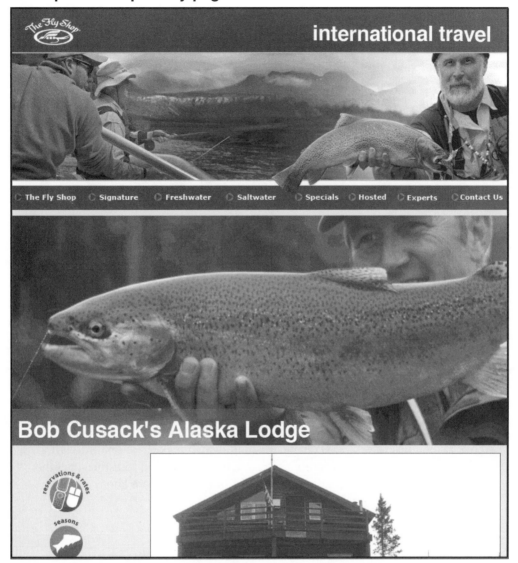

Guidelines for the effective use of space

- Keep the header relatively small.
- Prioritize the components for each page.
- Give the most important components the primary locations.

Description

- The most valuable space on each web page is the space above the fold. To get the most from it, you need to prioritize the components on each page and give the best locations to the highest-priority components.

Figure 14-6   Make the best use of web page space

Write for the web

Remember how web users use a web site. Instead of reading, they skim and scan. They want to get the information that they're looking for as quickly as possible, and they don't want to have to dig through several paragraphs of text for it. That's why writing for a web site is so different from writing for the printed page.

In figure 14-7, you can see a block of copy that isn't written for the web, followed by one that is. To present the same information in a way that is more accessible, the second example uses fewer words (135 to 177), which is the quickest way to improve your web writing. It also uses a numbered list to make it easy to find the flight information without having to dig through the text.

If you look through the other web writing guidelines, you'll see that they recommend what we implement in the figures of our books: an inverted pyramid style so the most important items are presented first; headings and subheadings to identify portions of the text; bulleted and numbered lists; tables for tabular information; and no headings with all caps. We do that so you don't have to read all of the text to review the information that you're looking for, and that's also the way web writing should work.

The last guideline is to make the text for all links as explicit as possible. For instance, "Find a job with us" is better than "Jobs", and "Apply for unemployment compensation" is better than "Unemployment". Remember that 30 to 40 percent of a user's clicks are likely to be on the Back button because a link didn't take him where he wanted. The more explicit your links are, the less that will happen.

Incidentally, the first example in this figure also illustrates poor typography. Above all, the text lines are 90 characters long, which makes the text difficult to read. In addition, three different font sizes are used in the first four lines, but the font sizes don't reflect the relative importance of the text. More about that in figure 14-9.

Writing that isn't for the web (177 words and 1041 characters)

The progressive air services you'll use to reach Cusack's Alaska Lodge are a wonderful reflection of your journey into the wilderness. First, you will fly a major jet service from near your home to Anchorage, Alaska; arriving here, most itineraries will mandate an overnight stay. The next morning you will board a small plane piloted by one of the fine bush pilots of Iliamna Air Taxi (often one of their Pilatus aircraft, a high-flying, very comfortable aircraft), for the transfer between Anchorage and the little village of Iliamna. Upon arriving, Iliamna Air Taxi's Iliamna crew will switch your gear from the mid-sized plane to a smaller, float-equipped Cessna or Beaver, and after a short wait, you will be on the final leg of your adventure, touching down on the lake's surface in front of Bob's lodge a short thirty minutes later. For the remainder of your week, Bob will be your pilot, flying you into amazingly beautiful country in his two small airplanes, giving you a peek into the enormity and grandeur of his corner of Alaska.

The same copy, but written for the web (135 words and 717 characters)

The three-part flight to Bob Cusack's Alaska Lodge is a fascinating journey into the Alaskan wilderness

1. You take a major jet service from your home to Anchorage, Alaska.
2. From Anchorage, you take the Iliamna Air Taxi to the little village of Iliamna. This flight will be piloted by one of the Air Taxi's fine bush pilots in a comfortable plane like the Pilatus.
3. In Iliamna, the Air Taxi's crew will switch your bags to a smaller, float plane like a Cessna or a Beaver. Then, after a short wait and a 30 minute flight, you will touch down on beautiful Lake Iliamna in front of Bob's lodge.

For the remainder of your week, Bob will be your pilot as he takes you into the beauty and grandeur of his corner of Alaska.

Web writing guidelines

- Use fewer words.
- Write in inverted pyramid style with the most important information first.
- Use headings and subheadings to identify portions of the text.
- Use bulleted lists and numbered lists to make information more accessible.
- Use tables for tabular information.
- Don't use all caps (all capital letters) for headings. Usually, it's best to capitalize only the first letter in a heading, plus any required capitalization.
- Make the text for all links as explicit as possible.

Description

- Web users skim and scan; they don't read like book readers do. So when you write for the web, you need to change the way you think about writing.

Figure 14-7   Write for the web

Chunk long pages into shorter pages

Remember that web site users don't like to scroll. So a general guideline for web page design is to limit the amount of scrolling to one-and-one-half or two times the height of the browser window. But what if you need to present more information than that?

The best solution is to use *chunking* to divide the content into logical pieces or topics that can be presented on separate web pages. This is illustrated by the example in this figure. Here, the copy for each book on the site has been broken down into six topics that are represented by the "About the book" links. If, for example, the user clicks on "What this book does", the first web page in this figure is displayed. Or, if the user clicks on "Meet the author", the second web page is displayed.

This approach lets the users select the topics that they're interested in so they have more control over their web site experience. This makes it easier for the users to find what they're looking for. And this reduces the need for scrolling. How much better this is than forcing the users to scroll through a long page of text trying to find what they're looking for.

Two pages with chunks of information about a book

What this book does

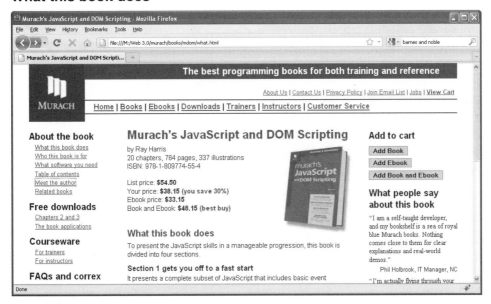

Meet the author

Description

- *Chunking* refers to the grouping of content into chunks that can be presented on separate web pages. This lets the users select the chunks of information that they're interested in.

- Chunking is one way to improve the web writing, make the information more accessible, and reduce the need for scrolling.

Figure 14-8   Chunk long pages into shorter pages

Know the basic principles of graphics design

Most web designers aren't graphics designers, but they should at least know the four basic principles of graphics design that are presented in figure 14-9. These principles are in common use on all of the best web sites, so it's easy to find examples of their use.

For instance, *alignment* means that aligning related items gives a sense of order to a web page, and all of the examples to this point in this chapter make extensive use of alignment. Similarly, *proximity* means that related items should be close to each other, and all of those examples illustrate this principle too. When proximity is applied to headings, it means that a heading should be closer to the text that follows it than the text that precedes it.

The principle of *repetition* means that you repeat some elements from page to page to give the pages continuity. This is natural for web pages, starting with the header, which is usually the same on all pages. This goes along with *contrast*, which is what draws your eye to a component. For instance, a component with a large heading or a yellow background will draw attention because it stands out from the other components of the page.

The home page in this figure illustrates what happens if you don't obey these principles. Because the principle of proximity isn't obeyed, the headings float above blocks of copy so it looks like the page consists of many small components. Because the contrast of the symbols in the middle of the page (what are they?) draws your eye to them, the user is drawn away from the text that matters. Besides that, the alignment isn't clean so the page looks disorganized.

If you aren't a graphics designer, you don't need to be intimidated by the use of these principles because there are thousands of good examples on the Internet. By copying them, you should be able to develop an attractive and inviting web site that delivers a high degree of usability.

But whether or not you're a graphics designer, you should at least get the typography right. That way, your readers are more likely to read what you've written. In section 1, you were introduced to many of the guidelines for effective typography, but this figure presents them again.

One common problem is text lines that are longer than 65 characters. This is illustrated by the first example in figure 14-7, which has 90 characters per line, and that makes the text unappealing and difficult to read. To fix that problem, you can increase the font size and shorten the line width. This is illustrated by the second example in figure 14-7.

Some less common problems are using a background image, using a background color that is too dark, centering text, and justifying text. Also, if you indent the first line of each paragraph, you don't need space between the paragraphs, but you do need space if you don't indent the first lines. Last, you should avoid the use of reverse type (white type on a dark background), especially for text, because it's difficult to read.

A home page that doesn't obey the graphics design principles

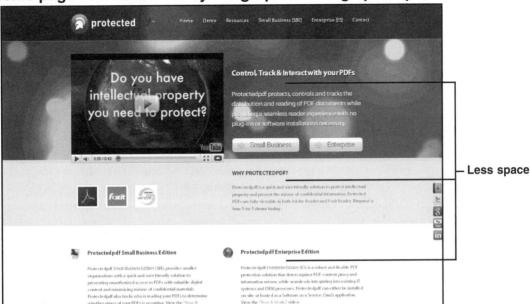

Four principles of graphics design

- *Alignment* means that items on the page should line up with each other.
- *Proximity* means that related items should be close together.
- *Repetition* means that you should repeat some elements from page to page to give the pages continuity.
- *Contrast* is what draws your eye to the components on a web page. If everything is the same, nothing stands out.

Typographical guidelines

- Limit the line length of paragraphs to 65 characters.
- Use a sans serif font in a size that's large enough for easy reading.
- Show the relationship between a heading and the text that follows by keeping them close.
- Use dark text on a light background, and don't use an image for the background.
- Don't center text and don't justify text.
- If you indent the first lines of paragraphs, you don't need space between the paragraphs.
- Don't use reverse type (white type on a colored background) for text.

Description

- If you aren't a graphics designer, you can at least implement the basic principles of graphics design and get the typography right. You can also get great ideas from the thousands of sites that are available on the Internet.

Figure 14-9   Know the basic principles of graphics design

Design methods and procedures

At this point, you should have a good idea of how the pages of a web site should look and work. That means you're ready to learn how to use the methods and procedures that will help you design a web site. But first, you should know how development teams are used.

The use of development teams

A large company's web site is usually designed and implemented by team members like those that are summarized in figure 14-10. To design the site, a typical team will consist of one or more web designers, one or more writers, a marketing specialist or two, and one or more graphics designers. Then, to implement the web site after it has been designed, a typical team will consist of HTML and CSS specialists, client-side programmers, server-side programmers, a database administrator, and a network administrator.

In short, you don't design a web site or even a portion of a web site by yourself when you work in a large shop. In contrast, a small web site may be designed and developed by a single person. In either case, though, you never work alone, unless you're designing your own web site. Instead, you review each phase of the design with the people you're developing it for: your boss, your client, the marketing team, or the other members of the design team.

This figure also summarizes the difference between a *web designer* and a *graphics designer*. This is an important distinction because they're two different jobs. In short, web designers participate in all phases of web design with the focus on usability. In contrast, graphics designers focus on the aspects of a web site that make it look more inviting and manageable so more people will use it.

In practice, then, good graphics design is an essential but relatively small part of the web design process. In fact, the trend is toward simplicity. So if you're designing a small site, don't be afraid to keep it simple.

A large web site that is managed by a team

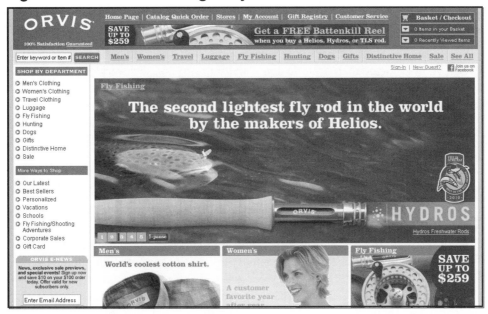

Typical members of a development team

For design
Web designers

Writers

Marketing specialists

Graphics designers

For implementation
HTML and CSS specialists

Client-side programmers

Server-side programmers

Database administrator

Network administrator

Web designers vs. graphics designers

- *Web designers* participate in all phases of web design.
- *Graphics designers* focus on the graphics that make web pages work better and look more inviting.

Description

- In a large company, a web site is usually designed and implemented by a team. In a small company, a single person is likely to do everything.
- Unless you're designing your own web site, you will be working with others who will review and evaluate your work, such as your boss, marketing specialists, your customer, or potential users.
- *Web designer* is a term that's often confused with *graphics designer*, but graphics design is a relatively small part of web design.

Figure 14-10   The use of development teams

Top-down design, stepwise refinement, and prototyping

For all but the simplest web sites, designing a web site is a challenging process. To complicate that, your design usually has to please several reviewers so you can't just design the pages and be done with them. You usually have to design, review, adjust the design, and repeat that loop until the site is done.

With that as background, figure 14-11 presents three methods that can help the design process go more smoothly. These are proven methods that have been used on all types of systems projects for many years. And they work for web site projects too.

The first method is *top-down design*. This just means that you should design the most critical elements of a system first. Then, you can work your way down through the less critical elements until the entire system is designed.

For a web site, the most critical elements are the home page and the primary content pages. For instance, the primary content pages for a commercial site are the product pages. The primary content pages for a community service site are usually the pages that describe the services that the site provides. After those pages have been designed, which includes the navigation between them, you can go on to the other sections or pages of the web site.

The second method is *stepwise refinement*. This just means that you can't design a web page in a single step. Instead, you need to work the page through successive levels of refinement on the way to the final page design. For instance, the designer often starts by developing several sketches for the design of a page. Then, when the reviewers agree on one of those approaches, the designer develops a simple version of the page using HTML and CSS that shows more detail. This refinement process continues until the final version of the page is agreed upon.

Stepwise refinement is illustrated by the two examples in this figure. The first example shows a rough sketch of what the home page for a community service site might look like. This can be a hand-drawn sketch or a computer-drawn sketch. The second example is a web page that is a later step in the design of the page. Although it is only partially implemented, it will give the reviewers a better idea of what the designer has in mind.

The third method is *prototyping*. This just means that you need to develop a working model (*prototype*) of the critical web pages as early in the design process as possible. Then, the reviewers can actually use the pages to see how they work. That usually will raise all sorts of concerns that can be resolved early in the design process when the cost of fixing the problems is relatively inexpensive. If you don't prototype the web site, critical issues are likely to be raised late in the process when they cost more to fix.

The second example in this figure illustrates what an early prototype might be. At this stage, only one of the speaker pages needs to be developed to show the navigation to a speaker page and back. But if you get that right, you've got the top-level of your design project under control.

The sketch of a home page

<table>
<tr><td colspan="2">Header</td></tr>
<tr><td colspan="2">Navigation bar</td></tr>
<tr><td>Selling copy</td><td>News items</td></tr>
<tr><td>Lecture 1 with thumbnail photo and brief intro
Lecture 2 with thumbnail photo and brief intro
Lecture 3 with thumbnail photo and brief intro
Lecture 4 with thumbnail photo and brief intro
Lecture 5 with thumbnail photo and brief intro
Lecture 6 with thumbnail photo and brief intro</td><td></td></tr>
<tr><td colspan="2" align="center">P.O. Box 5149, Fresno, CA 93755-5149 · (559) 444-2180</td></tr>
</table>

An early prototype for the home page

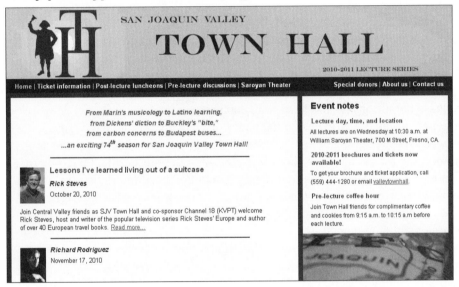

Description

- *Top-down design* means that you start with the most difficult aspects of a system and proceed downwards through the less critical aspects. For a web site, this usually means that you start by designing the home page and the primary content pages.

- *Stepwise refinement* refers to the process of making step-by-step improvements to the design with review and evaluation after each step. This often means that you start the design for the pages of a web site with rough sketches before you implement them with HTML and CSS.

- A *prototype* is a working model of a web page or a portion of a web site. This gives reviewers an accurate view of how the web pages will work. The benefit of *prototyping* is that you detect problems early in the development cycle when they cost less to fix.

Figure 14-11   Top-down design, stepwise refinement, and prototyping

The lifecycle of a web site

The diagram at the top of figure 14-12 represents the *lifecycle* of every web site or business system. First, you design the web site. Then, you implement it. Last, you maintain it, usually for many years. In fact, the cost of maintaining a web site is likely to be far more than developing it in the first place. That's why it's so important to develop the web site in a way that makes it easier to maintain.

To make a web site easier to maintain, you need to implement it with HTML for the content and CSS for the formatting. That's most important, and that's what you've learned to do throughout this book. Beyond that, you should only use tables for tabular information, not for page layout. And you shouldn't use HTML frames, which aren't presented in this book.

Perhaps most important, though, is to take the time to get the design right in the first place. Then, you should be able to enhance and improve the web site with minimal change to what's already in place.

Next, this figure presents a simple procedure for designing a web site. This procedure will be illustrated in a moment, but here's the general idea. Like you would with any system design project, step 1 has you define who is going to use the web site and what the goals of the web site are. As you do the steps that follow, these definitions should help you keep your focus.

In steps 2 through 5, you design the pages of the web site and the navigation between those pages. Here's where top-down design, stepwise refinement, and prototyping are essential. In short, you start with the most critical pages, move on to the less critical sections and pages, and you keep improving the design until everyone is satisfied and the prototype becomes the final design. Then, you can plan the directories for all of the files of the web site and go on to the implementation procedure.

In the implementation procedure in this figure, you start by developing the HTML and CSS templates for the pages of the web site. These should be at least partially complete as part of the design process, but some refinement is usually needed. These templates of course will make it easier to develop the web pages. Once they're done, you do the time-consuming work of developing the contents for all of the pages, and then implementing those contents with HTML. When all of the pages are ready, you test the entire site and deploy the web site to an Internet server as shown in the next chapter.

The last procedure in this figure is for maintaining a web site. In brief, you plan what the changes should be and then design, implement, and test them. If the changes are minimal, that may be all that's needed. But if the changes or enhancements are extensive, this might turn out to be another design project instead of a maintenance project. That's why it's so important to get the design right in the first place.

The lifecycle of a web site

How to make a web site easier to maintain

- Use HTML for the content and CSS for the page layout and formatting.
- Don't use tables for page layout. Only use tables for tabular information.
- Don't use frames (not presented in this book).
- Get the design right in the first place with full knowledge that each page is likely to be changed in the lifecycle of the web site.

A simple procedure for designing a web site

1. Define the audience and set the goals for the web site.
2. Design the home page.
3. Design the primary content pages.
4. Design the other pages.
5. Plan the navigation.
6. Plan the directories for the files of the site.

Top-down design, stepwise refinement, and prototyping

A simple procedure for implementing a web site

1. Develop the HTML and CSS templates for the pages.
2. Develop the web pages.
3. Test the entire site.
4. Deploy the site to a web server (see chapter 15)

A simple procedure for maintaining a web site

1. Plan the changes.
2. Design the changes.
3. Implement the changes.
4. Test the changes.

Description

- The *lifecycle* of all systems is (1) design, (2) implement, and (3) maintain. Often, more time is spent maintaining a web site than developing it in the first place.

Figure 14-12   The lifecycle of a web site

The design procedure applied to a small web site

To give you a better idea of how the design procedure in the last figure works, this topic steps you through the design of a small web site.

Define the audience and set the goals

Figure 14-13 presents the description of a community service organization called Town Hall. Each year, this organization brings six renowned speakers into the local community for lectures. This organization has been doing this for almost 75 years, and the lectures have enlightened and enriched the lives of the organization's members as well as students and non-members who attend the lectures. To balance its budget, this organization also relies on the donations from a core group of donors.

Before you can define the audience and goals of a web site, you need to get that type of information. Then, you can draft the definitions of the audience and goals as shown in this figure.

Usually, the *target audience* for a web site will consist of more than one type of visitor. In this case, that audience is defined as members, non-members, and donors. And usually there will be more than one goal for the web site. Because these definitions will guide the design of the web site, it's important to get them right and to get all of the design participants to agree on them.

About Town Hall

- Town Hall is a community service that runs six lectures each year that are available to all of the members of the community.
- The speakers for these lectures come from all over the country and are known experts in their fields.
- After each lecture, a luncheon is held in the same building and the speaker for the day answers questions from the audience.
- Eight days before each lecture, there's a meeting at the local library to discuss the subject of the lecture.
- Students are admitted to these lectures free.
- Town Hall will be celebrating its 75th anniversary in 2011.

The target audience

- Members of Town Hall
- Prospective members of Town Hall
- Donors and possible donors to Town Hall

The goals of the web site

- Provide all of the information that members need for attending the lectures.
- Provide all of the information that non-members need for attending one or more lectures.
- Convince non-members to become members.
- List current donors and encourage people to become donors.

Description

- Like all system projects, you start by defining what you're trying to do and who you're going to do it for.
- Before you can define the audience and set the goals for the site, you need to learn about the company or organization that the site represents.
- The people who you want to use your web site can be referred to as the *target audience*.

Figure 14-13   Define the audience and set the goals

Design the home page

By now, you should know how to go about the design of a home page. Start with sketches for different approaches to the page. Then, prototype an early version of the page. And get reviews after each step in the refinement process.

When you design the home page for a web site, you also have to make some decisions about the navigation for the web site. This is illustrated by the prototype for the home page in figure 14-14. Here, the navigation bar indicates what the sections or pages of the web site will be. And the main column in the body of the page will provide the navigation to each of the six speakers. This too should be part of the stepwise reviews.

Design the primary content pages

Next, you design one of the primary content pages. This is illustrated by the prototype for a speaker page in figure 14-14, and it should be linked with the home page. This will give the reviewers a better idea of how the web site is going to work, including how the navigation will work. In this case, the user needs to click on the Back button or the Home link in the navigation bar to return to the home page.

Remember that one of the guidelines in figure 14-4 is to design the home page so it is different from the other pages, and the two pages shown here follow that guideline. In this case, even the headers for these pages are different from the home page header. Although most web sites use the same header for each page of the site, that isn't always necessary.

An early prototype for the home page

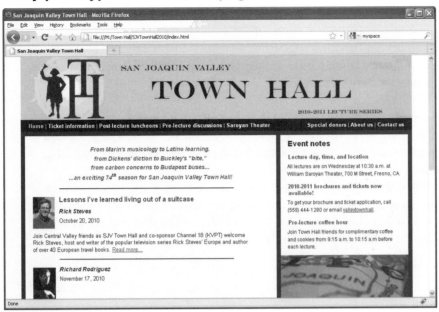

An early prototype for a primary content page

Description

- To get the design started, sketch or prototype the home page. After you agree on the design of the home page, sketch or prototype one of the primary content pages.

- Use stepwise refinement to get these pages working the way you want them to.

Figure 14-14   Design the home page and the primary content pages

Design the other pages

After you've got the basic design for the home and primary content pages done, you can design the other pages. For a large site, you may need to design one section of the rest of the site at a time. But for a small site like Town Hall's, the other pages are mostly independent pages that can be designed one at a time.

This is illustrated by the example in figure 14-15. This is the page that provides the information for getting tickets. In this case, the designer decided that this page should also show the dates for the lectures so the users won't have to switch back and forth between the home page and the tickets page.

Then, she decided that she should also provide links to the speaker pages. As a result, the user can go to a speaker page from either the home page or the ticket page, and that clearly improves the usability of the site. So here again, the design of a page leads to navigation decisions.

The ticket information page

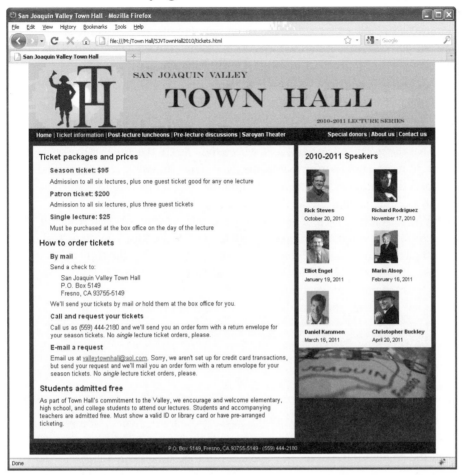

The other pages that are needed

- Post-lecture luncheon
- Pre-lecture discussions
- Saroyan Theater
- Special donors
- About us
- Contact us

Description

- After you've agreed on the design of the home page and the primary pages, sketch or prototype the other types of pages that are needed, working from the most important pages to the least important.
- Often, the pages for each section of a site are a separate design problem, and these pages don't have to be like the home page or the primary content pages.

Figure 14-15   Design the other pages

Plan the navigation

Whenever you have general agreement on how the navigation of the site should work, you can document the navigation by developing a *site plan*. This is illustrated by the first diagram in figure 14-16. This shows that the home page links to six speaker pages, and the about-us page links to two pages. Otherwise, the home page links go to single pages.

One of the benefits of developing a site plan is that it shows how many levels deep the navigation goes. In general, the deeper the navigation goes, the harder it is for the users to keep track of where they are in the site. So most site plans don't go more than four or five levels deep. Unfortunately, the deeper the site plan goes, the harder it is to create and maintain, and that often means that the site plan isn't an accurate representation of the navigation.

When you develop a site plan, you can use whatever symbols you want for the web pages. Also, you usually have to divide the site plan for a large web site over several pages. For instance, you can use one page to show the top two levels and maybe the third level for one of the sections of the site, and you can use other pages for the other sections of the site.

For a small web site, you may decide that you don't need a site plan. However, it can be useful when you're explaining the navigation to the people who are reviewing your design.

Plan the directories for the site

When all of the types of pages and the navigation are designed, you're almost ready to implement all of the pages. For instance, you will need to implement the pages for the other five speakers in the Town Hall web site. Before you do that, though, you should plan the directories that you're going to use for the files of your site.

For instance, the second diagram in figure 14-16 shows the plan for the directories of the Town Hall web site. Like most web sites, the top directory is the root directory. Beneath that, there is one directory for the style sheets of the web site and one for its images. Then, there is one directory for the speaker pages and one for the about-us pages. The last directory is for all of the independent, single pages of the site.

The benefit of planning the directories is that you will be able to find the files that you're working with more easily, and you will know where to put any new files that you create. For that reason, it makes sense to develop a preliminary plan for the directories early in the design process and enhance it as needed during the life of the project.

Here again, you may decide that you don't need a diagram for the directories that you're going to use. But you should at least create the directories that you're going to use on your computer or network early in the design process. That's especially true if you're working with other people on the design of the project.

The site plan for the web site

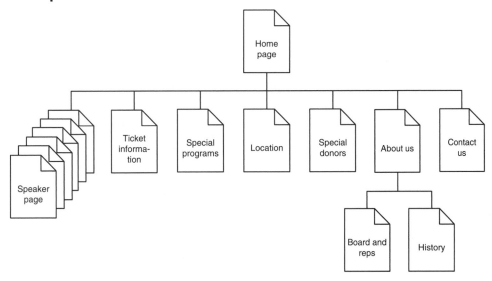

The directories for the web site

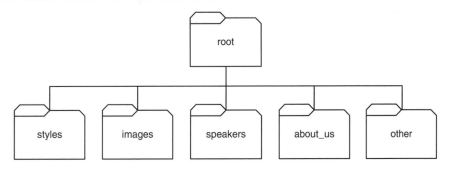

Description

- When you have general agreement on the way the pages of the web site are going to work, you can develop a *site plan* that shows all of the pages that the web site requires.

- The site plan not only shows the required pages, but also the number of levels that the user will be able to navigate. To some extent, the number of levels indicates how complicated the navigation is likely to be.

- After you agree on the site plan, you can diagram the directories for the files of the web site. This diagram should show the directories for the html, css, and image files, as well as any other types of files.

- If a site plan goes down another level, the directory structure usually does too.

Figure 14-16   Plan the navigation and the directories for the site

Perspective

If you apply all of the guidelines, methods, and procedures that you've just learned, you will go a long way towards designing and developing an effective web site. But there's a lot more to learn. If, for example, you're going to do the writing for the site, you should learn more about effective web writing. Or, if you're going to do the graphics design for the web site, you should learn more about graphics design. In short, designing and developing a web site is a challenging process that requires a wide range of skills.

Terms

usability	web designer
accessibility	graphics designer
breadcrumbs	top-down design
chunking	stepwise refinement
alignment	prototyping
proximity	system lifecycle
repetition	target audience
contrast	site plan

Summary

- When you design a web site, *usability* is the primary issue. That refers to how easy a web site is to use, and to a large extent that determines the success of the web site. To achieve usability, a web site needs to implement the current conventions for web site use.

- *Accessibility* refers to how accessible a web site is, especially for the disabled. For the visually disabled, the primary guideline is to use relative font sizes so the users can increase the font size in their browsers.

- The home page of a web site should be used to sell the site by emphasizing what's different about the site and why users should want to use it.

- To let the users know where they are as they navigate through a site, you can highlight the active links on the page, match the heading on the page to the link that led to it, or use *breadcrumbs*.

- Writing for the web isn't like writing for print. Instead, web writing should be written in inverted pyramid style, use headings and subheadings, and use bulleted and numbered lists.

- *Chunking* refers to the grouping of information into topics (chunks) that can be presented on separate web pages. This is a good way to convert one long page into two or more shorter pages.

- If you aren't a graphics designer, you should at least know the principles of *alignment*, *proximity*, *repetition*, and *contrast*. You should also know how to make the typography easy to read.

- With few exceptions, you will work with other people on the design of the site. In a large company, the design team may include web designers, writers, marketing specialists, and graphics designers.

- A *web designer* is involved with all aspects of web design. A *graphics designer* focuses on the graphics that make a web site look inviting and manageable.

- Three methods that should be used in the design of any non-trivial web site are: *top-down design*, *stepwise refinement*, and *prototyping*.

- The *lifecycle* of all systems consists of design, implementation, and maintenance. Because more time is likely to be spent on the maintenance than on developing the web site, you should design and implement a web site so it's relatively easy to enhance and maintain.

- When you design a web site, you start by defining its *target audience* and goals. Then, those definitions guide you as you design the home page, primary content pages, other pages, and navigation for the site.

- As you design the navigation for a web site, you can develop a *site plan*. Then, that site plan can be used to plan the directories for the files of the site.

15

How to deploy a web site

Once you've developed and tested a web site on your local computer, you're just a few steps away from making that web site available to anyone in the world who is connected to the Internet. To do that, you just need to transfer the files for your web site to a web server that's connected to the Internet.

How to get a web host and domain name

Before you can *deploy* (or *publish)* a web site to the Internet, you need to have access to a web server that's connected to the Internet. If you already have access to such a web server, you can use that server. Otherwise, you can search the Internet for a web host as described in this topic. If you want to register a domain name for your site, a web host can usually do that for you too.

How to find a web host

Figure 15-1 shows how to find a *web host,* or *web hosting service.* To do that, you can search the web for "web host" or "web hosting service". Then, you can follow the links until you find a web host that has all the features you need. For small web sites like the ones presented in this book, you only need a small amount of disk space. For larger web sites, you may need more disk space, access to a database server, and a server-side programming language such as PHP, JSP, or ASP.NET.

In addition, most web hosts provide one or more *FTP (File Transfer Proto-col)* accounts. This provides a way for you to transfer the files for your web site to and from your web host.

Most web hosts charge a monthly fee. For a small web site, the price is often less than $5 per month. Also, some web hosts provide some services for free. If you search the Internet, you'll find a wide range of services and prices.

If you already pay an *Internet Service Provider (ISP)* to connect to the Internet, you can check to see if it provides free web hosting as part of its monthly fees. If so, you can check to see if it provides the web hosting features that you need for your web site.

When you get a web host, you will receive an *IP address* in this format: 64.46.106.120. You can use this address to access your web site. Later, when you get your domain name, you can access your site with either the IP address or the domain name. Internally, the Internet uses IP addresses to address web sites, but people use domain names because they're easier to remember.

A web host

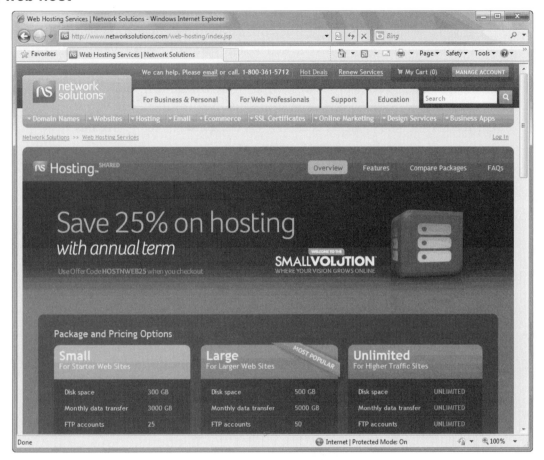

Description

- A *web host*, or *web hosting service*, provides space on a server computer that's connected to the Internet, usually for a monthly fee. You can use a web host to make your web site accessible via the Internet.

- *File Transfer Protocol* (*FTP*) allows you to transfer the files for your web site to and from your web host.

- To find a web host, search the web for "web host" or "web hosting service". Then, follow the links until you find a web host that has all the features you need.

- An *Internet Service Provider* (*ISP*) often includes free web hosting as part of its monthly fees. As a result, if you have an ISP, you can check to see if it provides the web hosting features that you need for your web site.

Figure 15-1   How to find a web host

How to get a domain name

If you're using a web host, you can often use its *domain name* to access your web site. For example, if your web hosting company has a domain name of

`olive.forest.net`

you may be able to access your web site using a *subdomain* like this:

`www.valleytownhall.olive.forest.net`

Or, you may be able to access your web site using a subdirectory like this:

`www.olive.forest.net/valleytownhall`

Either way, the domain name of the web host is included in the URL that's used to access your web site.

For most professional web sites, you'll want to get your own domain name. That way, you can access your web site without including the domain name of the web host in the URL. For example, you can access a web site with the domain name valleytownhall.com like this:

`www.valleytownhall.com`

To get a domain name, you can use a web site like Network Solutions as shown in figure 15-2. But first, you need to decide what extension you want to use for the web site. The .com extension was originally intended to be used for commercial web sites, .net was intended to be used for networking web sites, and .org was intended to be used for other organizations. However, many other extensions are now available, such as those for military (.mil), government (.gov), business (.biz), and television (.tv) web sites.

When you use a site like the one shown here, you typically enter one or more domain names. Then, the *domain name registry* is searched to see which of the names is available, and you can choose to purchase any available name for a specific amount of time. If you are using a web host, it may also provide a service like this.

A search for a domain name

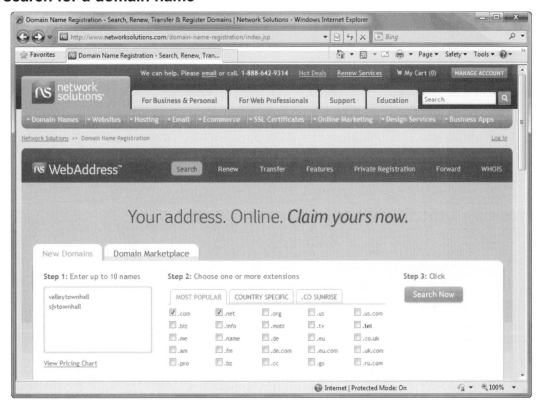

Description

- A *domain name* is a user-friendly name that's used to locate a resource that's connected to the Internet. For example, google.com is a domain name.

- A domain name can have one or more *subdomains*. For example, mail.google.com is a subdomain.

- The .com, .net, and .org extensions are popular endings for domain names. These extensions were originally intended to be used for commercial web sites (.com), networking infrastructure web sites (.net), and other types of organizations (.org).

- The *domain name registry* is a database of all registered domain names.

- If you are using a web hosting service, you can often use that service to register the domain name for you. To start, you can use your web hosting service to find a domain name that hasn't been registered yet. Then, you can have your web hosting service register that domain name for you.

Figure 15-2   How to get a domain name

How to transfer files to and from the web

Once you have a web host and domain name, you can publish your web site to the Internet by transferring the files for your web site from your local computer to the correct directory on the web host's server. To do that, you can use an FTP client like FileZilla, an IDE like DreamWeaver that includes an FTP client, or a tool for uploading files that's provided by your web host. To give you an idea of how FTP clients work, the next three figures show you how FileZilla Client works.

How to install FileZilla Client

Figure 15-3 shows how to install FileZilla Client. To do that, you can go to the FileZilla website and follow the instructions. Since FileZilla runs on the Windows, Mac, and Linux operating systems, the directions for installing it vary depending on your operating system.

An FTP program

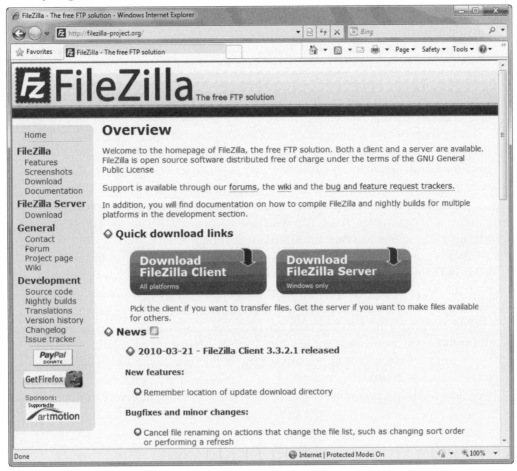

How to install FileZilla Client

1. Go to the FileZilla website (www.filezilla-project.org).
2. Click on the Download FileZilla Client link.
3. Follow the instructions to install the FileZilla Client application on your system.

Description

- FileZilla is a free FTP client application that runs on the Windows, Mac, and Linux operating systems.
- FileZilla supports basic FTP as well as FTP over SSL/TLS (FTPS) and SSH File Transfer Protocol (SFTP), which can be used for secure file transfers.

Figure 15-3   How to install the FileZilla FTP client

How to connect to a web site on a remote web server

Figure 15-4 shows how to use FileZilla to connect to your web site on your web host. To do that the first time, you use the Site Manager dialog box to create the new site and give it a name. Then, you specify the host name, server type, user name, and password for the site. Finally, you click the Connect button to connect to the site.

If the connection is successful, FileZilla displays a window like the one in the next figure. Otherwise, it displays an error message that you can use to troubleshoot the problem. If necessary, you can contact your web host for help with these FTP settings.

After you successfully connect to a site for the first time, you can easily connect to it again later. To do that, you just select the site name in the Site Manager dialog box and then click the Connect button.

When you use FileZilla Client, you usually set the default directories for the local and remote sites. For example, you set the default local directory to the root directory of the web site on your computer, and you set the default remote directory to the root directory for your web site on the web host. That makes it easy to work with the web site each time you connect to it. To set the default directories, you use the Advanced tab of the Site Manager dialog box.

Note that the name of the root directory on the remote site varies depending on how your web server is configured. As a result, you may need to ask your web host for help or do some experimenting to set the root directory correctly.

FileZilla's Site Manager dialog box

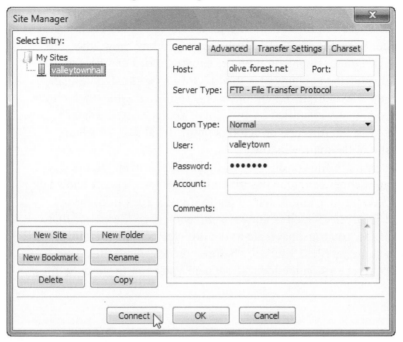

How to connect to a web site for the first time

1. Start FileZilla, and then use the File→Site Manager command to display the Site Manager dialog box.

2. Click the New Site button and enter a name for the site.

3. Enter the details needed to connect to the site, including the host name, user name, and password.

4. Click the Connect button to save the connection settings and connect to the site.

How to connect to a web site after it has been set up

- Open the Site Manager, click on the site name, and click the Connect button.

How to edit the settings for a web site

- Open the Site Manager, click on the site name, edit its settings, and click the OK button.

Description

- For the Server Type option, you typically use FTP. For sensitive data, though, you can use FTP over SSL/TLS (FTPS) or SSH File Transfer Protocol (SFTP).

- For the Logon Type option, you typically use Normal. See FileZilla help for a description of the other options.

- To set the default directories for the local and remote sites, you can use the Advanced tab.

Figure 15-4   How to connect to a web site on a remote web server

How to upload and download files

Figure 15-5 shows the FileZilla window after a connection has been made to a remote web site. Here, the right pane of the main window shows the directory tree for the remote site, along with the subdirectories and files in the root directory. To display the contents of a subdirectory, you can double-click on it, and to move up a level to the parent directory, you can double-click on the first directory (the one that's identified by two dots). You can use the same techniques to work with the files and directories on the local site, which are listed in the left pane of the main window.

To transfer one or more files or directories from your local site to the remote site, you can use the technique described in this figure. This is known as *uploading* files. You can use a similar technique to transfer files from the remote site to your local site, which is known as *downloading* files. Note that before you upload files, you must navigate to the directory on the remote site where you want to store the files. Similarly, before you download files, you must navigate to the directory on the local site where you want to store the files.

FileZilla when it is connected to a web host

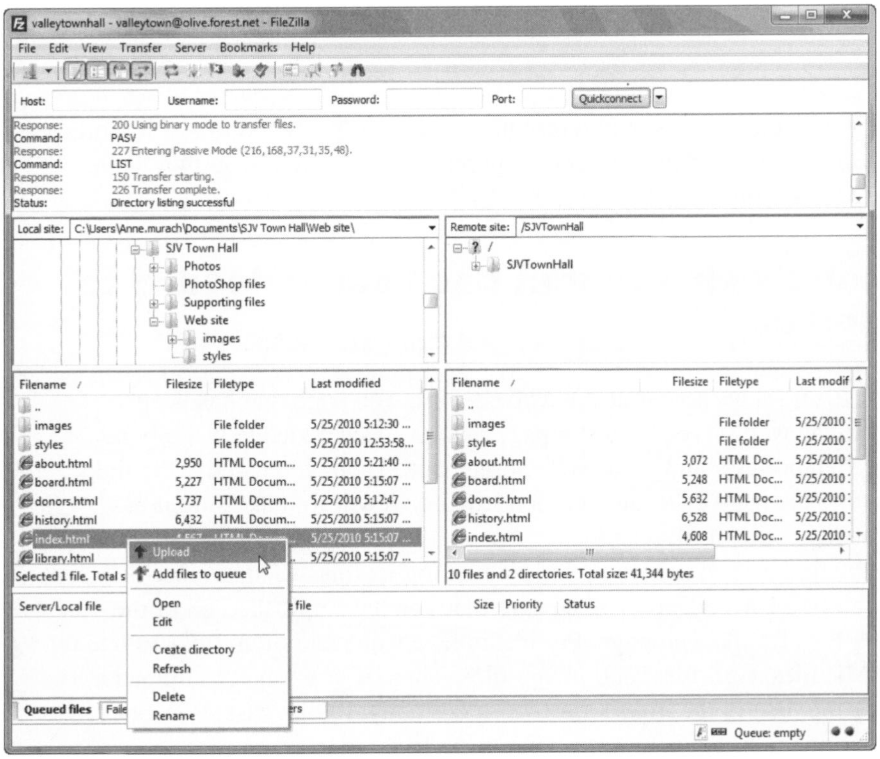

Description

- The top left pane of the main FileZilla window shows the directory structure of the local system, and the top right pane shows the directory structure of the remote system.

- If you select a directory in either directory tree, the subdirectories and files in that directory are displayed in the lower pane. Then, you can use that pane to navigate through the directories.

- The directories that are identified by two dots at the top of both lower panes represent the parent directories.

- To *upload* a file or directory from the local site to the remote site, display the directory on the remote site where you want the file or directory uploaded. Then, right-click on the file or directory in the local site and select the Upload command from the resulting menu.

- To *download* a file or directory from the remote site to the local site, display the directory on the local site where you want the file or directory downloaded. Then, right-click on the file or directory in the remote site and select the Download command from the resulting menu.

- You can also upload or download multiple files and directories by selecting them and then using the Upload or Download command.

Figure 15-5   How to upload and download files

Two other skills for deploying a web site

After you deploy your site to a remote web server, you need to test it. You also need to get your site indexed by the popular search engines so they will deliver people to your site.

How to test a web site that has been uploaded to the web server

Figure 15-6 shows how to test a web site or a web page that has been uploaded to the web server. To test a page that has been added to a site, you start your web browser and go to your home page. Then, you can use the links to navigate to the page that you've uploaded and view it to make sure it has been uploaded successfully.

You should also test the web page by clicking its links to make sure they work correctly. That way, you can be sure that you have uploaded all of the supporting files for the web page. For example, a web page often links to one or more HTML files, CSS files, and image files. Then, if you forget to upload a supporting file, one of the links won't work correctly. In that case, you can solve the problem by uploading the supporting file.

To test an entire web site that has been uploaded to a web server, you need to methodically review all of the pages of the site, starting with the home page. You also need to test every link on every page to make sure that all of them work. And you need to do this with all of the popular browsers.

A web site on the Internet

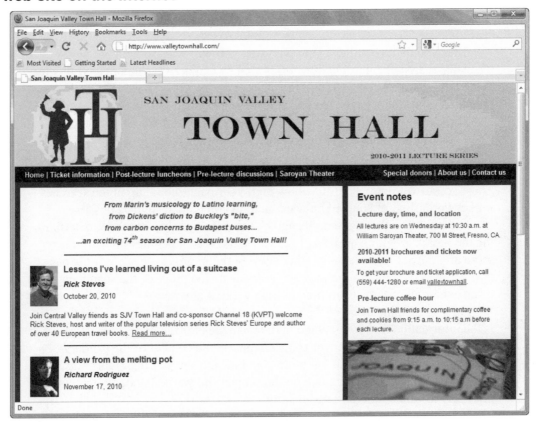

Description

- To test a web site or web page that has been uploaded to the Internet, start your web browser and navigate to the URL for the web site or page.
- To test a web page, click on all links to make sure they still work correctly. To test a web site, methodically review all of the pages and test all of the links on the site.

Figure 15-6   How to test a web site that has been uploaded to the web server

How to get your web site into search engines and directories

After you deploy and test your web site, you will want to get your pages into the major search engines and directories so they can deliver visitors to your site. To do that, you go to the URLs in the table in figure 15-7. These URLs take you to hidden submission pages like the Google page shown in this figure.

At the submission page, you only need to submit the URL of your home page. Then, if your site is linked properly, the search engine's "robot" will "crawl" through the rest of your pages by following the links in your site. As it crawls, the robot will score your pages based on their relevance to keywords. Those scores will later determine how high your pages come up in the searches for keywords, and of course you want them to come up as high as possible.

The trouble is that the search engines use different algorithms for determining the scores of your pages. For instance, some search engines improve the score of a page if it has links to other sites. Some improve the score if the pages of other web sites link to the page. To complicate the process, the search engines change their algorithms from time to time without any notice.

For some engines, one of the factors that helps determine the score of a page is the information that you include in the meta tags for the page (see figure 3-3 in chapter 3). Another factor for some engines is the content of the primary heading on the page. To find out more about the current scoring algorithms, you can search the web or buy a book on the subject. Be warned, though, that you are likely to find conflicting information.

If you don't want to include a web page in the indexing process, you can code a meta tag for the page like the one in this figure. For instance, you usually don't want your shopping cart pages included.

Once you've submitted your web site for indexing, you don't have to do it again, even if you've made significant enhancements to the site. That's because the robot for a search engine periodically crawls through all of the sites and indexes the pages again, sometimes with a new algorithm for scoring.

But what happens if you delete a page on your web site that has already been indexed? Unfortunately, it will still come up in the search results. Then, if somebody clicks on its link, the page won't be found and a 404 error page will be displayed. Although your web site will eventually be re-indexed without the deleted page, that may take a while.

One way to get around this problem is to delete the content from the page, but not the page itself. Then, you can add a meta tag that will redirect the user to another page like this:

```
<meta http-equiv="refresh" content="0" url="../backlist.html" />
```

Although there are other ways to handle this, this is a simple one.

Last, you should be aware that most web hosts offer statistics packages that tell you where your visitors are coming from. You can also buy third-party packages that do that. This data can help you figure out what's working…and what isn't working…so you can make changes that will improve your site.

The URLs for the major search engines and directory

Site name	Site type	Web URL
Google	Search engine	http://www.google.com/addurl/
MSN/Bing	Search engine	http://www.bing.com/webmaster/SubmitSitePage.aspx
Yahoo	Search engine	http://search.yahoo.com/info/submit.html
DMOZ	Directory	http://www.dmoz.org/add.html

The Google page for submitting your site

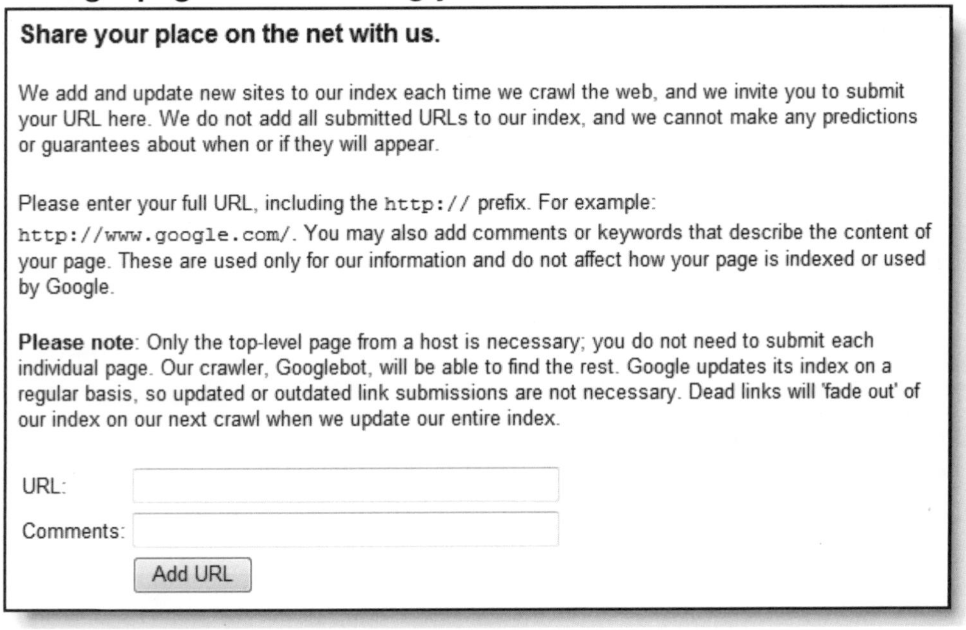

Share your place on the net with us.

We add and update new sites to our index each time we crawl the web, and we invite you to submit your URL here. We do not add all submitted URLs to our index, and we cannot make any predictions or guarantees about when or if they will appear.

Please enter your full URL, including the `http://` prefix. For example: `http://www.google.com/`. You may also add comments or keywords that describe the content of your page. These are used only for our information and do not affect how your page is indexed or used by Google.

Please note: Only the top-level page from a host is necessary; you do not need to submit each individual page. Our crawler, Googlebot, will be able to find the rest. Google updates its index on a regular basis, so updated or outdated link submissions are not necessary. Dead links will 'fade out' of our index on our next crawl when we update our entire index.

URL: [   ]

Comments: [   ]

[Add URL]

How to tell a robot not to visit a page

```
<meta http-equiv="robots" content="noindex, nofollow" />
```

Description

- After you have deployed and tested your site, you will want to get your pages into search engines and directories that can deliver visitors to your site. To do that for the three major search engines and the major directory, go to the URLs in the table above.

- Each search engine has a "robot" that crawls through the pages of your site and indexes them so they can be used by the search engine.

- Each search engine has its own algorithms for scoring pages, and those scores determine how high a page will be placed in the search results for specific keywords.

- If you don't want the robot to include a page in the index, you can add a meta tag for the page as shown above.

- Most web hosts offer statistics packages that track which sites and search engines are sending you visitors. You can also buy third-party statistics packages.

Figure 15-7   How to get your web site into search engines and directories

Perspective

If you understand the first 13 chapters of this book, you can write and test the HTML and CSS code for a web site on a local computer. If you understand this chapter, you can make your web site available to anyone in the world who can connect to the Internet. Now, it's up to you to dream up a web site that's worth sharing with the world!

Terms

deploy	IP address
publish	domain name
web host	subdomain
web hosting service	domain name registry
FTP (File Transfer Protocol)	upload a file
ISP (Internet Service Provider)	download a file

Summary

- To *deploy* (or *publish*) a web site, you can use a *web host*, or *web hosting service*, that will make your web site accessible from the Internet.

- You can use *File Transfer Protocol* (*FTP*) to transfer the files for your web site to and from your web host.

- An *IP address* uniquely identifies a web site, and so does a *domain name*.

- To find a *domain name* for your web site, you search the *domain name registry*, which is a database of all registered domain names.

- Once you have a domain name, you can have one or more *subdomains* that address portions of the domain.

- FileZilla is a free FTP client that runs on the Windows, Mac, and Linux operating systems. You use it to *upload* files from your computer to the web server and to *download* files from the web server to your computer.

- To test a web page that has been uploaded to the Internet, start your web browser, navigate to the URL for the web page, and click on all links to make sure they work correctly.

- To get your web site into a search engine, go to the URL for its hidden submission page. Then, its robot will crawl through your pages and score them for later searches that are based on keywords.

Appendix A

How to set up your computer for this book

This appendix shows how to install the software that we recommend for editing and testing the web pages and applications for this book. That includes Notepad++ as the text editor for Windows users, TextWrangler as the text editor for Mac OS users, plus the Firefox browser for both Windows and Mac OS users. This appendix also shows you how to download and install the source code for this book.

As you read these descriptions, please remember that most web sites are continually upgraded. As a result, some of the procedures in this appendix may have changed since this book was published. Nevertheless, these procedures should still be good guides to installing the software.

How to install a text editor

If you're already comfortable with a text editor that works for editing XHTML and CSS, you can continue using it. But otherwise, we recommend that you use Notepad++ on a Windows system or TextWrangler on a Mac OS system. Although you can get more powerful editors, both of these are free and they provide all of the capabilities that you need for developing web pages.

How to install Notepad++

Figure A-1 shows how to download and install Notepad++ on a Windows system. Since this is a typical text editor, you shouldn't have any trouble using it. In case it helps, though, chapter 2 gives you a quick introduction to it.

How to install TextWrangler

Figure A-1 also shows how to download and install TextWrangler on a Mac OS system. Since this is a typical text editor, you shouldn't have any trouble using it.

The web site address for downloading Notepad++

```
http://notepad-plus.sourceforge.net
```

How to install Notepad++

1. Go to the web site address above.
2. Click on the Download link at the top of the page, click on the "Binary files" link to expand it, and click on the "Download NotePad++ executable files" link.
3. Click on the latest version of the Installer file (e.g., npp.5.6.8.Installer.exe) and save it on your C drive.
4. Use Windows Explorer to find the Installer file on your C drive and double-click on it to run it. Then, follow the instructions.

The web site address for downloading TextWrangler

```
http://www.barebones.com/products/textwrangler
```

How to install TextWrangler

1. Go to the web site address above.
2. Click the Download Now button, then click the Download link for the Disk Image file that's right for your release of Mac OS. This will add the file to your download list.
3. Double-click the disk image on your desktop. This will open the disk image, which places a TextWrangler disk icon on the desktop. This will also open the TextWrangler disk window.
4. If the TextWrangler disk window doesn't appear, double-click the TextWrangler disk icon on the desktop.
5. In the TextWrangler disk window, drag the TextWrangler icon on top of the Applications folder icon. Then, close the TextWrangler window.
6. Drag the TextWrangler disk icon to the trash can to eject the disk image.
7. Browse to the Applications folder in Finder or press Command+Shift+A, and double-click the TextWrangler icon to start TextWrangler.
8. To keep the TextWrangler icon in your dock, control-click the icon, select Options, and select "Keep in Dock".

Discussion

- If you're using a Windows system, we recommend that you use Notepad++ for entering and editing HTML and CSS files.
- If you're using a Mac OS system, we recommend that you use TextWrangler for entering and editing HTML andCSS files.

Figure A-1   How to install Notepad++ or TextWrangler as your text editor

How to install Firefox

When you develop web pages and applications, you need to test them on all of the browsers that the users of the application are likely to use. For a commercial application, that usually includes Internet Explorer, Firefox, Safari for Macs, Opera, and Google's Chrome. Then, if an application doesn't work on one of those browsers, you need to fix it.

As you do the exercises for this book, though, you can test your web pages on just two browsers. Windows users should use Internet Explorer plus Firefox. Mac OS users should use Safari and Firefox. In practice, though, Mac OS users also need to test their pages on Windows systems with Internet Explorer because that's the browser that most people use.

Figure A-2 shows how to download and install Firefox. As you respond to the dialog boxes for the installer, we recommend that you make Firefox your default browser.

The web site address for downloading Firefox

```
http://www.mozilla.com
```

How to install Firefox

1. Go to the web site address above.
2. Click on the Download Firefox - Free button.
3. Save the exe file to your C drive.
4. Run the exe file and respond to the resulting dialog boxes.

Other popular browsers

- Opera
- Safari
- Chrome

Description

- Microsoft's Internet Explorer and Mozilla's Firefox are the most popular browsers today. That's why you should test all web pages on both of those browsers.
- If you have a Windows system, Internet Explorer will already be on your system, but you will have to install Firefox.
- Because Internet Explorer doesn't adhere to all of the current standards for web browsers and Firefox does, you are likely to find differences in the way these browsers render the same page.
- If a web page is rendered correctly on both browsers, it will probably work on other browsers too. To be thorough, though, you may also want to test each page on the other popular browsers.

Figure A-2   How to install Firefox

How to install and use the source code for this book

The next two figures show how to install and use the source code for this book. One figure is for Windows users, the other for Mac OS users.

For Windows users

Figure A-3 shows how to install the source code for this book on a Windows system. This includes the source code for the applications in this book, and the source code for the exercises.

When you finish this procedure, the book applications will be in the directory that's shown in this figure, and the exercises will be in the two directories that are shown in this figure. Then, when you do the exercises, you use the subdirectories and files in this directory:

```
c:\html_css
```

But you have backup copies of these subdirectories and files in this directory:

```
c:\murach\html_css\exercises
```

That way, you can restore the files for an exercise by copying the files from the second directory to the first.

The Murach web site

```
www.murach.com
```

The default installation directory for the source code on a Windows system

```
c:\murach\html_css
```

The Windows directories for the book applications and exercises

```
c:\murach\html_css\book_apps
c:\murach\html_css\exercises
```

The Windows directories for doing the exercises

```
c:\html_css\ch01
c:\html_css\ch02
...
c:\html_css\ch13
```

How to download and install the source code on a Windows system

1. Go to www.murach.com, and go to the page for *Murach's HTML, XHTML, and CSS*.

2. Click the link for "FREE download of the book applications." Then, click the "All book files" link for the self-extracting zip file. This will download a setup file named hcss_allfiles.exe onto your hard drive.

3. Use Windows Explorer to find the exe file on your hard drive. Then, double-click this file. This installs the source code for the book applications and exercises into the directories shown above.

   After it installs the book applications and exercises, the exe file copies all of the subdirectories of the exercises directory to c:\html_css, so you can use these subdirectories when you do the exercises.

How to restore an exercise file

- Copy it from its subdirectory in

  ```
  c:\murach\html_css\exercises
  ```

  to the corresponding subdirectory in

  ```
  c:\html_css
  ```

Description

- The exe file that you download stores the exercises in two different directories. That way, you can do the exercises using the files that are stored in one directory, but you have a backup copy in case you want to restore the starting files for an exercise.

Figure A-3   How to install the source code for this book on a Windows system

For Mac OS users

Figure A-4 shows how to install the source code for this book on a Mac OS system. This includes the source code for the applications in this book, and the source code for the exercises.

When you finish this procedure, the book applications will be in the directory that's shown in this figure, and the exercises will be in the two directories that are shown in this figure. Then, when you do the exercises, you use the subdirectories and files in this directory:

```
documents\html_css
```

But you have backup copies of these subdirectories and files in this directory:

```
documents\html_css\exercises
```

That way, you can restore the files for an exercise by copying the files from the second directory to the first.

The Murach web site

```
www.murach.com
```

The Mac OS directories for the book applications and exercises

```
documents\murach\html_css\book_apps
documents\murach\html_css\exercises
```

The Mac OS directories for doing the exercises

```
documents\html_css\ch01
documents\html_css\ch02
documents\...
documents\html_css\ch13
```

How to download and install the source code on a Mac OS system

1. Go to www.murach.com, and go to the page for *Murach's HTML, XHTML, and CSS*.

2. Click the link for "FREE download of the book applications." Then, click the "All book files" link for the regular zip file. This will download a setup file named hcss_allfiles.zip onto your hard drive.

3. Move this file into the Documents directory of your home directory.

4. Use Finder to go to your Documents directory.

5. Double-click the hcss_allfiles.zip file to extract the directories for the book applications and exercises. This will create a directory named html_css in your Documents directory that will contain the book_apps and exercises directories.

6. Copy the subdirectories in this directory

   ```
   documents\murach\html_css\exercises
   ```

   to this directory

   ```
   documents\html_css
   ```

   This is the directory that you'll use when you do the exercises.

How to restore an exercise file

- Copy it from its subdirectory in

  ```
  documents\murach\html_css\exercises
  ```

  to the corresponding subdirectory in

  ```
  documents\html_css
  ```

Description

- This procedure stores the exercises in two different directories. That way, you can do the exercises using the files that are stored in one directory, but you have a backup copy in case you want to restore the starting files for an exercise.

Figure A-4   How to install the source code for this book on a Mac OS system

Index

For more on Murach products, visit us at
www.murach.com

Books for web developers

Murach's HTML, XHTML, and CSS	$44.50
Murach's JavaScript and DOM Scripting	54.50
Murach's Java Servlets and JSP (Second Edition)	52.50
Murach's ASP.NET 3.5 Web Programming with C# 2008	52.50
Murach's ASP.NET 3.5 Web Programming with VB 2008	52.50

Books for Java and .NET developers

Murach's Java SE 6	$52.50
Murach's C# 2008	52.50
Murach's Visual Basic 2008	52.50
Murach's C++ 2008	52.50

Books for database programmers

Murach's Oracle SQL and PL/SQL	$52.50
Murach's SQL Server 2008 for Developers	52.50
Murach's ADO.NET 3.5, LINQ, and the Entity Framework with C# 2008	52.50
Murach's ADO.NET 3.5, LINQ, and the Entity Framework with VB 2008	52.50

Prices and availability are subject to change. Please visit our website or call for current information.

Our unlimited guarantee...when you order directly from us

You must be satisfied with our books. If they aren't better than any other
programming books you've ever used...both for training and reference...you can
send them back within 90 days for a full refund. No questions asked!

Your opinions count

If you have any comments on this book, I'm
eager to get them. Thanks for your feedback!

To comment by

E-mail:	murachbooks@murach.com
Web:	www.murach.com
Postal mail:	Mike Murach & Associates, Inc.
	4340 North Knoll Ave.
	Fresno, California 93722-7825

To order now,

 Web: www.murach.com

 Call toll-free:
1-800-221-5528
(Weekdays, 8 am to 4 pm Pacific Time)

 Fax: 1-559-440-0963

 Mike Murach & Associates, Inc.
Professional programming books

What software you need for this book

- To enter and edit HTML, XHTML, and CSS, you can use any text editor, but we recommend Notepad++ for Windows users and TextWrangler for Mac OS users. Both are available for free.

- To test the web pages that you develop on a Windows system, we recommend that you use Internet Explorer plus Firefox. On a Mac OS system, we recommend that you use Safari and Firefox. All of these browsers are free.

- To help you install these products, appendix A provides the web site addresses and procedures that you'll need.

- To help you use Notepad++, chapter 2 provides a short tutorial.

The downloadable applications and files for this book

- All of the applications and examples presented in this book.

- The starting files for the exercises in this book.

How to download the applications and files

- Go to www.murach.com, and go to the page for *Murach's HTML, XHTML, and CSS.*

- Click the link for "FREE download of the book applications."

- If you're using a Windows system, click the "All book files" link for the self-extracting zip file. That will download an exe file named hcss_allfiles.exe. Then, find this file in Windows Explorer and double-click on it. That will install the files for this book in this directory: c:\murach\html_css.

- If you're using a Mac, click the "All book files" link for the regular zip file. That will download a zip file named hcss_allfiles.zip onto your hard drive. Then, move this file into the Documents folder of your home folder, use Finder to go to your Documents folder, and double-click on the zip file. That will create a folder named html_css that contains all the files for this book.

- For more information, please see appendix A.